Welcome to t  nd

WELCOME TO THE 1998 TASTE OF SCOTLAND GUIDE. Its purpose is to help you experience to the full the richness and diversity of Scottish cuisine which is as varied as our landscape.

You will also discover something of the quality of Scottish produce, the fruits of that landscape and the seas which surround it.

Over the next 270 pages, you will find a selection of around 400 of the finest eating places in Scotland – some are among the finest in the world. Many old favourites appear, along with 59 new and welcome additions since last year.

When you eat in a Taste of Scotland establishment, you can be sure that one of our qualified Inspectors has been there ahead of you to make a thorough assessment and ensure standards meet our high expectations.

You may already be aware that every establishment listed here makes a marketing contribution. It's worth bearing in mind, however, that they do so only AFTER they have exceeded Taste of Scotland criteria. To maintain the Guide's credibility – and our own integrity – this philosophy is strictly observed.

We inspect around 500 places each year and only once these inspections have been completed do we know exactly how many will be included in the following year's Guide.

As you use this Guide, you will discover just how well you can eat in Scotland. If you like what you find, tell us.

Equally, if you encounter something you don't like, it's vital you let us know about that, too. If an establishment fails to maintain standards, we will act swiftly to withdraw its membership from the Scheme.

The current certificate is your guarantee that an establishment is a member of Taste of Scotland and will provide you with the highest levels of quality and service.
So… enjoy!

Amanda J Clark, Chief Executive

THE TASTE OF SCOTLAND
1998

This is to certify that

Allan Cottage

has been selected for membership of

The Taste of Scotland Scheme

in recognition of its commitment to the pursuit
of excellence in food preparation and service

*Taste of Scotland current members
are identified by the 1998
Certificate of Membership which
should be on display.*

A la carte.

THE GLENEAGLES HOTEL

ONE DEVONSHIRE GARDENS

THE ROYAL SCOTSMAN

BRITISH AIRWAYS' CONCORDE

The food at the country's finest establishments is just as often complemented by a bottle of Highland Spring natural mineral water, as it is complimented by the customers. Hardly surprising, considering its crisp, clean taste is the ideal accompaniment to haute cuisine everywhere. And it doesn't get much higher than on board Concorde.

Contents

TASTE OF SCOTLAND IS GRATEFUL
FOR THE CONTINUED SUPPORT OF:
STB · Scotch Quality Beef and Lamb Association
The Macallan · Highland Spring · Walkers Shortbread Ltd
Matthew Algie · Alexander Wines

TRADE BOARD MEMBERS
Laurie Black (Chairman, Taste of Scotland Board), **Fouters Bistro.**
Annie Paul, **Taychreggan Hotel.**
David Wilson, **Peat Inn.**

How to use this Guide

ENTRIES
All members are listed in the Guide in alphabetical order under the nearest town or village. Island entries are shown alphabetically under Isle.

DOGS/PETS
Some establishments welcome guests with their pets – we advise that you check in advance to avoid any difficulties.

ACCOMMODATION RATES
In the entries we state the number of rooms and whether special rates are available at particular times of the year. The DB&B (Dinner Bed and Breakfast) and B&B rates quoted are a guide to the prices charged. However some rates may change from time to time and you should request specific rates either by telephone or requesting a tariff to be sent out.

MEAL PRICES
£ symbols indicate the price category that the establishment has indicated to us they fall into.

They are as follows:
£ = up to £10 per person
££ = £10 –£20 per person
£££ = £20 –£30 per person
££££ = over £30 per person

LUNCHES
Lunchtime eating may be less for-mal in some establishments than others and thus the Taste of Scotland criteria extends to establishments who are open for a lighter lunch or bar snack. To avoid disappointment please establish when booking whether lunchtime opening is for dining room lunch or bar meals.

TIPS TO AVOID DISAPPOINTMENT
Make an advance reservation whenever possible. Mention that you are using the Taste of Scotland Guide. Check if price changes have taken place since publication of this Guide. If you are planning on paying by credit card – check that your card will be accepted.

COMMENTS
Taste of Scotland welcomes comments – both good and bad – about your experiences using this Guide.

However, if you have an unsatisfactory meal we would always advise that you speak to the person in charge at the establishment con-cerned and let them know of your disappoint-ment. It gives an immediate opportunity for the situation to be rectified or explained.

If this fails to resolve the problem, do write to Taste of Scotland about your experience. It is our policy to then pass a copy of your letter or comment form onto the establishment for investigation.

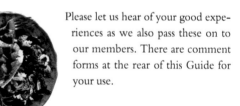

Please let us hear of your good expe-riences as we also pass these on to our members. There are comment forms at the rear of this Guide for your use.

GUIDE TO SYMBOLS

The symbols listed here indicate more information about the facilities available at each member establishment.

🏫 Number of rooms

🛏 Accommodation rates

SP Special rates available

✕ Information on meals

V Vegetarians welcome

🚭 Smoking restrictions

RQ Reservation required

UL Unlicensed

♀ Licensing status

👑 Scottish Tourist Board Crown grading

💳 Credit Cards

Ⅺ Proprietor or Manager

🕇 Children

♿ Facilities for disabled

⬧ Shipboard restaurant

🎪 Packed meals provided

🅿 No parking

🎷 Opening hours during local festival

🐕 Information on pets

🚩 Member of the Scotch Beef Club

Map Reference	
Address & Telephone Number, etc	**MOYNESS HOUSE** 6 Bruce Gardens, Inverness IV3 5EN Tel: 01463 233836 Fax: 01463 233836
How to get there	From A9 (north + south) and A862 Beauly, follow signs for A82 Fort William holiday route. Through Tomnahurich Street to Glenurquhart Road (A82), turn into Bruce Gardens diagonally opposite Highland Regional Council offices.
Brief description	**Lovely Victorian house in the centre of Inverness – close to Eden Court Theatre and Balnain House.**
Type of building **Style of cooking** **Inspector's comment**	• A detached villa built in 1880, formerly the home of Neil Gunn, the celebrated Scottish author. • First class home cooking. • "Stylish dishes contrasting with the traditional surroundings of Inverness."
Description	Moyness House is situated in a quiet residential part of Inverness, within ten minutes walk of the town centre and Eden Court Theatre. It is tastefully decorated and appointed in a way which respects the Victorian nature of the house, and retains its elegance. The bedrooms are charmingly decorated and have en suite facilities; the principal rooms are smart and spacious. A large garden to the rear of the house is also available for guests to enjoy. Moyness House is run by Jenny and Richard Jones – with Jenny being responsible for the cooking and her daily changing menus show flair and imagination. She goes to great lengths to source high quality Scottish produce, and treats her ingredients imaginatively, within a classic context – just as her many regular guests like it!
Seasonal limitations	Open all year except Christmas wk 🏫 Rooms: 7 with private facilities 🛏 DB&B £44–£52 B&B £26–£34 SP Special rates available ✕ Residents only ♀ Residents licence ✕ Dinner ££ V Vegetarians welcome 🕇 Children welcome 🚭 No smoking in restaurant
Menu specialities	**Smoked mackerel pâté with oatcakes. Medallions of venison with port wine sauce and onion marmalade. Warm raspberry and white chocolate cake with red fruit coulis.**
	STB Deluxe 👑 👑 👑 💳 Credit cards: Mastercard/Eurocard, Visa, Switch, Delta Ⅺ Proprietors: Richard & Jenny Jones

The Macallan Taste of Scotland Awards

THE 1997 WINNERS OF THE MACALLAN TASTE OF SCOTLAND AWARDS ARE:

HOTEL OF THE YEAR	The Wheatsheaf Hotel, Swinton
RESTAURANT OF THE YEAR	Let's Eat, Perth
COUNTRY HOUSE HOTEL OF THE YEAR	Knockinaam Lodge, Portpatrick
SPECIAL MERIT AWARD	**Best Tea-Room** Kind Kyttock's Kitchen, Falkland
SPECIAL MERIT AWARD	**Best Lunch** – Ballathie House Hotel, Kinclaven, nr Perth
THE MACALLAN PERSONALITY OF THE YEAR	Alan Craigie, Creel Restaurant and Rooms, St Margaret's Hope, Orkney

THE RUNNERS-UP ARE:

The Marcliffe at Pitfodels – Aberdeen
Hotel Eilean Iarmain – Sleat, Isle of Skye
Le Café St Honoré – Edinburgh
The Puppet Theatre – Glasgow
Kilmichael Country House Hotel – by Brodick, Isle of Arran
Newmiln – Perth
The Granary – Comrie
South Kingennie House – Kellas, by Broughty Ferry

Now in their eleventh year, the Awards were set up to encourage the pursuit of excellence and by so doing to encourage others to emulate the winners.

The Macallan Single Malt is renowned for its unique character and unrivalled quality and as such makes a perfect partner for these Awards.

Easter Elchies House, Home of The Macallan

The Awards are restricted to establishments which are listed in the Taste of Scotland Guide and thus are already highlighted as leaders in their specific category.

This year the judging for the Awards was an exceptionally difficult task with a record number of nominations coming in from all areas and for all types of establishments. It is a pleasure to be able to recognise the spectrum of all that is great about eating in Scotland – from the tea-rooms to the most elegant country houses.

We are delighted to announce the introduction of a new overall Award for Excellence, recognising an establishment from all of the 1997 winners which particularly impressed the judges. Our congratulations go to Knockinaam Lodge, the first winner of The Macallan Taste of Scotland Award for Excellence.

We now invite Taste of Scotland customers to once again nominate establishments of outstanding quality. Please use the coupons at the rear of this Guide to forward your nominations for The Macallan Taste of Scotland Awards 1998. Letters and postcards are also welcome. In addition, Taste of Scotland Inspectors are asked to nominate their favourite places throughout the inspection season.

The categories for the 1998 Awards will remain the same. As in the past the Special Merit Awards will be decided upon from the recommendations received.

Closing date for entries – 30 June 1998.

The 1997 Winners have been highlighted in the listings.

SCOTLAND

STB Quality Assurance

SINCE 1985 the Scottish Tourist Board has been inspecting hotels, guest houses, bed and breakfasts and self catering accommodation assessing the standards that visitors expect and helping owners and operators meet those standards.

In a two tier scheme, accommodation all over the country is visited annually and **GRADED for quality and CLASSIFIED for facilities**.

Grades are based on a wide ranging assessment of quality and service aspects. Each establishment is assessed on its own merits so that any type can achieve the highest grade.

DELUXE . . . . reflects an excellent overall standard
HIGHLY COMMENDED. . . . . . reflects a very good overall standard
COMMENDED. . . . . reflects a good overall standard
APPROVED. . . . . reflects an acceptable overall standard

These GRADES are awarded by the STB inspectors once they have checked all the important factors that contribute to quality in an establishment. Just as you would, they look for clean, attractive surroundings, well furnished and heated. They sample meals, sleep in the beds, and talk to the staff. Like you they know that quality should be assessed irrespective of the range of facilities on offer, they know the value of a warm and welcoming smile.

The CROWN CLASSIFICATION denotes the range of facilities on offer – things such as private bathrooms, lounges, meal provision and so on. From a basic LISTED classification up to FIVE CROWNS can be added. So more crowns mean more facilities.

The distinctive Thistle plaques show the awards made by the STB inspectors as a result of their independent annual assessment. For more information about grading and classification of accommodation in Scotland contact: Scottish Tourist Board, Thistle House, Beechwood Park North, Inverness IV2 3ED. Telephone: 01463 716996

Local Tourist Information

For specific information on a particular part of Scotland, contact the following:

Aberdeen and Grampian Tourist Board
Tel: 01224 632727 Fax: 01224 639836

**Angus and City of Dundee
Tourist Board**
Tel: 01382 434664 Fax: 01382 434665

**Argyll, the Isles, Loch Lomond,
Stirling, Trossachs Tourist Board**
Tel: 01369 701000 Fax: 01369 706085

Ayrshire and Arran Tourist Board
Tel: 01292 288688 Fax: 01292 288686

Dumfries and Galloway Tourist Board
Tel: 01387 250434 Fax: 01387 250462

Edinburgh and Lothians Tourist Board
Tel: 0131 557 1700 Fax: 0131 557 5118

**Greater Glasgow and Clyde Valley
Tourist Board**
Tel: 0141 204 4480 Fax: 0141 204 4772

**The Highlands of Scotland
Tourist Board**
Tel: 01463 723024 Fax: 01463 233044

Kingdom of Fife Tourist Board
Tel: 01592 750066 Fax: 01592 611180

Orkney Tourist Board
Tel: 01856 872856 Fax: 01856 875056

Perthshire Tourist Board
Tel: 01738 627958 Fax: 01738 630416

Scottish Borders Tourist Board
Tel: 01750 20555 Fax: 01750 21886

Shetland Tourism
Tel: 01595 693434 Fax: 01595 695807

Western Isles Tourist Board
Tel: 01851 703088 Fax: 01851 705244

For general enquiries please contact the
**Scottish Tourist Board,
23 Ravelston Terrace, Edinburgh
Tel: 0131 332 2433 Fax: 0131 343 1513**

SCOTLAND

FOOD FROM SCOTLAND
· WINNER ·
· 1996 ·
EXCELLENCE AWARD

SCOTTISH CHOICE

ESTABLISHED
·1864·
MATTHEW ALGIE
Tea & Coffee Merchants

BLENDED IN SCOTLAND FOR SCOTLAND™

MATTHEW A

88
PREMIUM
ROUND
TEA BAGS

BLENDED IN SCOTLAND
FOR SCOTLAND™

The Fine Cheeses of Scotland

THE CLIMATE and geography of Scotland are well suited to cheese-making. During the 13th century the Scots were known to be making a wide variety of cheese, but little has been recorded of their character until the 18th century. At one time cheese was made at many farmhouses and crofts, predominantly for domestic use or for payment of rent, but there was little financial return in this manner of cheesemaking, and the advent of improved transportation of milk altered this dramatically to the extent that by the 1970s farmhouse cheese-making in Scotland had virtually ceased entirely.

Although a few large modern creameries located at Lockerbie, Stranraer and Campbeltown today account for some 80% of total output, smaller creameries have survived on the islands of Bute, Arran, Islay, Mull, Gigha and Orkney. On Orkney can also be found the only surviving vestiges of truly traditional farmhouse cheesemaking in the British Isles, despite the incredible extent of official regulation of all dairies. These remote farmhouse cheeses have a quite distinctive taste and texture and are rarely available outwith Orkney. In addition over the last 30 years, cheesemaking has been re-established at several farms and small dairies across the country, representing Scotland's contribution to a more widespread revival of small scale artisan cheesemaking. Many of the cheeses named below are therefore of relatively recent origin or revival and have given the Scot's cheeseboard a variety and appeal which was lacking only a few years ago.

If you come across interesting local cheese when you eat out, it may be worth enquiring where it can be bought. A few of the small farm cheeses can be bought throughout Britain. The main supermarkets now stock some local cheese and the small number of specialist cheese shops in the main towns have extended their ranges in recent years.

Here are some names to look out for listed according to their geographical origin.

AYRSHIRE AND SW SCOTLAND
Scotland's most productive dairying region containing the largest creameries

Bonnet: mild, pressed goatsmilk cheese.
Burns: traditionally made, unpasteurised, distinctive mild Dunlop cheese.
Swinzie: unpasteurised, pressed, full flavoured ewes milk cheese. All made on a small dairy farm in Ayrshire.

Galloway: established large scale creamery Scottish cheddar made in Stranraer, Galloway.

Loch Arthur: traditional, unpasteurised, organic, cloth-bound cheddar made on a small community dairy farm near Dumfries.

Lockerbie: established large scale creamery cheddar made in Lockerbie.

There are also some locally made farmhouse cheeses which may change from year to year.

BORDERS AND LANARKSHIRE
Traditional hill farming region with a few small, but excellent farmhouse cheesemakers.

Bonchester: small unpasteurised coulommier style Jersey milk cheese.
Teviotdale: vignotte style, white moulded unpasteurised. Both made at a small farmhouse dairy at Bonchester Bridge.

Kelsae: unpasteurised, creamy Jersey milk pressed cheese with a texture similar to Wensleydale and **Stichill** with a crumbly Cheshire like texture. Both made in a tiny farm dairy near Kelso.

Lanark Blue: unpasteurised ewes milk cheese in the style of Roquefort. **Dunsyre Blue:** unpasteurised blue veined cows milk cheese. Both made on a small dairy ewes upland farm near Lanark.

CLYDE AND WESTERN ISLES
Includes many of Scotland's surviving island creameries by virtue of the historical difficulty (and cost) of moving fresh milk to market.

Arran: soft, creamy, medium cheddar made in the creamery on Arran.

Arran Blue: blue veined, semi soft cheese.
Crotin: small, young, white moulded soft cheese. Both made in a tiny creamery at Brodick, Arran.

Drumleish: buttery tasted, mild, uneven textured cheese.

Isle of Bute: medium cheddar. Made in the creamery on Bute.

Inverloch: pressed goats cheese in red wax, farmhouse made on the Isle of Gigha.

Mull of Kintyre: mature cheddar with a nutty flavour.

Highland: mature, pliable, smooth flavour and strong aftertaste. Made in the creamery (a former distillery) at Campbeltown.

Mull: traditional unpasteurised, cloth-bound farmhouse cheddar made at Tobermory on the Island of Mull.

EAST SCOTLAND AND PERTHSHIRE
Fine agricultural district with a remarkable range of fine cheese from just two cheesemakers in the area.

Bishop Kennedy: a 'Trappist' cheese washed in malt whisky to produce a distinctive orangey red crust and a strong creamy taste, runny when ripe, suitable for vegetarians.
Howgate Brie and **Howgate Camembert** (often referred to merely as Scottish Brie and Camembert): traditionally made, maturing to a runny sticky texture, suitable for vegetarians.
Pentland: white moulded soft cheese, creamy texture, made in small quantities and not widely available, suitable for vegetarians.
St Andrews: award winning soft cheese, mild creamy, full flavoured with characteristic golden rind, suitable for vegetarians.
Strathkinness: award winning Scottish mountain cheese, nearly 50 gallons of fresh, whole milk goes into one cheese, dense fruity flavour, matured 6-8 months, suitable for vegetarians, limited availability.

All made at the old farm dairy at Kinfauns Home Farm, in the Carse of Gowrie to the east of Perth, by Howgate Cheese, who pioneered the making of continental cheese in Scotland 30 years ago.

Gowrie: traditional cloth-bound unpasteurised cheddar and Ingle Oak Smoked Cheddar both from a small industrial unit in Perth.

NORTH AND NORTH EAST SCOTLAND
Mainly highland area with difficult climate for large scale commercial dairying but some diverse cheese-making.

Crowdie: fresh, traditional soft crofters cheese. **Galic**, **Hramsa** and **Gruth Dhu:** soft, fresh cheese with wild garlic, black pepper or other added ingredients. **Caboc:** Soft double cream cheese coated in pinhead oatmeal. All made for nearly 30 years in a small industrial unit in Tain, Ross-shire.

Caithness: a new, mild, Danish style waxed cheese (also smoked). Made on a small dairy farm in Lybster, Caithness.

Strathdon Blue: an entirely new blue veined cheese launched in 1997 and made in an industrial creamery in Aberdeen.

Orkney: Climate well suited to dairying and with long tradition and heritage of distinctive cheesemaking, ranging from the two commercial creameries to several small, seasonal farmhouse makers depending upon milk availability.

Orkney Cheddar: distinctive, smooth, even textured, pliable cheese with a history of at least two centuries. Made in two separate creameries in Kirkwall (Claymore) and in Evie (Swannay) in the north east of the Mainland.

There are several seasonal, but quite distinctive farmhouse cheeses available only locally and often known only by their makers' names.

St Andrews • Bishop Kennedy • Strathkinness

Pentland • Howgate Brie • Camembert

howgate

farmhouse cheesemakers

BY APPOINTMENT TO HER MAJESTY THE QUEEN
CHEESEMAKERS
HOWGATE DAIRY FOODS LIMITED, PERTHSHIRE

Kinfauns Home Farm
Kinfauns • Perthshire • Scotland • PH2 7JZ
Tel: (01738) 443440 Fax: (01738) 443439

In Search of the Perfect Espresso

IT'S STARTED. A trend which took off in Seattle has moved to London and is rapidly heading north. No longer will we tolerate the dirty, muddy excuse served up as coffee for so many years. Now people want good coffee and they want lots of it.

"As with food, the secret of good coffee lies in a combination of quality product and skilled production" enthuses David Williamson, Managing Director of Glasgow-based coffee company Matthew Algie. "The beans must be carefully chosen and blended and the perfect espresso can only be made by forcing water at the correct pressure and temperature through a tightly compact wad of eight grams of freshly ground coffee beans producing 1.7 fluid ounces of coffee in exactly 22 seconds". Wow! And just one more thing: the machine must be spotlessly clean.

There is no doubt that speciality coffees are here to stay and that gourmet roast and ground coffee are in increasing demand. Whereas people often drink ordinary coffee at home, they expect great coffee when they go out to dinner. Leading Scottish hotels and restaurants are now promoting a full menu of speciality coffees and even sending staff to the Speciality Coffee School where they discover not only the precise definition of the perfect espresso but, more importantly, how to replicate it in their own hotel, restaurant or cafe.

All great speciality coffees start with a great espresso – it's the building block from which speciality coffees are made and therefore has to be perfect. A quick tip – if your espresso does not have a thick hazelnut brown foam on top (the crema), something has gone wrong. It could be any one of 25 factors but a coffee expert should be able to correct the problem. From there the possibilities are endless. Take, for instance, Caffe Mocha – chocolate and espresso, filled with steamed milk and crowned with a swirl of whipped cream and chocolate shavings. It's delicious. Whipped cream, chocolate sauce, nutmeg, cinnamon, hazelnut and a measure of flavoured syrup can all be added to Lattes (a milky coffee, longer than a cappuccino) to create your own special brew.

One thing is for certain. It used to be that you could judge a restaurant on its pâté; now you can add coffee to the list. In fact, the quality of the coffee could soon be one of the main factors influencing choice in where to eat out in Scotland.

Spirit of Place

MALT WHISKY COMES FROM THE LAND. Made from only water and malted barley, it is also subtly influenced by the micro-climate of the place in which it is made and matured. Charles MacLean looks at the influence Strathspey has on *The Macallan*.

Harvesting The Macallan 'Golden Promise'

Speyside is the acknowledged heartland of malt whisky production. Today, the region contains two-thirds of the malt distilleries in Scotland: 59 in all. Aeneas MacDonald remarked in 1930 'It would be no true or, at least, no very discerning lover of whisky who could enter this almost sacred zone without awe'. This is as true today as it was then.

It is by no historical accident that Speyside has won pre-eminence. The low country between the mountains and the sea, called the Laich o'Moray and known as the Garden of Scotland, has wonderfully rich soils and an equable climate, while its northern latitude makes for long hours of daylight during the summer months. In other words, it is perfect barley growing country.

The peat clad hills which fence the Laich to the south supplied fuel in the days when peat fired the stills and dried the malt. And their relative inaccessibility made them an ideal sanctuary for illicit distillers. Generations of small farmers learned their craft in these hills. In one glen alone there were over 200 'private' stills in the early 1800s. Prior to 1824, however, there were only two licensed distilleries on Speyside. The many hundreds of others saw no need to 'enter' themselves, and cocked a snoot at the authorities. As the Rev. John Grant, minister at Tomintoul, wrote in his entry for the Statistical Account of Scotland (1790): "Tammtoul (sic) ... is inhabited by 37 families ...all of them sell whisky and all of them drink it."

Speyside's holy of holies is Strathspey, which lies between Grantown-on-Spey and Craigellachie, seventeen miles downstream. The parish of Knockando, which comprises the northern portion of Strathspey, climbs in wooded slopes from fertile meadows on the river bank until it becomes wild heather-clad moorland – the highest ground in Morayshire. There are many mineral springs in the parish, and the underlying rocks are granitic, schistose and sedimentary. Perfect conditions for whisky-making, and not surprisingly, there were many smugglers' lairs in these parts. The springs and burns which supplied them now provide production water for The Macallan.

The Macallan distillery lies on one of the few fords across the Spey and twice a year drovers herded their cattle over here from the rich Laich o'Moray to sell them at the Falkirk Trystes. Macallan Farm was a natural resting place, and drovers carried the reputation of the pure malt whisky made there far and wide. Because of its reputation, Alexander Reid, the owner of Macallan Farm was among the first on Speyside to take out a distilling license, only a year after the passing of the Excise Act of 1823, which made it reasonable to do so.

Although The Macallan lies so close to the Spey, the distillery's production water is not drawn from here. It comes direct from the source – pure, sweet and mineral rich – via four private bore holes. Malted barley comes from all over Scotland including the Laich o'Moray, and the distillery specifies a particular species – *Golden Promise*. This strain of barley is generally considered to be the best by brewers and distillers, but it is difficult to grow and gives only a low yield. As a result most farmers and distilleries have gone over to hybrid varieties. The Macallan will not admit of compromise, however. As David Robertson, the distillery manager says: "This involves us in considerable time and effort, as farmers must be financially persuaded to grow Golden Promise when they are aware that better farm yielding varieties are available to them. It is not uncommon for farmers to yield two tonnes per acre on Golden Promise, in comparison to three tonnes of a newer variety such as Prisma."

The distillery stands at c.400 feet above sea level. The air is absolutely pure: lichen clads the trees, a sure sign of the absence of air-borne pollution. The winters here are cold – Scotland's principal ski resort, Aviemore, is not far away – while the summers can be hot. Mean temperatures vary from -25°C to +25°C. While it is maturing, whisky does not like to be disturbed by wide swings in temperature. For this reason, The Macallan built a pioneering new maturation warehouse – the largest in Europe – which provides an environment of calm repose for the maturing malt.

Nobody knows for certain precisely how location influences the flavour of malt whisky, but regional differences are recognised and, as with some wines, connoisseurs can tell from the aroma and flavour of a malt just where it comes from, even if they might not be able to identify the precise distillery. Speyside is malt whisky's heartland and Strathspey the heart of that heartland. Just why such splendid malt whisky is made in this corner of the world defies scientific analysis but certainly owes something to the spirit of place.

For many years the most popular whisky among local people on Speyside has been The Macallan, and now the rest of the world has come to agree with them.

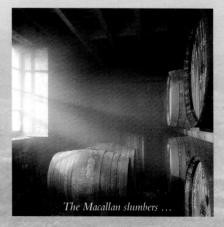

The Macallan slumbers …

Wine and Scottish Food:
A Marriage Made in Heaven

"The King sits in Dunfermling toune, Drinking the blude-reid wine...."

Sir Patrick Spens

WHAT THE KING ATE with his wine is sadly not recorded, but there would certainly have been no shortage of local delicacies to choose from, even in those far-off days. Succulent beef, hearty venison, flavoursome pheasant and grouse, gleaming oysters, sleek river trout – Scotland's wonderful natural larder is a real treasure trove to the growing number of food and wine enthusiasts who visit the country's hotels and restaurants every year.

Pairing food and wine in exciting, inventive ways has always been an important part of French culinary tradition – hardly surprising perhaps, in a nation that gave the world cordon bleu cooking and Chateau d'Yquem. Today, as wine becomes an increasingly popular drink at home, Scotland's chefs are following their partners in the Auld Alliance and including both red and white wine in a wide range of dishes, from soups and sauces to desserts. Innovation in the kitchen has been matched by innovation in the dining room, as restaurants acknowledge the need to offer customers a wisely chosen wine list which complements the menu and adds to their enjoyment of the meal.

Much has been written about food and wine matching, but the basic principles are actually quite simple. The first rule to remember is that there are no rules: just let your tastebuds be your guide. With relatively few exceptions, most foods can happily be paired with several different types of wine – so don't be afraid to try red wine with fish, or sweet white wine with cheese. As long as you choose wines with the same body, texture and depth of flavour as the food they are to be served with, you are unlikely to go wrong. As with cooking, experimentation is very much the name of the game – which is as it should be!

Jane Meek
Alexander Wines

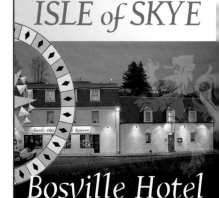

See entry Page 165

Walkers Shortbread –
Celebrating 100 Years of Scottish Taste

WALKERS SHORTBREAD LTD, the well known, distinguished Scottish family business, is celebrating its 100th birthday this year. Founded in 1898 by Joseph Walker as a tiny village bakery, the company has grown into a highly respected international bakery. Walkers found its place on the map at the end of the last century, when Joseph had to borrow enough money to buy some flour and rent a small baker's shop in the beautiful village of Aberlour-on-Spey, nestled in the heart of the Scottish Highlands.

Today, through the success of Joseph's first endeavour, Walkers Shortbread is world famous. It is still baked in the very same village, using traditional family recipes, but on a much larger scale. Joseph's grandchildren, James, Marjorie and Joseph have been running the business since the 1960s, a time when the demand for shortbread increased dramatically and accounts were opened with top stores such as Harrods and Fortnum & Mason.

Since the Sixties, the company has developed a reputation for Scottish heritage and quality worldwide and can be found in over 50 different countries in distinctive tartan packaging. Walkers uses modern technology mixed with age-old craftsmanship with traditional family recipes to produce luxury gifts and treats. Each Walkers product is made from the finest ingredients, without artificial additives, flavourings or colourings, certified Kosher (OUD) without animal fats and are suitable for vegetarians.

Choose from delicious Traditional Shortbread ranges in mouth-watering Almond, Hazelnut, Stem Ginger and Macadamia Nut Shortbread. Walkers Ginger Royals must be the ultimate in shortbread. The luxury shortbread rounds contain tangy, moist pieces of ginger, generously coated with smooth, rich, melt-in-the-mouth dark chocolate.

As well as shortbread, Walkers produces traditional style biscuits, cakes, oatcakes and meringues, available in beautiful tartan boxes and tins decorated with traditional Scottish paintings. Glenfiddich Cake is crammed with fruit, deliciously rich and moist with a generous measure of malt whisky. It is produced in co-operation with the famous distillery, situated near Walkers in the Spey Valley – an area now known as 'Quality Corner' because of the many family companies producing goods which have become world famous because they are outstanding examples of what Scotland has to offer.

Walkers looks forward to celebrating its centenary. New products will be launched for the special year which will make ideal gifts and treats.

BALBIRNIE HOUSE

PRIDE OF BRITAIN MEMBER

AA ★★★★ DE LUXE

SMALL LUXURY HOTELS OF THE WORLD

THE MACALLAN/
TASTE OF SCOTLAND
1996 HOTEL
OF THE YEAR

Wonderful food in the perfect setting, each and every day a range of mouth-watering dishes. Bistro style in the Gamekeepers, rather more formal in the main restaurant overlooking the lovely gardens. Every evening a feature speciality dinner with a multitude of choices on each course at a fixed price of £28.50. We look forward to welcoming you.

Why don't you visit Balbirnie and enjoy one of our special feature overnight stays?

Affordable luxury in idyllic surroundings. Take a stroll in the grounds, 400 beautiful acres of country park and golf course with lovely walks, browse through our fascinating Library, or use the hotel as a base, partake of pursuits such as golfing, riding or clay pigeon shooting or simply enjoy the relaxation. Have one of our all inclusive packages or let us tailor-make a break to suit your particular requirements.

**Balbirnie Park, Markinch,
by Glenrothes, Fife KY7 6NE.
Telephone (01592) 610066
Fax (01592) 610529**

♛ The National Trust for Scotland

Brodick Castle Restaurant
Isle of Arran

Visit magnificent Brodick Castle which is situated in an idyllic position overlooking the sea and surrounded by an 80 acre woodland garden.

Enjoy the best of home cooking and baking in the licensed restaurant which was once the original servant's hall in the heart of the Castle and where you will always be served with hospitality and a warm welcome.

Open daily, 11am – 5pm, 1st April or Good Friday (which ever is earlier) to 31 October.

**Brodick Castle, Isle of Arran, KA27 8HY
Tel: 01770 302202 Fax: 01770 302312**

See entry Page 149

See entry Page 72

A UNIQUE EXPERIENCE OF QUALITY IN THE COUNTRY

Brodie COUNTRYFARE

Restaurant	Bubbles
Quality Home Cooking	*For elegant ladies clothes*
❖	❖
Candle & Soap Shop	Kitchen & Tableware
❖	❖
Countrywear	Food Hall
Country clothing for men & ladies	*Wonderful Delicatessen & Scottish Produce*
❖	❖
Knitwear	Hopscotch
❖	*Children's clothing*
Toys, Stationery	❖
Curiosity & Interiors	Scottish Gifts

**Brodie Countryfare, Brodie, by Forres, Morayshire
Tel: 01309 641555
(approx. 7 miles East of Nairn on the A96)**

Coul House Hotel

Our views are breathtaking. The ancient 'Mackenzies of Coul' picked a wonderful situation for their lovely home. Today, Ann and Martyn will give you a warm Highland welcome. You'll enjoy the 'Taste of Scotland' food of chef Bentley, log fires, summer evening piper and 'Skye' and 'Hamish', the hotel's lovable labradors. Why not use our 'Highland Passport' to cruise on Loch Ness, visit Cawdor Castle, sail to the Summer Isles... or follow our 'Highland Heritage' trail to Glenfiddich Distillery, the Wildlife Park, Culloden Battlefield... for golfers, there's a 5-course holiday including championship Royal Dornoch... for anglers, we have our own salmon and trout fishing... there's pony trekking too.

Ring or write for our colour brochure.

Coul House Hotel
By Strathpeffer,
Ross-shire
Tel 01997-421487
Fax 01997-421945

See entry Page 223

See entry Page 94

CREEBRIDGE HOUSE HOTEL

Galloway,
South West Scotland

Built in 1760 this former shooting lodge to the Earl of Galloway is now an elegant 20 bedroom Country Hotel set in Newton Stewart in 3 acres of private gardens and woodland. 18 hole Golf course 400 yards from the front door. Private Salmon and Trout fishing on the Cree & Bladnoch rivers.

Choose from either the Garden Restaurant or our friendly local Bar where renowned Chef Proprietor Chris Walker and his team cook some of their Taste of Scotland Award winning dishes using fresh local produce. All rooms en suite with colour TV, direct dial phone etc.

Prices from £35.00 bed and breakfast each
Phone or Fax for our brochure
Tel: 01671 402121 Fax: 01671 403258
Email: creebridge.hotel@daelnet.co.uk
Website: www.creebridge.co.uk

See entry Page 195

See entry Page 233

THE SANDFORD

COUNTRY HOUSE HOTEL

The Sandford Hotel, one of the Kingdom of Fife's most picturesque, listed, country house hotels, is renowned for its fine Scottish and European cuisine and comfortable accommodation.

Seasonal dishes in particular, served in the oak beamed restaurant, are the hallmark of Head Chef, Steven Johnstone. An extensive wine list has been carefully chosen in order to complement the variety of dishes on the extensive table d'hôte menu.

The Sandford is located near to both St Andrews and Dundee, and provides an ideal venue for those touring, fishing, golfing or shooting in this region of Scotland.

Bar Lunch 12.00 to 2.30 pm
Bar Supper and Dinner 6.00 to 9.30 pm. Open January to December (inclusive).

The Sandford Country House Hotel
Newton Hill, Wormit, nr Dundee,
Fife DD6 8RG
Tel 01382-541802 • Fax 01382-542136

The Dundonnell Hotel

An 'oasis' in the West this long established family run hotel offers high standards in food and accommodation in a stunning lochside location, midway between Ullapool and Gairloch on Route A832. An ideal centre for relaxation and exploring an area where walking and wildlife are in abundance. Close to An Teallach and many other Munros; for garden enthusiasts Inverewe Gardens 30 mins drive.

Dundonnel Hotel, Little Loch Broom,
Nr Ullapool, Ross-shire, IV23 2QR
Tel: 01854 633204 Fax: 01854 633366
E-mail: selbie@dundonnnelhotel.co.uk
Web: http://www.sol.co.uk/d/dundonnelhotel

AA ★★★   **STB Highly Commended** RAC★★★

Pittodrie House Hotel

"Scottish Splendour at the Foot of Bennachie"

A baronial mansion set in the beautiful Aberdeenshire Countryside with 27 individually designed luxurious bedrooms, magnificent public rooms adorned with antiques and warmed by crackling log fires.

Both the dining room and bar lunch menu's offer the freshest of local produce cooked with care and flair. An extensive wine list and malt whisky collection accompany the fine food and exceptional service.

Relax in the walled garden, climb Bennachie, explore the whisky and castles trail – just some of the activities to enjoy.

Pittodrie House Hotel, Chapel of Garioch, Inverurie AB51 5HS
Tel: (01467) 681444, Fax: (01467) 681648

See entry Page 147

See entry Page 167

HOTEL EILEAN IARMAIN
Isle Ornsay Hotel

The Gaelic Inn on the Sea

*The Taste of Skye
- mostly landed at our own wharf. Oysters and prawns, lobsters and halibut. Relish our seafood and relax in a seaview room. Open all year. Centrally heated. Full menus and information available from:*

Effie Kennedy, Hotel Eilean Iarmain, Sleat, Isle of Skye, IV43 8QR.
Telephone: 014713 833332 Fax: 014713 833275

Dungallan House Hotel

GALLANACH ROAD, OBAN, PA34 4PD
TEL: 01631 563799 FAX: 01631 566711

 AA ★★ ❀
👑👑👑
STB Commended

George and Janice Stewart look forward to welcoming you to their lovely Victorian Villa set high above Oban. Only half a mile away from the town centre with all its facilities yet far enough to be at peace amidst 5 acres of steep craggy tree-lined cliffs and lawns

See entry Page 197

See entry Page 213

ENMORE HOTEL

E legant warm hotel with well tended gardens in enviable location overlooking the Firth of Clyde. Excellent inventive cooking by chef/patron using own garden produce and specialising in Taste of Scotland dishes. Good service and hospitality from very attentive staff and owners. Luxurious, pretty bedrooms, some with four-poster beds and jacuzzi. Comfortable public rooms with lots of flowers, books and log fires. Squash courts and conference facilities. Golf, fishing, stalking, water sports and Argyll Forest Park nearby. Ideal centre for exploring this undiscovered part of the Highlands yet only 1 hour from Glasgow Airport. Dogs and children welcome.

AA ★★❀
👑👑👑👑
STB Highly Commended
(THE TASTE OF SCOTLAND)

See entry Page 98

See entry Page 134

The Haven Hotel

The Haven Hotel is situated in one of the West Highland's most charming villages. The hotel was built a century ago as a merchant's residence and still retains its unique character. Behind its warm sandstone exterior, you'll find all the elements of a traditional West Highland welcome – friendly service, well-appointed rooms and delicious locally produced food.

Food in the hotel's restaurant represents Scottish cooking at its best with menus based on a wealth of excellent local produce. Fresh salmon, seafood and fish caught locally, prime Scottish Beef, Highland Venison, hill Lamb, home grown vegetables and soft fruits, home baking – these are starting points for cuisine which is simple, imaginative and delicious. An extensive wine list complements the superb menu which changes daily.

Romantic Hotel of Britain and Ireland Award 1997
 AA ★★ 77% ❀
Courtesy & Care Award   Special Merit Award

**3 INNES STREET, PLOCKTON, ROSS-SHIRE IV52 8TW
TELEPHONE** (01599) 544223, **FAX** (01599) 544467

THE HOLLY TREE HOTEL

F riendly family run hotel in breathtaking setting on the shores of Loch Linnhe. All bedrooms are ensuite and enjoy magnificent views across the loch to the Morvern peninsula. Delicious freshly prepared food is available all day from our 'Charles Rennie MacIntosh' style restaurant. A perfect touring base for Glencoe, Fort William and Oban.

ℋoustoun ℋouse
—— HOTEL & RESTAURANT ——
UPHALL • Nr EDINBURGH
★★★★

At Houston House, the traditional Scottish surroundings are matched by equally traditional Scottish hospitality. Whether you visit for relaxation, business or celebration, we know that you will wish to relive your experiences at Houstoun and we look forward to your return.

Full leisure facilities opening late 1998

Houstoun House Hotel, Uphall,
West Lothian EH52 6JS
Telephone 01506 853831
Fax 01506 854220

See entry Page 112

See entry Page 189

See entry Page 117

See entry Page 211

Inver Lodge Hotel

Lochinver, Sutherland, IV27 4LU.
Tel (01571) 844496 Fax (01571) 844395

The hotel commands panoramic views of Loch Inver Bay with great peaks of Sutherland: Cansip & Suliven in the background.

Inver Lodge offers high standards in service, accommodation, and cuisine, making the most of locally landed fish and crustacea, using the best Aberdeen Angus beef, Highland lamb and local venison.

Guests can enjoy free trout fishing in the most spectacular scenery. Salmon fishing is available for an additional fee.

Lochinver is an ideal base for touring the Northern Highlands with easy day trips to Inverewe Gardens, Smoo Caves and Dunrobin Castle. Numerous & famous golf courses are within an easy 1½ hours drive.

Please contact Nicholas Gorton for a brochure.

KNOCKENDARROCH HOUSE
STB
♛♛♛
   ★★ ⊛ 73%   Highly Commended

Higher Oakfield, Pitlochry, Perthshire,
Telephone: 01796 473473 Fax: 01796 474068
Email: knock@dial.pipex.com

A gracious Victorian mansion, family owned and run, with glorious views over Pitlochry and Tummel River and valley yet close to the town centre. Set in its own grounds surrounded by mature oaks, Knockendarroch affords a relaxed atmosphere with the high standards in food, wines and personal service. Lots to see and do locally including the festival theatre. The perfect base for sightseeing and touring. A non smoking hotel.

ARDANAISEIG HOTEL
by Loch Awe

IN A REMOTE PLACE
of quiet tranquillity and
almost surreal natural beauty,
where the slopes of Ben
Cruachan fall into the clear
waters of Loch Awe, there is a
small, luxurious and wildly
romantic old country house
hotel. It sits alone, overlooking
the mysterious islands and
crannogs of the Loch, in
deeply wooded gardens
teeming with wildlife

♕♕♕♕ HIGHLY COMMENDED

Kilchrenan by Taynuilt   Argyll
Scotland   PA35 1HE
Tel 01866 833333   Fax 01866 833222

Award winning chef
Douglas Wright has
compiled his menus
from the finest of
local and Scottish
ingredients. Whether
just passing or staying in the area you
are sure to return here be it for one of
his fine light lunches or a memorable
dinner. Every meal at
The Loft is special.

AA ✹ ✹   OPEN ALL YEAR

On the road to the golf course
Blair Athol, by Pitlochry, Perthshire
Tel 01796 491377 Fax 01796 481511

See entry Page 69

See entry Page 66

LOVAT ARMS HOTEL
BEAULY NR. INVERNESS IV4 7BS
TELEPHONE: (01463) 782313
FAX: (01463) 782862

*Friendly family managed hotel offering
great comfort and excellent value for
money, with Aberdeen Angus Beef and
North Country Cheviot lamb from our
own farm. 10 minutes from Inverness,
and central to the whole Highland area.
Bar Lunches, High Teas, Bar Suppers
and Lairds Table for Dinner.*

Take a Fresh Look at Malin Court

The Carrick Restaurant provides the best of modern Scottish food in a congenial and informal atmosphere. Chef takes only the finest ingredients and gently transforms them into exquisite lunches, high teas and dinners.

However if you would like to stay longer one of our 17 en suite bedrooms with sea views is the ideal base from which to explore Burns country. Malin Court is tucked away on the Ayrshire Coast overlooking Turnberry's famous golf course, Ailsa Craig and the mystical Isle of Arran. No matter how short your visit we're sure you'll find it all very refreshing.

MALIN COURT HOTEL & RESTAURANT
TURNBERRY, AYRSHIRE. KA26 9PB
TEL•01655 331457 FAX•01655 331072
Email•info@malincourt.co.uk
Iternet•http://www.malincourt.co.uk

AA ★★★
RAC HOTEL ★★★
Hospitality Comfort Restaurant
Best Western

See entry Page 230

See entry Page 78

Mansfield House Hotel

WEENSLAND ROAD, HAWICK.
TEL. 01450-373988

Standing in its own wooded grounds overlooking Hawick this charming Victorian House Hotel is now considered one of the best restaurants in the Scottish Borders.

The magnificent Dining Room which has been restored to its original glory makes dining out a real pleasure.

The menus which have a Scottish flavour feature the very best of local and Scottish produce and are complemented by an excellent wine list.

We are sure you will enjoy a memorable meal in the most memorable of surroundings.

See entry Page 139

See entry Page 75

Nivingston House

Award winning food, great golf, in landscaped peace and quiet

Nestling at the foot of the Cleish Hills and dating back to the year 1725, Nivingston is a peaceful haven within easy reach of Edinburgh, Glasgow and Perth. Situated in 12 acres of landscaped grounds in which guests can try their hand at golf, putting and croquet, the hotel provides every comfort and modern convenience.

Nivingston House,
Cleish Hills, Nr Kinross,
Tel 01577 850216 Fax 01577 850238

THE ROMAN CAMP HOTEL
CALLANDER FK17 8BG
TEL 01877-330003 FAX 01877-331533

Nestling in the heart of the beautiful Trossachs, the Roman Camp Hotel offers a magical mixture of gracious living and historic atmosphere.

Surrounded by 20 acres of superb gardens on the banks of the River Teith, the hotel's picturesque interior reflects the original charm of this 17th century building.

All bedrooms have private bathrooms, and facilities which make for a welcoming, comfortable stay. Guests can enjoy peace and tranquillity in a truly unique style.

Fresh produce and fine wines will tempt the most discerning diner and friendly personal service creates an atmosphere of leisured living.

The Roman Camp invites you to relax and enjoy the warmest of welcomes and the greatest of pleasure.

For brochure, tariff and reservations write, telephone or fax.

MANSFIELD HOUSE HOTEL

At the Mansfield House Hotel we have all you need to help you enjoy your holiday... good food, friendly service and a lovely atmosphere... they're all to be found at the Mansfield. So whether you're touring or golfing, shooting or fishing, alone or with a small group, give us a call. We will tell you about our 18 rooms, several with jacuzzis, and about our special rates for weekends and week-long holidays. We can make your mouths water with the food in our restaurants and you can enjoy our more than 50 malt whiskies and our real ales. We will help book your tee-off times at Tain, Royal Dornoch and many other nearby courses and pass on discounts. We can suggest touring itineraries and we can arrange car hire. In short, we will do anything and everything to ensure that you enjoy your stay at the Mansfield House Hotel.

AA ★★★ Scotland's Commended **RAC**★★★

STB
👑👑👑👑👑
Highly Commended

INVESTOR IN PEOPLE

RAC Merit
Awards
Restaurant &
Hospitality

SCOTSBURN ROAD, TAIN, ROSS-SHIRE IV19 1PR
TEL. 01862-892052 FAX. 01862-892260

See entry Page 225

See entry Page 41

See entry Page 169

See entry Page 228

THAINSTONE HOUSE HOTEL

**Thainstone Estate Inverurie Aberdeenshire AB51 5NT
Tel: 01467 621643 Fax: 01467 625084**

On A96 north of Aberdeen (8 miles from airport)

A country house hotel and country club near Aberdeen, winners of Taste of Scotland Scotch Lamb Challenge 1992. Four star and two RAC Rosettes.

**CONVERTED COUNTRY MANSION
COUNTRY HOUSE COOKING
"THAINSTONE RANKS AMONG THE BEST
COUNTRY HOUSE HOTELS IN SCOTLAND"**

This charming house has been modernised to become a comfortable hotel and country club. Behind its imposing facade the house has been radically altered to create a luxurious modern hotel and leisure centre. The Head Chef, Allan Donald (ex Gleneagles), offers both à la carte and table d'hôte menus in Simpson's Restaurant. There is an ambitious and bold feeling about many of the dishes; the presentation is influenced by nouvelle cuisine, but portion sizes and the quality of the raw materials are influenced only by the rich farming country within which Thainstone stands. You can also eat in Cammie's Bar, where the food and the atmosphere is more informal.

TRIGONY HOUSE HOTEL
THORNHILL

 👑👑👑 STB Highly Commended
RAC★★ *merit* **AA** ★★

A small Edwardian country house set in the beautiful Nithsdale Valley of Dumfries and Galloway.

Good food, comfort and hospitality. All bedrooms with en suite facilities. Elegant dining room. Cosy bar. Golf, shooting and fishing all nearby or why not simply relax and enjoy the Land of Burns.

**TRIGONY HOUSE HOTEL
Thornhill, Dumfriesshire DG3 5EZ
Tel: 01848 331211 Fax: 01848 331303**

Scottish Produce: Renowned for Quality

TRADITIONALLY, Scottish produce is famed throughout the world for its quality. From smoked salmon to whisky, shortbread to natural mineral water.

NATURAL MINERAL WATER, THE CLEAR CHOICE

Natural mineral water is the finest water on earth. But beware, not all bottled waters are 'natural mineral water'. For instance 'spring water' is often processed and treated before bottling and 'table water' can actually be mains or tap water. Natural mineral water like Highland Spring has the distinction of having nothing added or taken away. Except a little carbonation to make it sparkling. In fact, they don't even have to filter it. That happens naturally as it percolates its way through hundreds of layers of porous rock to the underground aquifers, where it waits to be collected.

With its unique purity and Scottish heritage, it's not surprising that Highland Spring is considered the ideal accompaniment not only to food, but to Scotland's other national drink, whisky. In fact, both the Scotch Whisky Association and The Scotch Malt Whisky Society recommend a splash of Highland Spring to bring the water of life, to life.

THE SOURCE OF HIGHLAND SPRING

Drawn from deep below the rolling Ochil Hills in Blackford, Perthshire, you could say that every rain shower is a delivery of Highland Spring. Though it takes another fifteen years for it to filter down through the rock layers to its underground source. On the way down, it absorbs the natural wholesome minerals which distinguish it from other waters. It's then bottled as it's found. Nothing is added, except maybe a bubble or two.

No wonder the Scottish Kings were known to favour its unique taste and purity. In fact, in 1488 King James IV of Scotland even ordered the celebration ale for his Coronation to be made from 'Blackford Water'. Though these days people seem to prefer it without the yeast and barley.

It does, however, still enjoy the same reputation both at home and abroad. In fact, visit the best eateries in Scotland and it won't just be the food that's sparkling. As a member of Connoisseurs Scotland, it's on tap, so to speak, in some of the country's most exclusive establishments. From the Gleneagles Hotel to The Old Course Hotel in St Andrews. But then it's used to keeping such lofty company. After all, it's also served on board Concorde.

Alexander Wines

WHOLESALE WINE MERCHANT AND SHIPPER

Deanside Road, Hillington, Glasgow G52 4XB
Tel: 0141 882 0039 Fax: 0141 882 0041

Scottish Agents for:

Laurent-Perrier *Champagne*
Remy-Pannier *Loire*
Henri Bourgeois *Sancerre*
Ch. Kirwan 3 eme Cru *Margaux*
Ch. de la Jaubertie *Bergerac*
Antonin Rodet *Burgundy*
Marques de Riscal *Rioja*
Hugh Ryman *Spain/Moldova*
Moreno Wine Importers *Spain*
Royal Tokay Wine Company *Hungary*
Cranswick Estate *Australia*
Simon Hackett *Australia*
Selaks *New Zealand*
Simonsig *South Africa*
Casablanca *Chile*

See article Page 20
See entry Page 83

Welcome To The Listings

ARDOE HOUSE HOTEL
South Deeside Road
Aberdeen AB12 5YP
Tel: 01224 867355
Fax: 01224 861283

B9077, 3 miles west of Aberdeen.

Just outside Aberdeen this baronial style hotel provides very good accommodation and hospitality.

- Scottish baronial mansion converted to a comfortable country house hotel.
- Modern and traditional Scottish cuisine.
- "An elegant, charming hotel close to Aberdeen."

Ardoe House is a classic Scots baronial granite mansion, with towers and corbelled bartizans, crow-stepped gables and crenellations. It was built in 1878 by a wealthy soap manufacturer, 'Soapie' Ogston, for his wife. As day turns to night Ardoe turns into a fairytale castle and it is a delight to relax in the original palatial rooms. The bedrooms have private facilities and there are also function rooms available for conferences and weddings. Dining is à la carte (or house menu if on an exclusive rate) from an extensive menu of unusually treated dishes and imaginative combinations. Chef Ivor Clark draws inspiration from classic French cooking, whilst using fresh Scottish produce. The hotel has 2 AA Rosettes. *(See advert Page 22.)*

Open all year
🏠 Rooms: 71 with private facilities
🛏 DB&B from £65   B&B from £45
SP Special rates available
✖ Food available all day £££
✖ Lunch ££
✖ Dinner £££
Ⓥ Vegetarians welcome
🧍 Children welcome
♿ Facilities for disabled visitors
🚭 No smoking in dining room

Fillet of salmon hot smoked with a lime and horseradish sauce. Loin of Scottish venison with beetroot and orange compote. Raspberry and Drambuie crème brûlée.

STB Highly Commended 👑 👑 👑 👑 👑
💳 Credit cards: Mastercard/Eurocard, Visa, Diners Club, Switch
👤 General Manager: Ewen Kirkpatrick

THE ATHOLL HOTEL
54 King's Gate
Aberdeen, Grampian
AB15 4YN
Tel: 01224 323505
Fax: 01224 321555

Follow signs for A96 north. Turn right at King's Gate roundabout, the hotel is situated ½ mile along King's Gate in the heart of the city's West End.

Comfortable and friendly city centre hotel.

- Traditional granite building.
- Traditional Scottish cooking.
- "A high standard of accommodation and quality service prevails in this personally owned and managed hotel."

The Atholl Hotel is under the personal supervision of Gordon Sinclair who has an eye for detail and high standards. The rooms are well-appointed and attractively decorated and the hotel has a comfortable and warm atmosphere – the staff are friendly and enthusiastic. The cooking is simple and straightforward with high quality products and there is much evidence of local quality produce. Menus change monthly with specials changing nightly depending upon local produce.

Open all year except New Year's Day
🏠 Rooms: 35 with private facilities
🛏 B&B £69.50–£78
SP Special rates available
✖ Lunch ££
✖ Dinner ££
Ⓥ Vegetarians welcome
🧍 Children welcome

Haggis in a potato nest with Drambuie cream sauce. Double loin of Highland lamb with a pear, port and tarragon purée. Chocolate cup with Glayva mousse garnished with local berries.

STB Highly Commended 👑 👑 👑 👑
💳 Credit cards: Mastercard/Eurocard, American Express, Visa, Diners Club, Switch
👤 Managing Partner: Gordon Sinclair

CALEDONIAN THISTLE HOTEL
Union Terrace
Aberdeen AB10 1WE
Tel: 01224 640233
Fax: 01224 641627

Follow signs to city centre, Union Terrace is located half-way along Union Street, Aberdeen's main thoroughfare.

Traditional city centre hotel.

- Town hotel in the heart of Aberdeen.
- Combination of traditional and Scottish cuisine with a strong European influence.
- "Scottish hospitality and innovative food in a city centre hotel."

This large, imposing Victorian hotel overlooks Union Terrace Gardens and is very close to Union Street, the main shopping street of the Granite City. It is well-appointed and tastefully decorated in a style which complements the architectural features; bedrooms are traditionally furnished and very comfortable. The Restaurant on the Terrace is of a high standard offering a well-balanced table d'hôte menu which features local fresh produce and is cooked with a Mediterranean influence under the expertise of Chef Martin Buhler. For less formal eating there is Elrond's Cafe, a spacious bar and restaurant which serves drinks, snacks and a bistro menu. The Caledonian Thistle is a very conveniently located base to explore all that Aberdeen has to offer.

Open all year
🏨 Rooms: 80 with private facilities
🛏 DB&B £59–£102   B&B £45.50–£88.50
SP Special rates available
✘ Food available all day ££
✘ Lunch except Sun Sat ££
✘ Dinner £££
Ⓥ Vegetarians welcome
🧍 Children welcome
♿ Limited facilities for disabled visitors – please enquire

Galantine of corn fed chicken. Halibut fillet en Papillote. Dark chocolate shell with white chocolate mousse on a blackcurrant coulis.

STB Commended 👑 👑 👑 👑 👑
💳 Credit cards: Mastercard/Eurocard, American Express, Visa, Diners Club
Ⓜ General Manager: Ewing Stewart

COURTYARD RESTAURANT
Alford Lane
Aberdeen AB1 1YD
Tel: 01224 213795
Fax: 01224 212961

In Aberdeen's West End, between Holburn Street and Albyn Place, just round the corner from Union Street.

A gourmet's paradise in central Aberdeen.

- City centre restaurant and bistro.
- Modern, creative Scottish cooking.
- "Every visit is a memorable dining experience at this Aberdonian restaurant."

The Courtyard on the Lane is a small stone building in a cobbled lane in Aberdeen's commercial district. It is a sanctuary of good food and a great discovery. Martha's Bistro (downstairs) has an informal atmosphere. Upstairs, the Courtyard Restaurant is more formal and encourages you to linger over lunch or dinner. Glenn Lawson and his young kitchen team have created a fresh and innovative menu with daily selections of fish, game and poultry. The same menu is served in both dining areas. It is advisable to book. Winner of The Macallan Taste of Scotland Restaurant of the Year 1994.

Open all year except first wk Jan
Closed Sun Mon
✘ Lunch except Sun Mon ££
✘ Dinner except Sun Mon £££
Ⓥ Vegetarians welcome
🧍 Children welcome
♿ Facilities for disabled visitors – bistro restaurant only
🚭 No pipes or cigars in dining areas

Pigeon terrine studded with leeks and oyster mushrooms. Grilled salmon on a risotto pancake with fresh tomato sauce. Chocolate walnut tart on a malt whisky anglaise.

💳 Credit cards: Mastercard/Eurocard, American Express, Visa, Mastercharge, Switch, Delta
Ⓜ Manager: Richard Hood

CRAIGLYNN HOTEL

36 Fonthill Road, Aberdeen AB11 6UJ
Tel: 01224 584050 Fax: 01224 212225
e-mail 106053,1542 @ compuserve.com
website http://www.craiglynn.co.uk

On corner of Fonthill Road and Bon Accord Street, midway between Union Street and King George VI Bridge. Car park access from Bon Accord Street.

An intimate and charming hotel, close to the centre of Aberdeen.

- An impressive late Victorian house built with local granite.
- Lovingly prepared Scottish cooking.
- "An elegant town house with exceptional architectural features."

Craiglynn Hotel was once the home of a wealthy Aberdeen fish merchant and has attractive rooms with high moulded ceilings and carved fire surrounds. These features have been carefully preserved by the hotel's owners, Chris and Hazel Mann, as have the parquet flooring and rose-wood panelling in the dining room (which was originally the billiard room). Service is friendly and attentive, and guests are made to feel part of the family. In the handsome dining room menus are short, since everything is prepared from fresh produce (even home-grown), and the cooking homely. The bedrooms are very comfortable and most have unique en suite facilities.

Open all year except Christmas Day + Boxing Day
🛏 Rooms: 9 (7 with private facilities)
🍴 DB&B £39.50–£75.50   B&B £25–£60
🍴 Non-residents – by reservation
♀ Restricted licence
✗ Dinner ££
Ⓥ Vegetarians welcome
🕂 Children welcome
✂ No smoking in dining room + bedrooms

Leek and coriander soup. Medallions of pork tenderloin in a crushed pepper, cream and white wine sauce. Aurchtydonald strawberries in a meringue basket with Drambuie ice cream.

STB Highly Commended 🏵 🏵 🏵
💳 Credit cards: Mastercard/Eurocard, American Express, Visa, Diners Club, Mastercharge, Switch
👤 Partners: Hazel & Chris Mann

FARADAY'S RESTAURANT

2 Kirk Brae, Cults
Aberdeen AB15 9SQ
Tel/Fax: 01224 869666

4 miles from Aberdeen on A96 to Cults.

Faraday's has a deserved reputation for the quality and originality of its cooking.

- Small, atmospheric restaurant in a tastefully converted Victorian electricity station.
- Traditional Scottish cooking, with European, Eastern and African influences.
- "A highly enjoyable eating experience – excellent in all aspects."

Michael Faraday, after whom this restaurant is named, was 'The Father of Electricity'. The choice of name is appropriate for a building which was, in Victorian times, an electricity sub-station supplying the district of Cults. The room is long and inviting: its panelled walls decorated with tapestries and memorabilia; its tables of polished wood, with brass candlesticks and linen napery. Vases of cut flowers embellish the window embrasures, and there is a minstrel's gallery at one end. John Inches, Faraday's owner/chef, presents a short menu (five main courses, changing weekly) which he describes as 'Scottish traditional', but which draws inspiration from his extensive travels in France and makes intelligent use of Eastern flavourings and presentation.

Open all year except Boxing Day + New Year's Day
Closed Sun Mon lunch
✗ Lunch except Sun Mon £-££
✗ Dinner except Sun Mon – special functions only ££
Ⓥ Vegetarians welcome
♿ Facilities for disabled visitors
✂ No smoking before 2 pm + 10 pm

Tossed summer salad of Scottish asparagus, leeks, warm new potatoes and crispy bacon. Pan-seared breast of marinaded pheasant with fresh thyme, flat cap field mushroom with haggis in a rich Madeira jus. Individual hazelnut pavlovas with rose-water ice and orange sugared strawberries and raspberries.

💳 Credit cards: Mastercard/Eurocard, Visa, Switch
👤 Chef/proprietor: John Inches

THE MARCLIFFE AT PITFODELS

North Deeside Road, Aberdeen AB15 9YA
Tel: 01224 861000 Fax: 01224 868860
e-mail – stewart@marcliff.win-uk.net

On A93 to Braemar. 1 mile from A92. 3 miles from city centre.

An outstanding country house hotel on the outskirts of Aberdeen.

- A large modern building tastefully in keeping with the older house it encompasses.
- Modern classic cooking with French influence and the best of Scottish ingredients.
- "Excellence abounds in all aspects of service, surroundings and cuisine."

The Marcliffe at Pitfodels is a clever combination of old and new. Its atmosphere is luxurious, and enhances modern design with antiques and baronial detailing – the spacious new foyer has a stone flagged floor, comfortable sofas and an open fire. The Marcliffe's proprietors, Sheila and Stewart Spence, are experienced hoteliers and this shows in the attention to detail and the high standard of service in every department. There are two restaurants: the Conservatory, and the Invery Room. Menus in both are well-balanced and extensive; and the cooking is accomplished. Fresh lobster is available from May to October. 100 malt whiskies and 400 wines available. One of 14 establishments shortlisted for The Macallan Taste of Scotland Awards 1997.

- - - - - -

    Open all year
🏨 Rooms: 42 with private facilities
🛏️ DB&B £82.50–£150   B&B £52.50–£125
SP Special rates available
✕ Lunch £££
✕ Dinner £££
Ⓥ Vegetarians welcome
⚘ Children welcome
♿ Facilities for disabled visitors
🚭 No smoking in Invery Room Restaurant
🐂 Member of the Scotch Beef Club

Char-grilled gravadlax set on a leek, potato and celeriac galette with a chive butter sauce. Herb crusted rack of lamb with beignets of rosemary stuffing and mint jus. Fresh peppered pineapple with rum and coconut ice cream.

STB Deluxe 👑 👑 👑 👑 👑
💳 Credit cards: Mastercard/Eurocard, American Express, Visa, Diners Club, Mastercharge, Switch
👤 Proprietors: Stewart Spence & Sheila Spence

MARYCULTER HOUSE HOTEL

South Deeside Road, Aberdeen AB12 5GB
Tel: 01224 732124 Fax: 01224 733510

B9077 Banchory-Aberdeen (South Deeside Road) c. 5 miles from Aberdeen, 1 mile west of B979 and B9077 junction. Signposted.

A historic country hotel outside Aberdeen.

- Country hotel on the banks of the River Dee.
- Good hotel cooking with French influences.
- "Fresh orchids and log fires await you in this country hotel on the banks of the River Dee."

In the early 13th century a powerful Anglo-Norman noble founded a preceptory (college) of the Knights Templar on the south bank of the Dee. The remains of the preceptory are incorporated into Maryculter House. The hotel has five acres of grounds on the banks of the river. The 23 bedrooms are all comfortable and tastefully decorated, as are the public rooms and bars. Food is served both in the bar, 'The Poacher's Pocket' and in the 'The Priory', a more formal dining room where the tables are charmingly dressed with linen and fresh orchids. The former's menu offers an interesting selection of well-priced bistro style food; the latter's is a solid table d'hôte menu (six main courses) with a broad choice of meat, poultry, fish and vegetarian dishes.

- - - - - -

    Open all year
🏨 Rooms: 23 with private facilities
🛏️ DB&B £55–£58   B&B £37–£45
SP Special rates available
✕ Food available all day £££
✕ Lunch ££
✕ Dinner £££
Ⓥ Vegetarians welcome
⚘ Children welcome
♿ Facilities for disabled visitors

Parcels of smoked salmon filled with smoked mackerel mousse and surrounded by a pickled cucumber and orange salad. Pan-fried medallions of venison on a redcurrant glaze garnished with pear fritters. Home-made malt whisky cheesecake on a fresh raspberry coulis with chantilly cream.

STB Commended 👑 👑 👑 👑
💳 Credit cards: Mastercard/Eurocard, American Express, Visa, Diners Club, Switch
👤 General Manager: Andrew Miller

LAIRHILLOCK INN & RESTAURANT
Netherley
by Stonehaven
Aberdeenshire AB39 3QS
Tel: 01569 730001
Fax: 01569 731175

Take A90 south from Aberdeen, pass Portlethen then take right hand turn for Durris for 3 miles.

A charming old coaching inn between Stonehaven and Aberdeen.

- Atmospheric country pub with restaurant.
- Modern cooking, with continental influences.
- "An imaginative menu, a comprehensive wine list and olde worlde atmosphere makes for a very enjoyable eating experience."

Lairhillock is a traditional small coaching inn (originally a farmhouse). It stands on the old Stonehaven-Aberdeen road, and was certainly there when Bonnie Prince Charlie took this road north to ultimate defeat at Culloden in 1746. The place has been extensively refurbished by its current owners, Frank and Anne Budd, in a way which enhances the original rustic features (low ceilings, dark beams, carved oak bar front, large open hearth with real log fires). Friendly, helpful staff complete the picture to make a very welcoming inn. Beef comes from a local farm; daily fish from Gourdon; fruits from local suppliers. Sauces are interesting and appropriate, and the overall treatment of the food sensitive and unusually good. An interesting wine list features some unusual wines, and some first growths. The Lairhillock is a great favourite with business people, locals and tourists.

Open all year except 25, 26 Dec, 1 + 2 Jan
✗ Lunch £
✗ Dinner ££
Ⓥ Vegetarians welcome
✿ Children welcome
♿ Facilities for disabled visitors

Prawns in a sauce from peppers, courgettes and Cajun spices. Ostrich steaks. Sticky toffee pudding.

▣ Credit cards: Mastercard/Eurocard, American Express, Visa, Diners Club, Mastercharge, Switch, Delta
◪ Proprietors: Frank & Anne Budd

THAINSTONE HOUSE HOTEL & COUNTRY CLUB
Inverurie, Aberdeenshire AB51 5NT
Tel: 01467 621643
Fax: 01467 625084

On A96 north of Aberdeen, 8 miles from airport – between Kintore and Inverurie.

A country house hotel and country club near Aberdeen, offering first class cooking and hospitality.

- Converted country mansion.
- Country house cooking.
- "Elegant surroundings, relaxed atmosphere, with a high standard of food and service."

This charming house has been modernised to become a comfortable hotel and country club. The Executive Chef Allan Donald offers both à la carte and table d'hôte menus in 'Simpsons' Restaurant. There is an ambitious and bold feeling about many of the dishes; the presentation is influenced by nouvelle cuisine, but portion sizes and the quality of the raw materials are influenced only by the rich farming country within which Thainstone stands. You can also eat in Cammie's Bar, where the food and atmosphere is more informal. The hotel has 2 AA Rosettes. *(See advert Page 32.)*

Open all year
▥ Rooms: 48 with private facilities
⌂ DB&B £66–£90   B&B £45–£80
ⓢⓟ Special rates available
✗ Food available all day ££-£££
✗ Lunch £££
✗ Dinner ££££
Ⓥ Vegetarians welcome
✿ Children welcome
♿ Facilities for disabled visitors
⌇ No smoking in restaurant

Game terrine studded with artichokes. Turban of Scottish salmon and lobster with rich crayfish and coriander sauce. Warm frangipane tart, mulled berries and clotted cream.

STB Highly Commended 👑 👑 👑 👑 👑
▣ Credit cards: Mastercard/Eurocard, American Express, Visa, Diners Club, Switch, Delta
◪ General Manager: M Jane Robertson

UDNY ARMS HOTEL
Main Street, Newburgh, Aberdeenshire AB41 6BL
Tel: 01358 789444
Fax: 01358 789012

On A975, 2½ miles off A92 Aberdeen-Peterhead,
15 minutes from Aberdeen.

A hotel situated in the centre of Newburgh village, overlooking the golf course. The hotel has a function suite and cafe bar.

- A traditional Victorian stone-built house with the style and character of an old village inn.
- Creative Scottish cooking.
- "Excellent food and friendly atmosphere fulfils the hotel's motto 'you simply can't help returning.'"

The Udny Arms Hotel overlooks the Ythan Estuary and has attracted sportsmen, nature lovers and tourists to the Aberdeenshire village of Newburgh for over 100 years. It is an unpretentious and intimate hotel, run by the Craig family, and the service is cheerful and efficient. Some recent changes to the building have made room for a cosy residents lounge. Dining is in the bistro, a split-level restaurant overlooking the lovely Sands of Forvie. The extensive à la carte menu changes every six weeks, and includes a handful of 'specials' which change daily. Meat and game come from the famous Bain of Tarves – and fish is a speciality. The hotel also has a brasserie-style restaurant, in the Parlour, with table d'hôte menu. Udny Arms has an AA Rosette and is a member of the Certified Aberdeen Angus Scheme.

Open all year except Christmas Night + Boxing Night
- ♨ Rooms: 26 with private facilities
- ⛱ DB&B £45–£50   B&B £30–£55
- 🆂🅿 Special rates available
- ✗ Lunch £-££
- ✗ Dinner £-££
- Ⓥ Vegetarians welcome
- ✷ Children welcome
- ♿ Facilities for disabled visitors

Home-cured gravadlax. Sauté scallops on wilted spinach with pesto sauce. The original sticky toffee pudding.

STB Commended 👑 👑 👑 👑
- 💳 Credit cards: Mastercard/Eurocard, American Express, Visa, Diners Club, Mastercharge, Switch, Delta
- 🅺 Proprietors: Denis & Jennifer Craig

HAWKCRAIG HOUSE
Hawkcraig Point, Aberdour
Fife KY3 0TZ
Tel: 01383 860335

From centre of Aberdour, take Hawkcraig Road (signed 'Silver Sands') through large car park, then to right, down very steep access to Hawkcraig Point.

Individual house with outstanding location and charming hosts.

- Whitewashed ferryman's house.
- Accomplished traditional cooking.
- "The adventurous approach to the house proved more than worth the effort for the spectacular situation and cooking."

This charming old whitewashed ferryman's house sits at the water's edge at Hawkcraig Point, next to the old harbour with lovely views of Aberdour Bay and Inchcolm Island's, 12th century abbey. Only half an hour from Edinburgh by road or rail and a pleasant hour's drive from Gleneagles, St Andrews and the East Neuk of Fife. Elma Barrie is a superb hostess whose accomplished cooking encourages guests to return again and again to enjoy the comfort and hospitality of Hawkcraig House. Not to be missed – Hawkcraig House puddings!

Open mid Mar to late Oct
- ♨ Rooms: 2 with private facilities
- ⛱ DB&B £45–£48   B&B £24–£26
- 🅷 Open to non-residents – booked meals only
- ♀🆄🅻 Unlicensed – guests welcome to take own wine
- ✗ Dinner – booked meals only £££
- Ⓥ Vegetarians welcome
- ✷ Children over 8 years welcome
- 🚭 No smoking throughout

Pittenweem chowder with fresh Finnan haddock and fresh crab salad. Prime Scottish roast beef and Yorkshire pudding. Chocolate brandy roulade.

STB Deluxe 👑 👑 👑
- 💳 No credit cards
- 🅺 Proprietors: Elma & Dougal Barrie

COSHIEVILLE HOTEL
by Aberfeldy
Perthshire PH15 2NE
Tel: 01887 830319

5 miles west from Aberfeldy on the B846 Kinloch Rannoch/Tummel Bridge road.

- One of Perthshire's oldest inns – over 1,000 years old.
- Traditional Scottish with flair and imagination.
- "A popular watering hole for locals and visitors alike with a discerning palate."

This is an interesting inn, south facing and overlooking the Perthshire countryside. Only five minutes from Aberfeldy it is ideally placed for many outdoor pursuits including walking, fishing, shooting etc. It is close to Ben Lawers and Schiehallion. The friendly small informal bar offers excellent cuisine with the same menu on offer in the bar as in the restaurant for those who prefer a more informal setting. The chef proprietor here has built up an excellent local reputation over the past six years and is committed to making use of the excellent fresh produce available locally.

```
        Open 5 Mar to 5 Nov, weekends only 5 Nov to
        5 Mar + open New Year
🏠      Rooms: 6 with private facilities
🛏      DB&B from £45    B&B £27.50–£32.50
SP      Special rates available
✕      Lunch £
✕      Dinner ££
Ⓥ      Vegetarians welcome
𝄃      Children welcome
𝄫      No smoking in restaurant
```

Crumble of smoked haddock and apple with a course mustard dressing. Collops of heather-fed venison with port and redcurrant sauce. Rich bread and butter pudding.

STB Commended ♕ ♕ ♕
- Credit cards: Mastercard/Eurocard, Visa, Switch
- Chef Proprietors: Dougie & Annemarie Harkness

FARLEYER HOUSE HOTEL
Aberfeldy
Perthshire
PH15 2JE
Tel: 01887 820332
Fax: 01887 829430

Follow signs to the Castle Menzies and Weem on the B846. The hotel is situated 1 mile past the castle on right.

An award-winning country house hotel in beautiful surroundings.

- A small, formal and intimate hotel, rightly renowned.
- Elegant Scottish cuisine.
- "Excellent Scottish cuisine with flair and imagination."

In the heart of the old Castle Menzies estate, Farleyer was built as a croft in the 16th century. Enlarged twice since then Farleyer retains its air of calm opulence. Thirty-four acres of grounds enhance the house's tranquillity. Its Bistro offers imaginative Scottish cooking in a relaxed and informal atmosphere. The set menus in the Menzies Restaurant make the most of the outstanding quality of local game, meat and fish.

```
        Open all year
🏠      Rooms: 19 with private facilities
🛏      DB&B £95–£120    B&B £75–£110
SP      Special rates available
✕      Food available all day £££
✕      Lunch ££
✕      Dinner ££££
Ⓥ      Vegetarians welcome
𝄃      Children welcome
♿      Facilities for disabled visitors
𝄫      No smoking in Menzies Restaurant
🐄      Member of the Scotch Beef Club
```

House-cured salmon, orange dressing. Loin of Perthshire lamb, Aberfeldy malt sauce. Sweet spiced crème brûlée, vanilla ice cream.

STB Deluxe ♕ ♕ ♕ ♕
- Credit cards: Mastercard/Eurocard, American Express, Visa, Diners Club, Switch, Delta
- General Manager: Andy Cole

GUINACH HOUSE

by The Birks, Aberfeldy
Perthshire PH15 2ET
Tel: 01887 820251
Fax: 01887 829607

On A826, south-west outskirts of Aberfeldy, on road to 'The Birks', Guinach is signposted from Urlar Road.

This small hotel is run by international Master Chef Bert MacKay and his wife, Marian.

- This Victorian house is set in three acres of secluded gardens and birch woods with stunning views across Perthshire.
- Sophisticated cuisine combining a range of national and international influences.
- "Hospitable hosts and first class cuisine."

Guinach House is a seven-roomed hotel immersed in the rolling countryside around Aberfeldy. It is an ideal location for those who simply wish to relax in tranquil surroundings and indulge in gastronomic inspiration. For those who prefer to build up an appetite more actively, there are nearby facilities for swimming, golf, fly fishing and riding. The MacKays are attentive and friendly hosts who run Guinach more like a home than a hotel. Bert's culinary expertise allows him to create rich and varied menus, while maximising on the availability of fresh local produce. Guinach has 2 AA Rosettes.

Open all year except Christmas Eve to 27 Dec
🏠 Rooms: 7 with private facilities
🛏 DB&B £65 B&B £42.50
✗ Dinner 4 course menu £££
Ⓥ Vegetarians welcome
🧒 Children welcome
🚭 No smoking in dining room

Grilled Strathtay cheese with rhubarb conserve. Medallions of venison set on bramble and port wine jus with chestnuts. Cinnamon and honey wafers with raspberries in Drambuie.

STB Highly Commended 👑 👑 👑
💳 Credit cards: Mastercard/Eurocard, Visa
👤 Proprietors: Mr & Mrs MacKay

BRAEVAL RESTAURANT

nr Aberfoyle, Stirling FK8 3UY
Tel: 01877 382 711 Fax: 01877 382 400

Situated on the A81, 1 mile outside Aberfoyle, next to the golf course.

A small restaurant owned by one of Scotland's most famous chefs.

- A country restaurant with a formidable reputation.
- Outstanding modern Scottish cooking.
- "An unforgettable gourmet experience."

Nick Nairn was the youngest Scottish chef ever to win a Michelin Star (in 1991, retained ever since). A former merchant seaman, he is self-taught (like so many leading chefs!) and opened Braeval with his wife, Fiona, in 1986. Since then he has won many awards. He presents a set four course menu (choice of desserts) at both lunch and dinner, and is happy to discuss special requirements (e.g. vegetarian) prior to arrival. The menus change daily according to the produce available – important, since Nick cooks in the straightforward modern manner which allows flavours to speak for themselves. He has evolved his own style: simple, but with flair and imagination.

Open all year except 1 wk Feb, 1wk Jun + 2 wks Oct
Closed Mon Tue
✗ Lunch Sun 4 course set menu ££: Thu to Sat 3 course set menu – bookings only ££
✗ Dinner Wed to Sat 4 course set menu £££
Ⓥ Vegetarians welcome – prior notice required
♿ Facilities for disabled visitors
🚭 Note: Guests are asked not to smoke pipes or cigars. Cigarettes permitted at coffee stage only
🐄 Member of the Scotch Beef Club

Seared sea bream with salad nicoise. Roast rump of lamb with pesto olive oil and tomato jus. Crème brûlée with rhubarb.

💳 Credit cards: Mastercard/Eurocard, Visa, Switch, Delta
👤 Proprietors: Nick & Fiona Nairn

THE SCOTTISH WOOL CENTRE
Riverside Car Park, Aberfoyle
Stirlingshire FK8 3UG
Tel: 01877 382850
Fax: 01877 382854

Adjacent to main car park in Aberfoyle, southern gateway to the Trossachs. 1 mile off A81 on A821.

Coffee shop, visitors centre with sheep show and craft shop.

- Coffee shop and restaurant.
- Home cooking.
- "Enjoy a sheep show, spinning demonstrations and good home cooking all under one roof."

The visitors centre presents 'The Story of Scottish Wool' – a live theatre display spanning 2,000 years, 'where all the stars are on four legs'. Next door is a craft display area, where you can watch spinners and weavers, a knitwear and woollens shop and a gift shop. Outside there is a kiddie's farm, and, at the weekends, sheepdog trials and pipe bands. The restaurant which is part of all this activity is self-service and provides meals all day. The baking is especially good, and snacks and light meals are its forte. It has a stable feel, with pine furniture and old photographs.

Open all year except Christmas Day + New Year's Day
- ⊎ Unlicensed
- ✗ Food available all day £
- ✗ Lunch £
- Ⅴ Vegetarians welcome
- ⅄ Children welcome
- ⅇ Facilities for disabled visitors

Cauliflower and black pepper soup. Scotch beef and mustard cobbler. Butterscotch sundae.

STB Commended Visitor Attraction
- ⊞ No credit cards
- ☒ Catering Manager: Joan S Battison

BIRKWOOD LODGE
Gordon Crescent
Aboyne
Aberdeenshire AB34 5HJ
Tel/Fax: 013398 86347

In Aboyne take the A93 towards Ballater. Gordon Crescent is the first lane on left after village green at Roman Catholic chapel.

High quality family run B&B.

- Victorian granite town house.
- Scottish home cooking.
- "A very friendly B&B with excellent home cooking."

Birkwood Lodge is a typical Victorian Deeside house in pink granite and the interior has many features typifying the exuberance of the period. Two of the bedrooms are en suite and attractively decorated and furnished. The public rooms are equally very comfortable and include such little extras as a game board and excellent reading materials. The Thorburn family are your hosts and have superb local knowledge to ensure that you do not miss any of the attractions in the area. Jim also lets fishing on the Dee which often influences items on the menu and Elizabeth is in charge of the cooking which is highly accomplished, using only the freshest produce. Menus are well-balanced and the food is flavoursome and presented in an appetising style.

Open all year
- ⊞ Rooms: 3 with private facilities
- ⊨ DB&B £42   B&B £24
- ✗ Residents only
- ⚲⊎ Unlicensed – guests welcome to take own wine
- ✗ Packed Lunch on request £
- ✗ Dinner ££
- Ⅴ Vegetarians welcome
- ⅄ Children welcome
- ⅄ No smoking in dining room + bedrooms

Fresh crab with avocado. Roast pheasant with skirlie. Lemon roulade.

STB Highly Commended 👑 👑 👑
- ⊞ No credit cards
- ☒ Owners: Jim & Elizabeth Thorburn

HAZLEHURST LODGE

Ballater Road, Aboyne
Aberdeenshire AB34 5HY
Tel: 013398 86921
Fax: 013398 86660
e-mail hazlehurst.lodge@nestorg.uk

On A93 on western side of Aboyne.

Traditional rose granite exterior with innovative design and artwork within.

- Victorian lodge to Aboyne Castle.
- Imaginative new Scottish cooking.
- "A unique dining experience – innovative and creative."

The traditional coach house exterior is charming but, in stunning contrast, it hides a wealth of modern art by internationally recognised Scottish artists, from the sculptures and paintings to the very furnishings around you – many specially commissioned. In a welcoming atmosphere, Anne Strachan combines traditional home cooking with an imaginative approach to sauces and accompaniments to create memorable dishes. Her wine list is selected from top growers, mainly French, and is very reasonably priced given the quality of the wines. There are three bedrooms, all individually designed, with full private facilities, plus a gallery and family accommodation in the adjoining cottage.

....

    Open Feb to Dec
🏠 Rooms: 5 with private facilities
🛏 B&B £27–£38
✕ Lunch + special occasions by arrangement
✕ Dinner £££
✁ No smoking in dining room

Paupiettes of sole with herbs served with a tomato salsa. Rack of lamb with a trouffle sauce. Floating meringue with plums.

STB Deluxe 👑 👑 👑
💳 Credit cards: Mastercard/Eurocard, American Express, Visa, Diners Club
🔑 Proprietors: Anne & Eddie Strachan

THE WHITE COTTAGE RESTAURANT

Dess, Aboyne
Aberdeenshire AB34 5BP
Tel/Fax: 013398 86265

On main A93 Aberdeen-Braemar, 2½ miles east of Aboyne.

Award-winning restaurant in the heart of Royal Deeside.

- Pink granite 150 year old converted cottage.
- Creative Scottish cooking.
- "Laurie and Josephine are dedicated to the presentation of first class Scottish food."

For over ten years Laurie and Josephine Mill have built a strong reputation with local clientele for their special style. Chef/proprietor Laurie Mill is enthusiastic about the best raw materials he can source and believes in allowing the intrinsic flavours to emerge simply on the plate. Fish and vegetables are minimally cooked, soup and stocks are long in the making and sauces complement rather than dominate. There is also a vegetarian menu. The cottage is delightful, in the winter log fires add to the intimacy and in the summer the conservatory and pond garden lends itself well to the relaxed atmosphere that pervades. This commitment to the food is also reflected in a carefully compiled wine list with wines from the old and new world and all reasonably priced. White Cottage has 2 AA Rosettes.

....

    Open most of the year except 24 Dec to 4 Jan
    Closed Mon
🏠 Room: 1 with private facilities
🛏 DB&B £46–£52   B&B £21–£26
🍷 Restaurant licence
✕ Lunch and supper except Mon £-££
✕ Dinner except Mon 4 course menu £££
Ⓥ Vegetarians welcome
♿ Facilities for disabled visitors
✁ No smoking in restaurant

Parfait of Strathdon chicken livers with Worcesterberry and port sauce. Steamed noisettes of Aberdeenshire lamb with chicken and thyme mousse. Dark chocolate roulade, white chocolate sorbet.

💳 Credit cards: Mastercard/Eurocard, Visa, Switch
🔑 Proprietors: Laurie & Josephine Mill

SUMMER ISLES HOTEL
Achiltibuie
Ross-shire IV26 2YG
Tel: 01854 622282
Fax: 01854 622251

A835 to Ullapool and beyond – 10 miles north of Ullapool turn left onto single track road to Achiltibuie. Village is 15 miles on (i.e. 25 miles from Ullapool).

Award-winning country hotel in the West Highlands.

* A country hotel in a converted croft house.
* Innovative modern Scottish cooking.
* "The very best of food, wine and comfort."

Achiltibuie is another world. The village itself is a straggle of white cottages at the end of which you find the hotel, facing out over the bay to the Summer Isles and the Hebrides beyond. It is an unlikely setting for an outpost of civilisation and fine cooking. Proprietors Mark and Gerry Irvine are natural hosts, and create an undemanding ambience in the hotel which ensures guests may relax easily. Dinner is served promptly at 8 pm from a simple menu, prepared daily by the chef, dependant upon fresh raw materials, and presented with skill and flair. To enhance the meal there is a very well sourced wine list, with up to 400 bins to choose from. Everyone who goes there leaves reluctantly, determined to return.

Open Easter to mid Oct
🛏 Rooms: 12 with private facilities
🛏 DB&B £79–£110   B&B £44–£75
✖ Food available all day £
✖ Lunch £££
✖ Dinner ££££
Ⓥ Vegetarians welcome
🧒 Children welcome
🚭 No smoking in restaurant + bedrooms

Carpaccio of Aberdeen Angus beef fillet, served with a piquant relish. Fresh Summer Isles lobster, served with a seafood cous cous and fresh basil. Hot steamed syrup pudding with home-made custard.

STB Highly Commended 👑 👑 👑
💳 Credit cards: Mastercard/Eurocard, Visa, Switch
🕴 Proprietors: Mark & Gerry Irvine

RESTAURANT BOUZY ROUGE
1 Rochsolloch Road
Airdrie
Lanarkshire
ML6 9BB
Tel: 01236 763853
Fax: 01236 770340

On the border between Airdrie and Coatbridge within easy access of Glasgow and Edinburgh.

Innovative town bistro.

* Ground floor of tenement building.
* Casual gourmet dining.
* "Great food – great atmosphere."

Deceptively large, this city bistro has style. Furniture is individually hand crafted by Scottish wood-craftsmen and sculptors and the food matches the interior being colourful, eclectic and having flavoursome appeal. Run by a young yet experienced husband and wife team with a second eaterie, already very popular, in Glasgow. This delightful brasserie is a welcome addition to the Guide.

Open all year except Christmas Day + New Year's Day
✖ Food available all day ££
✖ Lunch £-££
✖ Dinner ££
Ⓥ Vegetarians welcome
🧒 Children welcome
♿ Facilities for disabled visitors

Tartare of smoked chicken and smoked salmon with a spicy tomato salsa. Fresh Scottish ostrich on pommes dauphinoise with redcurrant and juniper reduction. Caramelised lemon tart with blackcurrant sorbet.

💳 Credit cards: Mastercard/Eurocard, American Express, Visa, Diners Club, Mastercharge, Switch, Delta
🕴 Proprietors: Alan and Audrey Brown

GEAN HOUSE
Tullibody Road, Alloa
Clackmannanshire
FK10 2HS
Tel: 01259 219275
Fax: 01259 213827

A907 from Kincardine Bridge or Stirling. Park
entrance on B9096 Tullibody, less than 5 minutes
from Alloa Town Hall roundabout.

A delightful, richly decorated, family-run hotel.

- Country house hotel.
- Modern cooking, with many influences.
- "Good quality food, well-presented."

Gean (the word is Scots for a wild cherry tree, and
refers to the number of these which surround the
house) is an unspoilt Edwardian mansion set in its
own grounds on the outskirts of Alloa. Built in 1912,
it is meticulously maintained by its owner Sandra
Frost who ensures Scottish hospitality in luxurious
surroundings. Friendly and well-run, very
reasonably priced, imaginative food, Gean House is
delightful. Twenty four hour service facility.

Open all year
🏠 Rooms: 7 with private facilities
🛏 DB&B £75–£82.50   B&B £60–£80
SP Special rates available
✗ Food available all day £
✗ Lunch ££
✗ Dinner £££
Ⅴ Vegetarians welcome
🕆 Children welcome
♿ Facilities for disabled visitors
✕ No smoking in dining room
🐂 Member of the Scotch Beef Club

**Duck and shitake mushroom rissoles. Roast
aubergine, pepper and sweet potato gallette.
Scottish summer berries in aspic and white wine.**

STB Highly Commended 🏴 🏴 🏴 🏴
💳 Credit cards: Mastercard/Eurocard, American
   Express, Visa, Diners Club, Delta, JCB
Ⅺ Manager: Andrea L Frost

DRUMNACREE HOUSE
St Ninians Road, Alyth, Perthshire PH11 8AP
Tel/Fax: 01828 632194

Turn off A926 Blairgowrie-Kirriemuir to Alyth.
Take first turning on left after Clydesdale
Bank – 300 yards on right.

**A small country hotel winner of the Glenturret
Perthshire Tourism Award 'Most Enjoyable
Restaurant Meal' and awarded 2 AA Rosettes for
food.**

- Converted mansion.
- Modern Scottish and international cooking.
- "Friendly small hotel, offering excellent
  hospitality and food."

Drumnacree House is situated at the foot of
Glenisla in the old market town of Alyth, which has
a southern aspect and is surrounded by raspberry
fields. Allan and Eleanor Cull run their hotel most
efficiently and create a relaxing atmosphere. They
both do the cooking and draw from their years of
international travel to create unusual menus as well
as more traditional ones all of which are
accompanied by home-grown organic vegetables
and herbs from the kitchen garden; the dishes
express a national content while being inspired by
foreign impulses and are attractively described and
presented. Allan also cures his own fish and game.

Open 1 Apr to 20 Dec
🏠 Rooms: 6 with private facilities
🛏 DB&B £49.50–£80   B&B £30–£55
SP Special rates available
♀ Restricted licence
✗ Dinner residents only Sun Mon: non-residents
   Tue to Sat ££
Ⅴ Vegetarians welcome – prior notice required
🕆 Children welcome
✕ No smoking in dining room + bedrooms
🐂 Member of the Scotch Beef Club

**Ravioli of Scottish snails with smoked bacon on a
bed of shredded lettuce. Spiced breast of pigeon
on a bed of cous cous with a chanterelle
mushroom sauce. Little pot of raspberry and
Cointreau cream.**

STB Highly Commended 🏴 🏴 🏴
💳 Credit cards: Mastercard/Eurocard, American
   Express, Visa
Ⅺ Proprietors: Allan & Eleanor Cull

B5 D5 A

INVERCRERAN COUNTRY HOUSE HOTEL
Glen Creran, Appin, Argyll PA38 4BJ
Tel: 01631 730 414 Fax: 01631 730 532
e-mail invercreran@dial.pipex.com

Just off A828 Oban-Fort William at head of Loch
Creran, 14 miles north of Connel Bridge.

**An idyllically positioned family-run hotel in the
wilds of Glen Creran.**

- Secluded country house with stylish appeal.
- Excellent quality Scottish cooking.
- "Uniquely styled mansion house hidden in Glen
  Creran."

The hotel commands stupendous mountain views,
built perched on a hillside enjoying uninterrupted
views over idyllic Glen Creran. The house itself is
strikingly different, cleverly designed to make the
most of its situation, yet not in the slightest out of
place in this secluded picturesque glen. Splendid
public rooms with spacious terraces, and large
comfortable bedrooms, contribute to the overall
feeling of luxury. The three generations of the
Kersley family who own and run the hotel do so with
unassuming charm and friendliness. The food lives
up to the high standards that mark this place
featuring local meats and seafood in traditional
recipes presented to delight the eye and please the
palate, served within a delightful dining room. To
fully appreciate the excellent food here it is
advisable to book ahead.

Open 15 Mar to 15 Nov
- ⊞ Rooms: 9 with private facilities
- ⇌ DB&B £80–£115   B&B £50–£85
- SP Special rates available
- ✕ Lunch ££ – booking essential
- ✕ Dinner ££££
- Ⓥ Vegetarians welcome
- ⚹ Children over 5 years welcome
- ⅋ Facilities for disabled visitors
- ⅟ No smoking in dining room
- 🐄 Member of the Scotch Beef Club

**Fresh langoustines and mussel terrine. Pan-fried
wild sea scallops served with a lime and prawn
butter. Oatmeal tulip basket filled with fresh soft
fruits.**

STB Deluxe ♕ ♕ ♕ ♕
- 💳 Credit cards: Mastercard/Eurocard, Visa
- ℕ Manager: Tony Kersley

LETHAM GRANGE RESORT
Colliston, Angus DD11 4RL
Tel: 01241 890373 Fax: 01241 890414

From A92, Arbroath, take A933 Brechin road and
turn right at Colliston to Letham Grange.

**A gracious and beautifully restored baronial
mansion.**

- A grand country house hotel preserving the best
  of the past.
- Modern/traditional Scottish cuisine.
- "A warm welcome awaits all who visit this
  scenic estate and splendid country house."

With its period features – original oak panelling,
sculptured ceilings, period paintings – faithfully and
carefully restored to their original splendour of 1884,
its Victorian builders would recognise a great deal at
Letham Grange. This is enhanced by modern
comforts and a range of outdoor pursuits from golf on
its rolling parkland estate, fishing, shooting,
tennis and indoor curling rink. In its magnificent
Rosehaugh Restaurant the hotel offers both à la carte
and table d'hôte dishes that draw on fresh local
produce, imaginatively cooked. Period conservatory
open for lunch and light meals all day in summer
months. The menus are well-balanced and
reasonably priced. The wine list extensive. The hotel
stocks over 90 single malt whiskies.

Open all year
- ⊞ Rooms: 41 with private facilities
- ⇌ DB&B £81.75–£97.75   B&B £62.50–£79
- SP Special rates available
- ✕ Food available all day ££
- ✕ Lunch £
- ✕ Dinner ££
- Ⓥ Vegetarians welcome
- ⚹ Children welcome
- ⅋ Facilities for disabled visitors

**Arbroath smokie – boned, smoked and sautéd in
onions wrapped in a pancake and served with
melted Orkney Cheddar. Char-grilled Aberdeen
Angus fillet with haggis croquettes and Drambuie
cream sauce. Panacotta with fresh Tayside berry
compote.**

STB Highly Commended ♕ ♕ ♕ ♕
- 💳 Credit cards: Mastercard/Eurocard, American
  Express, Visa, Diners Club, Switch, Delta
- ℕ General Manager: Alan T Wright

FAR VIEW COTTAGE
Kilchoan, Acharacle
Argyll PH36 4LH
Tel: 01972 510357

Corran Ferry to Salen on A861 then B8007 to Kilchoan. A few hundred yards from the Tobermory-Kilchoan Ferry. At Kilchoan turn left towards the ferry. Far View is about 400 yards from the Tobermory ferry jetty.

Comfort and hospitality in this remote and beautiful place.

- Extended keeper's cottage.
- Home style Scottish cooking.
- "Get away from it all to this haven of good food and friendly faces."

Rob and Joan Thompson own and run Far View, which takes its name from panoramic views to east, south and west, down the Sound of Mull, out to Tiree and across Kilchoan Bay. Originally a keeper's cottage it has been recently imaginatively extended with tasteful care which has successfully preserved the original character. Joan is an enthusiastic hostess who delights in producing appetising dishes, accompanied by the tastiest of sauces. Her home-made soups and desserts are delicious and seconds are often offered and accepted. Rob also cooks a substantial Scottish breakfast and his nutmeg potatoes and herbed sausage on a ring of apple are interesting and unusual. There is very much the feeling of staying in a friend's house here and a rare feeling of space and unhurried peace.

Open Apr to end Oct + Easter
- 🏠 Rooms: 3 with private facilities
- 🛏 DB&B £34–£45   B&B £28–£37
- SP Special rates available
- ✗ Packed lunches for residents £
- ✗ Dinner £-££
- ✶ Children over 12 years welcome
- ✗ No smoking throughout

Cucumber and mint soup with home-made wholemeal bread. Venison in a pear, blackcurrant and Marsala sauce. Mousse of fresh local raspberries with almond tuiles.

STB Highly Commended 👑 👑 👑
- No credit cards
- 🗶 Proprietors: Rob & Joan Thompson

FEORAG HOUSE
Glenborrodale
Acharacle
Argyll PH36 4JP
Tel: 01972 500 248
Fax: 01972 500 285

36 miles or 1 hour's drive from Corran Ferry on B8007.

A handsome new house on the shores of Loch Sunart in Glenborrodale.

- Luxury country house.
- Delightful home cooking.
- "An oasis of comfort and luxury set in breathtaking Highland scenery."

Feorag House (Feorag means squirrel in Gaelic) was designed and built by its present owners, Peter and Helen Stockdale, in 1994 on the wooded northern shore of Loch Sunart. It has a lovely situation, within yards of a rocky inlet and facing south. The view can best be appreciated from the large balcony attached to the sitting room, with open log fire, or in less clement weather, from the broad bay windows in the luxurious dining room. Altogether, the house has been sensitively designed, furnished and decorated to a high standard. The food is delicious: both Peter and Helen cook and bake on their Aga; everything is fresh and local. Do not miss afternoon tea served at 4.30 pm from silver teapots and fresh baking from the Aga. Their friendliness and hospitality is overwhelming. A real find!

Open all year
- 🏠 Rooms: 3 with private facilities
- 🛏 DB&B £49–£59   B&B £29.50–£39.50
- SP Special rates available
- ✗ Residents only
- Unlicensed – guests welcome to take own wine
- ✗ Dinner ££
- Vegetarians welcome – by arrangement
- ✶ Children over 10 years welcome
- ✗ No smoking in dining room + bedrooms

Seared scallops on a bed of rice noodles with mustard seed dressing. Roast rack of lamb with red wine sauce. Wild bramble and lemon mousse.

STB Deluxe 👑 👑 👑
- Credit cards: Mastercard/Eurocard, Visa, Switch
- 🗶 Proprietors: Peter & Helen Stockdale

MEALL MO CHRIDHE COUNTRY HOUSE
Kilchoan, West Ardnamurchan, Argyll PH36 4LH
Tel/Fax: 01972 510238

From Corran Ferry by A861, then along B8007 by the
side of Loch Sunart. On main road by shore, just
past post office.

A beautiful shoreline Grade II Listed Georgian house.

- Country house built in 1790 - originally a manse.
- Good Scottish home cooking at its best.
- "A breakfast to die for – wake up to some superb
  home baking treats."

Meall mo Chridhe (pro. 'me-al-mo-cree') means 'little hill of my heart'. Standing within its own 45
acres, it has splendid views over Kilchoan and the
Sound of Mull. Its resident owners, Roy and Janet
Smith are committed to providing their guests with
the very best, offering 'good food, peace and
tranquillity'. Dinner is by candlelight, in what was
originally the 'Marriage Room', sitting at a
magnificently antique dining table. The four course
set menu uses only fresh local produce;
vegetables, fruits and herbs are grown in the walled
garden. Janet uses her two Agas to great effect,
producing home cooking and baking to
tantalise every tastebud. Guests are made most
welcome at Janet's Daisy Chain craft studio with
many of Janet's hand-produced goods. The
adjoining farm shop has a selection of fresh home-
grown fruits and vegetables, as well as locally
supplied salmon, shellfish, cheeses and meats.

Open 1 Apr to 31 Oct
- 🏠 Rooms: 3 with private facilities
- 🛏 DB&B £69–£74   B&B £35–£40
- SP Special rates available
- UL ♀ Unlicensed – guests welcome to take own
  wine + spirits
- ✗ Dinner 4 course menu £££
- V Vegetarians welcome
- ☀ Children over 12 years welcome
- ✗ No smoking throughout

**Three cheese croustade: local cheeses wrapped in
fresh spinach, baked in filo pastry then served with
chilled fresh tomato salsa. Grilled fresh tuna served
on a bed of home-grown herb salad with mild
horseradish dressing. Steamed chocolate pudding
with rich chocolate sauce and poached kumquats.**

STB Highly Commended 👑 👑 👑
- ⊞ No credit cards
- 🅜 Proprietors: Roy & Janet Smith

LOCH MELFORT HOTEL
Arduaine, by Oban
Argyll PA34 4XG
Tel: 01852 200233
Fax: 01852 200214

On A816, 19 miles south of Oban.

**A country house with spectacular views and
gardens.**

- Stylish and friendly hotel with the emphasis on
  welcome.
- Fresh, imaginative Scottish cuisine.
- "A great place for wonderful fresh seafood."

Under its owners Philip and Rosalind Lewis, the
Loch Melfort Hotel deserves its growing reputation
and such past awards as 'Hotel of the Year
Scotland', 1992. It is dramatically situated with
panoramic views across Asknish Bay to the islands.
Originally the home of the Campbells of Arduaine,
the hotel has been sensibly and tastefully extended
to take maximum advantage of the magnificent land
and seascape. The renowned Arduaine Gardens
are adjacent to the hotel grounds. Both in its dining
room and Chartroom Bar, the hotel offers the best
of fresh local produce – particularly sea food and
shellfish – and an imaginatively balanced wine list.
The hotel has 1 AA Rosette.

Open all year except mid Jan to mid Feb
- 🏠 Rooms: 26 with private facilities
- 🛏 DB&B £45–£85.50   B&B £35–£65
- SP Special rates available
- ✗ Food available all day £
- ✗ Lunch (Chartroom Bar) £
- ✗ Dinner £££
- V Vegetarians welcome
- ☀ Children welcome
- ♿ Some facilities for disabled visitors
- ✗ No smoking in dining room

**Wild Loch Etive mussels marinière with cider,
cream and herbs. Roast guard of Borders Wedder
lamb with a herb and green peppercorn crust -
served with a sloe gravy. Fresh Scottish
strawberries and raspberries in sweetened red
wine.**

STB Highly Commended 👑 👑 👑 👑
- ⊞ Credit cards: Mastercard/Eurocard, Visa,
  Switch
- 🅜 Proprietors: Rosalind & Philip Lewis

ARISAIG HOUSE

Beasdale, by Arisaig, Inverness-shire PH39 4NR
Tel: 01687 450622 Fax: 01687 450626

Just off A830 Fort William-Mallaig, 1 mile past
Beasdale railway station.

One of the most distinguished hotels in the West Highlands.

- Scots baronial mansion luxuriously maintained.
- Innovative Scottish cooking.
- "A house of comfort and style, with an intriguing history."

Arisaig House was built in 1864. The garden falls, in formal terraces, down to the beach from which Bonnie Prince Charlie escaped to France. Ruth, John and Andrew Smither, owners, have very capable managers in Alison and David Wilkinson (their daughter and son-in-law) who maintain the highest standards. Public and private rooms are tastefully furnished; admirers of the Art Deco style will be captivated by their charm. Their priority is to provide 'peace and quiet and gentle luxury to the weary traveller'. Arisaig House's chef marries fresh local produce (notably, seafood from Mallaig) and personal inspiration, both table d'hôte and à la carte. Dinner in a formal way is a gourmet experience – lunch, whilst unusual in a hotel of this genre, is served in the dining room or on the terrace and can be anything from soup and sandwiches to more substantial fare. Arisaig House has 2 AA Rosettes.

Open 1 Apr to 31 Oct
🏠 Rooms: 14 with private facilities
🛏 B&B £65–£126
SP Special rates available
♀ Residential licence
✗ Lunch £££
✗ Dinner ££££ 4 course menu – booking essential
Ⓥ Vegetarians welcome
✳ Children over 10 years welcome
🚭 No smoking in dining room

Fricassée of squat lobsters and wild mushrooms in a Valerus truffle nage. Pot roasted Guinea fowl with water asparagus and saffron. Pear tarte tatin with honey ice cream.

STB Deluxe 👑 👑 👑 👑
Ⓔ Credit cards: Mastercard/Eurocard, American Express, Visa, Switch
Ⅺ Partner: Ruth Smither

THE OLD LIBRARY LODGE & RESTAURANT

Sea Front, Arisaig
Inverness-shire PH39 4NH
Tel: 01687 450651
Fax: 01687 450219

In centre of village on waterfront.

Little restaurant in a village setting.

- Small restaurant with rooms.
- Good, fresh natural Scottish cooking.
- "Once found – regularly sought out. Booking essential in evenings."

The Old Library Lodge and Restaurant enjoys an attractive situation on the waterfront in Arisaig with fine views out over the small Hebridean Isles. The building itself is a 200 year old stone built stable converted into a restaurant of character with accommodation attached. A cheerful and welcoming atmosphere prevails not least in the dining room where guests choose from a table d'hôte menu with a choice of five of everything – starters, main courses and puddings. The menu is fresh and well-balanced featuring, naturally enough, a wealth of locally caught fish and seafood attractively cooked and presented. The comfortable accommodation is in a wing of terraced bedrooms with balconies overlooking the terraced garden. Breakfast is something to look forward to.

Open 24 Mar to end Oct
Closed Tue lunch
🏠 Rooms: 6 with private facilities
🛏 DB&B from £56.50   B&B from £34
SP Special rates available
♀ Table licence
✗ Lunch except Tue
✗ Dinner £££
Ⓥ Vegetarians welcome – prior notice required

Mussel and fennel soup with home-made bread. Grilled duck breast marinated in honey and soy sauce. Rhubarb fudge crumble with cream or ice cream.

STB Highly Commended 👑 👑 👑
Ⓔ Credit cards: Mastercard/Eurocard, American Express, Visa, Switch, Delta
Ⅺ Proprietors: Alan & Angela Broadhurst

BALCARY BAY HOTEL

Shore Road, Auchencairn
Dumfries & Galloway
DG7 1QZ
Tel: 01556 640217/640311
Fax: 01556 640272

A711 Dalbeattie-Kirkcudbright to Auchencairn.
Then take 'no through road' signposted Balcary
(single track) for 2 miles.

Country house in idyllic setting.

- Superb country house dating back from 1625 set
  standing close to the beach of Balcary Bay.
- Modern Scottish cooking.
- "The perfect setting to enjoy good food."

This house stands in a splendidly exposed position
by the Solway Firth, in three acres of grounds. Under
the personal care of resident managers Graeme and
Clare Lamb the service is friendly and efficient, and
the hotel is maintained to accommodate guests in
considerable comfort. Most of the en suite
bedrooms have spectacular views. A short table
d'hôte menu is offered in the restaurant, featuring
fresh local specialities as well as an extensive à la
carte menu. The conservatory extension to the bar
is delightful for meals.

```
     Open Mar to mid Nov
🏠   Rooms: 17 with private facilities
🛏   DB&B £54–£76    B&B £48–£54
SP   Special rates available
✗    Lunch Sun – booking advisable £: Lunch Mon to
     Sat – by prior reservation only ££
✗    Dinner £££
Ⓥ    Vegetarians welcome
🖈    Children welcome
♿   Facilities for non-resident disabled visitors
🚭   Smoking discouraged
```

**Broccoli mousse with a goats cheese and walnut
dressing. Roast saddle of venison in a crème de
cassis sauce. Sticky ginger pudding with clotted
cream.**

STB Highly Commended 🏆 🏆 🏆 🏆
💳   Credit cards: Mastercard/Eurocard, American
     Express, Visa, Switch, Delta
🧑   Proprietors: The Lamb Family

ARDCHOILLE FARM GUEST HOUSE

Dunshalt, Auchtermuchty, Fife KY14 7EY
Tel/Fax: 01337 828414

On B936 just outside Dunshalt village, 1½ miles
south of Auchtermuchty. 1 hour's drive from
Edinburgh, 20 minutes from St Andrews or Perth.

**Comfortable family guest house in open
countryside.**

- A farmhouse built in 1957 where guests'
  comfort is a priority.
- Traditional, good home cooking, using only
  fresh ingredients.
- "Spotlessly clean, every home comfort and more
  – delicious food too."

From the embroidered linen napkins you can tell that
attention to detail is the aim of proprietors Donald and
Isobel Steven. They succeed in making you feel like a
guest in their own elegantly furnished home.
Wonderful home-made shortbread is available in the
bedrooms. Freshly prepared meals of local produce
are served at a long mahogany table set with fine
china and crystal in the comfortable dining room,
husband Donald serves the food that Isobel cooks.
Breakfasts are "the best we've ever had". Home-made
soups, vegetables from the garden, home baking,
preserves and home-made ice cream – a speciality –
can all be enjoyed here, as well as a selection of
Scottish cheeses. The personal touch is evident
throughout. Ardchoille's location makes it an excellent
base for touring, golf or just relaxing.

```
     Open all year except Christmas/New Year
🏠   Rooms: 3 with private facilities (2 en suite)
🛏   DB&B £45–£55    B&B £25–£35
UL ♀ Unlicensed – guests welcome to take own wine
✗    Dinner 4 course menu ££
🍴   Dinner for non-residents – by prior
     arrangement only
Ⓥ    Vegetarians welcome – prior notice required
🚭   No smoking throughout
```

**Dill blinis (warm herb pancakes) with smoked
seafood and crème fraîche dressing. Scotch lamb
fillets with creamy pesto, mustardy baked potatoes
with olives, shredded organic green vegetables.
Lime bavarois with passion fruit jelly.**

STB Highly Commended 🏆 🏆 🏆
💳   Credit cards: Mastercard/Eurocard, Visa, Delta,
     JCB
🧑   Proprietors: Donald & Isobel Steven

CORROUR HOUSE HOTEL

Inverdruie, by Aviemore
Inverness-shire
PH22 1QH
Tel: 01479 810220
Fax: 01479 811500

Inverdruie is a ½ mile from Aviemore, on road to Coylumbridge, Glenmore and Cairngorms.

A Victorian house hotel in the heart of the Highlands.

- Victorian house.
- Traditional Scottish.
- "Superb home cooking in a tranquil setting overlooking the Cairngorm Mountains."

Corrour House Hotel is an elegant family-run hotel which offers true Highland hospitality from its hosts David and Sheana Catto. The house stands in four acres of garden and woodland, overlooks Rothiemurchus Forest and enjoys fine views of the Cairngorm Mountains. The house is attractively furnished and decorated and is an excellent place from which to relax and enjoy the surroundings. The Cattos are friendly and accomplished hosts and the cooking is excellent making best use of local produce whether at breakfast or dinner.

Open 27 Dec to 31 Oct
🏫 Rooms: 8 with private facilities
🛏 DB&B £40–£55   B&B £25–£35
SP Special rates available
✕ Dinner ££
Ⓥ Vegetarians welcome
🕇 Children welcome
🚭 No smoking in dining room + some bedrooms

Smoked trout and horseradish mousse with warm walnut bread. Ballindalloch pheasant served with red wine, orange, redcurrant and garden herb sauce. Toasted almond and strawberry pavlova roulade with a summer fruits coulis.

STB Highly Commended 👑 👑 👑
💳 Credit cards: Mastercard/Eurocard, Visa
🅰 Proprietors: Mr & Mrs Catto

LYNWILG HOUSE

Aviemore, Inverness-shire PH22 1PZ
Tel/Fax: 01479 811685

A9 Perth-Inverness, take Lynwilg road 1 mile south of Aviemore.

A beautiful country house built in the 1930s.

- Country house overlooking the Cairngorms.
- Traditional Scottish cooking.
- "A combination of the best hospitality, cooking and location."

Lynwilg is an impressive country house, built by the Duke of Richmond, standing on high ground looking out over the Cairngorms. The house is set in four acres of attractively landscaped gardens with a well-planned kitchen garden providing much of the fruit, vegetables and herbs used in the daily changing menus. Marjorie Cleary presents a set menu each evening; her inventiveness and flair in the kitchen mean that every meal is special. Comfortable, well-furnished bedrooms (3 of which are en suite), roaring log fires, croquet on the lawn and fishing on a private loch are all indications of a relaxed country house style. A private self-catering cottage in the grounds sleeps four. Winner of The Macallan Taste of Scotland Special Merit Award for Outstanding Hospitality 1994.

Open New Year to 31 Oct
🏫 Rooms: 4 with private facilities
🛏 DB&B £48–£58   B&B £28–£35
SP Special rates available
🅰 Non-residents welcome subject to availability
🍷 Unlicensed – guests welcome to take own wine
✕ Dinner 4 course menu ££-£££
Ⓥ Vegetarians welcome
🕇 Children welcome
🚭 No smoking in restaurant

Cream of smoked trout and leek soup. Butterfly venison steak pan-fried, on a bed of garden greens, with a redcurrant and port wine sauce. Rosemary sorbet with almond tuile biscuits.

STB Deluxe 👑 👑 👑
💳 Credit cards: Mastercard/Eurocard, Visa
🅰 Proprietors/Owners: Alan & Marjory Cleary

THE OLD BRIDGE INN
Dalfaber Road
Aviemore PH22 1PU
Tel: 01479 811137
Fax: 01479 810270

At south end of Aviemore, take B970 ski road (Cairngorms) for 300 yards then take turning on left for another 300 yards.

A cosy Highland pub nestling beside the River Spey.

- A friendly informal place of great hospitality.
- Good pub food.
- "Busy, informal and friendly."

Only minutes on foot from the centre of Aviemore, the Old Bridge Inn has the air of a country pub. This quaint and unpretentious building offers pub food as it should be – freshly prepared and cooked. Proprietor Nigel Reid and Chef Norma Hutton concentrate on fresh local produce for their extensive and imaginative menu. Rightly popular, they even make their own ice cream. There is a special children's menu. In the evenings, the menu is based on food cooked on a large chargrill. In the summer the inn hosts regular Highland ceilidhs, with pipers and Scottish dancing. The summer of 1997 sees the final completion of a major extension and re-furbishment to satisfy continued demand. A new dining area for 40 guests, featuring exciting new menu concepts. Bookings accepted.

Open all year
- ✗ Lunch £
- ✗ Dinner ££
- Ⓥ Vegetarians welcome
- ⚲ Children welcome
- ⚹ Facilities for disabled visitors

Mussels in a leek broth. Venison casserole with a port and rowan jelly. Prune and almond tart.

- 🄲 Credit cards: Mastercard/Eurocard, Visa
- ⋈ Owner: Nigel Reid

THE ROWAN TREE RESTAURANT & GUEST HOUSE
Loch Alvie, by Aviemore
Inverness-shire PH22 1QB
Tel/Fax: 01479 810207

1½ miles south of Aviemore on old A9 (B9152) overlooking Loch Alvie.

Restaurant and guest house, with horn carving visitor attraction and all day tea-room.

- A small restaurant and guest house on Speyside.
- Traditional Scottish fare.
- "Friendly establishment offering good, fresh, home cooking and baking."

One of the oldest hotels in Strathspey, The Rowan Tree is fast establishing a reputation as a place to find traditional quality Scottish food. A four course table d'hôte dinner menu offers generous portions of dishes with a distinctly Scottish theme and there is a comfortable lounge to enjoy a pre-dinner drink and peruse the wine list. George and Gillian have added a tea-room offering delicious home baking, sandwiches and salads to complement the Speyside Horn and Country Crafts – visitor attraction where guests can see the traditional craft of horn carving and visit the craft shop.

Open 27 Dec to 1 Nov
Note: Jan to Mar open Fri Sat nights only
Closed Sun
- 🛏 Rooms: 10, 8 with private facilities
- 🛌 DB&B £40–£65   B&B £20–£35
- ⓈⓅ Special rates available
- ✗ Food available all day except Sun £
- ✗ Dinner except Sun – 4 course menu ££
- Ⓥ Vegetarians welcome
- ⚲ Children welcome
- ⌇ No smoking in dining room

Timbale of smoked venison and rowanberry jelly. Rowan Tree chicken with crème fraîche and coriander sauce. Almond and coffee ice cream sandwich with Amaretto ice cream.

STB Commended 👑 👑 👑
- 🄲 Credit cards: Mastercard/Eurocard, Visa, Mastercharge, Switch
- ⋈ Proprietors: George & Gillian Orr

CULZEAN CASTLE

Maybole, Ayrshire KA19 8LE
Tel: 01655 760274 Fax: 01655 760615

Culzean Castle is well signposted on Ayr to
Turnberry road. Take A77 towards Stranraer then
A719 towards Culzean.

**One of Scotland's most famous castles – a National
Trust property.**

- Listed building designed by Robert Adam.
- Traditional Scottish.
- "Unique establishment – authentic Scottish
  country house hospitality."

Culzean Castle is an unusual yet most welcome
addition to Taste of Scotland. The top floor was
Eisenhower's holiday home and now offers
accommodation and excellent hospitality. giving its
guests an opportunity to experience life in an
extremely well-preserved, 'living' castle. It is run by
Susan and Jonathan Cardale (who is Administrator).
Susan is an accomplished cook who uses only the
best produce, cooks it in a traditional Scottish style
and presents it well. It is well worth arriving early
as guests will then have time to see round the castle
on a most informative tour or explore the grounds.
House guests are also permitted to explore the castle
between 9 am and 10.30 am before the public arrive.
A wonderful experience in an historic building with
an atmosphere redolent of a bygone age.

Open mid Apr to mid Oct
- Rooms: 6, 4 with private facilities
- B&B £100–£210 (incl tea)
- SP Special rates available for group booking of
  whole apartment
- Non-resident dinner parties – by prior
  arrangement
- Unlicensed – complimentary drinks cupboard
- Dinner ££££
- Children welcome – prior arrangement
  required for children under 10 years
- Facilities for disabled visitors
- No smoking in dining room + bedrooms

**Seared salmon with potato pancake, sour cream
and spring onion dressing. Roast loin of lamb with
rosemary and red wine sauce served with seasonal
vegetables. Lemon roulade with passion fruit sauce.**

STB Highly Commended Visitor Attraction
- Credit cards: Mastercard/Eurocard, American
  Express, Visa
- Administrator: Jonathan Cardale

FOUTERS BISTRO RESTAURANT

2A Academy Street, Ayr
Ayrshire KA7 1HS
Tel: 01292 261391
Fax: 01292 619323

Town centre, opposite Town Hall.

Historic basement restaurant in Ayr.

- Converted bank vaults.
- Modern Scottish cooking.
- "Consistency and excellent cuisine have ensured
  Fouters popularity for over 24 years."

Situated in a converted basement of the 18th
century British Linen Bank building, in an old
cobbled lane opposite the Town Hall in Ayr, Fouters
has been a restaurant since 1973, and is one of the
best places to eat in south-west Scotland. Laurie
and Fran Black create a bright and cheerful
atmosphere; white walls and stencils give a casual,
continental feel to this underground sanctuary. It
has been one of the most popular restaurants in Ayr
since it opened. The style of cooking is inspired by
the traditional French kitchen, and makes good use
of the fish and shellfish from Ayr Fish Market, game
in season from local estates and top quality
Ayrshire beef and dairy products. Menus are
supplemented by daily 'chef's specials'. Fouters has
2 AA Rosettes.

Open all year except 25 to 27 Dec + 1 to 3 Jan
Closed Sun Mon
- Lunch except Sun Mon ££
- Dinner except Sun Mon £££
- Vegetarians welcome
- Special diets catered for
- Children welcome
- Member of the Scotch Beef Club

**Taste of Scotland Platter. Lobster and monkfish
thermidor. Fouters pavlova with summer fruits.**

- Credit cards: Mastercard/Eurocard, American
  Express, Visa, Diners Club, Mastercharge,
  Switch, Solo
- Owners: Laurie & Fran Black

MONTGREENAN MANSION HOUSE HOTEL

Montgreenan Estate
nr Kilwinning
Ayrshire KA13 7QZ
Tel: 01294 557733
Fax: 01294 850397

On A736, 4 miles north of Irvine.

A luxury country house hotel in its own grounds.

- An impeccably restored and maintained Georgian mansion.
- Fine modern/traditional Scottish cuisine.
- "A lovely country house hotel with impeccable standards of service and cuisine."

Built in 1817 by a wealthy tobacco baron, and set in 50 acres of secluded parklands and beautiful gardens, Montgreenan still retains the impressive architecture and decorative features of the period – down to white-aproned helpful staff. This well-run hotel combines Edwardian grandeur with informal comfort – and even has its own heliport. Based on the finest raw materials, the hotel offers excellent, innovative modern cuisine. Its wine list is unusually comprehensive, and will satisfy the most demanding connoisseur. Guests can also enjoy horse-riding, clay pigeon shooting and fishing. The hotel has 1 AA Rosette.

Open all year
🏨 Rooms: 21 with private facilities
🛏 DB&B £130 (min 2 nights stay)
　　B&B £100–£146
✗ Lunch ££
✗ Dinner £££
Ⓥ Vegetarians welcome
⚭ Children welcome
🚭 No smoking in restaurant

Venison sausage on a bed of skirlie with a game sauce and julienne of smoked venison. Fresh water salmon with flambéed king prawns and mussels in a light thyme sabayon. Rum and raisin cheesecake.

STB Highly Commended 👑 👑 👑 👑
💳 Credit cards: Mastercard/Eurocard, American Express, Visa, Diners Club, Mastercharge
Ⓝ Proprietor: Darren Dobson

NORTHPARK HOUSE HOTEL

Alloway Village, Ayr
Ayrshire KA7 4NL
Tel: 01292 442336
Fax: 01292 445572

Alloway Village, near Burns' cottage, 2 miles from Ayr town centre.

A charming, well-restored small country house hotel and restaurant in the heart of Burns' country.

- An award-winning, family-run establishment of excellent reputation.
- Outstanding and varied traditional cuisine.
- "A very attractive hotel offering high quality food and service."

Robert Burns was born almost next door to Northpark, an early 18th century farmhouse that has been sympathetically extended and converted. Surrounded by Belleisle's two fine golf courses, it stands in its own grounds. Although the hotel has five well-appointed bedrooms, it is best known for its four unique restaurants, grouped around a central conservatory which serves light meals and snacks. In each of the restaurants, both table d'hôte and à la carte menus offer the best of local produce cooked with flair but without pretension. With 95 bins, the wine list befits the cuisine.

Open all year
🏨 Rooms : 5 with private facilities
🛏 DB&B £77.50–£105　　B&B £62.50–£90
ⓈⓅ Special rates available
✗ Food available all day
✗ Lunch ££
✗ Dinner £££
Ⓥ Vegetarians welcome
⚭ Children welcome
♿ Facilities for disabled visitors
🚭 Two dining rooms non-smoking

Poached salmon on a spaghetti of cucumber. Roast loin of lamb wrapped in a Parmesan omelette with a rosemary jus. Warm soft centred chocolate pudding with caramelised banana.

STB Highly Commended 👑 👑 👑 👑
💳 Credit cards: Mastercard/Eurocard, American Express, Visa, Diners Club, Mastercharge, Switch
Ⓝ Proprietors: Rosamond & Graeme Rennie

THE STABLES COFFEE HOUSE
Queen's Court, 41 Sandgate
Ayr KA7 1BD
Tel: 01292 283704

To the rear of the old courtyard at the corner of
Sandgate and Newmarket Street.

A small, charming town centre restaurant and tea-room with garden in a courtyard dating back to the 18th century.

- Unmistakably Scottish fare and atmosphere in a charming corner of Ayr.
- Ethnic Scottish cooking.
- "A lovely range of home-made Scottish dishes and plenty of old world charm."

Proprietor Ed Baines is a man of firm opinions. At the Stables, a converted stable block built of local stone in the 1760s, he caters for those who wish distinctively Scottish fare, from tea and a scone to a full meal. You will find neither burgers, beans nor chips in his restaurant. The cakes, scones and iced cream are excellent and made on the premises, the family smokehouse at Craigrossie always produces something interesting. Enjoy a glass of Silver Birch wine with farm-made cheeses and fresh oatcakes or one of the traditional dishes listed below. This is an iconoclastic establishment, but what Ed Baines does, he does well. Children's toys and books available.

....

Open all year except 25, 26 Dec, 1 + 2 Jan
Note: Open Sun during summer only
✗ Food available all day £
✗ Lunch £
Ⓥ Vegetarians welcome
⚲ Children welcome
✄ Main dining room non-smoking + separate non-smoking dining room

Cullen skink. Tweed Kettle: casserole of salmon, mushrooms, celery and onions spiced with mace and cooked in white wine. Brown bread ice cream.

⊡ No credit cards
✗ Proprietor: Edward J T Baines

BALLACHULISH HOUSE
Ballachulish, Argyll PA39 4JX
Tel: 01855 811 266
Fax: 01855 811 498

From roundabout south of Ballachulish Bridge take
A828 Oban. Signed on left, 200 yards beyond
Ballachulish Hotel.

A traditional guest house dripping in antiques.

- An 18th century country house.
- Home cooking; local fish a speciality.
- "This house is steeped in history and offers peace, tranquillity and excellent hospitality."

Ballachulish House is steeped in history. It has been the seat of the Stewarts of Ballachulish since the 16th century, indeed the final order for the massacre of Glencoe was signed here. Today Ballachulish House offers quiet, peace and comfort to the traveller. The rooms are spacious and elegantly furnished with antiques; log fires throughout the year ensure a warm and relaxed ambience; the en suite bedrooms have spectacular views over Loch Linnhe and the Morven Hills and in keeping with the rest of the house are comfortable and well-decorated. The owners, Liz and John Grey, treat visitors to their home as personal guests. The dining room is situated in the oldest part of the house, has a low ceiling and looks out to the garden. A simple but elegant table d'hôte menu is presented, the food is carefully presented and well-balanced.

....

Open all Feb to Nov
🛏 Rooms: 5 with private facilities
🛏 DB&B £63–£65   B&B £38–40
♀ Restricted hotel licence
✗ Dinner 4 course menu £££
Ⓥ Vegetarians welcome
⚲ Children welcome
✄ No smoking in dining room + bedrooms

Mussels and mushrooms in puff pastry baskets. Fillet of pork with ginger and spring onions. Crêpes with Cointreau and orange butter.

STB Deluxe 👑 👑 👑
⊡ Credit cards: Mastercard/Eurocard, Visa, Switch, Delta, JVC
✗ Owners: Liz & John Grey

COSSES COUNTRY HOUSE

Ballantrae
Ayrshire KA26 0LR
Tel: 01465 831 363
Fax: 01465 831 598
e-mail 100636.1047@compuserve.com

From A77 at southern end of Ballantrae, take inland road signed to Laggan. Cosses is c. 2 miles on right.

Luxury bed and breakfast to the highest standards with superb cooking and hospitality to match.

* Converted farmhouse full of character.
* Gourmet country house cooking.
* "A truly welcoming Taste of Scotland."

Now a country house, dating from 1606, standing in 12 acres of glorious gardens and woodland in a fold in the hills, Cosses was built as a shooting lodge and became the home farm for nearby Glenapp Estate. It is the home of Robin and Susan Crosthwaite, and guests are made to feel they are part of the family. They grow their own vegetables, herbs and some fruit, and Susan – a Cordon Bleu Chef – presents delicious, four course, table d'hôte menus which feature local seafood and game, Scottish cheeses and home-made petit fours (the menus are often discussed with guests beforehand). Two cottage suites are provided within the courtyard and there is a double bedroom en suite within the house itself.

Open Feb to Nov
🏠 Rooms: 3 with private facilities
🛏 DB&B £50–£70　B&B £30–£48
SP Special rates available
✕ Dinner £££
🍴 Dinner for non-residents – by reservation only
Ⓥ Vegetarians welcome
🧍 Children welcome
🚭 No smoking in dining room

Ballantrae prawns rolled in Scottish smoked salmon in a piquant mayonnaise. Fillet of Scottish beef with a whisky, mushroom and cream sauce. Meringue baskets filled with Cosses berry fruits and served with melba sauce.

STB Deluxe 👑 👑 👑
💳 Credit cards: Mastercard/Eurocard, Visa
🧍 Proprietors: Susan & Robin Crosthwaite

BALGONIE COUNTRY HOUSE HOTEL

Braemar Place, Ballater AB35 5NQ
Tel/Fax: 013397 55482

Off A93 Aberdeen-Perth, on outskirts of village of Ballater.

A country house hotel in the heart of Deeside.

* Tranquil Edwardian mansion in four acres of mature gardens with views towards hills of Glen Muick.
* Traditional and innovative recipes using fresh local produce.
* "An idyllic retreat – first rate food, wine and hospitality."

Balgonie is five minutes' walk from Ballater on Royal Deeside, set in spacious gardens overlooking Ballater Golf Course. The resident proprietors, John and Priscilla Finnie, pride themselves on maintaining a friendly but unobtrusive service. The nine en suite bedrooms are very comfortable and tastefully furnished. The dining room is the heart of Balgonie providing an inviting cuisine using locally sourced fish and game. When in season, herbs and soft fruits from the garden are always found on the menu. French and German are spoken. The hotel has 2 AA Rosettes. Winner of Taste of Scotland Country House Hotel of the Year Award 1993.

Open 12 Feb to 5 Jan
🏠 Rooms: 9 with private facilities
🛏 DB&B £78–£88　B&B £49.50–£59.50
SP Special rates available
✕ Lunch – by reservation only ££
🍴 Dinner 4 course menu – non-residents by reservation £££
Ⓥ Vegetarians welcome – prior notice required
🧍 Children over 5 years welcome at dinner
🚭 No smoking in dining room

Salad of Scottish asparagus tips, avocado and smoked salmon finished with yoghurt and lime dressing. Fillet of Aberdeen Angus beef topped with horseradish sabayon and finished with a Madeira jus. Glazed lemon tart with blackcurrant coulis.

STB Deluxe 👑 👑 👑 👑
💳 Credit cards: Mastercard/Eurocard, American Express, Visa, Switch, Delta
🧍 Proprietor: John G Finnie

DARROCH LEARG HOTEL
Braemar Road, Ballater
Aberdeenshire AB35 5UX
Tel: 013397 55443
Fax: 013397 55252

½ mile from centre of village of Ballater, off A93.

Country house hotel on Royal Deeside with views of Cairngorms.

- Victorian period house overlooking Ballater and Royal Deeside.
- Modern Scottish cooking.
- "Excellent food using only the freshest local produce."

Darroch Learg was built in 1888 as a country residence when Royal Deeside was at its most fashionable. The hotel enjoys a wonderful situation, high up on a rocky hillside, with excellent views. The house has period charm and has retained the comfortable atmosphere of the family home it once was, with two drawing rooms (smoking and non-smoking). The dining room and spacious conservatory allow diners to enjoy the wonderful outlook south to the hills of Glen Muick. The short table d'hôte menu (three main courses) offers top quality local meat from the excellent local dealers confidently and expertly prepared in unusual combinations and sauces. The hotel has 3 AA Rosettes.

....

Open Feb to Dec closed Christmas
🏠 Rooms: 18 with private facilities
🛏 DB&B £56–£82   B&B £37.50–£57.50
✗ Food available all day £££
✗ Lunch £££
✗ Dinner ££££
Ⓥ◄ Vegetarians welcome – prior notice required
✶ Children welcome
♿ Facilities for disabled visitors – ground floor
🚭 No smoking in dining room

Fillet of halibut with risotto, crispy leeks and a mussel and saffron sauce. Fillet of Aberdeen Angus beef with braised oxtail, wild mushrooms, rosti potatoes and a tarragon sauce. Scottish strawberry cheesecake with white chocolate sorbet and strawberry sauce.

STB Highly Commended 👑 👑 👑 👑
💳 Credit cards: Mastercard/Eurocard, American Express, Visa, Diners Club, Switch
👥 Proprietors: Nigel & Fiona Franks

DEESIDE HOTEL
Braemar Road, Ballater
Aberdeenshire AB35 5RQ
Tel: 013397 55420
Fax: 013397 55357

On west side of Ballater, set back from A93 Braemar road.

A comfortable family hotel with a relaxed atmosphere.

- Pink granite town house.
- Traditional Scottish cooking.
- "A relaxed, friendly atmosphere with tasty traditional food."

The Deeside is an attractive pink granite building, set back from the main road with an informal well-maintained garden. It is a family-run establishment with nine en suite bedrooms, two of which are situated on the ground floor. The house is welcoming and in the sitting room there is an impressive painted frieze of wild animals; the original Victorian mantelpiece and tiled fireplace have been retained. Through an open archway from the lounge bar is the dining room with its varnished wooden floor and oil paintings of mountain scenery on the walls. In the evening, meals are available in both the restaurant and bar where you can also sample a good selection of Scottish real ales and malt whiskies.

....

Open 10 Feb to 2 Jan except Christmas Day + Boxing Day
🏠 Rooms: 9 with private facilities
🛏 DB&B £35–£40   B&B £20–£25
SP Special rates available
✗ Lunch Sun ££
✗ Dinner ££
Ⓥ Vegetarians welcome
✶ Children welcome
♿ Facilities for disabled visitors
🚭 No smoking in restaurant

Fish soups and chowders. Baked smoked fillet of haddock topped with cheese rarebit, tomato and pesto sauce. Clootie dumpling.

STB Commended 👑 👑 👑
💳 Credit cards: Mastercard/Eurocard, Visa, Switch
👥 Directors: Donald & Alison Brooker

GLEN LUI HOTEL
Invercauld Road, Ballater
Aberdeenshire AB35 5RP
Tel: 013397 55402 Fax: 013397 55545

Off A93 at western end of Ballater.

A town hotel with a country house appeal overlooking the golf course and Lochnagar.

- A country house style hotel standing in two acres of grounds.
- Modern Scottish cooking, with some French influences.
- "Scottish fare and French flair – a great combination."

A house which has been much added to, most recently by the addition of a wrap-around conservatory/restaurant overlooking the golf course. Accommodation is comfortable; service polite, friendly and well-trained. The courses on the extensive a la carte menu have a distinct French influence. But you forgive all when you discover the owner is himself French and the cooking is sublime. Each dish is presented with confidence and artistry. There is a very comprehensive wine list with vintage wines.

Open all year
Note: Possible renovation Jan/Feb – please telephone
- 🏠 Rooms: 19 with private facilities
- 🛏 DB&B £45–£55   B&B £29–£42
- SP Special rates available
- ✗ Lunch £
- ✗ Dinner £-££
- V Vegetarians welcome
- ☼ Children welcome
- ♿ Facilities for disabled visitors
- 🚭 No smoking in restaurant + bedrooms

Seared queen scallops served on a fine julienne of vegetables with a lemon and coriander dressing. Pan-fried noisette of venison served with a parfait of black pudding on a bed of red cabbage, edged with a juniper and port essence. Home-made cranachan ice cream served in a lacy biscuit on a pool of raspberry coulis garnished with fresh raspberries.

STB Highly Commended 👑 👑 👑 👑
- 💳 Credit cards: Mastercard/Eurocard, American Express, Visa, Mastercharge, Switch
- 👤 Proprietors: Serge & Lorraine Geraud

THE GREEN INN RESTAURANT WITH ROOMS
9 Victoria Road, Ballater, Aberdeenshire AB35 5QQ
Tel/Fax: 013397 55701

In centre of Ballater on village green.

A quality restaurant with rooms; Jeffrey and Carol Purves both have a justified reputation for delicious food in intimate and comfortable surroundings.

- A two-storey granite building, once a temperance hotel.
- Modern regional Scottish cooking, with good use of international influences.
- "Jeff and Carol consistently achieve the highest standards."

Jeff Purves' reputation is well-deserved: his cooking is innovative and imaginative, and he applies this to the excellent local produce available on Deeside. Chef specials change daily, often treat classic Scottish dishes in an unusual way and combine flavours with assured confidence. Jeff uses cream only when necessary, replacing sugar with honey, and so on – and he is also delighted by the challenge of vegetarian cooking, but requests advance warning to do it justice. Service from Carol is friendly and helpful in the intimate dining room. The Green Inn has 2 AA Rosettes. Winner of The Macallan Taste of Scotland Restaurant of the Year Award 1995.

Open all year except 2 wks Nov, Christmas Day + 26 to 28 Dec
Closed Sun Oct to Mar
- 🏠 Rooms: 3 with private facilities
- 🛏 DB&B £45–£49
- SP Special rates available
- ✗ Lunch Sun ££
- ✗ Dinner £££
- V Vegetarians welcome
- ☼ Children welcome
- ♿ Disabled access only
- 🚭 Smoking permitted at coffee stage only
- 🐄 Member of the Scotch Beef Club

A tartlet of Arbroath smokie with a fillet of smoked trout on salad leaves with a raw beetroot dressing. Tweed kettle. A warm chocolate mousse with pistachio ice cream.

STB Highly Commended 👑 👑 👑
- 💳 Credit cards: Mastercard/Eurocard, American Express, Visa Mastercharge
- 👤 Proprietors: J J & C A Purves

HAYLOFT RESTAURANT
Bridge Square, Ballater
Aberdeenshire AB35 5QJ
Tel/Fax: 013397 55999

Central Ballater, close to the bridge.

A highly atmospheric restaurant by the River Dee.

- Converted 19th century stables.
- Home cooking and fresh light meals.
- "The Hepburns' genuine enthusiasm for quality local produce and traditional cooking is evident."

The old stable building stands beside the river in the centre of town and has been converted into a licensed restaurant. The interior makes a theme of its former function, retaining many of the original features, with hay bales and items of riding tack decorating the room. The restaurant has a high wooden ceiling and has been set out on two levels with a long gallery running along one side. Pine tables and chairs, horse brasses and other paraphernalia add to the peculiar rustic atmosphere here. The varied menus offer both daily specials and traditional dishes (plus pizzas, pastas and children's specials), cooked simply with attention to presentation. The service is cheerful and there is a delicious range of home baking available during the day. In another part of the Hayloft building the UK's first indoor barbeque restaurant has just opened. You can select either chicken, salmon or steak from a chill display and cook it over a central barbeque – great fun!

Open mid Jan to end Nov + Christmas period
Note: Please book ahead if possible
Closed 1½ days during winter – please telephone
- ✗ Lunch £-££
- ✗ Dinner £-£££
- Ⓥ Vegetarians welcome
- ⚹ Children welcome
- ♿ Facilities for disabled visitors
- 🚭 No pipes or cigars
- 🐄 Member of the Scotch Beef Club

Marinated herrings. Escalope of venison. Grilled local salmon with parsley butter. Steaks.

- 💳 Credit cards: Mastercard/Eurocard, American Express, Visa, Diners Club, Mastercharge, Switch, Delta
- Ⓝ Proprietors: Brodie & Winnie Hepburn

RAVENSWOOD HOTEL
Braemar Road, Ballater
Aberdeenshire AB35 5RQ
Tel/Fax: 013397 55539

On the A93, western end of Ballater – a 10 minute walk from centre of village.

Small friendly hotel.

- Converted Victorian villa.
- Traditional Scottish hotel cooking.
- "Friendly hotel with good food and service."

Ravenswood Hotel is a small friendly family-owned Victorian hotel in the pretty village of Ballater which is already renowned as home to some of the best eating places in Scotland. The hotel is a splendid period building which retains many of its original features. The Fyfes offer simple good food, local produce well-cooked. Family service meals are offered in the dining room and the lounge bar (with fireplace) offers a selection of alternative dishes. Ravenswood is unpretentious, good value and a lovely place from which to explore Royal Deeside.

Open all year except 10 Nov to 5 Dec
- 🏨 Rooms: 8, 5 with private facilities
- 🛏 DB&B £32.50–£47.50   B&B £20–£35
- 🅢🅟 Special rates available
- ✗ Lunch ££
- ✗ Dinner ££
- Ⓥ Vegetarians welcome
- ⚹ Children welcome
- 🚭 No smoking in dining room

Cream of carrot soup. Pan-fried venison steak with a cream whisky and herb sauce. Strawberry and Drambuie shortcake.

STB Commended 👑 👑 👑
- 💳 Credit cards: Mastercard/Eurocard, American Express, Visa
- Ⓝ Owners: Fraser & Cathy Fyfe

Ballater, Royal Deeside   D4

STAKIS ROYAL DEESIDE & COUNTRY CLUB
Braemar Road, Ballater
Royal Deeside AB35 5XA
Tel: 013397 55858
Fax: 013397 55447

On A93 western end of Ballater, near Balmoral.

A resort hotel with full leisure and sports facilities.

- Victorian country house.
- Modern grand hotel with fine dining and bistro cooking.
- "The stylish ambience and excellent cuisine made the Oaks a memorable experience."

This house was built in the 19th century for the Keiller family (the inventors of marmalade) and has been converted into a modern resort hotel with time-ownership lodges and every imaginable facility. The food on offer has all the feel of a large hotel with a brigade of chefs working busily to support the restaurants. The Oaks is a classy formal restaurant, serving interesting and imaginative dishes prepared by Executive Chef, Paul Moran, both continental and classic influences are detectable in his beautifully presented dishes. In The Clubhouse Restaurant, which adjoins the pool area in the Leisure Club, the bistro style food is fast, comprehensive and unsophisticated – good grub for all the family, and some dishes may be taken away.

....

    Open all year
🏨 Rooms: 44 with private facilities
    DB&B £39–£89   B&B £29–£65
SP Special rates available
✕ Lunch (Clubhouse Restaurant) ££
✕ Dinner (Clubhouse Restaurant) ££
✕ Dinner (The Oaks) ££-£££
Ⓥ Vegetarians welcome
🖈 Children welcome
🚭 No smoking in The Oaks

Pigeon terrine studded with leek and French beans, truffle dressing and marmalade. Roasted seabass with tomato confit, cocotte potatoes, continental vegetables and vermouth sauce. Orange chibouste.

STB Highly Commended 👑 👑 👑 👑 👑
💳 Credit cards: Mastercard/Eurocard, American Express, Visa, Diners Club, Switch, Delta
🛇 General Manager: Richard McIntosh

Ballindalloch   D4   B

THE DELNASHAUGH INN
Ballindalloch
Banffshire AB37 9AS
Tel: 01807 500255
Fax: 01807 500389

From A9 Aviemore, take A95 via Grantown-on-Spey, or A941 from Elgin, to Ballindalloch.

A stylishly refurbished country inn on Speyside.

- Old drovers inn with a lovely situation.
- Creative home cooking.
- "Wonderful hospitality in an idyllic setting."

The Delnashaugh Inn dates back to the 16th century, when it provided rest and food for the drovers as they took their cattle to the markets in the south. Today it is popular with sportsmen, particularly fishermen: it stands within the Ballindalloch Estate and overlooks the valley of the River Avon, which joins the Spey not far from the hotel; fishing, shooting and stalking can be arranged. It was completely refurbished recently, in a way which respects the original atmosphere and character of the old inn. The inn's proprietors, David and Marion Ogden, present a tempting table d'hôte menu (three starters, three main courses), often featuring salmon and game from the estate. The traditional dishes are cooked with flair and imagination.

....

    Open mid Mar to end Oct
🏨 Rooms: 9 with private facilities
🛏 DB&B £60–£75   B&B £45–£60
✕ Lunch £
✕ Dinner £££
Ⓥ Vegetarians welcome – prior notice required
🖈 Children welcome
♿ Facilities for disabled visitors

Smoked haddock mousseline served on a bed of lemon dressed leaves. Roast breast of local wild duck served with an apple and cider sauce. Fresh raspberry sable served with a malt whisky cream.

STB Highly Commended 👑 👑 👑 👑
💳 Credit cards: Mastercard/Eurocard, Visa
🛇 Proprietors: David & Marion Ogden

MONACHYLE MHOR

Balquhidder, Lochearnhead, Perthshire FK19 8PQ
Tel: 01877 384 622
Fax: 01877 384 305

11 miles north of Callander on A84. Turn right at
Kingshouse Hotel – 6 miles straight along glen road.

**A small, award-winning farmhouse hotel in the
Perthshire hills.**

- Family-run establishment of great character .
- Modern Scottish cooking.
- "This hotel is dedicated to gastronomic
  excellence."

In Rob Roy country of mountains and lochs,
Monachyle Mhor sits in its own 2,000 acres in the
heart of the Braes o' Balquhidder. The hotel's views
over Lochs Voil and Doine are breathtaking.
Proprietors Rob and Jean Lewis fully deserve their
reputation for hospitality. All rooms are comfortable
and have bathrooms en suite. Both the restaurant
and cosy bar serve imaginative, good food that
makes the best of fresh, local produce – offering
game from the estate, fish from the West Coast and
the finest Scottish meat cooked with a French
influence by chef, Tom. Interesting, discerning wine
list. Monachyle Mhor has 2 AA Rosettes. There are
also three self-catering cottages, equipped and
appointed to the same high standards as the hotel.
(See advert Page 236.)

Open all year
🛏 Rooms: 10 with private facilities
🛏 B&B £30–£40
✕ Food available all day £-£££
✕ Lunch ££
✕ Dinner £££
Ⓥ Vegetarians welcome
🚭 No smoking in restaurant

**Pan-fried breast of pigeon on pearl barley and
bramble stock reduction. Mixed breasts of wild
duck with citrus and peppercorn dressing.
Chocolate Marquis.**

STB Commended 👑 👑 👑
💳 Credit cards: Mastercard/Eurocard, Visa,
   Switch
👤 Proprietor: Jean Lewis

TOR-NA-COILLE HOTEL

Inchmarlo Road
Banchory
Aberdeenshire AB31 4AB
Tel: 01330 822242
Fax: 01330 824012

Situated on the A93 Aberdeen to Braemar road, 18
miles from Aberdeen's city centre.

**Attractive hotel set in pleasant, well-tended
gardens**

- Victorian country house hotel.
- Traditional Scottish cooking.
- "A friendly hotel with good food and service."

Tor-Na-Coille Hotel is an attractive, ivy clad
Victorian mansion standing in its own wooded
grounds set back from the A93. It is a friendly,
professionally run hotel and is a very suitable place
from which to base and explore the surrounding
Deeside area. The restaurant is attractive where
fresh local produce is used, simply presented with
good flavour and texture. Menus are well-balanced
offering good choice and served by helpful and
professional staff.

Open all year except 25 to 28 Dec
🛏 Rooms: 23 with private facilities
🛏 DB&B £69.50–£81   B&B £45–£56.50
SP Special rates available
✕ Food available all day ££
✕ Lunch £
✕ Dinner £££
Ⓥ Vegetarians welcome
🧒 Children welcome
♿ Facilities for disabled visitors
🚭 Smoking areas in dining room

**A warm salad of pigeon breast, bacon. lentils,
salad leaves and quail eggs. Smoked fillets of
haddock served on steamed new potatoes and
leeks with an Arran mustard sauce. Brandy snap
basket filled with Atholl brose on warm
butterscotch sauce.**

STB Commended 👑 👑 👑 👑
💳 Credit cards: Mastercard/Eurocard, American
   Express, Visa, Diners Club, Switch, Delta
👤 Owner: Roxanne Sloan-Maris

BANFF SPRINGS HOTEL
Golden Knowes Road
Banff
Aberdeenshire AB45 2JE
Tel: 01261 812881
Fax: 01261 815546

On the western outskirts of Banff, overlooking the beach of Boyndie Bay on the A98 Banff to Elgin road.

- Modern hotel.
- Traditional Scottish cooking.
- "A friendly hotel with a superb view of the Buchan coastline, and what a sunset from the restaurant!"

Banff Springs Hotel is a modern purpose built property which has undergone recent refurbishment. It is in a superb location with wonderful views of the Buchan coastline and is in an excellent location to explore the surrounding area. The restaurant is a particularly good place from which to enjoy the views (and is attractively set out for dinner with crisp and co-ordinating linen). The cooking uses only good local fresh ingredients and is presented and prepared well by a chef who obviously cares and understands his subject. There is a pleasant atmosphere in this hotel with staff who are keen to ensure that guests enjoy their stay.

Open all year except Christmas Day
- 🛏 Rooms: 31 with private facilities
- 🛏 DB&B £44–£70.45   B&B £29–£52.50
- SP Special rates available
- ✕ Lunch £
- ✕ Dinner ££
- Ⓥ Vegetarians welcome
- 术 Children welcome
- ♿ Facilities for disabled visitors
- 🚭 No smoking in restaurant

Marinated salmon with warm salad of new potato, fromage frais and deep-fried leek. Escalope of venison with port wine and blackcurrant sauce, straw potatoes and wild berry tartlet. Fresh fruits of the forest crepe with chantilly cream.

STB Commended 👑 👑 👑 👑
- 💳 Credit cards: Mastercard/Eurocard, American Express, Visa, Switch, Delta
- 🅽 Proprietor: Nicola Antliff

PERTHSHIRE VISITOR CENTRE
Bankfoot
Perth
PH1 4EB
Tel: 01738 787696
Fax: 01738 787120

8 miles north of Perth on A9. Follow signs for Bankfoot.

Just off the A9, this is a good place to break a journey.

- Waitress service restaurant, plus shop and 'Macbeth Experience'.
- Country kitchen restaurant with good home cooking.
- "An excellent venue for all the family."

'The Macbeth Experience', which is the focus of this visitor centre, is a multi-media exploration of Scotland's mis-judged 11th century warrior king. Next door is a well-stocked shop (knitwear, glass, books, foods, whisky, gifts and souvenirs) and a comfortable friendly restaurant, offering freshly made soups, desserts and a varied selection of home baking as well as a selection of freshly cooked meals listed on a blackboard. There is a large car park adjacent and a children's play area.

Open all year except Christmas Day + New Year's Day
- ✕ Food available all day £
- ⚲ Table Licence
- Ⓥ Vegetarians welcome
- ♿ Facilities for disabled visitors

Soup of the day. Venison casserole in a red wine and mushroom gravy served with a selection of fresh vegetables. Cloutie dumpling.

- 💳 Credit cards: Mastercard/Eurocard, Visa
- 🅽 Proprietors: Wilson & Catriona Girvan

CHRIALDON HOUSE HOTEL

Station Road
Beauly
Inverness-shire IV4 7EH
Tel: 01463 782336

On A862 main road through Beauly, close to the square. 12 miles from Inverness.

A small hotel just off the main street in the centre of Beauly; an ideal touring base for the Highlands.

- Red sandstone Victorian detached town house.
- Scottish home cooking.
- "Ideal base for touring with excellent home cooking."

Surrounded by a very well-tended garden in the town of Beauly, the Chrialdon is elegant yet informal with spacious rooms in a homely environment. The hotel is run by Nicoll and Valerie Reid, who are welcoming and helpful hosts and who pay attention to the small details and needs which make for a memorable stay. They offer short but well-balanced menus, using only such fresh produce as is seasonally available; the cooking is simple, creative and tasty – and extremely good value for money. The Chrialdon has a good local reputation. *(See advert Page 25.)*

    Open all year except Christmas Day
🏠 Rooms: 9, 6 with private facilities
🛏 DB&B £38–£48   B&B £20–£30
SP Special rates available
✕ Residents only
✕ Dinner ££
Ⓥ Vegetarians welcome
✄ No smoking in dining room

Hot buttered shrimps and wild mushrooms in filo pastry shells. Venison medallions in a rich port and juniper berry sauce. Glen mist – a subtle blend of meringue cream and Drambuie.

STB Commended ♛ ♛ ♛
💳 Credit cards: Mastercard/Eurocard, Visa
Ⓜ Proprietors: Nicoll & Valerie Reid

LOVAT ARMS HOTEL

Beauly
Inverness-shire IV4 7BS
Tel: 01463 782313
Fax: 01463 782862

On A862, 11 miles from Inverness in Beauly centre.

Superior small town hotel.

- Elegant town hotel.
- Modern Scottish cooking.
- "This hotel makes the best use of Scottish authenticity."

The name Beauly derives its name from 'beau lieu' or beautiful place. The Lovat Arms is a stylish family-owned hotel in the centre of a picturesque small market town. The remains of Beauly Priory, built around 1230 and visited by Mary Queen of Scots, makes an ideal picnic location. The food is very well-cooked and presented by Head Chef Donald Munro who uses his skills to present local produce in innovative ways for good value for money. The hotel is an ideal place from which to explore Beauly or Moray Firth with their natural beauty and wide variety of wild life. *(See advert Page 30.)*

    Open all year
🏠 Rooms: 22 with private facilities
🛏 DB&B £40–£65   B&B £35–£47
SP Special rates available
✕ Food available all day ££
✕ Lunch ££
✕ Dinner £££
Ⓥ Vegetarians welcome
🧍 Children welcome
♿ Facilities for disabled visitors – please telephone
✄ No smoking in dining room

Loch Fyne oysters with lime hollandaise. Collops of Strathconnon venison with sloe gin and redcurrant sauce. Home-made sticky toffee pudding with Drambuie cream.

STB Commended ♛ ♛ ♛ ♛
💳 Credit cards: Mastercard/Eurocard, Visa
Ⓜ Proprietor: William Fraser

BORGIE LODGE HOTEL

Skerray, Bettyhill, Sutherland KW14 7TH
Tel/Fax: 01641 521 332

Take A836 for 7 miles from Tongue, turn left at the Torrisdale Road. Borgie Lodge is ½ mile along on the right.

A traditional hunting and fishing lodge in pleasant gardens on Scotland's northern seaboard.

- Spacious country house hotel.
- Home cooking – local fish a speciality.
- "A wonderful recluse with the best of home cooking."

Quiet and secluded, Borgie Lodge has been the home of Peter and Jacqui MacGregor for four years. In this time the hunting and fishing lodge has been tastefully upgraded to provide comfortable accommodation while keeping its traditional Highland image by way of Clan Sutherland tartan carpets, sporting prints and crackling log fires. A self-taught cook, Jacqui makes excellent use of the Caithness beef and lamb available to her, and the daily changing choice dinner menu will often feature the salmon and brown trout caught by the guests! Should you decide to contribute to the dinner menu, Borgie Lodge has salmon fishing rights on the Rivers Borgie and Halladale and boats for wild brown trout on the hotel's 20 hill lochs! Shooting and stalking on the 12,600 acre Tongue Estate. Peter can supply all the necessary ghillies, equipment and tuition.

Open all year except 24 Dec to 3 Jan
🛏 Rooms: 6 with private facilities
🛏 DB&B £62.50–£72.50   B&B £40–£50
✖ Lunch £
✖ Dinner £££
Ⓥ Vegetarians welcome
🧒 Children welcome
🚭 No smoking in dining room + bedrooms

Seared peppered salmon with cucumber pickle. Roast fillet of lamb with Cumberland sauce. Hazelnut meringue gâteau filled with fresh raspberries and cream.

STB Highly Commended 👑 👑 👑
💳 Credit cards: Mastercard/Eurocard, Visa
👤 Proprietors: Peter & Jacqui MacGregor

HARTREE COUNTRY HOUSE HOTEL

Biggar
Lanarkshire ML12 6JJ
Tel: 01899 221027
Fax: 01899 221259

Just off A702 on western outskirts of Biggar.

Country house hotel in peaceful surroundings.

- Old sandstone baronial mansion.
- Good Scottish cooking.
- "Good Scottish fare served in modern style."

Hartree is an historic country house with parts dating from the 15th century, although it is mainly Victorian and set in seven acres of peaceful wooded countryside. It is not far from Biggar, and offers a good base from which to tour this part of the Borders. The house is charming and has retained many baronial features in its interior – heavy mouldings and panelling, a marble floor in the lobby, and carved fireplaces. The grand dining room offers an interesting menu with daily changing 'specials' and many Scottish specialities. Almost equidistant from Edinburgh and Glasgow. Over 100 whiskies.

Open Mar to Dec
🛏 Rooms: 12 with private facilities
🛏 DB&B £41–£65   B&B £25–£50
SP Special rates available
✖ Dinner £-££
Ⓥ Vegetarians welcome
🧒 Children welcome

Smoked venison with Glenfiddich dressing. Pan-fried medallions of beef fillet layered with wild mushrooms topped with brandy cream sauce. Drambuie parfait with fresh raspberries and redberry sauce.

STB Commended 👑 👑 👑 👑
💳 Credit cards: Mastercard/Eurocard, American Express, Visa, Diners Club, Mastercharge, Switch, Delta
👤 Proprietors: John & Anne Charlton
Robert & Susan Reed

SKIRLING HOUSE
Skirling
Biggar
Lanarkshire
ML12 6HD
Tel: 01899 860274
Fax: 01899 860255
e-mail skirlinghouse@dial.pipex.com

In Skirling village overlooking the village green.
2 miles from Biggar on A72.

Architecturally unique, this splendid house is also wonderfully hospitable.

- Small deluxe guest house overlooking the village green in Skirling.
- Good home cooking.
- "Deluxe guest house offering hospitality and good home cooking with a 'Taste of Scotland'"

Private houses in the Arts and Crafts style are not common in Scotland, and to find one which retains so many of its original features is a great joy. The house was built in 1908 for Lord Gibson Carmichael and is now the home of Bob and Isobel Hunter, for whom nothing is too much trouble if it makes your stay more enjoyable. Bob presents a four course set menu each evening (guests preferences are sought in advance), based upon the fresh produce available locally that day; he cooks with a light touch and his dishes are very well-executed. The house cellar provides a selection of fine wines. Everything is home-made, including breads, ice cream and preserves. "This place is a real gem."

....

  Open 1 Mar to 31 Dec
🏠 Rooms: 3 with private facilities
🛏 DB&B £44–£56.50   B&B £27.50–£39
♀ Restricted hotel licence
✗ Lunch – by arrangement only
✗ Dinner 4 course menu ££
Ⓥ Vegetarians welcome
& Restricted access
↙ No smoking throughout

Balsamic fruits. Rack of Borders lamb in a pecan crust. White chocolate mousse in a praline basket.

STB Deluxe 🏵 🏵 🏵
⊟ No credit cards
🕴 Proprietors: Bob & Isobel Hunter

THE HOUSE OF BRUAR LTD
by Blair Atholl
Perthshire PH18 5TW
Tel: 01796 483236
Fax: 01796 483218

7 miles north of Pitlochry on the side of A9 at Bruar. Restaurant services A9.

An astonishing emporium of the 'best of Scottish'.

- Self-service restaurant.
- Home cooking and baking.
- "Wonderful for shopping, excellent for eating and a beautiful walk nearby."

The House of Bruar is a large, splendidly designed (inspired by Victorian hunting lodges) and expensively built (dressed stone, slate roof, astragal windows, etc) 'emporium' selling the very best of Scottish country products. It includes a cashmere hall, a cloth room, a wildflower nursery, country wear hall, food hall and 200 seater cafe/restaurant. Play and picnic areas are also provided. The lengthy blackboard menus offer snacks and full meals, with many classic Scottish dishes; the cooking is fresh and accomplished; breads, cakes and scones are freshly baked. A cheerful place for the whole family to break a journey.

....

  Open all year except Christmas Day +
  New Year's Day
✗ Food available all day
Ⓥ Vegetarians welcome
⚹ Children welcome
& Facilities for disabled visitors
↙ No smoking throughout

Home-baked cakes and scones. Fresh salmon, honey roast hams, filled crusty pies and Aberdeen Angus beef.

⊟ Credit cards: Mastercard/Eurocard, American Express, Visa, Mastercharge, Switch, Delta
🕴 Chef: Ian Bremner
🕴 Restaurant Managers: Susan Booth & James McMenemie

THE LOFT RESTAURANT
Golf Course Road
Blair Atholl, Perthshire
PH18 5TE
Tel: 01796 491377
Fax: 01796 481511

Take B8079 off A9, 5 miles north of Pitlochry. In village take golf course road by Tilt Hotel, the Loft is 50 yards on right.

Character bistro in historic village.

- A 19th century hay loft converted into a fine restaurant.
- Elegant Scottish.
- "A new look loft with Chef Douglas doing a fine job."

Located in a quiet side street off the main road through Blair Atholl is the Loft, a restaurant which is full of surprises and not to be bypassed! Climb the stairs, through the stable-style door and you will see an entirely refurbished eaterie retaining all the characteristics of twisted old beams, stone walls and oak flooring. Well thought out and fitted to high standards it forms a delightful setting in which to sample the excellent cuisine of Head Chef/Patron Douglas Wright. The menus, which change throughout the day, are refreshing and appealing to suit all levels of appetite. Advance bookings, especially for evenings, is strongly advised. New for 1998 is the conservatory bar and roof terrace. The Loft has 2 AA Rosettes. *(See advert Page 30.)*

    Open all year
✖ Morning coffee to late dinner available
✖ Lunch £
✖ Dinner ££
Ⓥ Vegetarians welcome
✦ Children welcome
✗ No smoking in restaurant

Caesar salad with thin slices of marinated tuna. Roast chump of local lamb with crushed garlic potato and shallot confit. Bread and butter pudding with vanilla anglaise.

▣ Credit cards: Mastercard/Eurocard, American Express, Visa, Diners Club, Mastercharge, Switch, Delta, JCB
▮ Head Chef/Patron: Douglas Wright

WOODLANDS
St Andrews Crescent, Blair Atholl
Perthshire PH18 5SX
Tel: 01796 481 403

A9, 7 miles north of Pitlochry. 100 yards down left turn in centre of Blair Atholl.

A charming guest house in Blair Atholl.

- Attractive country house.
- Good home cooking.
- "No wonder visitors return again and again - here you will find the essence of all that is best in Scotland."

Sheltered in its own gardens down a small lane off the main Blair Atholl thoroughfare, Woodlands is a warm and welcoming home. Here is a lady who knows her Scottish foods – and has broadcast her knowledge on TV and radio the length and breadth of the British Isles – and probably beyond. Her heart is in Scotland and her guests return again and again to hear her wonderful yarns and enjoy her cooking. A true taste of Scotland – the essence of all that is best in Scotland. A lady with eclectic taste and great charm. This is no ordinary B&B so relax and enjoy its idiosyncrasies. Gaelic spoken.

N.B. Opening times variable, depending on filming commitments
▥ Rooms: 3
⬗ DB&B £35–£40   B&B £20–£23
▣ ⚥ Unlicensed – guests welcome to take own wine
✖ Dinner ££
✖ Dinner for non-residents by arrangement
Ⓥ Vegetarians welcome

Warm pigeon breast served with a damson dressing and garnished with bacon. A halibut parcel layered with fresh leeks, tomatoes and citrus juices. Atholl Brose.

▣ No credit cards
▮ Proprietor: Dolina MacLennan

ALTAMOUNT HOUSE HOTEL
Coupar Angus Road
Blairgowrie
Perthshire PH10 6JN
Tel: 01250 873512
Fax: 01250 876200

Take A923 to Coupar Angus from centre of the town. The hotel is 500 yards on right hand side and is well-signed.

A comfortable family-run hotel offering good food.

- A stone built house within lovely grounds.
- Modern Scottish cooking.
- "A truly welcoming place where proprietors open their home to their guests and succeed in making your stay memorable."

Altamount Hotel is a lovely old Georgian house built in 1806 and set in six acres of its own well-tended gardens. The house has all the tranquillity of a country house hotel but is only 500 yards from the centre of Blairgowrie. New owner, Robert Glashan, is an accomplished host and makes every effort to ensure that his guests feel at home in his home. The cooking is in a modern style, well-presented using the best local produce and offering good value for money. Menus are well-balanced and are regularly updated with a new à la carte being introduced to offer even more choice for guests.

Open all year
Rooms: 7 with private facilities
DB&B £45–£60   B&B £30–£45
Special rates available
Food available all day ££
Lunch ££
Dinner £££
Vegetarians welcome
Children welcome
Facilities for disabled visitors
No smoking in dining room

Risotto of smoked haddock. Roast pigeon with green lentils, smoked bacon and a game gravy. Banana tart with home-made rum and raisin ice cream.

STB Commended
Credit cards: Mastercard/Eurocard, American Express, Visa, Switch, Delta
Proprietor: Robert & Sally Glashan

CARGILLS RESTAURANT & BISTRO
Lower Mill Street
Blairgowrie
Perthshire PH10 6AQ
Tel: 01250 876735

At the Square in the centre of Blairgowrie, turn left off A93 Perth-Braemar road into Mill Street. Cargills is behind the car park, 200 yards down on the left.

An attractive bistro in a converted grain store.

- Converted mill store of old stone.
- Modern Scottish cooking with some European influence.
- "Friendly, welcoming bistro with imaginative food combinations."

The old grain store with original stone exterior has been attractively converted into a modern bistro/restaurant with some original fittings such as metal pillars left as a feature. The arched door leads into a spacious area with polished wooden floor and attractive dark green wooden tables and chairs. There is a bar in the corner and a blackboard shows daily choices in addition to the menu. The menu offers an impressive selection of dishes all reasonably priced and a short wine list complements this. An ideal venue for an informal lunch or dinner which could be followed by a riverside stroll to Cargills Leap – a few hundred yards away!

Open all year except 11 to 26 Jan incl
Closed Sun after 7 pm + Mon
Lunch ££
Dinner ££
Vegetarians welcome
Children welcome
Facilities for disabled visitors

Hot smoked Westmill trout on salad Nicoise. Rump of roe deer, forest mushrooms, Denrosa honey and grain mustard sauce. Lemon chiffon cake, brûlée and Blairgowrie raspberries.

Credit cards: Mastercard/Eurocard, Visa, Switch, Delta
Chef/Proprietor: Willie Little

HEATHBANK – THE VICTORIAN HOUSE

Boat of Garten, Inverness-shire PH24 3BD
Tel: 01479 831 234

Situated in village of Boat of Garten.

Country house set in heather and herb gardens run by Graham and Lindsay Burge.

- Victorian house with painstakingly designed interiors.
- Skilled, imaginative cookery with fine attention to detail.
- "A trained professional is obviously at the stove - Graham Burge's cooking delights all of the senses."

Built at the turn-of-the-century, Heathbank retains much of its period charm. Bedrooms, including two with four-poster beds, are beautiful and filled with Victoriana. The cooking is highly individual and owes much to the many years which proprietor, Graham Burge, has spent working as a trained chef gathering the ideas and expertise which guests can now enjoy at Heathbank. Attention to detail is paramount. At dinner one can expect fresh soups, roulades and terrines, home-made bread, local game and fish, Scottish beef and lamb and of course glorious puddings with little regard to calorie values! Presentation is stylish, surroundings in Charles Rennie Mackintosh style are stunning and with Lindsay Burge front of house, a visit to this establishment will always be an enjoyable experience. Graham is a member of the Association Culinaire Française and the Scottish Chefs' Association.

Open Mar to Oct + New Year period
🛏 Rooms: 7 with private facilities
🛏 DB&B £45–£60   B&B £25–£38
♀ Restricted licence
🍴 Packed lunches available £
✕ Dinner 4 course menu ££-£££
🍴 Non-residents – booking essential
Ⓥ Vegetarians welcome
✹ Children over 10 years welcome
✌ No smoking throughout

Spiced coconut soup, home-made bread. Strathspey pheasant in port with apricots and thyme. Chilled double chocolate soufflé: dark chocolate flavoured with Drambuie, white chocolate with vanilla.

STB Highly Commended 👑 👑 👑
💳 No credit cards
👤 Proprietors: Lindsay Burge
         & Graham Burge AHCIMA

THE GRAPE VINE RESTAURANT & CAFE BAR

27 Main Street, Bothwell
Lanarkshire G71 8RD
Tel: 01698 852014
Fax: 01698 854405

On main street in Bothwell, ½ mile off M74 (East Kilbride exit).

Relaxed cafe bar bistro.

- Restaurant and village bar.
- Good standard cooking.
- "Ideal for all meal occasions at affordable prices."

The Grape Vine is in the centre of the picturesque conservation village of Bothwell. Whether for informal dining – a light meal or snack in the bar – or a more leisurely experience in the restaurant, both are available all day. Menus are creatively prepared to include a wide selection of tantalising choices.

Open all day, all year except Christmas Day,
Boxing Day, 1 + 2 Jan
✕ Food available all day ££
✕ Lunch £
✕ Dinner ££

Gâteau of haggis with Drambuie. Roast loin of lamb with cous-cous and wild berries. Tart tatin with cheesecake cream.

💳 Credit cards: Mastercard/Eurocard, American Express, Visa, Diners Club, Switch
👤 Proprietor: Colin Morrison

THE OLD MANOR HOTEL
129 Henderson Street
Bridge of Allan
Stirlingshire
FK9 4RQ
Tel: 01786 832169
Fax: 01786 833990

Just outside the centre of Bridge of Allan on the main road to Stirling.

A friendly, family-run hotel.

- Converted old manor house.
- Modern Scottish.
- "Warm hospitality and excellent food."

Rita and Terry Butcher purchased the Old Manor two years ago and since then they have put considerable effort into improving and upgrading this well-established family-run hotel. Extensive refurbishment on the ground floor has been tastefully done with modern and clever touches – including many photographs and memorabilia from Terry's football career. Good quality bar meals are available and the restaurant serves an à la carte menu which changes regularly. High teas can also be provided and a small private room is available for private parties.

Open all year
🏠 Rooms: 7, 6 with private facilities
🛏 DB&B £65   B&B £35–£55
SP Special rates available
✗ Food available all day £££
✗ Lunch ££
✗ Dinner £££
Ⓥ Vegetarians welcome
🏃 Children welcome
♿ Wheelchair access

Warm scallop mousse set on spinach and star anise fumet. Marinaded halibut with lemon grass and artichoke. Apple and mango charlotte with sultana and nutmeg anglaise.

STB Commended 👑 👑 👑 👑
💳 Credit cards: Mastercard/Eurocard, American Express, Visa, Mastercharge, Switch
👤 Proprietor: Terry Butcher

BRODIE COUNTRYFARE
Brodie, by Forres
Moray IV36 0TD
Tel: 01309 641 555
Fax: 01309 641 499

On A96 between Forres and Nairn.

Popular self-service restaurant.

- Restaurant within a shopping complex.
- Home baking and traditional meals.
- "A popular tourist attraction with a good selection of Scottish produce."

This is a country style theme restaurant within the Brodie Countryfare complex. Excellence is the hallmark here from the quality products sold to the food presented. Ideal for a rainy day when you can browse through all the lovely gifts on sale and then eat a meal (at any time of the day), either outside in the garden or inside in the eating area which has a conservatory. The à la carte menu offers freshly made soups and baking, salads and a long list of snacks and desserts; the 'chef's specials' are more substantial. *(See advert Page 24.)*

Open all year except Christmas Day,
Boxing Day, 1 + 2 Jan
♀ Licensed
✗ Food available all day £
✗ Lunch £
Ⓥ Vegetarians welcome
🏃 Children welcome
♿ Facilities for disabled visitors
🚭 Restaurant is non-smoking with small smoking area

Home-made cock-a-leekie soup. Salmon steaks with dill. Blinkbonny Delight: locally produced fresh fruits, meringue and cream.

💳 Credit cards: Mastercard/Eurocard, Visa, Switch
👤 Proprietor: Kathleen Duncan

AR DACHAIDH

Badnellan
Brora, Sutherland
KW9 6NQ
Tel/Fax: 01408 621658

A9 into the village of Brora then turn at sign at bridge to Badnellan, Gordonbush and Balnacoil. Take third turning on right,1 mile, and follow road to last house.

A peaceful crofting house with excellent hospitality.

- Traditional croft house.
- Traditional cooking with an Italian twist.
- "A crofting retreat run by hosts who make it a home-from-home."

Ar Dachaidh is a delightful croft house located at the end of a track road. The style is informal and friendly with the emphasis very much on guest comfort. Kath MacDonald, your host, is an accomplished cook and enjoys devising menus using the best of local produce. Packed lunches are also available for guests who wish to make the best of the excellent location for touring the surrounding countryside.

Open all year
🏠 Rooms: 3
🛏 DB&B £27   B&B £15
SP Special rates available
🍴 Residents only
♀ Unlicensed
✕ Packed lunch £
✕ Dinner ££
Ⓥ Vegetarians welcome
ᛪ Children welcome
🚭 No smoking in dining room

Local queen scallops in a saffron sauce served with seed bread. Brora rabbit with mustard, served with minted Scottish new potatoes, mange tout and sweetcorn. Whisky coffee chocolate cake with home-made Drambuie ice cream.

STB Commended Listed
💷 No credit cards
👤 Owner: Kath MacDonald

ROYAL MARINE HOTEL

Golf Road
Brora, Sutherland
KW9 6QS
Tel: 01408 621252
Fax: 01408 621181

On the A9 from Golspie to Helmsdale. At Brora cross bridge over River Brora and take Golf Road on right. Follow the road – hotel is on left.

Centrally situated hotel for everyone's needs.

- Sporting hotel.
- Traditional with a modern influence.
- "A superb holiday hotel with indoor sporting attractions."

The Royal Marine Hotel was built in 1913 and commands a fine position overlooking the mouth of the River Brora and adjacent to Brora's 18 hole James Braid Links Golf Course. Guests may also fish from the hotel's own boat on Loch Brora. The hotel has recently added a leisure complex which includes an indoor swimming pool, sauna, steam room, gymnasium and Garden Restaurant; conference and meeting facilities are also available. The Royal Marine Hotel is an ideal base for touring the Northern Highlands and Orkney, and exploring nearby visitor attractions. The Royal Marine Hotel has 1 AA Rosette.

Open all year
🏠 Rooms: 22 with private facilities
🛏 DB&B £50–£75   B&B £40–£60
SP Special rates available
✕ Food available all day ££
✕ Lunch £
✕ Dinner £££
Ⓥ Vegetarians welcome
ᛪ Children welcome
♿ Facilities for disabled visitors
🚭 No smoking in restaurant

Cullen skink. Pan-fried collop of beef fillet served over a potato haggis cake, finished with a Clynelish whisky sauce. Walnut tart with honey and brown bread ice cream.

STB Highly Commended 👑 👑 👑 👑
💷 Credit cards: Mastercard/Eurocard, American Express, Visa, Diners Club, Switch
👤 Managing Director: Robert Powell

SOUTH KINGENNIE HOUSE
Kellas, by Broughty Ferry
Dundee DD5 3PA
Tel: 01382 350 562

From A92 Dundee-Arbroath, take B978 to Kellas
then road to Drumsturdy to signpost for South
Kingennie, 2 miles.

Converted farmhouse.

- A quiet and formal restaurant in a tranquil
  country setting.
- Skilful, traditional Scots cooking.
- "A relaxing country venue for a delicious meal."

Originally a farmhouse, South Kingennie deserves
its excellent local reputation. Owned and run by
Peter and Jill Robinson, it serves inexpensive and
imaginative table d'hôte meals in a long, elegant
dining room. With the recent addition of an
attractive extension, the room is light and airy with
views over the garden and beyond. Peter's stylish
and imaginative cooking is matched by Jill's
supervision of the front of the house. Atmosphere
and service are relaxed and friendly. The wine list is
comprehensive. Tasting notes are clear and helpful.
Although in the countryside, South Kingennie is
within close proximity of Dundee. One of 14
establishments shortlisted for The Macallan Taste
of Scotland Awards 1997.

....

Open all year except Boxing Day, 1 Jan,
last wk Jan + first wk Feb
Closed Sun evening + Mon
✕   Lunch except Mon £-££
✕   Dinner except Sun Mon £££-££££
Ⓥ   Vegetarians welcome
⚢   Children welcome
⚬   Facilities for disabled visitors
⤜   No smoking in restaurant

**Salad of avocado and pigeon breast with mustard
dressing. Loin of new season lamb with rosemary
sauce and redcurrants. Lemon bavois with citrus
sauce and sorbet.**

▣   Credit cards: Mastercard/Eurocard, Visa,
    Mastercharge, Switch, Delta
⋈   Proprietors: Peter & Jill Robinson

LOCH FYNE OYSTER BAR
Cairndow
Argyll PA26 8BH
Tel: 01499 600217/600264
Fax: 01499 600234

A83 Glasgow-Oban-Campbeltown, at head of Loch
Fyne near Cairndow.

**Renowned seafood restaurant, fish shop and
garden centre.**

- Converted farm steading.
- Fresh seafood.
- "Unadulterated local seafood served at its best
  in a converted steading."

In 1978 John Noble and Andrew Lane started a
business which sets out to make the best possible
use of the wonderful fish and shellfish of Loch Fyne,
historically the most famous fishing loch on the
West Coast (during the mid-19th century 670 boats
were based here, and its oyster-beds supplied all
Edinburgh). Their plan was to re-establish the
oyster beds and, as well as offering them for sale
generally, to establish an oyster bar on the loch
where people could sample them, and other
seafood – cooked, cured, or simply served for the
purist on ice. The restaurant eschews 'haute
cuisine'; dishes are very simply prepared, so the
fresh natural flavour of the seafood can be enjoyed.
Meals served throughout the day, and the adjacent
shop (and tree nursery) permits 'carry-outs'. Winner
of The Macallan Taste of Scotland Special Merit
Award for Achievement 1995.

....

Open all year except Christmas Day +
New Year's Day
✕   Food served all day
Ⓥ   Vegetarians welcome

**Six oysters baked with garlic and breadcrumbs.
Bradan rost served with a whisky and horseradish
sauce. Lemon pavlova.**

▣   Credit cards: Access/Mastercard/Eurocard,
    Visa, Diners Club, Switch, Delta
⋈   Proprietors: Loch Fyne Oysters Ltd

ROMAN CAMP HOTEL
Off Main Street, Callander
Perthshire FK17 8BG
Tel: 01877 330003
Fax: 01877 331533

At the east end of Callander main street from Stirling, turn left down 300 yard drive to hotel.

A favourite stopping place of Queen Victoria.

- Close to the town, yet set on the banks of the River Teith.
- Outstanding Scottish cuisine.
- "A country house steeped in history and tranquillity."

Designed and built for the Dukes of Perth in 1625, the Roman Camp has been a hotel since 1939. Under the guidance of Eric and Marion Brown, it maintains its atmosphere of elegance. With its 20 acres of beautiful gardens, old library and secret chapel, the hotel offers the peace of the past alongside every possible modern convenience. The dining room, hung with tapestries and lit by candles, boasts a particularly fine painted ceiling. The best of fresh local produce is imaginatively used to create the finest Scottish cuisine, complemented by an excellent wine list. Service is unhurried and impeccable, the food is first class. Roman Camp has 2 AA Rosettes. *(See advert Page 31.)*

Open all year
- 🏠 Rooms: 14 with private facilities
- 🛏 DB&B £78.50–£113.50   B&B £44.50–£79.50
- SP Special rates available
- ✕ Lunch ££
- ✕ Dinner 4 course menu ££££
- Ⓥ Vegetarians welcome
- 🕭 Children welcome
- 🕭 Facilities for disabled visitors
- ✕ No smoking in dining room

Roast sea bass with confit of fennel and sauté bouillabaisse. Peppered loin of lamb with morelle ravioli and roasted sweetbreads. Chocolate and orange soup with mango ice cream.

STB Highly Commended 🏵 🏵 🏵 🏵
- ⊞ Credit cards: Mastercard/Eurocard, American Express, Visa, Diners Club, Mastercharge, Switch, Delta
- Ⅺ Proprietors: Eric & Marion Brown

BALEGREGGAN COUNTRY HOUSE
Balegreggan Road
Campbeltown
Argyll PA28 6NN
Tel/Fax: 01586 552062

Off A83 from outskirts of Campbeltown, follow farm road for ½ mile. Go through farmyard to top of hill.

A Victorian villa with careful home cooking.

- Substantial stone villa.
- Careful home cooking.
- "A delightful blend of genuine welcome, comfort and the best of Scottish food, sourced locally and used imaginatively."

The history of Balegreggan House dates back to mid 1800s when it was built and named after the Gaelic 'Bhaile Ghriogan' meaning 'Place of the Rocks'. Since then the house has been tastefully extended and passed through the hands of several caring owners. Now it is in the safe hands of Sarah Urquhart, Chef/Proprietor, and her husband, Bruce, who both work very hard to offer excellent Scottish hospitality. Bruce is an attentive host and Sarah's good home cooking will ensure first time visitors find their way back.

Open all year
- 🏠 Rooms: 4 with private facilities
- 🛏 DB&B £60–£65   B&B £40–£45
- SP Special rates available
- ♀ Restricted licence
- ✕ Dinner £££
- Ⓥ Vegetarians welcome
- 🕭 Facilities for ambulant disabled visitors – residents only
- ✕ No smoking throughout

Seared local king scallops served with a sauternes sauce. Pan-fried Barbary duck with a piquant raspberry sauce. Hot chocolate soufflé.

STB Highly Commended 🏵 🏵 🏵
- ⊞ Credit cards: Mastercard/Eurocard, Visa
- Ⅺ Proprietor: Sarah Urquhart

11 PARK AVENUE
11 Park Avenue
Carnoustie
Angus DD7 7JA
Tel/Fax: 01241 853336

Park Avenue runs from the main street in Carnoustie towards the railway and beach. Follow signs for free parking.

An excellent small town restaurant.

- Converted Victorian masonic hall.
- Modern Scottish cooking.
- "An elegant restaurant offering the best of Scottish cuisine."

Described by our Inspector as the "jewel in Carnoustie's crown" – 11 Park Avenue offers a most pleasurable eating experience. The restaurant is small, situated in the centre of Carnoustie and is pleasingly decorated and thoughtfully laid out. All food served here is home-made from the brown rolls to start – to the ice cream at the finish. Chef/Proprietor Stephen Collinson is a highly decorated chef and runs a fine restaurant. This is one place that deserves a long successful life. 11 Park Avenue has 1 AA Rosette.

Open all year except 25, 26 Dec + first wk Jan
Closed Sun Mon + Sat lunch
✗ Dinner except Sun Mon ££
Ⓥ Vegetarians welcome
⚲ Children welcome
↙ Smoking area in restaurant
🐄 Member of the Scotch Beef Club

Terrine of Arbroath smokie and smoked salmon. Fillet of Aberdeen Angus on a polenta crouton with salsa and Madeira sauce. Iced orange and Cointreau soufflé with caramel sauce.

💷 Credit cards: Mastercard/Eurocard, American Express, Visa, Diners Club
🍴 Chef/Proprietor: Stephen Collinson

CARRADALE HOTEL
Carradale, Argyll PA28 6RY
Tel/Fax: 01583 431 223

From Tarbert (Loch Fyne) 26 miles via A83, B8001 and B842. From Campbeltown about 17 miles on B842.

A country hotel in a pretty garden setting.

- Country hotel in its own grounds.
- Innovative/traditional cooking.
- "A wide range of dishes with strong Scottish influence can be enjoyed formally and informally."

Quite the most prominent feature of the village, the Carradale Hotel occupies a splendid location above the harbour in its own grounds and gardens. You will be kindly received by Marcus and Morag Adams who have been steadily improving the hotel's facilities over the past few years. The menus present local fish and meat with unusual and accomplished coulis and sauces. The cooking has a delightful freshness about it and each dish is well-balanced. Carradale offers pleasant beach and forest walks. The hotel has squash courts, sauna, solarium, mountain bikes, game fishing and an adjacent 9-hole golf course.

Open all year except 23 to 26 Dec
🛏 Rooms: 14 with private facilities, 3 children's rooms (adjacent to parents' rooms) + 1 family suite
🛏 DB&B £37–£54 B&B £20–£39
SP Special rates available
✗ Food available all day ££
✗ Lunch £
✗ Dinner ££
Ⓥ Vegetarians welcome
⚲ Children welcome
↙ No smoking in restaurant

Steamed Carradale landed langoustines, garlic and chive butter. Roasted local pheasant, rosti potatoes, spiced red cabbage, port and mushroom jus. Home-made banana and butterscotch ice cream.

STB Commended 👑 👑 👑
💷 Credit cards: Mastercard/Eurocard, Visa
🍴 Proprietors: Marcus & Morag Adams

DALRACHNEY LODGE HOTEL
Carrbridge, Inverness-shire PH23 3AT
Tel: 01479 841252 Fax: 01479 841382

Leave A9 at Carrbridge junction and follow A938 for
1½ miles, continue through village for 20 yards –
Dalrachney is on right.

Victorian shooting lodge in peaceful setting.

* Country hotel, formerly a hunting lodge of the
  Countess of Seafield.
* Traditional Scottish cooking: extensive bar meal
  menu.
* "Ideally situated whether it is for relaxation or for
  outdoor pursuits."

Dalrachney Lodge is a traditionally built Highland
shooting lodge standing in 16 acres of peaceful
grounds on the banks of the River Dulnain. Decor
throughout the hotel is of a high standard with
comfortable, spacious bedrooms and well-
maintained public rooms. There are also two self-
contained houses within the grounds which are
available on a self-catering or serviced basis. The
Lodge Restaurant is a typical period dining room
with a bright, open outlook. At lunch a wide-
ranging bar menu is presented, augmented by a dish
of the day – this can be eaten in the restaurant or in
the bar. For dinner, both à la carte and table d'hôte
menus are offered. Provision is made for anyone
with food allergies and special needs and there is
always a good vegetarian choice.

Open all year
🏠 Rooms: 16 with private facilities
🍴 DB&B £45–£70   B&B £25–£50
✗ Lunch ££
✗ Dinner 5 course menu £££
Ⅴ Vegetarians welcome
🕇 Children welcome
🚭 No smoking in restaurant

**Mussels with a garlic, butter, spinach, Parmesan
and parsley topping. Medallions of venison with a
redcurrant, cranberry and cream sauce.
Raspberries with Glayva, oatmeal, meringue and
cream.**

STB Highly Commended 🏆 🏆 🏆 🏆
💳 Credit cards: Mastercard/Eurocard, American
   Express, Visa, Mastercharge, Switch, Delta
Ⅺ Proprietor: Helen Swanney

CRAIGADAM
Castle Douglas
Kirkcudbrightshire
DG7 3HU
Tel/Fax: 01556 650233

2 miles north of Crocketford on the A712.

A luxury farmhouse set in the Galloway Hills.

* Farmhouse.
* Delightful home cooking.
* "An elegant country house within working farm
  with most welcoming and accomplished
  hostess."

Guests may relax in the comfortable and tastefully
furnished Craigadam and soon forget city stresses.
The house is set on a hill off a main road with good
views of the Galloway Hills. Celia Pickup is your
host and partner in the business and is an excellent
cook making best use of local produce such as
smoked duck, venison and Solway salmon and also
baking her own breads. Dinner is served in the oak-
panelled dining room at a long oak table and guests
dine together completing the feeling of traditional
farmhouse living.

Open all year except Christmas Eve to 2 Jan
🏠 Rooms: 3 with private facilities
🍴 DB&B £36–£39   B&B £22–£25
ⓤ Unlicensed
✗ Food available all day ££
✗ Dinner ££
Ⅴ Vegetarians welcome
🕇 Children welcome
🚭 No smoking in bedrooms

**Smoked venison with home-made chutneys. Wild
duck with sour cherry sauce. Iced Grand Marnier
creams with brandy snap crunch.**

STB Commended 🏆 🏆 🏆
💳 No credit cards
Ⅺ Partner: Celia Pickup

CHIRNSIDE HALL COUNTRY HOUSE HOTEL
Chirnside, nr Duns
Berwickshire TD11 3LD
Tel: 01890 818 219
Fax: 01890 818 231

Between Chirnside and Foulden on A6105. 1 mile east of Chirnside.

A luxury country house hotel.

* Sandstone Victorian mansion house.
* Imaginative Scottish cuisine with strong French emphasis.
* "A truly delightful country house with excellent cuisine in luxury surroundings."

This classical country house is set in beautiful Borders countryside over-looking the Cheviot Hills to the south. Everything at Chirnside Hall is on a grand scale – from massive mahogany doors – to the carpeted, carved stone staircase. The food is described by our Inspector as refined, innovative and skilful with a good choice of quality ingredients. Interesting and contemporary combinations alongside more traditional dishes given an innovative touch. Chirnside has 2 AA Rosettes.

....

Open all year
🏨 Rooms: 10 with private facilities
🛏 DB&B £62.50–£67.50   B&B £45–£50
SP Special rates available
✗ Food available all day £
✗ Lunch – booking essential ££
✗ Dinner – booking essential ££
V Vegetarians welcome
🕏 Children welcome
✗ No smoking in dining room

Warm salad of Orkney king scallops and smoked bacon with toasted pine nuts. Rack of Borders lamb with spring cabbage on a garlic and rosemary sauce. Iced Glayva and biscuit soufflé with shortbread.

STB Highly Commended 🏵 🏵 🏵 🏵
💳 Credit cards: Mastercard/Eurocard, American Express, Visa, Switch, Delta, JCB, Diners Club
🗡 Proprietors: Alan & Karla White

NIVINGSTON HOUSE
Cleish, Kinross-shire KY13 7LS
Tel: 01577 850216
Fax: 01577 850238

From M90, junction 5, take B9097 towards Crook of Devon. Hotel is 2 miles from junction 5.

A Victorian mansion standing in 12 acres of gardens.

* Country house hotel.
* Good country house cooking.
* "Beautiful setting for a lovely meal – relax in style."

Nivingston House is a tranquil place, standing as it does in 12 acres of gardens, with fine views over the rolling countryside, yet it is only a couple of miles from the M90. The building is a pleasing example of an old Scottish country house which has been extended with care, using different styles of architecture. Its location is ideal for reaching Edinburgh and Glasgow, not to mention St Andrews and the north. The atmosphere is comfortable and welcoming, with log fires and broad armchairs. In the pleasant, candlelit dining room, you will enjoy good quality country house cuisine, with interesting sauces. Nivingston House has 1 AA Rosette. *(See advert Page 31.)*

....

Open all year
🏨 Rooms: 17 with private facilities
🛏 DB&B £77.50–£120   B&B £55–£75
SP Special rates available
✗ Lunch ££
✗ Dinner £££
V Vegetarians welcome
🕏 Children welcome
♿ Facilities for disabled visitors
✗ Smoking discouraged
🐂 Member of the Scotch Beef Club

Hot West Coast scallops wrapped in Ayrshire bacon with a light curry mayonnaise. Breast of Perthshire pheasant roasted with a prune and whisky sauce. Drambuie and honey cheesecake.

STB Highly Commended 🏵 🏵 🏵 🏵
💳 Credit cards: Mastercard/Eurocard, American Express, Visa, Mastercharge, Switch, Delta
🗡 Managers: Peter & Agnes Aretz
🗡 Proprietors: The Nivingston Partnership

DUNLAVEROCK HOUSE
Coldingham Bay
Coldingham
Berwickshire TD14 5PA
Tel/Fax: 018907 71450

Take A1107 to Coldingham and then follow signs to
Coldingham Bay.

**Small deluxe country house hotel overlooking the
sea-topped sands of Coldingham Bay.**

- Late Victorian villa.
- Innovative home cooking.
- "A delightful escape from it all where skilled
  cooking by caring hosts make your stay
  unforgettable."

Leslie and Donald Brown travelled all over Scotland
to find this little haven which opened four years
ago. The house has six spacious individually
decorated, en suite bedrooms and every effort has
been taken to make guests as comfortable as
possible. Leslie and a small dedicated team prepare
meals to a very high standard using the very best of
local produce. Menus are compiled daily,
depending upon availability and guests' preference.
The Browns are superb hosts, the good food,
warmth and hospitality encourages guests to
re-visit time after time. Winner of The Taste of
Scotland Scotch Lamb Challenge Competition
Category 1 1997.

Open 1 Feb to 2 Jan except 22 to 26 Dec
- ⌂ Rooms: 6 with private facilities
- 🍽 DB&B £48–£70
- SP Special rates available
- ✗ Dinner ££
- Ⓥ Vegetarians welcome
- ⚘ Children over 9 years welcome
- ⚙ Facilities for disabled visitors
- ⚗ No smoking in dining room

**Sweet onion tartlet. Escalopes of salmon on
sautéed leeks with dill and lime butter.
Raspberries and lemon mousse layered on a
shortbread round on raspberry coulis.**

STB Highly Commended ♛ ♛ ♛
- ⊞ Credit cards: Mastercard/Eurocard, Visa, JVC
- ⋈ Proprietors: Donald & Leslie Brown

THE DEIL'S CAULDRON
27 Dundas Street, Comrie
Perthshire PH6 2LN
Tel: 01764 670352

On A85 west end of Comrie.

Lounge bar/restaurant in Comrie.

- 18th century town building.
- Auld Alliance cooking.
- "Good home cooking enjoyed by locals and
  visitors alike."

The Deil's Cauldron is an attractive bar and
restaurant which has been created from a 200 year
old Listed building in the village. There is a rugged
charm about the interior, with its exposed stone
walls lined with prints and old photographs. Two
dining rooms (one for non-smokers) offer intimate
and comfortable surroundings in which to enjoy
fresh local produce interestingly and skillfully
prepared. Lunch may be taken in the garden on fair
days. There is a choice of home-cooked dishes
which will accommodate all tastes, appetites and
pockets. The restaurant is popular amongst locals
and visitors. Watch out for excellent daily specials.
Winner of 'Glenturret Tourism Award For Most
Enjoyable Restaurant Meal in Perthshire'.

Open all year except Christmas Day +
31 Dec to 2 Jan
Note: Nov to Mar advisable to check
opening times
Closed Tue
- ✗ Lunch except Tue – booking preferred £
- ✗ Dinner except Tue – booking preferred ££
- Ⓥ Vegetarians welcome
- ⚘ Children welcome – by arrangement
- ⚗ Separate dining room for non-smokers

**Grilled Stilton and avocado salad. Medley of
seafood with saffron butter sauce. Dark chocolate
mousse with kumquat and brandy sauce.**

- ⊞ Credit cards: Mastercard/Eurocard, American
  Express, Visa, Switch, Delta
- ⋈ Proprietors: Robert & Judith Shepherd

THE GRANARY
Drummond Street, Comrie
Perthshire PH6 2DW
Tel: 01764 670838

On main street of Comrie (A85 west of Crieff) –
opposite garage.

**A small, welcoming coffee shop on the main street
of Comrie.**

- A charming little tea-room/coffee shop with the
  comfortable air of an Edwardian coffee shop.
- Good home baking.
- "Coffee shop offering the most excellent array of
  freshly baked products and home-made
  preserves."

The Granary is an old fashioned building in the
centre of the bustling village of Comrie. The large
windows with sunny flowered curtains look
towards the Perthshire hills and the antique
mahogany counter is laden with a mouth-watering
display of home baking. Local watercolours
decorate the walls, and a rich collection of home-
made jams and chutneys crowd the shelves.
Proprietors Liz and Mark Grieve have made The
Granary a special place with a warm and
welcoming atmosphere, tempting customers with a
delicious choice of food such as home-made ice
cream and a large selection of cakes, biscuits and
puddings. There is a good selection of ground
coffees and teas (including fruit and herbal
infusions). The full menu is available all day and
visitors can purchase cakes, scones, breads and
preserves to carry out. One of 14 establishments
shortlisted for The Macallan Taste of Scotland
Awards 1997.

Open 28 Feb to 28 Oct
Closed Mon except Bank Holiday Mondays
🔲 Unlicensed
✗ Food available all day Tue to Sat:
  afternoon Sun £
✗ Lunch £
🔲 Vegetarians welcome
⚘ Children welcome
♿ Facilities for disabled visitors
🚭 No smoking throughout

**Tomato and basil soup. Open sandwich salad
platter served on home-made soda bread.
Raspberry and almond torte.**

💳 No credit cards
Ⓜ Proprietors: Mark & Elizabeth Grieve

TULLYBANNOCHER FARM FOOD BAR
Comrie
Perthshire PH6 2JY
Tel: 01764 670827

½ mile west of Comrie on A85.

**A popular, informal bistro/restaurant on the banks
of the river Earn.**

- A self-service, relaxed and ideal place to break
  your journey.
- The best of farmhouse cooking.
- "Excellent selection of food available all day
  long."

Just outside the picturesque village of Comrie,
Tullybannocher is ideally placed for those enjoying
a drive along Loch Earn. It stands in beautiful
woodland, is easy to pull in to and offers ample car
parking. The decor of this large log cabin is simple.
It offers a wide range of inexpensive and freshly-
prepared meats, fish and quiches and simple but
good salads. The smell of home baking is refreshing
and real. In fine weather, the rustic tables on the
restaurant's rolling lawn are understandably
popular. Self-service during the day. Table service
for diners in the evening (6 pm – 9 pm).

Open 1 Apr to 14 Oct
♀ Restaurant licence
✗ Food available all day £
✗ Lunch £
✗ Dinner ££
🔲 Vegetarians welcome
⚘ Children welcome
🚭 Smoking area in restaurant

**Home made pork pâté flavoured with juniper
berries and white wine. Home-made steak pie
made with Guinness. Traditional Scottish cloutie
dumpling with cream.**

💳 Credit cards: Mastercard/Eurocard, Visa,
  Switch
Ⓜ Proprietor: Peter Davenport

CRAIGELLACHIE HOTEL

Victoria Street,
Craigellachie,
Moray AB38 9SR
Tel: 01340 881204
Fax: 01340 881253

On A941/A95, 12 miles south of Elgin.

An imposing hotel in its own grounds just off the main square of the village, with the River Spey at the foot of the garden.

- A large 19th century country hotel.
- Country hotel cooking.
- "A country hotel in the heart of Speyside."

Located at the heart of Whisky Country, within the attractive Speyside village of Craigellachie, this imposing hotel is decorated to a high standard and in excellent taste. Welcoming, comfortable and well-run, its elegant interior is matched by attentive and unobtrusive service. The bedrooms, some with four-poster beds and all with private facilities, have lovely views over the river and countryside beyond. The hotel also has an exercise room, sauna and beauty salon. The kitchen uses fresh produce as far as practicable, and carefully sources delicacies from all around Scotland – from Ayrshire smoked bacon to Sheildaig shellfish. The hotel has recently introduced a choice of a la carte restaurants; for fine dining the Ben Aigan and the Rib Room where the speciality is a 32oz single rib steak! Craigellachie has 2 AA Rosettes.

Open all year
- 🛏 Rooms: 30 with private facilities
- 🛏 B&B £54.50–£65
- SP Special seasonal rates available
- ✗ Lunch £-£££
- ✗ Dinner 4 course menu £-££££
- Ⅴ Vegetarians welcome
- 🛠 Children welcome
- ⚘ No smoking in Ben Aigan restaurant
- 🐄 Member of the Scotch Beef Club

Warm salad of lobster, leeks and new potatoes, beurre blanc. Seared venison loin, red onion and fig tatin, thyme jus. Hot prune and whisky soufflé.

STB Highly Commended 👑 👑 👑 👑
- 💳 Credit cards: Mastercard/Eurocard, American Express, Visa, Diners Club, Mastercharge, Switch, Delta
- ⋈ General Manager: Duncan Elphick

CAIPLIE GUEST HOUSE

53 High Street
Crail, Fife
KY10 3RA
Tel/Fax: 01333 450564

On main street in centre of village.

Small and friendly guest house on the High Street.

- Terraced 19th century townhouse.
- Traditional home cooking.
- "Informal guest house offering a warm welcome and home comforts."

This small but comfortable guest house is set on the main street of this attractive fishing village in the East Neuk of Fife. Recently refurbished and under new ownership since 1996 the house is comfortable with many small touches from the friendly and helpful proprietors. The dining room on the ground floor overlooks the main street and is light and airy.Cooking is good home-style with a commitment to good, fresh quality ingredients.

Open 1 Mar to 30 Nov
- 🛏 Rooms: 7, 3 with private facilities
- 🛏 DB&B £28.50–£34.50   B&B £16–£22
- SP Special rates available
- ⋈ Non-residents by arrangement
- ✗ Dinner ££
- Ⅴ Vegetarians welcome
- 🛠 Children welcome
- ⚘ No smoking in dining room

Orcadian oatmeal soup. Sauté of chicken breast with smoked bacon, leeks and honey. Drambuie spiced pears.

STB Commended 👑
- 💳 No credit cards
- ⋈ Owners: Sandra & Sandy Strachan

HAZELTON GUEST HOUSE
29 Marketgate, Crail
Fife KY10 3TH
Tel/Fax: 01333 450250

In town centre opposite tourist office and Tolbooth, A917.

A town guest house in Crail.

- Victorian terraced house.
- Creative Scottish cooking using fresh local produce.
- "Comfortable guest house offering delightful home cooking."

Hazelton is situated in the centre of Crail opposite the famous 16th century Tolbooth in Marketgate. Owners Alan and Rita Brown extend a warm welcome to their guests whom they accommodate in seven warm comfortably furnished bedrooms. The dining room overlooking Marketgate is airy and well-appointed. Breakfast is chosen from a well-balanced traditional menu. The set four-course dinner menu changes daily and is imaginative and interesting, always including fresh fish or seafood and red or white meat dishes, home-smoked specialities appear frequently. The Browns' attention to detail combined with the relaxed and friendly atmosphere and the high standard of Rita's award-winning culinary skills ensure that guests return time and again. National winner of 'New Covent Garden Soup Co. and Scotland on Sunday 1996 Recipe Competition'.

Open mid Feb to end Oct
- 🏠 Rooms: 7
- 🛏 DB&B £32–£35   B&B £16–£19
- SP Special rates available
- ✗ Residents only
- ✗ Dinner except Mon Tue – unless by prior arrangement ££
- ✗ It is requested that guests book their dinner table by 4 pm
- Ⓥ Vegetarians welcome – with advance notice
- ⚹ Dinner menu not suitable for children

Venison liver and bacon salad with orange sesame dressing. Herb-crusted haddock with crab and dill saffron sauce. Cranachan ice cream in oat biscuit basket with red berries.

STB Commended Listed
- ⊟ No credit cards
- ⋈ Proprietors: Alan & Rita Brown

ALLT-CHAORAIN HOUSE
Crianlarich
Perthshire FK20 8RU
Tel: 01838 300283
Fax: 01838 300238

Off A82, 1 mile north of Crianlarich on Tyndrum road.

Small country house in beautiful gardens with dramatic views.

- Informal country house.
- Home cooking.
- "Highland hospitality and good food served here in this excellent touring location."

This house is perched on a hill in its own grounds overlooking the scenic countryside of Benmore and Strathfillan. Its owner, Roger McDonald, runs the hotel personally and takes pride in maintaining an unobtrusive, homely atmosphere. Each evening he presents a different dinner menu for guests in the charming wood-panelled dining room where you will share one of three large tables with others staying in the hotel. The dishes are interesting, with a strong traditional Scottish theme; the cooking is much appreciated by guests. A 'trust' bar is available in the attractive drawing room where a log fire burns throughout the year.

Open 17 Mar to 1 Nov
- 🏠 Rooms: 7 with private facilities
- 🛏 DB&B £53–£58   B&B £35–£40
- SP Special rates available
- ✗ Residents only
- ✗ Dinner ££
- Ⓥ Vegetarians welcome
- ♿ Facilities for disabled visitors
- ⚥ Smoking in sun lounge only

Cauliflower and Stilton soup. Leg of lamb steak. Poached oranges in a Drambuie sauce.

STB Commended 👑 👑 👑
- ⊞ Credit cards: Mastercard/Eurocard, American Express, Visa, Switch, Delta
- ⋈ Proprietor: Roger McDonald

CRIEFF VISITORS CENTRE

Muthill Road, Crieff
Perthshire PH7 4HQ
Tel: 01764 654014
Fax: 01764 652903

On A822 leading out of Crieff to the south. 15 miles from Gleneagles Hotel by road and less than 1 hour from Edinburgh or Glasgow.

A visitors centre with a number of attractions.

- Self-service, cafeteria style restaurant.
- Home baking and light meals.
- "Friendly, popular visitors centre with a number of attractions."

This self-service, 180 seat, restaurant is part of a visitor complex of showroom, shops, audio-visual display and garden centre beside two rural factories producing thistle pattern Buchan pottery and Perthshire paper-weights. The restaurant itself is a large, light and airy building, with glass, brick and pine being used most successfully in its design and construction. It is a very busy establishment and is self-service. The range of food on offer goes from familiar starters, to soups, hot main courses, fresh salads and ending with an impressive array of home baking. It is good value and the produce used is all local and fresh, ideal for the family as there are special children's meals on the menu.

Open all year except 25, 26 Dec, 1 + 2 Jan
✕ Food available all day £
✕ Lunch £
Ⓥ Vegetarians welcome
Ⓚ Children welcome
♿ Facilities for disabled visitors

Home-made soups. Haggis, neeps and tatties. Daily dishes. Fresh home baking.

STB Commended Visitor Attraction
⊞ Credit cards – showroom only
Ⓜ Managing Director: Neil Drysdale

GLENTURRET DISTILLERY

The Hosh, Crieff, Perthshire PH7 4HA
Tel: 01764 656565 Fax: 01764 654366

A85 Crieff to Comrie road. Just over 1 hour from Edinburgh (M9) and Glasgow (M8).

Restaurant in a converted distillery building, offering a range of good quality food for both formal and informal occasions.

- An 18th century bonded warehouse in the grounds of Scotland's oldest distillery.
- Traditional Scottish fare.
- "Excellent selection of hot food available - the desserts are a real treat."

Glenturret makes a strong claim to being Scotland's oldest distillery. It was established in 1775 although the site was used by illicit distillers and smugglers long before then. The first distillery to encourage visitors, it now attracts over 220,000 people per annum, with a heritage centre, exhibition museum and shop as well as the restaurant. The Smugglers Restaurant, with the Kiln Room conversion at one end, is on the first floor of the converted warehouse and is self-service but has high standards of cooking. The Pagoda Room extends from the other end and offers a more formal setting, and efficient and friendly waitress service. In good weather visitors can sit at tables on the terrace. The menus feature Highland venison, beef and salmon. Coffee, afternoon tea and home baking are also available during the day. Dinners and parties are welcome at Glenturret by prior arrangement. *(See advert Page 34.)*

Open all year except 25, 26 Dec, 1 + 2 Jan
✕ Food available all day £
✕ Lunch ££
Ⓜ Dinner – by private arrangement only ££££
Ⓥ Vegetarians welcome
Ⓚ Children welcome
♿ Facilities for disabled visitors
🚭 Complete facilities are no smoking but a smoking area is provided in Smugglers Restaurant

Glenturret smoked salmon. Local venison in illicit whisky sauce. Cranachan (oatmeal, cream and raspberries flavoured with the Glenturret Original Malt Liqueur) and the Glenturret award-winning whisky ice cream.

STB Highly Commended Visitor Attraction
⊞ Credit cards: Mastercard/Eurocard, American Express, Visa, Switch
Ⓜ Director of Tourism: Derek Brown

SATCHMO'S RESTAURANT

32 High Street
Crieff, Perthshire
PH7 3BS
Tel/Fax: 01764 656575

In Crieff town centre opposite tourist office and town clock.

Lively bistro offering modern Scottish cooking among jazz memorabilia.

- Listed building c. 1900 – old British Linen Bank.
- Modern Scottish cooking.
- "A unique new place - good food and great music."

Satchmo's opened early in 1997 under its new chef proprietor Bill McGuigan. The building has many of the original features from its previous life as a bank cleverly integrated to complement the style of the bistro. Wood panelling, high ceilings, wooden flooring make an excellent backdrop for the jazz instruments (trumpet, clarinet etc) and other memorabilia create a lively atmosphere. The cooking is highly skilled, Bill changes the menu every week depending upon produce available and is obviously enthusiastic and accomplished in this task offering a mixture of light and more substantial dishes at each course. This is a most lively and welcome addition to Taste of Scotland, and in the summer live music is yet another feature.

Open all year
Closed Sun evening + Mon during winter
✕ Food available all day ££
✕ Lunch £
✕ Dinner ££
Ⓥ Vegetarians welcome
✻ Children welcome

Satchmo's West Coast mussels with shallots, herbs and cream. A dry spiced Letham chicken breast with new potatoes on a lemon butter sauce. Lemon tart with cinnamon ice cream.

⊞ Credit cards: Mastercard/Eurocard, American Express, Visa, Switch, Delta
ℵ Proprietors: T H Fergusson & Co (Restaurant's) Ltd

CRINAN HOTEL

Crinan, Lochgilphead, Argyll PA31 8SR
Tel: 01546 830261 Fax: 01546 830292

A82 Glasgow-Inveraray, then A83 to Lochgilphead. Follow A816 (Oban) for c. 5 miles, then B841 to Crinan.

One of Scotland's most famous hotels, consistently good.

- Country hotel with a spectacular location.
- Classical Scottish cooking with French influence.
- "A unique hotel with heaps of character and a well deserved reputation for its cuisine."

The tiny village of Crinan lies at the north end of the Crinan Canal which connects the Firth of Clyde (via Loch Fyne) to the Atlantic. The white family-owned hotel rises conspicuously above the holding basin and has stupendous views over a pattern of islands to the north and west. The hotel's small and exclusive Lock 16 Restaurant is in the top storey of the building and its picture windows enjoy the view to the full. Seafood is the speciality here. It is freshly landed daily below the hotel. Indeed so much does the chef rely on the catch of the day that he will often not know until 5 pm what his menu will be. The hotel's main restaurant, the Westward, offers a delicious table d'hôte menu (prefaced by the local shipping forecast!) which features prime beef, wild venison and hill lamb, as well as fish. The celebrated Lock 16 Restaurant has a bar alongside it, and displayed here are paintings by Frances Macdonald (Mrs Ryan).

Open all year except Christmas
🛏 Rooms: 22 with private facilities
🛏 DB&B £105–£120   B&B £75–£90
SP Special winter rates available
✕ Lunch £
✕ Dinner (Westward Restaurant) £££
✕ Dinner (Lock 16 mid Apr to end Sep only) except Sun Mon booking essential ££££
Ⓥ Vegetarians welcome
✻ Children welcome
♿ Facilities for disabled visitors

Mussels marinière. A selection of local seafood with cheese and fruit. Profiteroles with a butterscotch sauce.

STB Highly Commended 👑 👑 👑 👑
⊞ Credit cards: Mastercard/Eurocard, American Express, Visa, Switch
ℵ Proprietors: Nick & Frances Ryan

THE ROYAL HOTEL CROMARTY

Marine Terrace, Cromarty
Ross-shire IV11 8YN
Tel/Fax: 01381 600217

A9 past Inverness, Kessock Bridge 2 miles
turn right.

Traditional family-owned Scottish country house hotel.

- Seafront hotel with verandah.
- Traditional Scottish cooking.
- "A friendly hotel with good food."

This traditional hotel has been around for over 150 years and overlooks the beach and harbour of the ancient and historic village of Cromarty (most bedrooms share this splendid view – watch out for the bottle-nosed dolphins which live in the Cromarty Firth). The public rooms are pleasantly furnished and the dining room is bright and sunny. Friendly, well-trained staff offer an à la carte menu which features classic Scottish dishes. The food is simply presented but of a high standard. Children's selection on menu.

Open all year
🏨 Rooms: 10 with private facilities
🛏 DB&B £40–£50   B&B £27.50–£30
SP Special rates available
✖ Lunch ££
✖ Dinner ££
Ⓥ Vegetarians welcome
🧒 Children welcome
♿ Facilities for disabled visitors – ground floor only

Deep fried haggis balls. Venison venture. Grannie's juicy apple pie.

STB Commended 👑 👑 👑
💷 Credit cards: Mastercard/Eurocard, American Express, Visa, Mastercharge
🅺 Proprietors: John & Brenda Shearer

THE BAYVIEW HOTEL & RESTAURANT

Seafield Street, Cullen
Banffshire AB56 4SU
Tel: 01542 841031
Fax: 01542 841731

A98 between Banff and Fochabers – overlooking Cullen Harbour.

A really charming hotel in a picturesque fishing village on the Moray Firth.

- A small town hotel converted from a quayside house commanding magnificent views over the harbour and the bay beyond.
- Imaginative and honest cooking.
- "A convivial atmosphere with well-cooked local produce."

A delightful typical East Coast townhouse, close to the harbour at Cullen with lovely views over the Moray Firth. This is a pleasant haven from which to explore the surrounding countryside and historic local fishing villages. Proprietors Malcolm and Patricia Watt are 'hands on' in the Bayview with a keen understanding of what it takes to make a pleasurable stay for their guests. Their chef makes full use of the hotel's location by maximising on the excellent choice of fresh fish available daily, and the à la carte menus feature an excellent variety of fresh produce, imaginatively presented.

Open all year except Christmas Day
🏨 Rooms: 6 with private facilities
🛏 DB&B £37.50–£67.50   B&B £25–£40
SP Special rates available
✖ Food available all day £-£££
✖ Lunch £-££
✖ Dinner ££-£££
Ⓥ Vegetarians welcome
🧒 Children welcome
🚭 No smoking in restaurant

Savoury carrot and cheese parcel. Venison en croûte filled with herb mousse and served with port sauce. Sticky toffee pudding with local cream.

STB Commended 👑 👑 👑 👑
💷 Credit cards: Mastercard/Eurocard, American Express, Visa, Switch
🅺 Owners: Malcolm & Patricia Watt

THE SEAFIELD ARMS HOTEL

19 Seafield Street, Cullen
Banffshire AB56 4SG
Tel: 01542 840791
Fax: 01542 840736

Situated on A98 (main road through Cullen) up from town square.

A charming and well-appointed old town hotel offering comfort and relaxation.

- A 17th century coaching inn in the heart of Cullen.
- Traditional Scottish cooking with modern influences.
- "A warm welcome with friendly efficient service."

The Seafield Arms is an impressive former coaching inn, built by the Earl of Seaforth in 1822. The statistical Account of Scotland in 1845 stated: "The Seafield Arms... has no superior between Aberdeen and Inverness." The character and hospitality of this hostelry are still evident. The staff are smart, polite and attentive; the accommodation comfortable and traditional. The place is popular with local people and the bar offers a range of over 100 whiskies to enjoy before a roaring fire. A wide ranging menu caters for all ages and preferences.

Open all year
🏨 Rooms: 23, 22 with private facilities
🛏 B&B £26–£30
✖ Lunch £
✖ Dinner £££
Ⅴ Vegetarians welcome
🕇 Children welcome
♿ Facilities for disabled visitors
🚭 No smoking in dining room

Stir-fried garlic king prawns with white wine cream sauce. Medallions of venison with fruits of the forest sauce. Chocolate bread and butter pudding with Tia Maria custard.

STB Highly Commended 🏴 🏴 🏴 🏴
💳 Credit cards: Mastercard/Eurocard, American Express, Visa, Switch, Delta
🅺 Proprietors: Herbert & Alison Cox

EDEN HOUSE HOTEL

2 Pitscottie Road, Cupar
St Andrews
Fife KY15 4HF
Tel: 01334 652 510
Fax: 01334 652 277

Overlooking Haugh Park, just outside Cupar town centre, on main A91 road to St Andrews, hotel at junction with Pitscottie Road.

Victorian mansion with traditional cooking.

- Stone built merchants house.
- Fresh foods simply cooked.
- "Attractive business hotel and particularly popular with golfers."

Eden House Hotel has style. The house itself is Victorian – built for a merchant and reflecting the pompous grandeur favoured by the period. It has been very well refurbished, in a way which respects the original but allows for modern comforts. It also has an 'annexe' in the road-side gate-house. The Vizan family run the hotel with enthusiasm and attention to detail. The cooking makes use of local meat and fish and favours interesting and richly flavoured sauces. Eden House has 1 AA Rosette.

Open all year
Closed Sun lunch
🏨 Rooms: 11 with private facilities
🛏 DB&B £47–£54   B&B £31–£37
SP Special rates available
✖ Lunch £-££
✖ Dinner ££
Ⅴ Vegetarians welcome
🕇 Children welcome
♿ Facilities for disabled visitors
🚬 Smoking area in restaurant

Oriental beef: thin slices of fillet of beef cooked twice with garlic, coriander and limes served with a salad of fresh coriander leaves, tomatoes and sliced chillies. Loin of venison with a cranberry and cassis sauce. Rich chocolate mousse with blackberries and biscuit.

STB Commended 🏴 🏴 🏴
💳 Credit cards: American Express, Visa
🅺 Proprietors: Laurence & Mary Vizan

OSTLERS CLOSE RESTAURANT
Bonnygate, Cupar
Fife KY15 4BU
Tel: 01334 655574

Small lane directly off A91 main road through town.

Many years success at consistently high standards are very apparent in this small and friendly restaurant.

- An intimate ground floor 'cottage'.
- Elegant Scottish cuisine using fresh Scottish produce.
- An intense integrity pervades the excellence of Jimmy and Amanda's cooking and produces the very best of Scottish cuisine today."

Nestling in a lane or 'close' just off the market town of Cupar's main street, Ostlers is a simply and unpretentiously decorated small restaurant. Chef/proprietor Jimmy Graham deserves the excellent reputation he has earned for his imaginative cooking over the past 15 years. His treatment of fish and shellfish is outstanding, but he applies the same flair to Scottish meat and game. Jimmy has a particular passion for wild mushrooms and these are to be sought after if on the menu. Given such quality, a meal here – complemented by a good wine list – is excellent value for money. Amanda Graham looks after guests with courtesy and charm. Ostlers has 3 AA Rosettes.

Open all year except Christmas Day,
Boxing Day, 1 Jan + first 2 wks June
Closed Sun Mon
✗ Lunch except Sun Mon ££ – booking advised
✗ Dinner except Sun Mon £££
Ⓥ Vegetarians welcome – please mention at booking
⚘ Children welcome
⚐ Smoking restricted until all diners at coffee stage
🐄 Member of the Scotch Beef Club

Seared West Coast scallops on a bed of Glamis seakale with a butter sauce. Roast saddle of roe venison with wild mushrooms on a red wine sauce. Trio of summer fruit desserts.

⊞ Credit cards: Mastercard/Eurocard, American Express, Visa, Mastercharge, Switch, Delta
⋈ Proprietors: Jimmy & Amanda Graham

BRAIDWOOD'S RESTAURANT
1 Mile, nr Dalry, North Ayrshire KA24 4LN
Tel: 01294 833544

A737 Kilwinning-Dalry. On southern outskirts of Dalry, take road to Saltcoats for 1 mile and follow signs.

An outstanding restaurant deep in the Ayrshire countryside.

- A converted 18th century miller's cottage surrounded by rolling farmland.
- Innovative modern Scottish cooking.
- "An outstanding small restaurant – a joy to visit."

The owners have been described simply as 'two of Scotland's best younger chefs'. They are both highly qualified, with impressive track records (Shieldhill, Murrayshall, Peat Inn, Inverlochy Castle, etc.) and demonstrate their skills daily in wonderfully original combinations of flavour, textures and unusual ingredients. Their table d'hôte menus give an unexpected, and wholly successful, twist to classic dishes. Raw materials are carefully sourced locally. A truly gourmet experience. Braidwood's has 2 AA Rosettes. Winner of The Macallan Taste of Scotland Special Merit Award for Newcomers 1995.

Open last wk Jan to last wk Sep + second wk Oct to 31 Dec except Christmas Day
Closed Sun pm, Mon + Tue lunch
♀ Table licence
✗ Lunch except Mon Tue ££
✗ Dinner except Sun Mon £££
Ⓥ Vegetarians welcome – prior notice required
⚘ Children over 12 years welcome
⚐ No smoking throughout
🐄 Member of the Scotch Beef Club

A warm terrine of lemon sole, scallops and lobster, chive and horseradish hollandaise. Butter roasted baby Guinea fowl on a wild mushroom risotto and thyme jus. Iced caramelised pecan nut parfait, fresh raspberry coulis.

⊞ Credit cards: Mastercard/Eurocard, American Express, Visa, Switch, Delta
⋈ Owners: Keith & Nicola Braidwood

SCORETULLOCH HOUSE HOTEL
Darvel, Ayrshire KA17 0LR
Tel: 01560 323331
Fax: 01560 323441

Turn off A71 at eastern end of Priestland, near
Darvel. Follow signs – approx 1 mile from A71.
20 minutes south of Glasgow.

**A small well-restored hotel and restaurant in the
Ayrshire countryside.**

- Converted from 15th century farm.
- Traditional Scottish cuisine.
- "Wonderful home-cooked dishes in a family-run
  establishment of highest standards."

Scoretulloch House Hotel, run by Donald and Annie
Smith, lies high on a hill with superb views of the
Loudoun valley and offers good Scottish hospitality
and excellent cooking. The house was established
before 1500, collapsed into ruin and has now been
painstakingly and authentically rebuilt within the
original stone walls to provide comfort in an old
Scots country house. This is the place that 'they
could not find during their travels round the world'
and if you are weary of 'sameness' Scoretulloch will
restore your faith. Annie is a talented cook who is
keen not to tamper with natural flavours and tends to
use good traditional style rather than be influenced
by modern trends. A very hospitable place where
other interests may also be engaged in such as
country pursuits of fishing, walking, studying birds all
of which Annie and Donald take part in themselves.
Scoretulloch House Hotel has 2 AA Rosettes.

Open all year except Christmas Day +
New Year's Day
- 🛏 Rooms: 4 with private facilities
- 🍴 DB&B £63–£93   B&B £44.50–£75
- SP Special rates available
- ✗ Lunch except Mon Tue ££
- ✗ Dinner except Mon Tue £££
- V Vegetarians welcome
- ⌀ No smoking in restaurant

**Fresh local mushrooms au gratin. Beef Black
Velvet: a dark casserole of black Angus beef
marinated in a delicious Guinness gravy. Little pots
of caramel.**

STB Deluxe 👑 👑 👑 👑
- 💳 Credit cards: Mastercard/Eurocard, American
  Express, Visa, Mastercharge, Switch, Delta
- 🕴 Proprietor: Donald Smith

DAVIOT MAINS FARM
Daviot
Inverness IV1 2ER
Tel/Fax: 01463 772215

On B851 (B9006) to Culloden/Croy, 5 miles south
of Inverness.

Category B Listed farmhouse on a working farm.

- Early 19th century Highland farmhouse.
- Creative home cooking.
- "Margaret Hutcheson endeavours to find the
  best produce to tempt her guests."

Daviot Mains is a lovely and most unusual farmhouse in that it is almost completely square and
built around a courtyard. One of only three of its
type in Scotland, this is the warm and friendly home
of Margaret and Alex Hutcheson, with log fires in
the public rooms. Licensed, guests can enjoy wine
with Margaret's excellent home cooking.
Ingredients are meticulously sourced to provide
only the best of Highland meat and fish. Portions, as
one might expect on a working farm, are generous.
At 10 pm guests are offered a supper of tea and the
day's home baking such as scones, shortbread or
sponges.

Open all year except Christmas Eve,
Christmas Day, 31 Dec + New Year's Day
Note: Dinner not served Sun Sat Apr to
Sep incl.
- 🛏 Rooms: 3, 2 with private facilities
- 🍴 DB&B £30–£35   B&B £18–£23
- SP Special rates available
- ♀ Licensed
- ✗ Dinner except Sun ££
- V Vegetarians welcome – prior notice required
  Special diets on request
- ⚹ Children welcome
- ⌀ No smoking throughout

**According to season – home-made soups, fresh
local salmon and trout, Scottish meats, vegetables
and cheeses. Local fruits and home-made
puddings.**

STB Highly Commended 👑 👑
- 💳 Credit cards: Mastercard/Eurocard, Visa
- 🕴 Proprietors: Margaret & Alex Hutcheson

KINKELL HOUSE

Easter Kinkell, by Conon Bridge
Dingwall, Ross-shire IV7 8HY
Tel: 01349 861270
Fax: 01349 865902

1 mile from A9 on B9169, 10 miles north
of Inverness.

A well-appointed hotel with a reputation for high class cooking.

- Small country house hotel.
- Country house cooking.
- "Imaginative Scottish cooking with family hospitality in a country hotel."

Once a large farmhouse, Kinkell House stands in its own grounds on the Black Isle, overlooking the Cromarty Firth, towards Ben Wyvis and the hills of Wester Ross. It is the home of Marsha and Steve Fraser, and retains the atmosphere of a private house, with appropriate period furnishings and log fires. The excellence of Marsha's cooking has won Kinkell an AA Rosette, which is presented in interesting and well-balanced à la carte menus for lunch and dinner (five main courses; changing daily) featuring fresh local produce with both classic and innovative treatments. The restaurant is popular, and non-residents are asked to book in advance.

Open all year
- ⊞ Rooms: 7 with private facilities
- ⨝ DB&B £54–£59   B&B £34–£39
- ⓢⓟ Special rates available
- ⨎ Lunch – by reservation ££
- ⨎ Dinner – by reservation ££
- Ⓥ Vegetarians welcome
- ☂ Children welcome
- ♿ Facilities for disabled visitors
- ⌁ No smoking in dining room + bedrooms

Leek and smoked haddock chowder. Black Isle new season lamb fillet pan-fried with a sauce of port and bramble. Iced honey and whisky cream served with shortbread.

STB Highly Commended 🏵 🏵 🏵 🏵
- 💳 Credit cards: Mastercard/Eurocard, Visa
- 🅽 Proprietors: Marsha & Steve Fraser

TULLOCH CASTLE HOTEL

Tulloch Castle Drive
Dingwall, Ross-shire
IV15 9ND
Tel: 01349 861325
Fax: 01349 863993

Overlooking the town of Dingwall, ½ mile from town centre.

A castle hotel overlooking Dingwall.

- Castle hotel.
- Traditional with modern twist.
- "A wonderful castle hotel full of character."

Tulloch Castle dates back to the 12th century and commands magnificent views of the county of Dingwall and surrounding countryside. The castle is now owned and run by Ken and Margaret MacAulay and has an established reputation for providing excellent hospitality whether you are on business or pleasure – or a bit of both. The castle has ample characterful public and private rooms all tastefully decorated and maintained in keeping with the surroundings. Cooking is traditional with some modern influences and makes excellent use of local produce – as such the kitchen team have already scooped Highland Chef of the Year and Commis Young Chef of the Year.

Open all year
- ⊞ Rooms: 19 with private facilities
- ⨝ B&B from £39.50
- ✗ Food available all day £-££
- ✗ Lunch £
- ✗ Dinner ££
- Ⓥ Vegetarians welcome
- ☂ Children welcome
- ♿ Facilities for disabled visitors

Terrine of pheasant and rabbit studded with wild mushrooms and pistachio nuts. Steamed fillet of River Conon salmon wrapped in spinach leaves set on a bed of red pepper salsa, cordoned with a warm red wine vinaigrette. Warm compote of fresh local strawberries served in a tuile basket, with home-made whisky and ginger ice cream.

STB Approved 🏵 🏵 🏵
- 💳 Credit cards: Mastercard/Eurocard, American Express, Visa
- 🅽 Partner/Owner: Ken MacAulay

THE OPEN ARMS HOTEL

The Green, Dirleton
East Lothian EH39 5EG
Tel: 01620 850 241
Fax: 01620 850 570

From Edinburgh take coast road to Gullane and North Berwick. Dirleton is 2 miles between them.

A traditional country hotel with good food and accommodation – ideal for golfers.

- Late 1800s sandstone building – originally farmhouse.
- Modern Scottish.
- "Traditional family-run hotel, good food and accommodation in pleasant surroundings."

The Open Arms is set in the sleepy hamlet of Dirleton, opposite Dirleton Castle and village green. Long a favourite of its Edinburgh neighbours the Open Arms offers a warm friendly atmosphere in surroundings reminiscent of a country home in a renovated farmhouse. Local salmon is a particular favourite served with East Lothian vegetables. There is a good accompanying wine list, with thoughtfully selected vintages and fairly priced. Awarded 2 AA Rosettes.

....

    Open all year
🏨 Rooms: 10 with private facilities
🛏 DB&B £60–£94.50   B&B £30–£74.50
SP Special rates available
✗ Lunch £-££
✗ Dinner ££-£££
Ⓥ Vegetarians welcome
⚘ Children welcome
♿ Limited facilities for disabled visitors
🚭 Smoking discouraged: cigars + pipes not permitted

Fillets of Loch Awe trout with an orange and dill glaze, served with an avocado and pepper salad. Rack of 'Scottish Hill' lamb with a rosemary, onion and redcurrant confit. Drambuie cream parfait with a cherry and blueberry compote.

STB Highly Commended 🏅 🏅 🏅 🏅
💳 Credit cards: Mastercard/Eurocard, Visa, Mastercharge, Switch, Delta
🄼 Proprietors: Tom & Emma Hill

DORNOCH CASTLE HOTEL

Castle Street
Dornoch
Sutherland, IV25 3SD
Tel: 01862 810216
Fax: 01862 810981

From Inverness take A9 north for 43 miles, then 2 miles north of Dornoch Firth Bridge turn right onto A949. Dornoch 2 miles. The castle is on right opposite the Cathedral.

A castle hotel in the centre of Dornoch.

- Late 15th, early 16th, century castle.
- Traditional cooking.
- "Excellent location, caring staff and good Scottish cuisine."

Dornoch Castle dates back to the late 15th century and was formerly the Palace of the Bishops of Caithness. Dornoch Cathedral is directly opposite the hotel. A new wing was added to the building over 20 years ago and offers most of the accommodation – all of which are en suite. The hotel is run by Michael Ketchin who ensures that the needs of his guests are met and exceeded – whether they are in the area for business, pleasure or golf! The cooking is typically Scottish using obviously local produce and cooking it well with interesting accompaniments.

....

    Open 3 Apr to 31 Oct
🏨 Rooms: 17 with private facilities
🛏 DB&B £56–£64.50   B&B £35–£43.50
SP Special rates available
✗ Lunch £
✗ Dinner £££
Ⓥ Vegetarians welcome
⚘ Children welcome
🚭 No smoking in Bishops' Room Restaurant

Broccoli and carrot mousse provençale. Rosettes of beef Benbhraggie. Ecclefechan butter tart.

STB Commended 🏅 🏅 🏅 🏅
💳 Credit cards: Mastercard/Eurocard, American Express, Visa, Mastercharge, Switch, Delta
🄼 Proprietor: Michael Ketchin

MALLIN HOUSE HOTEL

Church Street, Dornoch
Sutherland IV25 3LP
Tel: 01862 810335
Fax: 01862 810810
e-mail address mallin.house.hotel@zetnet.co.uk

Down to centre of town, turn right.

Comfortable town hotel popular with golfers.

- Family-run hotel close to historic golf course.
- Traditional Scottish hotel cooking.
- "Ideally situated for many outdoor pursuits."

The hotel is a mere 200 yards from the Royal Dornoch Golf Course, one of the finest and oldest links courses in the world. As you would expect, it is very popular with golfers: its bar, in particular, is a refuge from the rigours of the course, with an exceptionally good range of bar meals including lobster and a special 'malt of the month' promotion. An extensive à la carte menu offers a good choice of local produce with superb, locally caught seafood as something of a speciality. Food is imaginatively prepared with unusual sauces and accompaniments. The restaurant itself has magnificent views of the Dornoch Firth and the Struie Hills. Accommodation is very comfortable including a residents' lounge.

Open all year
🏨 Rooms: 10 with private facilities
🛏 DB&B £48–£55   B&B £30–£35
✗ Lunch ££
✗ Dinner £-££
Ⓥ Vegetarians welcome
🕇 Children welcome
♿ Facilities for disabled visitors

Avocado crumble served with mango salsa. Aberdeen Angus rib eye steak. Crème caramel.

STB Commended 👑 👑 👑
💳 Credit cards: Mastercard/Eurocard, American Express, Visa, Switch, Delta
👤 Proprietors: Malcolm & Linda Holden

THE ROYAL GOLF HOTEL

The First Tee
Dornoch
Sutherland IV25 3LG
Tel: 01862 810283
Fax: 01862 810923

From A9, 2 miles into Dornoch town square, straight across crossroads, 200 yards on right.

The hotel is appropriately named, being adjacent to the first tee.

- Seaside golfing hotel.
- Innovative Scottish cooking.
- "Ideally situated for touring, golfing and relaxing."

The Royal Golf is a traditional Scottish hotel, within yards of the first tee of the famous golf course of the same name, and having a broad, picture-windowed modern extension overlooking the course and the sandy beaches of the Dornoch Firth beyond. The restaurant also benefits from this splendid view. Here Chef Jeanette Weatheritt presents a well-priced table d'hôte menu featuring local fish, poultry, beef and lamb. The cooking is first rate and presentation attractive.

Open 1 Mar to 31 Dec
🏨 Rooms: 25 with private facilities
🛏 DB&B £40–£80   B&B £42–£60
SP Special rates available
✗ Lunch £
✗ Dinner 4 course menu £££
Ⓥ Vegetarians welcome
🕇 Children welcome

Rich cream of cauliflower and Orkney cheese soup. Trio of Isle of Skye seafood to include salmon, sole and cod set on a tomato and tarragon sauce. Fresh fruit pavlova set on a red berry compot and topped with cream.

STB Commended 👑 👑 👑 👑
💳 Credit cards: Mastercard/Eurocard, American Express, Visa, Diners Club, Mastercharge
👤 General Manager: Donald MacLeod

THE OLD MONASTERY RESTAURANT
Drybridge, Buckie
Banff AB56 5JB
Tel/Fax: 01542 832660

Turn off A98 at Buckie Junction onto Drybridge Road. Follow road for 3 miles – do not turn right into Drybridge village.

Converted Benedictine monastery with stunning views and exquisite food.

- A lovingly converted monastery within its own grounds.
- A blend of classical French and Scottish.
- "The finest food, wine and hospitality can be found within these walls."

Originally built in 1904 as a holiday retreat for the Benedictine monks from Fort Augustus Abbey – The Old Monastery Restaurant was converted in 1980 and has acquired an excellent reputation both locally and abroad for its exquisite food. The views overlook the western mountains and Moray Firth, and stepping into the monastery you enter a world where the eating experience is the harmonisation of body and soul in an atmosphere of comfort and relaxation. Menus change seasonally and feature locally sourced Scottish produce. Two AA Rosettes and gold medal-winning chefs make this a very special place indeed.

Open all year except 2 wks Nov + 3 wks Jan
Closed Sun Mon
✘ Lunch except Sun Mon ££
✘ Dinner except Sun Mon ££££
Ⓥ Vegetarians welcome – prior notice advised
⚱ Children over 8 years welcome
⚬ No smoking in restaurant

Seared North Sea scallops with fennel butter sauce. Noisettes of Banffshire lamb with red onion and rosemary marmalade. Strawberry moussecake with sweet and sour strawberries and peppercorn syrup.

⊞ Credit cards: Mastercard/Eurocard, American Express, Visa, Mastercharge, Switch
Ⓚ Partners: Maureen & Douglas Gray

DRYBURGH ABBEY HOTEL
Dryburgh, Melrose
Roxburghshire TD6 0RQ
Tel: 01835 822261
Fax: 01835 823945

Off A68 at St Boswells onto B6404. 2 miles turn left onto B6356. Continue for 1½ miles, hotel signposted.

A splendid luxury hotel in the Scottish Borders with leisure facilities and comfortable accommodation.

- Scottish baronial red sandstone mansion on the banks of the River Tweed.
- International and modern Scottish cuisine.
- "Extensive modern cooking using local produce served in baronial surroundings."

In a tranquil setting on the banks of the River Tweed, adjacent to the ruins of the historic Abbey, this mansion has been restored and converted into a first class hotel, including indoor heated swimming pool. The Tweed Restaurant is situated on the first floor, with views over the lawns and gardens to the river: a spacious, elegant room with decorative cornicing and ornate chandeliers. The Head Chef, Patrick Ruse, offers a table d'hôte menu (lunch and dinner) which changes daily, and uses only fresh local produce. During the day and evening a range of light meals is also available, served in the lounge or bar.

Open all year
🛏 Rooms: 26 with private facilities
🛏 DB&B £52.50–£92.50   B&B £47–£71
SP Special rates available
✘ Food available all day £-££
✘ Lunch £-££
✘ Dinner ££-£££
Ⓥ Vegetarians welcome
⚱ Children welcome
♿ Facilities for disabled visitors
⚬ No smoking in restaurant

Pheasant and orange terrine with spiced onion chutney. Grilled Scottish salmon with basil creamed potato and mango scented cream. Rhubarb and strawberry crunch parfait.

STB Highly Commended 👑 👑 👑 👑 👑
⊞ Credit cards: Mastercard/Eurocard, American Express, Visa, Mastercharge, Switch, Delta, JCB
Ⓚ General Manager: John Sloggie

A TASTE OF SPEYSIDE
10 Balvenie Street, Dufftown
Banffshire AB55 4AB
Tel/Fax: 01340 820860

50 yards from the Clock Tower on the road to Elgin.

Popular restaurant on the whisky trail.

- Informal town restaurant.
- Good wholesome Scottish fare.
- "This restaurant, situated in the whisky capital of the world, makes the best use of fresh local ingredients."

The restaurant is situated in malt whisky heartland and was originally set up as a whisky tasting centre and restaurant. To this day one of its major attractions is the superb selection of malt whiskies on offer. Situated close to the centre of Dufftown the restaurant revels in its Scottishness, evident in its tartan inspired decor and style of cuisine, but in a tasteful, rather than a mawkish way. You will find simple fare that makes the most of local ingredients, cooked and presented with style. This is home cooking at its best, enhanced by a well-chosen wine list with a predominance of reasonably priced New World wines. Awarded 1 AA Rosette.

Open 1 Mar to 14 Nov
✘ Food available all day £
✘ Lunch £
✘ Dinner ££
Ⓥ Vegetarians welcome
⚐ Children welcome

Smoked pigeon with horseradish cream. Wild duck breast with rhubarb and juniper sauce. Heather honey and malt whisky cheesecake with double cream.

💳 Credit cards: Mastercard/Eurocard, American Express, Visa
Ⓝ Partners: Joseph Thompson, Raymond McLean & Peter Thompson

AUCHENDEAN LODGE HOTEL
Dulnain Bridge
Inverness-shire PH26 3LU
Tel/Fax: 01479 851 347

On A95, 1 mile south of Dulnain Bridge.

A charming Highland country hotel.

- Edwardian hunting lodge, with a great view over the Spey.
- Original, talented, eclectic cooking.
- "A unique dining experience – no wonder guests return here year after year."

Auchendean was built just after the turn of the century as a sporting lodge and has architectural details from the Arts and Crafts Movements. The present owners, Eric Hart and Ian Kirk, are convivial professionals dedicated to giving their guests a full dining experience. Before dinner you are served drinks in the drawing room and meet the other diners and choose from a splendid selection of over 40 malt whiskies. Both Ian and Eric share the cooking; Eric is a keen mycologist and finds over 20 varieties of edible wild mushrooms locally; the hotel's garden also provides vegetables (including six varieties of potato!), salads, herbs and honey. Eggs are supplied by the hotel's own hens. Wild berries, mountain hare, rabbit, pigeon, mallard, pheasant and home-cured gravadlax are specialities. The menu changes every night but always balances a simple main course with something more exotic. As a New Zealander Ian has created an extensive cellar including over 50 special wines from his home country. French spoken.

Open all year except Jan
🛏 Rooms: 8, 5 with private facilities
🛏 DB&B £37–£73   B&B £17–£49
SP Special rates available
🍱 Pre-booked packed lunch £
✘ Dinner £££
Ⓥ Vegetarians welcome – prior notice required
⚐ Children welcome
♿ Facilities for non-residents only
🚭 No smoking in dining room + one lounge

Wild cep soufflé. Pigeon breast with Madeira sauce. Liquorice and vanilla ripple ice cream.

STB Highly Commended 👑 👑 👑
💳 Credit cards: Mastercard/Eurocard, American Express, Visa, Diners Club
Ⓝ Proprietors: Eric Hart & Ian Kirk

LOW KIRKBRIDE FARMHOUSE
Auldgirth
Dumfries DG2 0SP
Tel/Fax: 01387 820258

From Dumfries take A76 Kilmarnock for 2 miles, then B729 to Dunscore. Beyond Dunscore at crossroads go right. After 1½ miles take first left. Farm first on left.

Farmhouse bed and breakfast set amidst rolling Dumfries pastures.

- Farmhouse family-bed and breakfast.
- Good home cooking.
- "Farmhouse B&B offering good food and hospitality."

This is a working farm with a prize-winning herd of Friesian cattle and lots of sheep, so there is much to entertain those who love the countryside and farming life. The traditional farmhouse has beautiful views and has a lovingly tended garden to the front. The guest rooms are comfortable with a domestic appeal about them. Dinner is provided for residents with substantial helpings of wholesome home-made dishes using home-grown produce wherever possible. Zan and her family cook, serve and entertain you in their friendly and happy home.

Open all year except Christmas Day
🏠 Rooms: 2
🛏 DB&B £26   B&B £15
🆂🅿 Special rates available
✗ Residents only
🆄🅻 Unlicensed
✗ Dinner ££
Ⓥ Vegetarians welcome
🕇 Children welcome
🚭 No smoking in bedrooms

Broccoli and Stilton soup. Roast home-reared Belted Galloway beef. Scotch trifle.

STB Commended Listed
🅴 No credit cards
🅺 Proprietors: Joe & Zan Kirk

SANDFORD COUNTRY HOUSE HOTEL
Newton Hill, Wormit
Fife DD6 8RG
Tel: 01382 541802
Fax: 01382 542136

4 miles south of Dundee on A92 (formerly A914) at junction of B946 signposted Wormit.

An historic 20th century building on the Tay.

- Country house hotel.
- Scottish/French modern cuisine.
- "Warm and friendly country house hotel providing good quality cooking with flair and enthusiasm."

Originally built for the Valentine family of Dundee (post-card manufacturers) this Listed building stands in five acres of gardens and has been carefully and lovingly cared for over the years. Now under the ownership of the Cowan family this care continues both in the level of hospitality offered and the standard of cooking which are both excellent. The emphasis is very much on a combination of Scottish and continental flavours and there is also great attention to the small details which take skill and commitment to prepare – like hand-made sweets and petits fours for example. Sandford is also an excellent base from which to enjoy the outdoor pursuits of the Newton Hill Outdoor Centre next door. *(See advert Page 26.)*

Open all year
🏠 Rooms: 16 with private facilities
🛏 DB&B £52.50–£85   B&B £35–£70
🆂🅿 Special rates available
✗ Food available all day £-£££
✗ Lunch £-£££
✗ Dinner £-£££
Ⓥ Vegetarians welcome
🕇 Children welcome
🚭 No smoking in restaurant

Asparagus risotto with rocket, Parmesan shavings, balsamic vinegar and extra virgin olive oil. Seared turbot with roast fennel, pesto oil, saffron nage and tapenade beignet. Whisky cream cheese parfait with crisp shortbread, rhubarb compote and fresh raspberries.

STB Highly Commended 👑 👑 👑 👑
🅴 Credit cards: Mastercard/Eurocard, American Express, Visa, Diners Club, Mastercharge, Switch, Delta
🅺 Proprietor: G Cowan

DAVAAR HOUSE HOTEL AND RESTAURANT

126 Grieve Street, Dunfermline
Fife KY12 8DW
Tel: 01383 721886/736463
Fax: 01383 623633

From M90, junction 3, A907 Dunfermline. Straight on through town, over Sinclair Gardens roundabout, 3rd right into Chalmers Street, 2nd left into Grieve Street.

Popular family-run hotel in quiet residential area.

- Large Georgian house.
- Home cooking.
- "A welcoming atmosphere and quiet competence pervades this place."

Davaar House was built at the turn of the century and retains such features as a splendid oak staircase, marble fireplaces and elaborate cornices. It is centrally situated in a residential area of Dunfermline. There is an appealing, chintzy appearance to the hotel which stands in lovely gardens. The food is cooked by Doreen Jarvis and her daughter Karen who create traditional dishes with intuitive flair and, using the best fresh vegetables, supplied by Jim and their son Kyle who own a fruit and vegetable business.

Open all year except 23 Dec to 6 Jan
Closed Sun
🏠 Rooms: 9 with private facilities
🛏 DB&B £54–£68   B&B £35–£50
SP Special rates available
♀ Restricted licence
✕ Lunch (Dec only) except Sun ££
✕ Dinner except Sun £££
V Vegetarians welcome
ᵏ Children welcome
♿ Facilities for disabled visitors
🚭 No smoking in restaurant + 1st floor bedrooms

Cream of spinach and nutmeg soup. Tay salmon rolled in oatmeal, toasted with lemon butter. Summer fruits marinated in cherry brandy presented in shortcake basket.

STB Commended 👑 👑 👑
💳 Credit cards: Mastercard/Eurocard, Visa, Switch, Delta
Ⅺ Proprietors: Doreen & Jim Jarvis

KEAVIL HOUSE HOTEL

Main Street, Crossford
nr Dunfermline
Fife KY12 8QW
Tel: 01383 736258
Fax: 01383 621600

Crossford lies on the A994 Dunfermline-Kincardine Road, 2 miles west of Dunfermline. Hotel is just off main street.

Well-established hotel with excellent leisure facilities.

- Country hotel with modern additions.
- Modern Scottish cooking.
- "Quiet, comfortable and attractive surroundings."

Crossford village is just outside Dunfermline, and Keavil House is on the Main Street, standing in 12 acres of gardens and woods. As well as having two restaurants to choose from, the hotel also has a swimming pool, gym and sauna/solarium, etc. Staff are smart and well-trained; rooms are very comfortable. There is a choice of à la carte or table d'hôte menus which offer both traditional and more adventurous dishes, all of them well-cooked and presented. Keavil is part of the Best Western group of hotels, but is much, much better than the average. Keavil has 1 AA Rosette.

Open all year
🏠 Rooms: 33 with private facilities
🛏 DB&B £52.50–£72.50   B&B £49–£84
SP Special rates available
✕ Food available all day
✕ Lunch £
✕ Dinner £££
V Vegetarians welcome
ᵏ Children welcome
♿ Facilities for disabled visitors
🚭 No smoking throughout

Home soused brown trout. Venison cutlets in a herb bread crumb with a rowan berry jelly. Heather honey and almond waffles with an elderberry syrup.

STB Commended 👑 👑 👑 👑
💳 Credit cards: Mastercard/Eurocard, American Express, Visa, Diners Club, Switch
Ⅺ Manager: Mark Simpkins

STAKIS DUNKELD HOUSE RESORT HOTEL
Dunkeld, Perthshire PH8 0HX
Tel: 01350 727771 Fax: 01350 728924

A9 to Dunkeld, hotel lies c. 1 mile east of village.

A popular country house hotel set in idyllic surroundings.

- Highly regarded as offering the best of the old and the new.
- Outstanding Scottish cuisine with flair.
- "An excellent blend of old and new, something for those keen on outdoor pursuits and also those who prefer more luxurious surroundings."

Built originally for the Seventh Duke of Atholl, this Edwardian house has been sympathetically extended and restored to form a rare combination of country house and luxury hotel. The hotel sits within its own 280 acre estate on the banks of the River Tay and has a private 2-mile salmon beat. An excellent leisure centre includes an indoor pool. Outdoors, the hotel offers all-weather tennis courts, a croquet lawn and clay-pigeon shooting. Menus in the dining room are intended to satisfy the most discerning of palates. The table d'hôte menu offers four choices for each course. It should be noted that during the quiet season the dining room is not always available at lunchtime but the bar is there for your enjoyment and a good range of dishes is available. Dishes are well-balanced and use fresh, local ingredients. Presentation and service round off a pleasurable experience. There is a Sunday night ceilidh (dinner-dance) with 'Taste of Scotland' menu.

Open all year
- 🏨 Rooms: 86 with private facilities
- 🛏 DB&B £65–£135.75   B&B £55–£109.75
- SP Special rates available
- ✕ Food available all day £
- ✕ Lunch from £
- ✕ Dinner from £££
- Ⓥ Vegetarians welcome
- ★ Children welcome
- ♿ Facilities for disabled visitors

Warm salad of Perthshire pigeon and blackcurrant dressing. Roast fillet of monkfish and scallop, lime and garlic butter sauce. Iced Drambuie and raspberry parfait.

STB Commended 🏴 🏴 🏴 🏴 🏴
- 💳 Credit cards: Mastercard/Eurocard, American Express, Visa, Diners Club, Mastercharge, Switch
- 🗡 Hotel Manager: Dick Beach
- 🗡 Executive Chef: Robert Lintott

THE ANCHORAGE HOTEL & RESTAURANT
Shore Road, Ardnadam
Holy Loch, Dunoon, Argyll PA23 8QG
Tel/Fax: 01369 705108

3 miles out of Dunoon on A815 heading north.

A recently refurbished lochside hotel.

- Very pretty whitewashed Victorian house.
- Scottish food imaginatively cooked.
- "The visitor is assured of impeccable service and excellent cuisine in this charming and tranquil hotel."

On the banks of the Holy Loch sits this white Victorian house which was bought by Dee and Tony Hancock five years ago. Since then they have both worked hard to renovate and refurbish and Tony completed the building of a charming conservatory/dining room which overlooks a well-laid out and most attractive garden. The decor is attractive and their attention to detail has resulted in a delightful, tasteful and comfortable place to stay. This dedication also extends to their well-planned menus which offer dishes carefully selected to make use of a wide range of local produce including shellfish, venison and game. The Anchorage is an enjoyable place to stay with its panoramic views across the loch and attentive professional hosts.

Open all year
- 🏨 Rooms: 5 with private facilities
- 🛏 DB&B £42.50–£55   B&B £27.50–£40
- ✕ Lunch £
- ✕ Dinner £££
- Ⓥ Vegetarians welcome
- ★ Children welcome
- ♿ Facilities for disabled visitors
- 🚭 No smoking throughout

Roast Isle of Arran king scallops served on a bed of courgette ribbons with a warm orange, ginger and dill sauce, topped with aubergine crisps. Perthshire pork fillet wrapped in Parma ham and sage sautéed and served with a Marsala wine and pineapple sauce on a pasta ribbon bed. White chocolate and kahlua sponge.

STB Highly Commended 🏴 🏴 🏴
- 💳 Credit cards: Mastercard/Eurocard, Visa, Delta
- 🗡 Owners: Dee & Tony Hancock

THE ARDENTINNY HOTEL

Ardentinny, Nr Dunoon,
Argyll PA23 8TR
Tel: 01369 810 209
Fax: 01369 810 241

12 miles north of Dunoon. From Gourock-Dunoon
ferry, take A815 then A880. Or scenic drive round
Loch Lomond A82 and A83 then A815 through
Strachur, and over hill to Ardentinny.

Rural family-run hotel.

* 18th century coaching inn.
* Traditional Scottish cooking.
* "A wonderful old coaching inn full of
  atmosphere."

This delightful droving inn built in the 1700s lies on a
small promontory on Loch Long and is surrounded
by the glorious Argyll Forest Park. The hotel's
gardens stretch down to the lochside and pier for
those arriving by yacht (the hotel has its own
moorings). Informal lunches and suppers can be
eaten in the Buttery or patio garden, or guests may
prefer a more formal dinner in the relaxed
atmosphere of the dining room. The food is really
good, the atmosphere friendly and welcoming.
Despite the buzz from the hotel, tranquillity
surrounds and the views of the loch and mountains
are most soothing.

Open all year
🏠 Rooms: 11 with private facilities
🛏 DB&B £59–£79   B&B £39–£55
SP Special rates available
✕ Food available all day £££
✕ Lunch £
✕ Dinner £££
V Vegetarians welcome
🕭 Children welcome
✕ No smoking in dining room

**Own hot smoked 'Loch Striven' salmon with chive
and turmeric dressing. Best end of Argyll lamb
with a rosemary and red wine reduction. Grilled
nectarines with honey and walnut cream.**

STB Commended 👑 👑 👑 👑
£ Credit cards: Mastercard/Eurocard, Visa,
   Mastercharge, Switch, Delta
Ⅺ Proprietors: Mr & Mrs P Webb
   Family-run by Bob & Anne Rennie

ARDFILLAYNE HOUSE

West Bay, Dunoon
Argyll PA23 7QJ
Tel: 01369 702267
Fax: 01369 702501

1 mile from Dunoon centre on Innellan road at end
of promenade.

Country house on the outskirts of Dunoon.

* Country house.
* Scottish/French cooking.
* "Fine Scottish cuisine to be enjoyed in an
  atmosphere of old world charm."

A traditional country house situated in a 16 acre
wooded estate on an elevated position overlooking
the Firth of Clyde on the outskirts of Dunoon, the
hotel retains the atmosphere of a bygone era. The
interior of the house is crammed with antique
furniture, Victoriana, bric-a-brac and an interesting
collection of clocks. Beverley's Restaurant is
decorated with lace, crystal and silverware, the
menu is locally sourced i.e. venison, seafood, wild
boar. Service is formal and the cooking applies
classical French techniques to traditional Scottish
recipes. Bill McCaffrey, the owner, buys his wine by
his own careful selection at wine auctions.
Ardfillayne has 1 AA Rosette.

Open all year
🏠 Rooms: 7 with private facilities
🛏 DB&B £60–£90   B&B £35–£55
SP Special rates available
🍴 Open for dinner – advance booking
   requested £££
V Vegetarians welcome – prior notice required
✕ No smoking in restaurant

**Sliced smoked chicken breast in a lime cassis.
Wild boar in a cherry and ginger sauce. Dark
chocolate and brandy gâteau.**

STB Deluxe 👑 👑 👑 👑
£ Credit cards: Mastercard/Eurocard, American
   Express, Visa, Diners Club
Ⅺ Proprietor: Bill McCaffrey

CHATTERS

58 John Street, Dunoon
Argyll PA23 8BJ
Tel: 01369 706402

On John Street, Dunoon, opposite the cinema.

Charming, award-winning small restaurant in popular seaside resort.

- Town restaurant in converted traditional cottage.
- Traditional French influenced Scottish cooking.
- "A charming restaurant in which to enjoy the most excellent cuisine and a welcome of genuine warmth and friendliness."

Now in its seventh year of operation in the capable hands of Rosemary MacInnes this restaurant has picked up several awards. The young chefs are very enthusiastic, original and extremely competent. Credible and well-balanced à la carte menus are presented for lunch and dinner (six starters, six main courses); every dish is an unusual and successful combination of flavours and textures, and each demonstrates considerable talent. There is also a lounge extension opening out onto a small garden, used for pre-lunch/dinner drinks and coffee. In spite of its excellence and distinction, Chatters has a friendly, informal atmosphere and is very popular with locals for coffee and afternoon tea, with home baking. Winner of The Macallan Taste of Scotland Special Merit Award for Enterprise 1994.

Open Mar to mid Jan except Christmas Day, Boxing Day + New Year's Day
Closed Sun
♀ Table licence
✕ Lunch £-££
✕ Dinner ££-£££
⌇ Smoking in lounge only

Baked tartlet of wild mushrooms and asparagus set on a tarragon cream reduction. Roast loin of lamb with mille feuille of sweet potato on a wild mushroom essence. Chocolate and hazelnut terrine on a fresh raspberry coulis.

💳 Credit cards: Mastercard/Eurocard, Visa
🅜 Proprietor: Rosemary Anne MacInnes

ENMORE HOTEL

Marine Parade, Dunoon
Argyll PA23 8HH
Tel: 01369 702230
Fax: 01369 702148
e mail enmorehotel@btinternet.com

On seafront near Hunters Quay Ferry, approx 1 mile from town centre.

Very comfortable small hotel in its own grounds facing the sea.

- 18th century villa.
- Modern Scottish cooking.
- "A comfortable hotel with a very personal touch."

Originally built in 1785 as a country retreat for a wealthy Glasgow businessman, the house has been enlarged over the years into a luxurious small hotel. It has ten en suite bedrooms, and the public rooms are attractively furnished with reproduction period pieces. There is a colourful garden, a squash court, a private beach and golf and fishing are within easy reach. The limited choice menu guarantees the freshness of the produce – 'creel caught crayfish' and Loch Fyne scallops – and the hotel's own garden provides herbs and vegetables. Chef/proprietor, David Wilson, has an AA Rosette, and is always looking for new ways to produce and present great ingredients. His wife, Angela, puts as much care into making sure your stay is happy as he does into his menus. *(See advert Page 28.)*

Open all year except 22 to 29 Dec
🛏 Rooms: 10 with private facilities
🛏 DB&B £70–£95   B&B £49–£75
ⓢ Special rates available
✕ Food available all day £-£££
✕ Lunch ££-£££
✕ Dinner £££
Ⓥ Vegetarians welcome
⚲ Children welcome
♿ Facilities for disabled visitors – non-residents only
⌇ No smoking in dining room

Gingered scallops with shredded deep-fried greens. Fillet of lamb with haggis sauce. Strawberry and peach compote with heather cream.

STB Highly Commended 😋 😋 😋 😋
💳 Credit cards: Mastercard/Eurocard, American Express, Visa, Mastercharge, Switch, Delta
🅜 Proprietors: Angela & David Wilson

36

36 Great King Street
Edinburgh EH3 6QH
Tel: 0131 556 3636
Fax: 0131 556 3663

Great King Street is off Dundas Street, the continuation of Hanover Street – 5 minutes from Princes Street.

Very modern restaurant in elegant Georgian basement.

- Contemporary interior design within New Town elegance.
- Best contemporary Scottish cooking.
- "This enchanting restaurant sets every sense tingling!"

A stunningly different modern restaurant. Although in a basement it is light, bright and airy. The minimalist, beautifully designed interior with modern yet comfortable furniture makes for a delightful atmosphere. The staff are all well-trained, professional but with an extra friendly quality which removes any pretentiousness often found in 'better' restaurants. They are rightly proud of their restaurant and this is conveyed in their manner. The cooking is skilful, by Chef Malcolm Warham, who uses the best fresh ingredients and his imagination to come up with inspired dishes. It is described as intrinsically Scottish with worldly influences.

....

    Open all year
✕ Lunch £-££
✕ Dinner ££
Ⓥ Vegetarians welcome
⚲ No smoking in restaurant

Carpaccio of prime Scottish beef with a Parmesan and basil cream. Roast canon of lamb with a sweet pepper, sausage and garlic fritter. A light rhubarb mousse set on a shortcake biscuit with a sweet ginger sauce.

⊞ Credit cards: Mastercard/Eurocard, American Express, Visa, Diners Club, Mastercharge, Switch, Delta
🅗 Restaurant Manager: Sophie Bagshaw

ATRIUM

10 Cambridge Street
Edinburgh EH1 2ED
Tel: 0131 228 8882
Fax: 0131 228 8808

Within Saltire Court, sharing entrance with Traverse Theatre, adjacent to Usher Hall.

Outstanding and individual modern restaurant of some style.

- Modern building – glass walls to 'Atrium'.
- Outstanding modern Scottish cooking.
- "A testament to forward thinking restaurant design and cuisine."

From its specially-designed oil-lamps to its overall decor, the Atrium is a striking example of modern Scottish design. Appropriately, the imaginative cooking here is as distinctive as the restaurant it serves. The restaurant's talented Chef/proprietor, Andrew Radford, has seen his success recognised informally by a devoted clientele. He has won a number of awards, including The Macallan Personality of the Year Award 1994. The restaurant he started offers an à la carte menu that is based on fresh local produce and changes twice daily. The Atrium also offers a snack menu available at lunchtime and in the evening for pre-theatre meals. Both menus are inspired, creative and well balanced, as befits the Atrium's deserved reputation: one of Edinburgh's foremost restaurants. Head Chef Glyn Stevens is an award-winning chef recognised by other leading organisations. Winner of The Taste of Scotland Scotch Lamb Challenge Competition Category 2 and Overall Winner 1997.

....

    Open all year except 1 wk Christmas
    Closed Sun
✕ Lunch except Sun Sat ££
✕ Dinner except Sun £££
Ⓥ Vegetarians welcome
⚲ Children welcome

Quail breast, olive oil mash, leek gravy. Whole roast sea bass, fine herb salad. Caramelised banana flan and vanilla cream.

⊞ Credit cards: Mastercard/ Eurocard, American Express, Visa, Switch, Delta
🅗 Proprietors: Andrew & Lisa Radford

THE BALMORAL HOTEL

1 Princes Street, Edinburgh EH2 2EQ
Tel: 0131 556 2414 Fax: 0131 557 3747

Princes Street at the corner of North Bridge at East End of Princes Street.

Edwardian luxury brought elegantly up to date.

- Sumptuous, elegant and distinguished hotel
- Variety of impeccable cuisines
- "A living landmark symbolising the epitome of excellence and quality."

Since its opening as the North British Hotel in 1902, The Balmoral has maintained its reputation as the embodiment of hospitality and ease. The hotel purchased by Rocco Forte early in 1997 and under this new ownership many improvements are planned. New Executive Chef Jeff Bland (formerly Cameron House, Loch Lomond) oversees the hotel's principal restaurant – the spacious and elegant No. 1 Princes St. – offering outstanding classically-orientated cooking which is exquisitely presented and served. Alternatively, the hotel's Brasserie offers an all day service of light meals and snacks. Bar lunches are available in NB's Bar. In the Palm Court lounge enjoy afternoon tea whilst a harpist plays. For food, ambience and service, this hotel deserves its reputation for all round excellence. The Balmoral has 2 AA Rosettes. Winner of The Macallan Taste of Scotland Hotel of the Year Award 1995.

Open all year
- 🏨 Rooms: 189 with private facilities
- 🛏 DB&B £169–£579   B&B £155–£565
- SP Special rates available
- ✗ Food available all day £££
- ✗ Lunch £-££££
- ✗ Dinner ££-££££
- Ⓥ Vegetarians welcome
- 🕿 Children welcome
- ♿ Facilities for disabled visitors
- 🚭 No smoking area in restaurants
- 🐂 Member of the Scotch Beef Club

Millefeuille of duck foie gras and potato rösti, Madeira sauce. Grilled sea bass with caviar, asparagus and artichoke ragoût. Grand Marnier soufflé with citrus sorbet.

STB Deluxe 👑 👑 👑 👑 👑
- 💳 Credit cards: Mastercard/Eurocard, American Express, Visa, Diners Club, Mastercharge, Switch, Delta, JCB
- 👤 General Manager: Stefan Bokaemper

BLUE BAR CAFE

10 Cambridge Street
Edinburgh
EH1 2ED
Tel: 0131 221 1222
Fax: 0131 228 8808

Adjacent to the Usher Hall. On the first floor of Saltire Court, above the Atrium and Traverse Theatre.

Modern, stylish bar cafe.

- Modern - part of theatre development.
- Appealing contemporary bistro style.
- "An assembly of food to set the taste buds tingling."

Unusually located within this unique theatre venue, this very stylish bar cafe is new to Edinburgh having just opened in July 1997. The brainchild of Andrew and Lisa Radford – proprietors of The Atrium (also located in the same building) – Blue aims to cater for the discerning diner who is looking for a more informal, whilst still an exceptionally high quality experience. The style of the interior is minimalist with space and light the key features. Well-designed and with some unusual features including oak tables for which the wood was imported from the Dordogne for this specific use. John Mark Rutter is Head Chef and was overall winner of the The Taste of Scotland Scotch Lamb Challenge competition 1997. The cooking is highly skilled and the menus offer great choice ranging from innovative soups and sandwiches to main meals.

Open all year except 1 wk Christmas
- ✗ Food available 12 noon –12 pm £
- ✗ Lunch £
- ✗ Dinner £
- Ⓥ Vegetarians welcome
- 🕿 Children welcome
- ♿ Facilities for disabled visitors

Mushroom risotto with pan-fried black pudding. Charred salmon and baba ganouj. Banana toffee biscuit ice cream.

- 💳 Credit cards: Mastercard/Eurocard, American Express, Visa, Switch
- 👤 Proprietor: Andrew Radford

CALEDONIAN HOTEL

Princes Street
Edinburgh EH1 2AB
Tel: 0131 459 9988
Fax: 0131 225 6632

West end of Princes Street at junction with
Lothian Road.

**A sumptuous city centre hotel that sacrifices
nothing to size.**

- Ex grand 'railway' hotel.
- Fresh, lively and world class.
- "An outstanding city centre hotel with the
  highest standards of excellence."

The 'Caley' has been a landmark and an Edinburgh
institution since it opened its doors in 1903. La
Pompadour Restaurant is situated immediately
above the hotel's front door, and affords engaging
views over the busy West End of Princes Street.
The Chef de Cuisine has combed old manuscripts
and investigated how Scottish cooks applied and
adapted classic methods in order to compose a
menu which is described as 'Legends of the
Scottish Table'. Service is state-of-the-art; the wine
list is exceptional; and the flavours are out of this
world. Downstairs there is Carriages – a modern
brasserie-style restaurant. *(See advert Page 25.)*

Open all year
⊞ Rooms: 246 with private facilities
🛏 B&B £70–£150
SP Special rates available
✗ Lunch (Carriages) ££
✗ Dinner (Carriages) ££
✗ Dinner (La Pompadour) ££££
Ⅴ Vegetarians welcome
🕇 Children welcome
♿ Facilities for disabled visitors
🚭 Smoking areas in restaurants
🐄 Member of the Scotch Beef Club

**Woodland mushrooms and Roquefort salad with
fried polenta. Pan-fried fillet of turbot with char-
grilled courgette in a lime and basil sauce.
Delicate summer pudding with a medley of ripe
berries.**

STB Highly Commended 👑 👑 👑 👑 👑
💳 Credit cards: Mastercard/Eurocard, American
Express, Visa, Diners Club, Switch, Delta
🙎 General Manager: Stephen Carter

CHANNINGS BRASSERIE

South Learmonth Gardens
Edinburgh
EH4 1EZ
Tel: 0131 315 2225/6
Fax: 0131 332 9631

From Central Edinburgh – Princes Street, West End,
cross Dean Bridge into Queensferry Road, then
right, just before pedestrian lights, into South
Learmonth Avenue and then right at the bottom.

**Charming private hotel of character in quiet
residential area.**

- Edwardian terraced town house.
- Innovative modern Scottish cooking.
- "Fresh flavours from around the world come
  together with style."

Originally five terraced townhouses in a smart
Edwardian terrace, Channings is a privately owned
hotel with the atmosphere of a gentleman's club.
The attractive features of the buildings have been
retained in the conversion, and furniture and
fabrics are tasteful; bedrooms are individually
designed. In the Brasserie, the interesting menus
change with the seasons and draw inspiration from
old classic European dishes. The ingredients are
fresh, and the house 'specials' are original and
delicious. Appropriate wines are suggested for
each dish. The atmosphere of the Brasserie is
relaxed and pleasant, and the garden adjacent to it
is used in the summer. The bar offers a wide range
of malt whiskies. Channings has 1 AA Rosette.

Open all year except 24, 26 + 27 Dec
⊞ Rooms: 48 with private facilities
🛏 DB&B on request   B&B £95–£120
SP Special rates available
✗ Lunch £
✗ Dinner ££
Ⅴ Vegetarians welcome
🕇 Children welcome
🚭 No smoking in brasserie

**Seared halibut fillet perched on pickled vegetables,
carrot and ginger oil. Glazed peppered duck with
pakchoi and crispy polenta cake. Chocolate torte
with a tuile basket of pistachio ice cream.**

STB Highly Commended 👑 👑 👑 👑
💳 Credit cards: Mastercard/Eurocard, American
Express, Visa, Diners Club, Mastercharge,
Switch, Delta
🙎 Proprietor: Peter Taylor

CREELERS SEAFOOD BISTRO BAR & RESTAURANT

3 Hunter Square, Royal Mile
Edinburgh
EH1 1QW
Tel: 0131 220 4447/4448
Fax: 0131 220 4149

The Square surrounds the back of the Tron Kirk on the Royal Mile at intersection with Bridge Street.

Seafood bistro bar and restaurant.

- Informal style in the heart of the Old Town.
- Innovative, contemporary cooking.
- "Up-to-date seafood menu offered in informal style."

A sister establishment to Creelers in Brodick (Isle of Arran – see entry), Tim and Fran James bring fresh fish and home smoked products from the island to their restaurant in the heart of Edinburgh, just off the High Street. The bistro bar has an informal atmosphere, with quiet decor and murals of Arran; the restaurant is more formal and exhibits the work of local and Arran artists (for sale) – an excellent feature here. Downstairs is a private room, seating 12–15 people. Head Chef Stuart Allan presents a lightweight table d'hôte menu and a lengthy à la carte menu, for lunch and dinner, featuring game and vegetarian dishes as well as Scottish seafood.

Open all year except Christmas Day,
Boxing Day + 2nd wk in Jan
Closed Sun Oct to Jun
🎷 Food available all day during Edinburgh
   Festival only £
✗ Lunch £
✗ Dinner ££-£££
Ⓥ Vegetarians welcome
🅿 No parking

A warm tartlet of creamed smoked haddock on tomato and basil coulis. Fillet of turbot on a bed of sautéed leeks with asparagus on a light lime beurre blanc. Lemon posset with fruit and shortbread.

💳 Credit cards: Mastercard/Eurocard, Visa, Switch
🎫 Proprietors: Fran & Tim James & Co Ltd

DRUM & MONKEY

80 Queen Street
Edinburgh
EH2 4NF
Tel: 0131 538 8111
Fax: 0131 220 5077

West end of Queen Street in New Town at corner with North Charlotte Street.

Fun, friendly yet stylish city bistro.

- Georgian ground floor and basement restaurant.
- Best contemporary bistro cooking.
- "Great atmosphere, excellent food, good value dining."

This establishment appears to be a wine bar at street level at first glance and indeed the ground floor is a popular meeting place with local business people and visitors where the atmosphere is relaxed and lively. Downstairs in the restaurant there is a slightly more formal feel, with much dark woodwork, gothic style niches and pew benches. This atmosphere is further enhanced by excellent service that manages to blend speed and efficiency with charm and friendliness. The cooking is contemporary, to a very high standard demonstrating good skills, and best use is made of quality ingredients.

Open all year except 25, 26 Dec, 1 + 2 Jan
Closed Sun evening
✗ Food available all day ££
✗ Lunch except Sun Sat ££
✗ Dinner except Sun ££
Ⓥ Vegetarians welcome
🧒 Children welcome
♿ Facilities for disabled visitors – limited

Avocado mousse, wrapped in gravadlax with a grain mustard dressing. Venison medallions with braised red cabbage, rösti potatoes and port jus. Sticky toffee pudding.

💳 Credit cards: Mastercard/Eurocard, American Express, Visa, Diners Club, Switch
🎫 Restaurant Manager: Claire Alderson

DUBH PRAIS RESTAURANT
123b High Street
Edinburgh EH1 1SG
Tel: 0131 557 5732
Fax: 0131 557 5263

Edinburgh Royal Mile, opposite Holiday Inn Crowne Plaza.

Genuine Scottish basement restaurant.

- Intimate basement.
- Contemporary Scottish cooking.
- Cooking here shows a real passion for fresh native ingredients."

Walking down the Royal Mile which leads from Edinburgh Castle to Holyrood Palace, look out for the sign of the black pot (in Gaelic 'dubh prais') down a few steps on the left in the High Street. Its imaginative chef/owner, James McWilliams, presents a well-balanced à la carte menu which devotes itself entirely to Scottish seasonal produce and regional recipes. The restaurant is popular with locals and tourists alike, and the dishes offered are described with patriotic fervour and are cooked using simple methods as the freshest produce requires.

Open all year except 2 wks Christmas + 2 wks Easter
Closed Sun Mon
- ✗ Lunch except Sun Mon £
- ✗ Dinner except Sun Mon £££
- Ⓥ Vegetarians welcome
- ☇ Children welcome
- ✰ Guests are asked not to smoke cigars or pipes

West Coast broth: light seafood soup flavoured with chilli. Fillets of ostrich, with thyme and wild mushroom sauce. Sticky toffee pudding.

- ▣ Credit cards: Mastercard/Eurocard, American Express, Visa, Mastercharge, Switch, Delta, JCB
- Ⅺ Chef/Proprietor: James McWilliams
- Ⅺ Proprietor: Heather McWilliams

DUCK'S AT LE MARCHE NOIR
2/4 Eyre Place
Edinburgh EH3 5EP
Tel: 0131 558 1608
Fax: 0131 556 0798

At the northern end of Dundas Street lies Eyre Place. Duck's lies near the junction of the two.

A relaxed and intimate Scottish restaurant with a hint of 'the garlic'.

- Highly regarded, cosy and intimate.
- Excellent modern French/Scottish cuisine.
- "A restaurant with some style and a flair for presentation."

Proprietor Malcolm Duck established this stylish restaurant which is tucked away in a quiet corner of the New Town. Award-winning chefs produce innovative and excellent Scottish-style cooking from fresh, local ingredients and the exceptional menu is well-presented with French undertones. Malcolm Duck takes justifiable pride in his extensive and spectacular wine list. Duck's at Le Marche Noir is relaxed and restful with attentive service, fresh flowers, candlelight and crisp linen all contributing to the ambience. Regional food and wine evenings from around the world are held once a month. A private dining room and special menus are available. The restaurant has 2 AA Rosettes.

Open all year except 25 + 26 Dec
- ✗ Lunch ££
- ✗ Dinner £££
- Ⓥ Vegetarians welcome
- ☇ Children welcome
- ♿ Facilities for disabled visitors
- ✰ No smoking room in restaurant

Haggis wrapped in filo on a bed of sweet potato with a thyme jus. Roast rack of lamb with onion confit and a port wine sauce. Hazelnut and apricot steam pudding garnished with caramelised oranges.

- ▣ Credit cards: Mastercard/Eurocard, American Express, Visa, Diners Club, Switch, Delta, JCB
- Ⅺ Proprietor: Malcolm Duck

HALDANES RESTAURANT

39A Albany Street
Edinburgh
EH1 3QY
Tel: 0131 556 8407

At the east end of the city centre – off Broughton Street.

Stylish restaurant in elegant Georgian New Town basement.

- Basement restaurant.
- Best modern Scottish cuisine.
- "The success of these award-winning owners deserves to be repeated here in Edinburgh."

Haldanes is a newly refurbished restaurant which has the feel of a country house hotel or country club. Run by George and Michelle Kelso, who previously ran award-winning Ardsheal House in Appin, the basement has a light and airy feel and has been tastefully furnished and decorated in keeping with the style of the building. Michelle continues to be front of house – a true professional who understands the meaning of good service and is committed to providing just that. George is masterful in the kitchen where he applies a light touch to excellent local produce with innovation and style.

Open all year
Closed lunch Sun Sat
✗ Lunch except Sun Sat ££
✗ Dinner £££
Ⓥ Vegetarians welcome
⯏ Children welcome
⌇ No smoking in restaurant

Pan-fried crab cakes with tomato salsa. Medallions of Highland venison served with a redcurrant and rosemary sauce. Caramelised lemon tart.

💷 Credit cards: Mastercard/Eurocard, American Express, Visa, Mastercharge, Switch, Delta
Ⓜ Proprietor/Chef: George Kelso

HENDERSON'S SALAD TABLE

94 Hanover Street
Edinburgh EH2 1DR
Tel: 0131 225 2131
Fax: 0131 220 3542

2 minutes from Princes Street under Henderson's wholefood shop, at the junction with Thistle Street.

Busy informal, city centre wholefood eaterie.

- Lively, informal, cosmopolitan basement bistro in New Town.
- Innovative and interesting vegetarian cuisine.
- "An appetising array of exciting, fresh vegetarian choices."

Henderson's was an established institution long before wholefoods became popular and its enviable reputation for excellent and inexpensive fare is as well deserved now as in Janet Henderson's day. The atmosphere here is always congenial and the counter-served helpings generous. Vegetarian salads, savouries, quiches and puddings are freshly prepared and eagerly consumed throughout the day with an unusual selection of real ales and wines, some Scottish and many organic also on offer. Henderson's still actively run by the family, appeals to all ages proving that wholefoods can be fun, especially Monday to Saturday nights when 'real' musicians enliven the wine bar.

Open all year except Christmas Day,
Boxing Day, 1 + 2 Jan
Closed Sun except during Edinburgh Festival
✗ Food available all day except Sun £
✗ Lunch except Sun £
✗ Dinner except Sun £
Ⓥ Vegans welcome
⯏ Children welcome
⌇ No smoking in main restaurant + wine bar areas

Celery and Dunsyre Blue soup with nutty malt bread. Spinach and lentil layered pancake served with tomato and basil sauce. Fresh and dried fruits with soured cream and stem ginger.

💷 Credit cards: Mastercard/Eurocard, American Express, Visa, Switch, Delta, JCB
Ⓜ Proprietors: The Henderson Family

HOLIDAY INN CROWNE PLAZA
80 High Street, The Royal Mile, Edinburgh EH1 1TH
Tel: 0131 557 9797 Fax: 0131 557 9789

Centre of the Royal Mile tourist area.

A new building designed to look old on Edinburgh's High Street.

- Large city centre hotel.
- Modern Scottish cuisine with European overtones.
- "A fine restaurant in a cosmopolitan hotel on Edinburgh's Royal Mile."

The Holiday Inn Crowne Plaza has been heralded 'the finest example of Scottish mediaeval architecture built in recent times'. Sympathetically designed to blend perfectly with its ancient neighbours, the building incorporates four original Royal Mile Closes. The hotel has two restaurants named after such Royal Mile Closes: Carrubber's bistro, which has an airy village square feel with window boxes and hand-painted murals, serves a selection of dishes from an international buffet – the ideal place to relax with friends; Advocates' is a stylish à la carte restaurant incorporating a striking turret feature looking out onto the Royal Mile. The tranquil elegant surroundings are ideal for enjoying a sumptuous speciality menu accompanied by a fine selection of wines. Under the guidance of Jean-Michel Gauffre, one of Scotland's top chefs, both restaurants are achieving an excellent reputation for fine food and convivial atmosphere.

Open all year except 24 to 27 Dec
🛏 Rooms: 238 with private facilities
🛏 DB&B from £71.50   B&B from £55
✕ Food available all day ££
✕ Lunch ££
✕ Dinner £££
Ⓥ Vegetarians welcome
🧍 Children welcome
♿ Facilities for disabled visitors

Salmon and truffle ravioli with citrus fruits, roquette leaves and lobster dressing. Collops of Highland venison with herb crust on a parsnip and chestnut crumble. Warm apple tart and cinnamon ice cream.

STB Highly Commended 👑 👑 👑 👑 👑
💳 Credit cards: Mastercard/Eurocard, American Express, Visa, Diners Club, Mastercharge, Switch, Delta, JCB
🍴 Food & Beverage Director: Jean-Michel Gauffre

HOWIES RESTAURANT
63 Dalry Road
Edinburgh
EH11 2BZ
Tel: 0131 313 3334

On the south side of Dalry Road, between Richmond Terrace and Caledonian Road, two minutes from Haymarket.

Small, informal restaurant offering smart bistro food.

- Bistro within old commercial and residential buildings.
- Modern Scottish with French influences.
- "Well flavoured food, presented with skill and integrity."

Howies has successfully gained a niche in the market with its appetising fare at reasonable prices. Much of its success lies in its idiosyncratic nature: off-beat location, eclectic selection of tables, chairs and even cutlery! Great care, however, is taken over the daily changing menus to create appealing choices. In keeping with its slightly spartan bistro character, customers may bring their own wine if they wish (£1.30 corkage charge).

Open all year except 25, 26 Dec, 1 + 2 Jan
Closed Mon lunch only
✕ Lunch except Mon £
✕ Dinner ££
Ⓥ Vegetarians welcome
🧍 Children welcome
♿ Facilities for disabled visitors

Pheasant, duck and bacon terrine, with blueberry compote. Pork fillet medallions, pan-fried in oatmeal with braised red cabbage and jus of pear, coriander and calvados. Banana crème brûlée.

💳 Credit cards: Mastercard/Eurocard, American Express, Visa, Switch, Delta

IGG'S RESTAURANT

15 Jeffrey Street
Edinburgh EH1 1DR
Tel: 0131 557 8184
Fax: 0131 441 7111

Jeffrey Street lies between the Royal Mile and
Market Street, behind Waverley Station.

Lively, stylish restaurant with a continental atmosphere.

- Elegant L-shaped restaurant.
- Many authentic Spanish dishes.
- "An elegant blend of contemporary Scottish-Spanish cuisine."

A small friendly owner-run restaurant in the heart of Edinburgh's Old Town – Igg's is an attractive and comfortable restaurant, decorated with taste. It is difficult to know whether to describe it as a Scottish restaurant with Spanish influences or vice versa. Tables are attractively dressed with linen; lighting is subtle. Iggy Campos, is enthusiastic, generous and laid back – an excellent host who sets a relaxed tone in his stylish little restaurant. At lunchtime a tapas menu is available as well as a good priced three/four course table d'hôte and à la carte evening menu. Igg's has 1 AA Rosette.

Open all year except 1 to 3 Jan
Closed Sun
✗ Lunch except Sun ££
✗ Dinner except Sun £££
Ⓥ Vegetarians welcome
✻ Children welcome
♿ Wheelchair access

Bresola of venison with beetroot and walnut compote. Fillet of monkfish grilled with olive oil and pink peppercorns. A light Marquise of white and dark chocolate mousse soaked in Tia Maria, with a sharp raspberry sauce and served with vanilla cream.

▣ Credit cards: Mastercard/Eurocard, American Express, Visa, Diners Club, Switch, Delta, JCB
Ⓜ Owner: Iggy Campos

JACKSON'S RESTAURANT

209-213 High Street
Royal Mile, Edinburgh
EH1 1PL
Tel: 0131 225 1793
Fax: 0131 220 0620

On the north side of the upper Royal Mile near to Cockburn Street.

Atmospheric cellar restaurant in Edinburgh's Old Town.

- Cellar restaurant with more formal dining upstairs.
- Modern Scottish cooking.
- "Contemporary Scottish cuisine in the heart of the capital."

Jackson's is on the High Street, the original thoroughfare and market place of the ancient city of Edinburgh. The cellar restaurant is open for both lunch and dinner, offering table d'hôte and à la carte menus (à la carte only in the evenings during the Festival) and its location attracts many tourists in this busy area. There is a bistro style feel to the cellar with alcoves, stone walls, pine tables, tapestries and discreet lighting. Upstairs there is a more formal dining room which can also be hired for private dinners. The table d'hôte 'business' lunch is creative and very well-priced; the à la carte majors on Scottish dishes, treated in unusual and original ways.

Open all year except Christmas Day + Boxing Day
✗ Lunch £
✗ Dinner ££££
✻ Extended hours during Edinburgh Festival
Ⓥ Vegetarians welcome

Pan-fried fillet of monkfish, black truffle dressing. Tender collops of ostrich on rich bramble and wild game jus. Wild raspberry and Drambuie brûlée.

▣ Credit cards: Mastercard/Eurocard, American Express, Visa, Switch, Delta
Ⓜ Proprietor: Lyn MacKinnon

KEEPERS RESTAURANT
13B Dundas Street
Edinburgh EH3 6QG
Tel/Fax: 0131 556 5707
Mobile: 0410 434812

At the southern end of Dundas Street, near the junction with Abercromby Place.

Elegant cellar restaurant with friendly atmosphere.

- Series of three adjoining cellar rooms.
- Traditional Scottish cooking.
- "Freshly prepared, honest Scottish ingredients served with enthusiasm."

As its name suggests, this well-established restaurant specialises in game – supported by fish, shellfish and prime meat. The cooking is traditional, with good sauces and rich jus; the menus are both table d'hôte (four starters, four main courses) and à la carte and the dishes are naturally presented. Although centrally located, just down the hill from George Street, Keepers has an attractive intimacy. The wine list is well-chosen and reasonably priced. The restaurant serves lunch and dinner on a table d'hôte and à la carte basis. Individual rooms (or, indeed, the entire place) can be booked for private or business functions.

Open all year
Closed Sun, Mon lunch + Sat lunch unless by prior arrangement
🍴 Note: Parties by prior arrangement
✘ Lunch except Sun Mon Sat £
✘ Dinner except Sun £££
Ⓥ Vegetarians welcome
⚘ Children welcome
🚭 No smoking area by request

Apricot stuffed quail in a red pepper coulis. Pan-fried scallops in a mustard sauce topped with a herb biscuit. Home-made Glayva ice cream in a chocolate cup with blackcurrant syrup.

💳 Credit cards: Mastercard/Eurocard, American Express, Visa, Switch
🅽 Proprietors: Keith & Mairi Cowie

LE CAFÉ SAINT-HONORÉ
34 North West Thistle Street Lane
Edinburgh
EH2 1EA
Tel: 0131 226 2211

Centre of Edinburgh, just off Frederick Street, 3 minutes from Princes Street. At Frederick Street end of lane.

Charming Parisian-style bistro serving fashionable Franco-Scottish dishes.

- Small relaxed restaurant.
- Contemporary Scottish cuisine.
- "A delightful oasis of French style, using best fresh Scottish foods."

Café St Honoré is located in a service street parallel to George Street. It was formerly an authentic French restaurant, was decorated accordingly and still has a Gallic charm. Its owners favour a more Scottish style of cooking, making good use of the produce available, although there are French influences in the preparation. The lunch and dinner menus change daily and are à la carte – realistically limited to about half a dozen starters and the same number of main courses, and very reasonably priced. The cooking is adventurous and highly professional; interesting combinations and fresh, innovative sauces appear regularly. Chef Chris Colverson is an outstanding vegetarian cook, and is delighted to prepare vegetarian dishes if given notice (they don't generally appear on the menu). One of 14 establishments shortlisted for The Macallan Taste of Scotland Awards 1997.

Open all year except Christmas Day, Boxing Day, 2 wks Easter and 1 wk Oct
Closed Sun except during Edinburgh Festival
✘ Lunch ££
✘ Dinner £££
Ⓥ Vegetarians welcome
⚘ Children welcome
🚭 No smoking area in restaurant
🅿 No parking

Crab and lobster with basil, tomato and artichoke. Noisette of venison with a parsnip purée and deep-fried leeks. Tarte tatin with vanilla ice cream.

💳 Credit cards: Mastercard/Eurocard, American Express, Visa, Diners Club, Mastercharge, Switch, Delta
🅽 Proprietors: Jerry Mallet & Chris Colverson

LE CHAMBERTIN RESTAURANT

21 George Street
Edinburgh EH2 2PB
Tel: 0131 459 2306
Fax: 0131 226 5644

City centre of Edinburgh, at eastern end of George Street between St Andrews Square and Hanover Street.

Accessible yet exclusive restaurant within an excellent hotel.

- An elegant, gourmet restaurant with a relaxed ambience.
- Modern/traditional Scottish cuisine with world influences.
- "Stylish and elegant yet very soothing – an oasis of calm delight in a busy world!"

Although within the highly regarded George Inter-Continental Hotel, Le Chambertin has developed a formidable reputation of its own, not least for its excellent and fairly priced business lunches. Restaurant Manager Barnaby Hawkes makes the most of the restaurant's grand and gracious ethos. Tables are well spaced out amid a splendid blue decor. The atmosphere is unhurried, calm. Menus are creative and well-balanced, with a good selection of game, fish, beef and lamb. Le Chambertin is fully air-conditioned. The excellent value wine list reflects the range of such gourmet cuisine. Chef de Cuisine, Klaus Knust, is a member of the prestigious Confrerie de Chaine des Rotisseurs. Le Chambertin has 1 AA Rosette.

Open all year except Boxing Day, 1 + 2 Jan
Closed Sun + Sat lunch
- ✘ Lunch except Sun Sat £££
- ✘ Dinner except Sun £££
- Ⓥ Vegetarians welcome
- ⚘ Children welcome
- ♿ Facilities for disabled visitors
- ⚯ No smoking area in restaurant

Selection of hors d'oeuvre from the cold table. Baked peppered salmon with a tossed green salad and Champagne dressing. Scottish and continental cheeses, oatcakes and grapes.

- 💳 Credit cards: Mastercard/Eurocard, American Express, Visa, Diners Club, Mastercharge, Switch, Delta
- 🗵 Restaurant Manager: Barnaby Hawkes

MARTINS RESTAURANT

70 Rose Street North Lane
Edinburgh EH2 3DX
Tel: 0131 225 3106

In the north lane off Rose Street between Frederick Street and Castle Street.

A first class restaurant tucked away in a back street.

- Small city centre restaurant.
- Creative contemporary Scottish cooking.
- "The restaurant prides itself on the integrity of its raw materials and it pays off."

Generally regarded as one of the best places to eat in Edinburgh, Martin and Gay Irons established their restaurant in 1983. It is small and discreet, tucked away in a cobbled service lane parallel to Princes Street, in the very heart of the city. Its modest exterior gives no clue to the excellence within: the interior is bright, fresh and pastel-hued, decorated with fresh flowers and good contemporary pictures, and cleverly lit; the dining room is a pleasure to behold. Chef Forbes Stott creates innovative dishes which allow the true flavours of the essential ingredients to come through (Martins buys its produce carefully, mainly from small producers). His menus are healthy and well-balanced, his style light; organic and wild foods are favoured. The exceptional cheeseboard, which is famous in its own right, features farmhouse unpasteurised Scottish and Irish cheeses. Service is good. Martins sets out to provide a 'total gourmet experience' – and succeeds. Martins is Runner-up in The Taste of Scotland Scotch Lamb Challenge Competition Category 2 1997.

Open all year except 23 Dec to 16 Jan, 26 May to 3 Jun + 28 Sep to 7 Oct
Closed Sun Mon
- ✘ Lunch except Sun Mon Sat ££-££££
- ✘ Dinner except Sun Mon £££-££££
- Ⓥ Vegetarians welcome – prior notice required
- ⚯ No smoking in dining areas

Savoury tartlet of wild mushrooms and broad beans. Roast saddle of venison with celeriac rösti, red cabbage and a juniper and thyme sauce. Toasted oatmeal parfait with a raspberry jelly.

- 💳 Credit cards: Mastercard/Eurocard, American Express, Visa, Diners Club, Mastercharge, Switch, Delta
- 🗵 Proprietors: Martin & Gay Irons

THE ROCK RESTAURANT
78 Commercial Street
Commercial Quay
Leith
Edinburgh EH6 6LX
Tel: 0131 555 2225
Fax: 0131 555 1116

From city centre follow signs to Leith. At bottom of Leith Walk take left into Junction Street, right at mini roundabout to Commercial Street. Turn first left to Dock Place then left into Commerical Quay.

Modern city restaurant overlooking new Scottish Office building.

- Modern stylish restaurant.
- Modern Scottish cooking.
- "An excellent city restaurant in fashionable Leith."

The Rock Restaurant is situated in probably the most fashionable area of Edinburgh, in a new development. It is run by John Mackay (formerly of the Rock Cafe in Howe Street) and his business partner and chef Peter Banks (formerly from Martins Restaurant, Edinburgh). This new restaurant offers exceptionally good food, all freshly prepared and presented in a modern style. Fans of the Rock Cafe will be pleased to know that the excellent burgers are still available – however this new menu also offers other delights for the gourmet using interesting combinations of spices and influences from other corners of the world. The restaurant is elegant, tasteful and modern in decor and the staff are friendly, polite and efficient.

Open all year except 24 Dec - 4 Jan incl
Closed Sun night, all day Mon + Sat lunch
✕ Lunch £-££
✕ Dinner ££-£££
Ⓥ Vegetarians welcome

Honey glazed confit of duck with potato galette and buttered leeks. Fillet of salmon baked in Chinese spices served with shredded leeks and broccoli in its own juices. Raspberry crème brûlée with a raspberry, mint and orange salad.

💳 Credit cards: Mastercard/Eurocard, American Express, Visa, Switch
🔥 Senior Partners: John Mackay & Peter Banks

THE ROUND TABLE
31 Jeffrey Street
Edinburgh EH1 1DH
Tel: 0131 557 3032

Off the Royal Mile and less than 5 minutes walk from Waverley Station.

An ideally located city centre restaurant-bistro.

- Unpretentious, no frills, inexpensive eating.
- Plain traditional cooking.
- "Good honest cooking in an informal bistro."

With its fine views over the city to the north, The Round Table takes its name from the shape of the tables on which it serves its simple, good fare. The ambience is informal and fun. No money has been wasted on creating a theme or pseudo-atmosphere: what you see is what you get. The cooking is based on fresh Scottish meats and fish. The lunch menu offers a fixed price option of outstanding value. The simple, two page wine list is well-chosen and fairly priced. Downstairs is a small private, non-smoking room available for private parties of up to 14.

Open all year except Christmas Day, Boxing Day + 1 Jan
✲ Closed Sun except during Edinburgh Festival
✕ Lunch except Sun £
✕ Dinner except Sun ££
Ⓥ Vegetarians welcome
☆ Children welcome

Norwegian style herring salad. Fillets of beef with shallots and red wine sauce. Scottish cheese plate.

💳 Credit cards: Mastercard/Eurocard, Visa, Mastercharge
🔥 Proprietors: Anne & Robert Winter

SHERATON GRAND HOTEL

1 Festival Square
Edinburgh EH3 9SR
Tel: 0131 229 9131
Fax: 0131 229 6254

Vehicle access Western Approach Road, 500 yards from junction of Princes Street and Lothian Road. Pedestrian entrance off Festival Square.

Popular and busy city centre hotel.

* Modern yet stylish.
* Scottish/International .
* "Every modern comfort and facility provided with superb cooking."

The Sheraton Grand Hotel is a modern hotel; and no expense has been spared in its furnishing and decoration; there is a 'Leisure Club' with pool, sauna, solarium and gym. The staff are extremely professional and well-trained, but they are also helpful and friendly. The hotel has two restaurants; The Grill Room and The Terrace. The latter overlooks Festival Square (and its fountain) and offers a sophisticated brasserie style menu. The former is formal and intimate: Executive Chef, Nicolas Laurent, is ex Waldorf, London, and brings international expertise to the finest raw ingredients available. The Grill Room has 3 AA Rosettes.

Open all year
🏨 Rooms: 261 with private facilities
🛏 DB&B £197.50–£234   B&B £162.50–£199
✖ Lunch (The Terrace) ££ (The Grill Room) ££
✖ Dinner (The Terrace) ££ (The Grill Room) ££££
Ⓥ Vegetarian menus available in both restaurants
🧒 Children welcome with special menu available
♿ Facilities for disabled visitors
🚭 Pipes and cigars after 9pm in The Grill Room
🚭 No smoking area in The Grill Room
🚭 Smoking is discouraged in The Terrace
🐄 Member of the Scotch Beef Club

Lasagne of red mullet with langoustines and red pepper coulis. Assiette of suckling pig with Xeres Vinegar and an Alsace pinot noir sauce. Pistachio macaroon with crème brûlée and dried strawberries.

STB Deluxe 👑 👑 👑 👑 👑
💳 Credit cards: Mastercard/Eurocard, American Express, Visa, Diners Club, Mastercharge, Switch
🍴 Executive Chef: Nicolas Laurent
🍴 Restaurant Manager: Jean-Philippe Maurer

STAC POLLY

8-10 Grindlay Street
Edinburgh
EH3 9AS
Tel: 0131 229 5405
Fax: 0131 558 8552

Opposite Sheraton Hotel off Lothian Road, 100 yards from Usher Hall and Lyceum Theatre.

Charming city centre restaurant offering stylish Scottish cuisine.

* Ground floor restaurant in residential street, close to Edinburgh Castle.
* Modern/Scottish cuisine.
* "A real treat to enjoy Scotland's produce so expertly presented."

Stac Polly, from which this restaurant takes its name, is a magnificent mountain on Scotland's West Coast. Proprietor Roger Coulthard, who also runs the restaurant of the same name in Dublin Street, has tastefully decorated Stac Polly to reflect the heather-clad hills, with tartan curtains to make for an air of cosiness. The strength of Stac Polly's menu is its originality. Chef Steven Harvey compiles menus which take full advantage of Scotland's glorious larder to provide exciting interpretations of modern and traditional Scottish cuisine. From a full to a light meal, choice and service are excellent. The wine list is small but selective and moderately priced and is complemented by a comprehensive malt whisky and Scottish beer list. Private rooms available by arrangement.

Open all year incl Sun
✖ Lunch £
✖ Dinner ££
Ⓥ Vegetarians welcome
🚭 Smoking area in restaurant

Salad of smoked duck with ogen melon, crispy bacon and sautéed potatoes with seasonal leaves laced with a mustard and lemon dressing. Baked loin of Border lamb coated in a honey mustard and herb crumble topped with a minted red wine sauce. Cranachan made with fresh cream, raspberries, toasted oatmeal, heather honey and Drambuie.

💳 Credit cards: Mastercard/Eurocard, American Express, Visa, Mastercharge
🍴 Proprietor: Roger Coulthard

THE WITCHERY BY THE CASTLE
Castlehill, Royal Mile
Edinburgh EH1 1NE
Tel: 0131 225 5613
Fax: 0131 220 4392

At the Castle end of the Royal Mile, just a few feet
from the castle entrance, opposite Camera
Obscura.

**Historically sited stylish restaurant with
fashionable food.**

- Formal restaurant.
- Stylish modern Scottish cuisine.
- "Exciting modern Scottish cuisine in a fabulous
  setting – bewitching!!"

The Witchery is situated right by the entrance to
Edinburgh Castle on a site that was once the
centre of witchcraft in the Old Town. It has been
decorated with immense style and taste and The
Secret Garden, converted from a former school
playground, is one of the most romantic dining
spots in the city. Lunch and dinner are table d'hôte
and à la carte with a choice of stylish and
interesting dishes. James Thomson's wine list is
spectacular with a large selection of excellent
wines from all the wine-growing countries. The
Inner Sanctum suite has its own private dining
room.

Open all year except Christmas Day
- 🏠 Rooms: 1 suite with private facilities
- ✕ Lunch ££
- ✕ Dinner £££
- 🗓 Reservations advisable

**Salad of cumin, cured loin of lamb with tomatoes
and coriander. Confit of tuna with herb risotto and
red pepper tapenade. Iced pear parfait with ginger
snaps.**

- 💳 Credit cards: Mastercard/Eurocard, American
  Express, Visa, Diners Club, Switch
- 🧑 Proprietor: James Thomson

DALHOUSIE CASTLE
Bonnyrigg, nr Edinburgh
Midlothian EH19 3JB
Tel: 01875 820153
Fax: 01875 821936

A7, 7 miles south from Edinburgh or north from
Galashiels. Signposted from traffic lights on A7 at
B704 junction. ½ mile journey.

**Historic castle hotel dating from 13th century,
family seat of Ramsays of Dalhousie.**

- Historical building with superb features.
- Traditional Scottish and French cooking.
- "Steeped in history with real atmosphere yet
  offering modern luxuries."

Splendour and history surrounds this 13th century
castle which was built over 700 years ago by the
Ramsays of Dalhousie. Situated amongst acres of
forest, parkland and pasture yet close to Edinburgh
and gateway to the north. Dalhousie is a memorable
place to visit. In a unique dungeon setting the
cooking is traditional Scottish with French
influences serving fresh local produce at its best.
Extensive classical function and conference rooms.

Open all year except 3 wks Jan
- 🏠 Rooms: 29 with private facilities
- 🛏 DB&B £79.50–£112   B&B £55–£87.50
- 🆂🅿 Special rates available
- ✕ Food available all day ££
- ✕ Lunch from £
- ✕ Dinner £££
- Ⓥ Vegetarians welcome
- 🧒 Children welcome
- 🚭 No smoking in dining room

**Curried West Coast mussels, roasted pepper and
lychees. Roast breast of chicken on a bed of haggis
and edged with a swede and ginger cream. Warm
scotch pancake with butterscotch ice cream and
cinnamon anglaise.**

STB Highly Commended 👑 👑 👑 👑 👑
- 💳 Credit cards: Mastercard/Eurocard, American
  Express, Visa, Diners Club, Switch, Delta
- 🧑 Director & General Manager: Neville Petts

HOUSTOUN HOUSE HOTEL

Uphall, West Lothian EH52 6JS
Tel: 01506 853831 Fax: 01506 854220

Just off A89 Edinburgh-Bathgate at Uphall.

Traditional Scottish baronial house with all modern luxuries.

* 16th century tower house in ancient grounds
* Country house cuisine.
* "Comfortable and elegant historic house offering high standards of comfort and cooking."

The core of the house is a substantial, early 16th century tower, built by Sir John Shairp, advocate to Mary Queen of Scots, and lived in by his descendants for 350 years. Its gardens were laid out in the 18th century, and include a 20 foot high yew hedge planted in 1722 and a cedar tree which is even older. Extensions and additions to the house – including the Houstoun Suite for banqueting and conferences – have been done sympathetically. The restaurant is situated in the former drawing room, library and great hall on the first floor – each of them delightful rooms, with 17th and 18th century panelling and plasterwork, beautifully furnished with antiques and pictures. The chef presents a sophisticated and well-balanced table d'hôte menu at lunch and dinner. His cooking is first class, and this is complemented by an award-winning wine list. *(See advert Page 29.)*

Open all year
🏚 Rooms: 73 with private facilities
🛏 DB&B £65–£95   B&B £45–£75
🆂🅿 Special rates available
✗ Lunch except Sat ££
✗ Dinner 4 course menu £££
Ⓥ Vegetarians welcome
✶ Children welcome
♿ Facilities for disabled visitors
🚭 No smoking dining room available

Salmon ravioli with crab, ginger and coriander mousseline. Red mullet on a tomato and herb risotto. Hot rhubarb and cinnamon soufflé on a ginger sabayon.

STB Highly Commended 👑 👑 👑 👑 👑
💳 Credit cards: Mastercard/Eurocard, Visa, Diners Club, Mastercharge, Switch
👤 General Manager: Irene Tilley

JOHNSTOUNBURN HOUSE HOTEL

Humbie, nr Edinburgh
East Lothian EH36 5PL
Tel: 01875 833696
Fax: 01875 833626

From A68 Edinburgh-Jedburgh 2 miles south of Pathhead, turn at Fala (hotel is signposted) – 2 miles on right.

A peaceful, charming country house hotel only 15 miles from Edinburgh.

* A beautifully restored and maintained Scottish baronial mansion
* Scottish cuisine.
* "Good Scottish cuisine offering the best local produce."

Built below the rolling Lammermuir Hills in 1625, Johnstounburn House stands in its own extensive, lovely grounds. The staff are welcoming and friendly, as is the ambience – open log fires, panelled and comfortable rooms. The hotel is a Thistle Country House Hotel. The table d'hôte dishes are excellent, making the most of good, local produce. The wine list is large – 70 bins – and concentrates on French and European wines.

Open all year
🏚 Rooms: 20 with private facilities
🛏 DB&B £70–£159   B&B £45–£120
🆂🅿 Special rates available
🍴 Lunch – reservation required ££
🍴 Dinner – reservation required £££
Ⓥ Vegetarians welcome
✶ Children welcome
🚭 No smoking in dining room

Sliced smoked Tobermory trout. Roast Ayrshire duck breast with an orange and Grand Marnier syrup. Poached pear on butterscotch, crème chantilly.

STB Commended 👑 👑 👑 👑
💳 Credit cards: Mastercard/Eurocard, American Express, Visa, Diners Club, Mastercharge
👤 General Manager: Ken Chernoff

MARRIOTT DALMAHOY HOTEL
& COUNTRY CLUB RESORT
Kirknewton
Midlothian EH27 8EB
Tel: 0131 333 1845
Fax: 0131 333 1433

7 miles west of Edinburgh along A71.

A large hotel and country club with two golf courses, sophisticated leisure facilities and comfortable accommodation.

- Restored Georgian country house in well-landscaped grounds just outside Edinburgh.
- International hotel cuisine.
- "A smart but relaxed country club atmosphere pervades this comfortable hotel."

Dalmahoy is the family home of the Earl of Morton, who converted it into a luxurious hotel about six years ago. The formal Pentland Restaurant is an elegant Regency style room, beautifully furnished, with splendid views towards the Pentland Hills. The menu is extensive, well-balanced and beautifully presented. The Marriott Dalmahoy also has a bistro style restaurant in the Leisure Centre. The hotel has 2 AA Rosettes.

Open all year
🏨 Rooms: 151 with private facilities
🛏 DB&B £62–£95　B&B £42–£75
SP Special rates available
✕ Food available all day ££££
✕ Lunch except Sat £££
✕ Dinner except Sat £££
Ⅴ Vegetarians welcome
🕴 Children welcome
♿ Facilities for disabled visitors
🚭 No smoking in restaurants
🐄 Member of the Scotch Beef Club

Flash-fried tiger prawns with black tagliatellini. Fillet of Aberdeen Angus beef char-grilled and topped with a pink peppercorn essence. Mille-feuille of praline cream.

STB Highly Commended 👑 👑 👑 👑 👑
💳 Credit cards: Mastercard/Eurocard, American Express, Visa, Diners Club, Switch, Delta
👤 Executive Chef: Mr Asson

THE MILL HOUSE
Temple, Midlothian EH23 4SH
Tel/Fax: 01875 830 253

Temple is 3 miles off A7 on B6372. Turn right after village sign. Mill House is beside church on right hand side.

Set in a charming riverside garden within conservation area of Knights Templar enclave.

- House of fine architectural detail refurbished in 1710.
- Skilled Scottish cooking.
- "Cordon Bleu cooking in a relaxed atmosphere in a most interesting and historic setting."

Mill House is set in a riverside garden within the conservation area of The Knights Templar. The garden has botanical interest throughout the year. Spring flowers and camomile lawn garden is open to the public on set days in the summer season. The house itself is interesting with fine architectural detail dating from its refurbishment in 1710. The interior is decorated to a high standard, very comfortable and offering many thoughtful additions for the guests. Caroline Yannaghas is a most welcoming hostess and treats her guests exceptionally well. Her cooking is highly accomplished, she is Cordon Bleu trained and uses only the best quality ingredients. A most relaxing place to stay.

Open Apr to Sep
🏨 Rooms: 3, 1 with private facilities
🛏 DB&B from £70　B&B from £35
SP Special rates available
🍴 Note: Available for dinner parties/Directors' Lunches
🍴 Non-residents – by arrangement
🍷 Unlicensed – wine supplied, if required
✕ Lunch – on request £££-££££
✕ Dinner £££-££££
Ⅴ Vegetarians welcome
🕴 Children over 14 years welcome
🚭 No smoking throughout

Hot asparagus mousse with chervil sauce. Rack of Scottish lamb with topping of onion and mint purée, served with garlic and port sauce. Apple tart with its own sorbet.

STB Highly Commended 👑
💳 No credit cards
👤 Proprietor: Mrs Caroline Yannaghas

NORTON HOUSE HOTEL

Ingliston, Edinburgh, Midlothian EH28 8LX
Tel: 0131 333 1275 Fax: 0131 333 5305

Take A8 west from Edinburgh – 6 miles from city centre – signposted on A8 just after airport turnoff.

Relaxed, yet efficient country house hotel with very high standards.

- Victorian mansion set in its own 55 acres of parkland.
- Gourmet/Scottish cooking.
- "A peaceful and luxurious retreat just minutes from city centre."

Recently refurbished in luxurious style, this 19th century country house is a Listed building. The hotel is part of Richard Branson's Virgin Hotel Collection. The hotel has two restaurants: The Gathering Bar and Bistro which offers a high quality family menu in a walled garden with a barbecue area 200 yards from hotel, and the Conservatory Restaurant. This is an extremely elegant, flower filled conservatory, which has been awarded two AA Rosettes for the excellence of its cooking. An experienced team of chefs cook the food for both venues and in the Conservatory you will be treated to an extensive à la carte menu, a lunch/dinner table d'hôte menu and a short Taste of Scotland menu. The dishes are imaginative – a combination of the unusual and the traditional, but even the latter are given a creative twist.

Open all year
- Rooms: 47 with private facilities
- DB&B £65   B&B £110–£175
- SP Special rates available
- ✗ Food available all day £-£££
- ✗ Lunch except Saturday ££
- ✗ Dinner from £££
- Ⓥ Vegetarians welcome
- ⚲ Children welcome
- ⚹ Facilities for disabled visitors
- ⤢ No smoking area in restaurant

Tartar of salmon with a Pernod and dill infusion. Seared loin of Border lamb with broccoli mousse and rosemary juice. Lemon and lime soufflé with lemon tuile biscuit.

STB Highly Commended 🏅 🏅 🏅 🏅 🏅
- Credit cards: Mastercard/Eurocard, American Express, Visa, Diners Club, Mastercharge, Switch
- General Manager: Alan P Campbell

MANSEFIELD HOUSE HOTEL

Mayne Road, Elgin
Moray IV30 1NY
Tel: 01343 540883
Fax: 01343 552491

Just off A96 in Elgin. From Inverness, drive towards town centre and turn right at first roundabout. At mini-roundabout, hotel on right.

A popular family-run hotel and restaurant.

- Town house hotel in country setting.
- Traditional Scottish cooking, with some French influences.
- "A very friendly hotel with a high standard of food and service."

Close to the centre of Elgin, this completely refurbished and restored former manse provides a comfortable retreat. It has excellent facilities to suit the commercial and private guest and the restaurant is especially popular with the local business community. The Head Chef, Scott Hood, presents a well-priced à la carte menu made up of classic Scottish dishes, using market available fish, meat and vegetables. The quality of his cooking has been recognised by an AA Rosette.

Open all year
- Rooms: 20 with private facilities
- DB&B £55–£85   B&B £55–£65
- SP Special rates available
- ✗ Lunch £
- ✗ Dinner £££
- Ⓥ Vegetarians welcome
- ⚲ Children welcome
- ⚹ Facilities for disabled visitors
- ⤢ No smoking in restaurant

Haggis gâteau: local haggis, creamed potatoes and neeps served with a whisky cream sauce. Darne of Moray Firth halibut lightly steamed, presented on a crayfish sauce. Warm sticky toffee pudding with toffee sauce.

STB Highly Commended 🏅 🏅 🏅 🏅
- Credit cards: Mastercard/Eurocard, American Express, Visa, Switch
- Owners: Mr & Mrs T R Murray

ROTHES GLEN
Rothes,
by Elgin, Morayshire
AB38 7AQ
Tel: 01340 831 254
Fax: 01340 831 566

Beside the A941, 6 miles south of Elgin and 3 miles north of Rothes.

Excellent country house hotel within a castle style building.

- Turreted baronial mansion.
- Traditional Scottish with modern influences.
- "This castle like building offers tranquillity and a superb dining experience."

Resident proprietors, Michael MacKenzie and Frederic Symonds have made a remarkable impression on Rothes Glen. They have a commitment to high standards and use of fresh Scottish produce that is immediately apparent. The building itself is very impressive and stands in ten acres of well-kept mature grounds with Highland cattle in fields fronting the hotel. Inside all is tranquillity with many of its fine Victorian features being retained. Cooking is accomplished by a chef who is highly skilled and taking courage from the new owners to broaden the menus and experiment with more modern combinations whilst still making the most of the excellent local produce to hand in Moray. Rothes Glen has 2 AA Rosettes.

Open all year
- Rooms: 16 with private facilities
- DB&B £70–£100   B&B £50–£80
- Lunch ££
- Dinner £££
- Vegetarians welcome
- Children welcome
- No smoking in dining room
- Member of the Scotch Beef Club

Gratin of fresh local crab served with pink grapefruit. Medallions of roe deer with red cabbage marmalade and a piquant sauce. Ecclefechan tart with yoghurt cream.

STB Highly Commended 👑 👑 👑 👑
- Credit cards: Mastercard/Eurocard, American Express, Visa
- Resident Proprietors: Michael MacKenzie & Frederic Symonds

THE OLD SCHOOLHOUSE RESTAURANT
"Tigh Fasgaidh," Erbusaig, Kyle
Ross-shire IV40 8BB
Tel/Fax: 01599 534369

Outskirts of Erbusaig on Kyle-Plockton road.

Delightful restaurant with three en suite bedrooms.

- A charming 19th century schoolhouse in its own grounds on the picturesque road between Kyle and Plockton.
- Imaginative modern cooking.
- "A charming dining out experience."

This old school has been tastefully converted by the owners Calum and Joanne Cumine into a small restaurant with three bedrooms, each of which is restfully decorated. The conversion has been sensitively done, and retains the character of the place, and the feel of the past, while providing the level of comfort required by today's guests. The cooking is imaginative and versatile, and makes good use of the wonderful fish, shellfish, meat and game so readily available in this unspoiled corner of the West Highlands. The menu is reasonably priced and the owners are delighted to cater for vegetarians. It is no wonder that this small restaurant has such a big reputation locally.

Open Easter to end Oct
- Rooms: 3 with private facilities
- B&B £19–£26
- Special rates available
- Dinner ££-£££
- Vegetarians welcome
- Children welcome
- Facilities for disabled visitors – restaurant only
- No smoking in restaurant

Smoked meats platter: venison, ham, lamb and duck served with fresh melon jelly. Local scallops served with bacon in a rich Glayva sauce. Raspberry pavlova.

STB Highly Commended 👑 👑 👑
- Credit cards: Mastercard/Eurocard, American Express, Visa, Switch, Delta
- Proprietors: Calum & Joanne Cumine

FINS SEAFOOD RESTAURANT

Fairlie, Largs, Ayrshire KA29 0EG
Tel: 01475 568989
Fax: 01475 568921

On A78, 1 mile south of Fairlie near Largs.

Fish farm, smokehouse, farm shop, cookshop and bistro/seafood restaurant.

- Renovated farm bistro.
- Imaginative, modern fish cookery.
- "Wonderful seafood in an informal country restaurant"

Fins is part of Fencebay Fisheries in Fairlie and fish of all kinds are cured and smoked by traditional methods; an agreement with the oyster farm across the way also provides them with scallops, prawns and other seafood (since they also have a fishing boat). So the fish at Fins is landed daily. The enterprise, owned by Jill and Bernard Thain, won the Scottish Seafood Product of the Year Award 1995 at the Scottish Food Proms. Chef Gillian Dick's lunch and dinner menus are à la carte, supplemented by a blackboard 'catch of the day' (there is also a steak dish for non-'fishies'). The cooking is modern and accomplished. The restaurant itself is situated in an old barn, very tastefully decorated (with a fishy theme), bright, friendly and cheerful. Service is excellent. A thoroughly good fish restaurant.

....

Open all year except Christmas Day,
Boxing Day + New Year's Day
Closed Mon
✗ Lunch except Mon ££
✗ Dinner except Mon £££
Ⓥ Vegetarians welcome
⚘ Children welcome – lunch only
⚹ Facilities for disabled visitors
⚞ Diners are requested to refrain from smoking
until after 2.30pm (lunch) + 9pm (dinner)

Scallop and artichoke soup. Poached duo of turbot and salmon with asparagus and a light squat lobster sauce. Home-made ice creams with speciality of Fins – prune and Armagnac.

⊞ Credit cards: Mastercard/Eurocard, American Express, Visa, Diners Club, Mastercharge, Switch, Delta
Ⓜ Owner: Jill Thain

THE GRANGE MANOR

Glensburgh Road
Grangemouth
Stirlingshire
FK3 8XJ
Tel : 01324 474836
Fax : 01324 665861

Just off M9. To Stirling – exit at junction 5, follow A905 for 2 miles (to Kincardine Bridge). To Edinburgh – exit at junction 6, turn right, 200 metres on right

Stately hotel on the outskirts of Grangemouth.

- Old manor with tasteful modernisation.
- Modern Scottish cuisine.
- "A good blend of old traditions with new - and great Scottish hospitality."

The Grange Manor is a stately old manor run by the Wallace family. Bill Wallace, an experienced and charming hotelier, enjoys personally greeting his guests and ensures that they feel at home in this comfortable hotel. Chef Ken Wilson offers fresh Scottish produce with inventive presentation and a simple but classic style of cooking. Both à la carte and table d'hôte eating is provided where game and fish feature with light and imaginative sauces, alongside traditional meats and poultry. The Grange Manor has 1 AA Rosette.

....

Open all year
🛏 Rooms: 37 with private facilities
🛌 DB&B £83.50–£98.50   B&B £60–£75
SP Special rates available
✗ Food available all day £££
✗ Lunch ££
✗ Dinner £££
Ⓥ Vegetarians welcome
⚘ Children welcome
⚹ Facilities for disabled visitors

Confit of gigot of Scottish rabbit with a shallot and fine bean salad. Pan-seared venison on pearl barley risotto with a gâteau of sweet potato. Orange croissant butter pudding with fresh custard and mint syrup.

STB Commended 👑 👑 👑 👑
⊞ Credit cards: Mastercard/Eurocard, American Express, Visa, Diners Club, Mastercharge, Switch, Delta
Ⓜ Proprietor: Bill Wallace

INCHYRA GRANGE HOTEL
Grange Road, Polmont
Falkirk FK2 0YB
Tel: 01324 711911
Fax: 01324 716134

Take B9143, junction 5, M9 motorway. Situated on border of Polmont/Grangemouth.

Extended country house hotel with function rooms and leisure facilities.

- Fully modernised and extended country house.
- Good hotel cooking.
- "Centrally based hotel with all facilities – ideal for business or touring."

Inchyra Grange traces its origins to the 12th century, but its internal lay-out and furnishings are modern. It stands in five acres of garden and park, and has a popular leisure club with swimming pool, sauna and steam baths, multi-gym, solarium and resident beautician. There are two restaurants: the first is in the Leisure Club, and features 'healthy meals and snacks'; the main restaurant specialises in classic Scottish cooking and offers extensive à la carte and table d'hôte menus. The hotel's central situation near Falkirk makes it popular as a business venue, for meetings and conferences, not to mention business lunches, and it also does a good trade in functions. A function room for 450 has just been completed. *(See advert Page 29.)*

Open all year
- 🏠 Rooms: 109 with private facilities
- 🛏 DB&B £59.50–£62.50   B&B £30–£55
- ✕ Food available all day £££
- ✕ Lunch except Sat ££
- ✕ Dinner £££
- Ⓥ Vegetarians welcome
- ✦ Children welcome
- ♿ Facilities for disabled visitors
- ✔ No smoking in restaurant

Tempura of Scottish langoustines with a coriander and papaya salsa. Pan-seared fillet of seabass with a saffron barley broth. Bitter chocolate torte with a hot whisky sauce.

STB Highly Commended 👑 👑 👑 👑 👑
- 💳 Credit cards: Mastercard/Eurocard, American Express, Visa, Diners Club, Mastercharge, Switch
- 🏅 General Manager: Mr Andy Burgess

KIND KYTTOCK'S KITCHEN
WINNER MACALLAN SPECIAL MERIT AWARD 1997 – BEST TEA-ROOM
Cross Wynd, Falkland
Fife KY15 7BE
Tel: 01337 857477

A912 to Falkland. Centre of Falkland near the Palace, turn up at the Square into Cross Wynd.

Bustling cottage tea-room in a uniquely historic village.

- Traditional Scottish tea-room in terraced cottage.
- Excellent home baking.
- "The tea room of your dreams – everything home-made and delicious."

Kind Kyttock's is situated in a charming 17th century terraced cottage overlooking the cobbled square in one of Scotland's most picturesque villages. Its two rooms are most attractive – comfortable, informal and cheerful, with a 'country tea-room' feel. And this is precisely what Kind Kyttock's is, a tea-room of outstanding quality, which has frequently won the Tea Council's Award for Excellence. Bert Dalrymple is its owner/cook, his baking is divine – including scones, oatcakes, pancakes and other Scottish delicacies – and as well as this he preserves his own fruits, jams, pickles and chutneys, roasts his own meats for sandwiches, makes his own soups, etc. No wonder the place is so popular with locals, and you can buy baking to take away when it is available.

Open all year except Christmas Eve to 5 Jan
Closed Mon
- ✕ Food available all day except Mon £
- Ⓥ Vegetarians welcome
- ✦ Children welcome
- ✔ No smoking throughout

Home-baked pancakes, scones, fruit squares, shortbread, wholemeal bread, stovies, cloutie dumpling. Locally grown vegetables used in Scotch broth and at salad table. Selection of teas available.

- 💳 Credit cards: Mastercard/Eurocard, Visa
- 🏅 Owner: Bert Dalrymple

CHAPELBANK HOUSE HOTEL
69 East High Street, Forfar
Angus DD8 2EP
Tel: 01307 463151
Fax: 01307 461922

Town centre – Forfar. 15 miles north of Dundee on A90.

A family-run hotel with an emphasis on service.

- Small, town centre hotel.
- Good, traditional home cooking.
- "High standards throughout, a most enjoyable meal experience."

Built in 1865 on the main road leading through the market town of Forfar, Chapelbank was once the home of the town's doctor. The present owners, Duthie and Edith Douglas, have converted and furnished it well. Standards of fittings are high throughout and the Douglas' take a special pride in their cuisine. Calm and spacious, the dining room is popular with local non-residents as a place where fair prices and fresh, straightforward produce meet in both a table d'hôte and an extensive à la carte menu. From a warm welcome to a simple but varied wine list, from freshly prepared porridge and cream among other things for breakfast, to service that is friendly and capable, Duthie and Edith know what they are doing and do it well.

Open 21 Jan to 4 Oct + 14 Oct to 31 Dec
Closed Sun evening + Mon
🛏 Rooms: 4 with private facilities
🚪 DB&B £54–£68 B&B £36–£50
♀ Restricted hotel licence
✗ Lunch except Mon £
✗ Dinner except Sun Mon ££
Ⓥ Vegetarians welcome
木 Children welcome
⅋ Facilities for disabled visitors
✑ No smoking in dining room + bedrooms

Roulade of chicken and duck with salad and spicy onion marmalade. Peppered Angus fillet steak finished with green peppercorns, brandy and cream. Fresh strawberry pavlova.

STB Highly Commended 👑 👑 👑 👑
💳 Credit cards: Mastercard/Eurocard, American Express, Visa, Switch, Delta, JCB
🗈 Owners: Duthie & Edith Douglas

KNOCKOMIE HOTEL
Grantown Road, Forres, Moray IV36 0SG
Tel: 01309 673146
Fax: 01309 673290

1 mile south of Forres on A940. 26 miles east of Inverness.

A timeless and elegant hotel overlooking the Royal Burgh of Forres.

- A rare example of Arts and Crafts Movement architecture – an elegant villa built in 1914 around an earlier building.
- The best of Scottish cooking with French influences.
- "First class Scottish produce, well-cooked and served in comfortable and interesting surroundings."

Ideally placed for visiting the castles, stately homes and distilleries of the north-east, this gracious country house offers guests first-rate accommodation and dining facilities. Part of the hotel's landscaped gardens are set aside to supply herbs and salad leaves; vegetables are grown locally, to order. Knockomie's resident director is Gavin Ellis, who is knowledgeable, courteous and hospitable, and his staff are smart and well-trained. The daily changing table d'hôte menu is carefully selected; the food is all local and fresh; cooking is 'modern classic'. The wine list is of especial interest – very well-priced, with some wonderful rarities; over 80 whiskies are also listed. Knockomie has 2 AA Rosettes.

Open all year except Christmas Day
🛏 Rooms: 16 with private facilities
SP Special rates available
✗ Lunch £
✗ Dinner 5 course menu £££
Ⓥ Vegetarians welcome
木 Children welcome
✑ No smoking in dining room
⅋ Facilities for disabled visitors
🐂 Member of the Scotch Beef Club

Wild mushroom and water asparagus terrine with a dill cream sauce. Pan-fried West Coast scallops with marinated cous cous and coriander beurre blanc. Drambuie iced soufflé.

STB Highly Commended 👑 👑 👑 👑
💳 Credit cards: Mastercard/Eurocard, American Express, Visa, Diners Club, Mastercharge, Switch, Delta, JCB
🗈 Resident Director: Gavin Ellis

RAMNEE HOTEL
Victoria Road, Forres, Moray IV36 0BN
Tel: 01309 672410 Fax: 01309 673392

A96 Inverness-Aberdeen, off bypass at roundabout at eastern side of Forres – 500 yards on right.

An attractive 'country house in town' conveniently close to the centre of Forres.

- Edwardian private house with a high standard of accommodation and hospitality.
- Fresh local produce well-presented in modern style.
- A distinguished family-run hotel with well-cooked local produce."

The Ramnee Hotel was built in 1907 as a private residence for Richard Hamblin returning to Scotland after a long career in the Indian Civil Service. Set in two acres of carefully landscaped gardens, the hotel enjoys a central location in Forres, a charming Victorian spa town on the Morayshire and Nairnshire border. The hotel's 20 bedrooms are tastefully furnished and fitted with all the extras you would expect in a first rate establishment. Food in Hamblin's Restaurant is characterised by generous portions imaginatively presented. A table d'hôte menu is available at lunchtime and there is a choice of excellent value table d'hôte and steak menus at dinner. The accompanying wine list is extensive and well-chosen. Lighter, more informal meals are available in Tippling's cocktail lounge. Ramnee has 1 AA Rosette.

....

Open all year except Christmas Day + 1 to 3 Jan
- ⌂ Rooms: 20 with private facilities
- 🛏 DB&B £51–£97.50   B&B £31.50–£69.50
- SP Special rates available
- ✗ Lunch £
- ✗ Dinner £££
- Ⓥ Vegetarians welcome
- ⚹ Children welcome
- ✘ No smoking in restaurant

Roulade of fresh and smoked salmon presented with a spinach and lime butter sauce. Saddle of lamb with caramelised shallots and a light garlic jus. Crème brûlée.

STB Highly Commended 🏵 🏵 🏵 🏵
- ⊞ Credit cards: Mastercard/Eurocard, American Express, Visa, Diners Club, Switch, Delta
- 👤 Director: Garry W Dinnes

BRAE HOTEL
Bunoich Brae, Fort Augustus
Inverness-shire PH32 4DG
Tel: 01320 366289
Fax: 01320 366702

300 metres off A82. Turn left to Bunoich Brae just before leaving Fort Augustus heading north to Inverness on A82.

In an elevated position overlooking Fort Augustus this is a family-run hotel with a period atmosphere and a warm welcome.

- A Victorian manse with fine views.
- International modern cooking.
- "A relaxed stay enhanced with high quality food cooked with flair and imagination."

This restored Victorian building stands in its own pretty grounds, looking out over Fort Augustus and the Great Glen, with spectacular views of the Caledonian Canal, River Oich and Loch Ness. The resident owners, Andrew and Mari Reive want their hotel to be a 'home from home' and go to great lengths to put their guests at ease. The enclosed verandah is ideal to sit in and lounge away wet days with a good book and the dining room is light and airy. Mari Reive is a talented chef and describes her style of cooking as 'international'. Her eclectic menus feature fresh fish, seafood and game from nearby Loch Lochy. Guests are also offered the very best of home-made breads and breakfast marmalade. The Brae Hotel has 1 AA Rosette.

....

Open mid Mar to Oct
- ⌂ Rooms: 7 with private facilities
- 👥 Non-residents – prior booking recommended
- ✗ Dinner ££-£££
- Ⓥ Vegetarians welcome – prior notice required
- ⚹ Children over 7 years welcome
- ✘ No smoking in dining room

Warm scallop and bacon salad. Spiced venison fillet with spiced cranberry sauce. Banana caramel meringue torte.

STB Highly Commended 🏵 🏵 🏵
- ⊞ Credit cards: Mastercard/Eurocard, American Express, Visa, Switch, Delta, JCB
- 👤 Owners: Andrew & Mari Reive

CRANNOG SEAFOOD RESTAURANT
Town Pier, Fort William
PH33 7NG
Tel: 01397 705589
Fax: 01397 705026

Fort William town pier – off A82 Fort William town centre bypass.

Founded by fishermen, this restaurant serves the finest Scottish seafood.

- Seafood restaurant.
- Fresh seafood, cooked simply.
- "Crannog is second to none for its fresh seafood."

The Fort William branch of Crannog is a small, octagonal, red-roofed building on the pier at Fort William. The decor is simple – white walls, blue carpet, comfortable chairs – and the room has splendid views over Loch Linnhe. When they are not admiring the view, diners can sometimes watch the catch being landed direct into the kitchen – and soon afterwards enjoy the freshest imaginable seafood. This is Crannog's philosophy: very fresh seafood in friendly surroundings. It works, and the restaurant is very popular, so it is advisable to book.

Open all year except Christmas Day + 1 Jan
- ✗ Lunch £
- ✗ Dinner ££
- Ⓥ Vegetarians welcome
- ✦ Children welcome
- ♿ Facilities for disabled visitors
- ✘ Smoking area in restaurant

Smoke house starter with a tangy lemon mousse. Pan-fried monkfish with a hint of Pernod and cream. Walnut tart.

- ⊞ Credit cards: Mastercard/Eurocard, Visa, Switch
- ◪ Managing Director: Finlay Finlayson

LITTLE LODGE
North Erradale, Gairloch
Wester Ross IV21 2DS
Tel: 01445 771237

Take B8021 from Gairloch towards Melvaig for 6 miles, situated ¼ mile beyond turning to North Erradale.

A charming converted crofthouse.

- Whitewashed crofthouse.
- Traditional Scottish and innovative cooking.
- "In every respect the Little Lodge offers Highland hospitality at its best."

Little Lodge stands on a heather-clad peninsula with splendid views towards the Torridon Mountains and Skye. Di Johnson and Inge Ford are charming and welcoming hosts, and have restored their home in a way which best displays its original features. All bedrooms are en suite. Outside, their own hens, sheep and goats roam; their garden provides vegetables and herbs. Di's imaginative marinades and sauces enhance the excellent seasonal local produce (especially freshly-landed fish from Gairloch itself), while Inge's home-made bread, oatcakes, yoghurt and preserves make breakfast a special treat. Little Lodge is an idyllic retreat with superb cuisine which has earned Di and Inge much praise. Winner of The Macallan Taste of Scotland Special Merit Award for Hospitality 1996.

Open Apr to Oct
- ▥ Rooms: 3 with private facilities
- ⇌ DB&B £45–£48
- SP Special rates available
- ✗ Residents only
- Ⓤ ♀ Unlicensed – guests welcome to take own wine + spirits
- ✗ Dinner ££
- Ⓥ Vegetarians welcome – by prior arrangement
- ✦ No children
- ✘ No smoking throughout

Wild venison pâté with sourdough baguette. Roasted monkfish with a garlic, fresh lime and tamari jus served on fine pasta. Blackcurrant parfait with raspberry coulis.

STB Highly Commended 🏵 🏵 🏵
- ⊞ No credit cards
- ◪ Proprietors: Di Johnson & Inge Ford

MYRTLE BANK HOTEL

Low Road, Gairloch
Ross-shire IV21 2BS
Tel: 01445 712004
Fax: 01445 712214

Close to the centre of Gairloch, just off B2081.

Seafront hotel in spectacular setting.

- Modern village hotel.
- Traditional Scottish cooking.
- "Combined good standards with pleasant informal atmosphere."

Myrtle Bank Hotel is a modern village hotel set amongst spectacular scenery in the centre of Gairloch in a quiet cul-de-sac. Its location makes it an ideal exploring base. The hotel has been run by local proprietors for 11 years and is popular with both locals and visitors to the area. The cooking is good and provides popular dishes in a simple, traditional style. Seafood is particularly tasty given the local catch! The extension of the restaurant and bar area is planned for later this year.

Open all year except New Year's Day
🏨 Rooms: 12 with private facilities
🛏 DB&B £51–£57   B&B £36–£42
SP Special rates available
✕ Lunch £
✕ Dinner £££
Ⓥ Vegetarians welcome
🕏 Children welcome
♿ Facilities for disabled visitors
🚭 No smoking in dining room

Herb crêpes stuffed with asparagus and cheese glazed with hollandaise sauce. West Coast lemon sole, lined with smoked salmon coated with bearnaise sauce. Orange and Grand Marnier parfait.

STB Commended 👑 👑 👑 👑
💳 Credit cards: Mastercard/Eurocard, American Express, Visa, Switch
🅝 Proprietors: Iain & Dorothy MacLean

THE OLD MILL HIGHLAND LODGE

Talladale
Loch Maree
Ross-shire
IV22 2HL
Tel: 01445 760271

On A832 at Talladale – 10 miles north of Kinlochewe and 10 miles south of Gairloch.

Converted old mill now Highland lodge.

- Attractive converted mill.
- Skilled home cooking.
- "Delightful food, hospitality and comfort awaits the traveller in this idyllic part of the Scottish scenery."

The Old Mill Highland Lodge is set in a delightful, peaceful haven overlooked by the impressive grandeur of the Mountain Slioch and surrounded by two acres of landscaped garden through which meanders a Highland stream and where glorious flowers, trees and shrubs abound. This is a charming and elegantly furnished house where Joanna and Chris Powell look after their guests with genuine warmth and charm. Chris is an enthusiastic cook and produces imaginative and colourful dishes utilising much locally sourced Highland produce, while Joanna uses her experience in the wine trade to complement the mouthwatering dishes with just the right wine. No TV or radio disturbs the tranquillity here where you can be at one with nature – and watch with delight the pinemarten who visits the kitchen sill each evening to eat bread and jam!

Open all year except 15 Oct to 15 Dec
🏨 Rooms: 6 with private facilities
🛏 DB&B £45–£65   B&B £35–£45
SP Special rates available
🅟 Residents only
✕ Dinner £££
Ⓥ Vegetarians welcome - by prior arrangement
🚭 No smoking throughout

Puff pastry tartlet with local monkfish. Fillet of Highland beef with a wholegrain mustard cream sauce. Eve's pudding with home-made cinnamon ice cream.

STB Highly Commended 👑 👑 👑
💳 No credit cards
🅝 Partners: Chris & Joanna Powell

INCHBAE LODGE HOTEL

by Garve
Ross-shire IV23 2PH
Tel: 01997 455269
Fax: 01997 455207

Situated on A835 Inverness-Ullapool road. 6 miles north west of Garve.

A small family-run hotel with a panoramic view of Ben Wyvis.

- Small country hotel.
- Modern Scottish cooking.
- "Wonderful location, views and cooking!"

A former Victorian hunting lodge. It stands in seven acres of lovely wild garden, including its own island with free trout fishing in the River Blackwater and clay pigeon shooting available, by arrangement. The lodge has an intimate cottage feel with bags of character. The 12 rooms are divided between the lodge itself and a cedar wood chalet nearby. The owners, Patrick and Judy Price, go to great lengths to make their guests comfortable. Patrick's menus are inventive with a choice of two starters, main course and pudding and table d'hôte; produce is all fresh and imaginatively cooked. Inchbae has 1 AA Rosette.

Open all year except 24 to 30 Dec
🏨 Rooms: 12 with private facilities
🛏 DB&B £56–£61   B&B £33–£38
SP Special rates available
✗ Lunch £
✗ Dinner 5 course menu £££
Ⓥ Vegetarians welcome
🎅 Children welcome
🚭 No smoking in dining room + bedrooms

Smoked salmon pots stuffed with fresh salmon, herbs and cream cheese. Pot roast pigeon braised slowly in red wine and brandy. Rhubarb fudge crumble.

STB Commended 👑 👑 👑
💳 Credit cards: Mastercard/Eurocard, Visa
👤 Proprietors: Patrick & Judy Price

CALLY PALACE HOTEL

Gatehouse-of-Fleet
Dumfries & Galloway DG7 2DL
Tel: 01557 814341
Fax: 01557 814522

1 mile along B727 from Gatehouse-of-Fleet exit off A75 Dumfries-Stranraer, 30 miles west of Dumfries.

Grand and imposing country house hotel.

- Palatial hotel overlooking its own loch and golf course.
- Fine traditional Scottish cooking.
- "With its golf course and swimming pool this is an excellent place to bring the family."

Approached by a long, sweeping drive through beautiful woodland, this mansion stands in its own 150 acres of grounds. Its marble pillars, floors and tables combine with gilt and fine plasterwork to recall the grandeur of the 18th century. The hotel's public rooms are elegant and grand, with fine views over the landscaped grounds. The traditional dining room offers flowers, candles and music from the grand piano. Menus concentrate on selecting and presenting good, fresh, local produce with style. A snack menu is available all day and a popular high tea is available for 'tiny guests'. Both menus change daily. There is putting, tennis and croquet outside and a swimming pool sauna and jacuzzi inside.

Open 7 Mar to 3 Jan
🏨 Rooms: 56 with private facilities
🛏 DB&B £60–£83   B&B £45–£56
SP Special rates available
✗ Food available all day £
✗ Lunch ££
✗ Dinner £££
Ⓥ Vegetarians welcome
🎅 Children welcome
♿ Facilities for disabled visitors
🚭 No smoking in dining room

Roast breast of pigeon with green peppercorn jus. Escalope of Cree salmon baked in a puff pastry lattice with a prawn and vegetable stir fry. White chocolate and caramelised hazelnut delight.

STB Deluxe 👑 👑 👑 👑
💳 Credit cards: Mastercard/Eurocard, Visa, Switch
👤 General Manager: Jennifer Adams

GLAMIS CASTLE
Estates Office
Glamis, by Forfar
Angus DD8 1RJ
Tel: 01307 840 393
Fax: 01307 840 733

6 miles west of Forfar on A94. From Edinburgh
81 miles, from Glasgow 93 miles.

**A self-service restaurant in the old kitchens
of the castle.**

- Picturesque historic castle.
- Traditional Scottish cooking.
- "An impressive display of Scottish home-bakes
  and light meals."

Glamis Castle is the family home of the Earls of
Strathmore and Kinghorne and has been a royal
residence since 1372. The building is a five storey
L-shaped tower block which was re-modelled in the
17th century and contains magnificent rooms with a
wide range of historic items. The restaurant is on
the ground floor in the converted old kitchens and
has retained many of the original fixtures and
fittings. It is a self-service operation with a
blackboard featuring 'daily specials' and excellent
home-cooked and baked dishes.

Open 29 Mar to 25 Oct – otherwise by
appointment only
✖ Food available all day £
✖ Lunch £
Ⓥ Vegetarians welcome
⚲ Children welcome
♿ Facilities for disabled visitors

**Home-made pâté. Salmon and spring onion
quiches. Home baking.**

STB Highly Commended Visitor Attraction
💳 No credit cards
Ⓜ Castle Administrator: Lt Col P J Cardwell Moore

---

78 ST VINCENT
78 St Vincent Street
Glasgow G2 5UB
Tel/Fax: 0141 248 7878

On the corner of West Nile Street and St Vincent
Street. Only a few minutes walk from both Queen
Street and Central Stations.

**Contemporary styled city restaurant in carefully
restored historic building.**

- Spacious dining in adapted Phoenix
  Assurance building.
- Modern cosmopolitan cooking.
- "Modern Scottish cuisine at a modest price."

Located in the well-known 'Phoenix Building' this
cosmopolitan restaurant is predominantly French
with a Scottish flavour. However there are also
influences from Japan and the Middle East which
combine to offer an eclectic menu. The carefully
restored interior features an original marble
staircase, some amazing metal work and a stunning
mural by Glasgow artist Donald McLeod. 78 St
Vincent offers excellent food, wine and ambience at
very reasonable prices.

Open all year except Christmas Day, 1 + 2 Jan
Closed Sun lunch
✖ Lunch except Sun £
✖ Dinner ££
Ⓥ Vegetarians welcome
⚲ Children welcome
♿ Facilities for disabled visitors
⚭ Separate smoking area

**Langoustine bisque with a rouille croûton. Fillet of
sole with a sorrel cream and chilled cucumber.
Banana and butterscotch pavlova.**

💳 Credit cards: Mastercard/Eurocard, American
Express, Visa, Switch, Delta
Ⓜ Director: Mike Conyers
Ⓜ Manager: Caron Jardine

BABBITY BOWSTER

16-18 Blackfriars Street
Glasgow G1 1PE
Tel: 0141 552 5055
Fax: 0141 552 7774

In the heart of Glasgow's merchant city – at the East End of city centre.

An atmospheric hotel with good Scottish fayre.

- An Adam building c. 1790.
- Scottish cooking.
- "Fine fresh produce, traditional dishes with a modern touch."

Babbity Bowster is a splendid building on the site of what was originally a monastery. It takes its unusual name from a dance 'The Babbity Bowster' from the late 18th century 'babbity' meaning 'bob at the' and 'bowster' being a bolster or large pillow. Babbity Bowster is described as a cafe/bar/hotel/restaurant and it performs all of these functions with an atmosphere of excitement and is known as one of the 'in places' in Glasgow's city centre. Though casual in appearance Babbity Bowster provides good quality meals all day, both in the Schottische Restaurant and in the bar and garden area. Quality food, good drink and intellectual conversation is the key to the success of this place together with Fraser Laurie's personal supervision.

Open all year except Christmas Day +
New Year's Day
Note: Restaurant closed Sun
🛏 Rooms: 6 with private facilities
🛌 DB&B £60–£85   B&B £45–£65
✕ Food available all day £
✕ Lunch £
✕ Dinner ££-£££
Ⓥ Vegetarians welcome
🧒 Children welcome

Fresh asparagus and tomato salad with pine nuts and raspberry dressing. Seasonal fish stew, a combination of salmon, halibut, prawns, mussels and scallops in a rich tomato and basil sauce. Traditional cloutie dumpling.

💳 Credit cards: Mastercard/Eurocard, American Express, Visa
🗝 Owner: Fraser Laurie

THE BRASSERIE

176 West Regent Street
Glasgow G2 4RL
Tel: 0141 248 3801
Fax: 0141 248 8197

Approach via Bath Street from city centre; turn left into Blythswood Street then left into West Regent Street. From outwith city, follow one way systems via Blythswood Square to West Regent Street.

City centre restaurant and brasserie.

- Restaurant in the heart of Glasgow.
- Modern Scottish cooking.
- "Informality combined with elegance."

This elegant brasserie lies close to both Glasgow's theatreland and its mercantile centre and is popular both with businessmen at lunchtime and theatre goers in the evening. The Brasserie has an impressive pillared facade, and inside there is a horseshoe bar and dining area with a Victorian atmosphere. It has an air of restrained elegance and the à la carte menu reflects this, with a good choice of freshly cooked dishes, both brasserie-style and more substantial. Flair, continental influences and modern cooking styles are evident, and the service is excellent.

Open all year except Christmas Day,
Boxing Day, New Year's Day + 2 Jan
Closed Sun
✕ Food available all day except Sun ££
✕ Lunch except Sun ££
✕ Dinner except Sun ££
Ⓥ Vegetarians welcome
🧒 Children welcome

Half dozen oysters natural or Rockefeller. Supreme of halibut with lime butter. Crème brûlée.

💳 Credit cards: Mastercard/Eurocard, American Express, Visa, Diners Club, Switch
🗝 Manager: Ryan James

THE BUTTERY
652 Argyle Street, Glasgow G3 8UF
Tel: 0141 221 8188
Fax: 0141 204 4639

Junction 19, M8 – approach by St Vincent Street and Elderslie Street.

Gourmet restaurant – in old tenement style.

- Converted tenement building.
- Innovative Scottish cooking.
- "One of Glasgow's most famous restaurants – wonderful food and excellence in every respect."

The Buttery is a perennial favourite and continues to be one of Glasgow's premier restaurants. The outside of this old tenement building gives no clue to the interior, which has a unique character, with pieces of church furniture and Victoriana lending the whole of the restaurant an air of comfort and charm. Polite, well-informed and unobtrusive service characterises The Buttery, which is efficiently run by Jim Wilson, a man with a reputation for high standards. Chef Willie Deans' à la carte menus are an appetising balance of traditional Scottish dishes treated in a novel way and with unusual combinations, exquisitely presented with lots of interesting textures and flavours. He also presents outstanding vegetarian and dessert menus. The luncheon menu is excellent value. The Buttery has 2 AA Rosettes. *(See advert Page 234.)*

Open all year except Christmas Day + New Year's Day
Closed Sun
✗ Lunch except Sun Sat ££
✗ Dinner except Sun £££
Ⓥ Vegetarians welcome
✄ Smoking of pipes + cigars is preferred in the bar

Pan-fried scallops on lemon grass cous cous and clarified lobster butter. Highland venison with vegetarian haggis on a raspberry and whisky jus. The Buttery Grand Dessert.

💳 Credit cards: Mastercard/Eurocard, American Express, Visa, Diners Club, Switch, Delta
🄽 Manager: Jim Wilson

THE CABIN RESTAURANT
996-998 Dumbarton Road
Whiteinch
Glasgow G14 9RR
Tel: 0141 569 1036

From Glasgow city take Clyde expressway, pass Scottish Exhibition & Conference Centre to Thornwood Roundabout. Follow sign to Whiteinch (½ mile). Restaurant on right-hand side.

A Victorian 'front room' on Dumbarton Road.

- Small city restaurant.
- Modern Scottish, with continental influences.
- "A brilliant restaurant – innovative cuisine and 'hostess extraordinaire' – Wilma!

The restaurant is the original front room of an Edwardian tenement building, and is decorated accordingly, with original Art Deco features, a sideboard with china ornaments, old pictures and mirrors. The atmosphere is informal and cheerful. Dishes from the table d'hôte menu (five starters, seven main courses) are cooked to order; the cooking technique is creative, confident and to a very high standard; menus change daily, according to what is available in the market. About 9 pm, Wilma arrives to hostess and to sing one hour later. She is larger than life, first visited the restaurant shortly after it opened, and now returns nightly to encourage guests to sing along and let their hair down. The BBC made a half hour TV programme about her in Las Vegas! Chef David Dempsey is now in charge of the kitchen.

Open all year except 1 to 14 Jan + 15 to 30 Jul
Closed Sun Mon
✗ Lunch except Sun Mon Sat £
✗ Dinner except Sun Mon £££
Ⓥ Vegetarians welcome
♰ Children welcome
♿ Facilities for disabled visitors
✄ Pipes and cigars not permitted

Loch Fyne mussel and saffron soup with red pimento pepper. Aberdeen Angus beef fillet with a ragout of wild mushrooms, braised onions and thyme scented jus. Hazelnut sponge filled with a dark chocolate mousse served with Mascarpone, redcurrant, Cointreau and vanilla syrup.

💳 Credit cards: Mastercard/Eurocard, Visa
🄽 Proprietors: Mohammad Abdulla & Denis Dwyer

CATHEDRAL HOUSE HOTEL
28/32 Cathedral Square
Glasgow G4 0XA
Tel: 0141 552 3519
Fax: 0141 552 2444

Take junction 15 from M8. Follow signs for Glasgow Cathedral. Hotel situated on Cathedral Square.

Small city hotel in baronial Listed building.

- Unusual hotel and restaurant in historic part of Glasgow.
- Modern Scottish.
- "Select little restaurant offering excellent food and historic ambience."

Cathedral House Hotel is located within a beautifully restored historic building and is within sight of Glasgow Cathedral and The Provands Lordship (Glasgow's oldest house). It is therefore a must for those with an interest in Glasgow's architectural heritage. Within the hotel there are two choices of dining for the visitor. The Restaurant on the first floor offers an elegant location to enjoy good modern Scottish cuisine in comfortable surroundings. This area along with the rest of the hotel has been tastefully refurbished, retaining original features in a stylish way. The bar/bistro on the ground floor offers more informal surroundings in which to enjoy food all day and is a lively and popular meeting place.

Open all year except Christmas Day,
Boxing Day + New Year's Day
Restaurant closed Sun
🏠 Rooms: 8 with private facilities
🛏 B&B from £45
🆂🅿 Special rates available
🆅 Vegetarians welcome
✖ Food available all day
✖ Lunch (Cafe Bar) ££
✖ Dinner (Cafe Bar): (Rest except Sun) £££
☆ Children welcome
♿ Limited facilities for disabled visitors in Cafe Bar only

Char-grilled peppers with feta. Grilled salmon in a light lemon and mustard sauce. Chocolate bread and butter pudding.

STB Commended Listed
💳 Credit cards: Mastercard/Eurocard, American Express, Visa, Diners Club, Switch, Delta
👤 Manager: Gregor Munn

CITY MERCHANT
97 Candleriggs
Glasgow G1 1NP
Tel: 0141 553 1577
Fax: 0141 553 1588

Facing City Halls in Candleriggs, in Glasgow's Merchant City. Candleriggs on right going east along Ingram Street.

Established seafood restaurant in converted former Post Office.

- City centre restaurant.
- Modern Scottish.
- "Informal maritime ambience and wonderful fresh seafood."

Candleriggs has been upgraded, the City Halls renovated and now opposite the City Merchant Restaurant has expanded, doubling its capacity to cope with demand. This restaurant is not only popular with the business community but also shoppers and visitors. The restaurant specialises in seafood, but also offers game, prime Scottish steaks and vegetarian dishes. Daily fish market 'extras' are offered on the blackboard: Loch Etive mussels and oysters, king scallops, lobster and turbot as well as exotics such as red snapper. Lots of other fish and shellfish on offer on any day. The wine list is extensive with a choice of over 60 bins, but a 'bin-end' blackboard offers excellent value.

Open all year except Christmas Day, 1 + 2 Jan
✖ Food available all day £-££
✖ Lunch £-££
✖ Dinner ££-£££
🍴 Booking advisable
🆅 Vegetarians welcome
☆ Children over 6 years welcome
♿ Facilities for disabled visitors
🚭 No smoking area in restaurant

Scallops and squid in ginger and oyster sauce with sesame seeds. Collops of venison and ostrich on a potato and chive scone, Madeira sauce and rowan jelly dressing. Mixed berries with toasted oats in Drambuie cream, home-made shortbread.

💳 Credit cards: Mastercard/Eurocard, American Express, Visa, Diners Club, Mastercharge, Switch
👤 Executive Head Chef: Andrew Cumming
👤 Proprietors: Tony & Linda Matteo

THE DRUM AND MONKEY
93-95 St Vincent Street
Glasgow
G2 5TL
Tel: 0141 221 6636
Fax: 0141 204 4278

On corner of St Vincent and Renfield Street –
approx 100 yards from Central Station.

City bar and bistro in converted bank building.

- Bank building.
- Modern Scottish.
- "Warm atmosphere enhanced by Victorian styling and memorabilia."

The Drum and Monkey was originally a downtown bank but today it has a warm and comfortable ambience where shoppers rest on wicker chairs and leather couches. A fine selection of beers especially real ales and continental lagers is readily available. Bar food is available, with a simpler menu thereafter of freshly prepared to order filled sandwiches and wholesome salads. But for the real food experience the adjoining bistro provides more elaborate lunches and dinners in the most intimate of settings, combining modern dishes with the more traditional Scottish classics. The Drum and Monkey was named 'Pub of the Universe' in 1995.

Open all year except 25, 26 Dec, 1 + 2 Jan
- ✗ Food available all day ££
- ✗ Sun brunch available in bar
- ✗ Lunch except Sun ££
- ✗ Dinner ££
- Ⓥ Vegetarians welcome
- ♿ Facilities for disabled visitors

Salad of poached egg, black pudding and smoked bacon. Fricassée of Scottish seafood, saffron potatoes and dill. Chocolate and toffee crème brûlée.

- 💳 Credit cards: Mastercard/Eurocard, American Express, Visa, Diners Club, Switch, Delta
- Ⓜ Bistro Manager: Lucie Moran

FROGGIES
53 West Regent Street
Glasgow
G2 2AE
Tel: 0141 572 0007
Fax: 0141 572 1117

From George Square take St Vincent Street, turn third right into Hope Street, then first right into West Regent Street.

French/Cajun restaurant in the heart of Glasgow.

- A spacious, city centre bistro/restaurant and bar.
- Eclectic cuisine.
- "Glasgow restaurant with French/American influence."

Froggies has the unforced style and vibrant atmosphere of a cafe/restaurant in Lyons or New Orleans. It is well supported by the local business community. Jean-Louis Turpin, its Toulouse-born proprietor, says that his goal is "to de-mystify the forbidding atmosphere of some French restaurants. To achieve this the restaurant offers a selection of French and Cajun dishes, using fresh Scottish produce." His chef, Philippe Avril (from Marseilles) presents a distinguished à la carte menu, a table d'hôte menu and a 'Repas d'Affaire'. All are very well-priced. Froggies recently opened a theme bar, 'New Orleans', within the restaurant. The menu includes an exciting selection of French, Cajun and Creole dishes using, as always, the best Scottish produce.

Open all year except Christmas Day,
Boxing Day, 1 + 2 Jan
Closed Sun
- ✗ Lunch except Sun £
- ✗ Dinner except Sun ££
- Ⓥ Vegetarians welcome
- ☓ Children welcome
- ⌇ Smoking area in restaurant

Thinly sliced grilled smoked salmon on a bed of lambs lettuce and fresh egg tagliatelle salad. Roast breast of Guinea fowl flambeed in Armagnac with a duo of black and white grapes. Strawberry creme brulee baked with fresh strawberry pieces.

- 💳 Credit cards: Mastercard/Eurocard, American Express, Visa, Switch, Diners Club, Delta
- Ⓜ Owner: Mr Jean-Louis Turpin

GLASGOW HILTON INTERNATIONAL

Camerons Restaurant, 1 William Street
Glasgow G3 8HT
Tel: 0141 204 5555 Fax: 0141 204 5004

Access from M8 to hotel, or via Waterloo Street and Bishop Street from city centre.

20-storey landmark in central Glasgow.

- International hotel with a leisure centre, shopping mall and beauty salon.
- Grand hotel cooking.
- "Luxury city centre hotel which meets its award-winning reputation."

This very luxurious city centre hotel lives up to its international reputation as one of Glasgow's best. Camerons Restaurant provides relaxed high quality dining in a traditional restaurant. Concentrating on the best and freshest Scottish produce Chef Mizzen cooks seafood and game to exceptional standards developing the flavours of the produce and complementing them with interesting accompaniments, served in the elegance of a hunting lodge. Within the hotel there is also Minsky's New York Brasserie which is an original delicatessen serving a wide variety of food all day long. Raffles Bar is set in the old Colonial style with ceiling fans and window shutters and The Scotch Bar has an impressive selection of malt whiskies. Awarded 'Executive Travel Magazine Hotel of the Year 1996'. Camerons has 2 AA Rosettes.

Open all year
- 🏤 Rooms: 319 with private facilities
- 🛏 B&B from £105
- ✗ Lunch (Camerons) except Sun Sat £££: (Minsky's) from £
- ✗ Dinner (Camerons) ££-££££: (Minsky's) from £
- Ⓥ Vegetarians welcome
- 🕯 Children welcome
- ♿ Facilities for disabled visitors
- 🚭 No smoking area in restaurant
- 🐄 Member of the Scotch Beef Club

Hot smoked Shetland salmon on wilted greens and syboes. Racklet of lamb with a thyme mousse, on a ragoût of woodland mushrooms and sauté potatoes. Iced Blairgowrie raspberry cranachan with lemon butter shortbread.

STB Deluxe 👑 👑 👑 👑 👑
- 💳 Credit cards: Mastercard/Eurocard, American Express, Visa, Mastercharge, Switch
- 👤 General Manager: Jean-Pierre Mainardi

GLASGOW MOAT HOUSE

Congress Road
Glasgow G3 8QT
Tel: 0141 306 9988
Fax: 0141 221 2022

Situated on the banks of the River Clyde, next to the SECC.

A luxurious ultra-modern skyscraper hotel in city centre, on banks of the River Clyde.

- Large, modern skyscraper hotel in the heart of Glasgow.
- Modern international cuisine.
- "This luxury hotel offers comfort, cuisine and service to the highest standard."

The Glasgow Moat House takes its theme from its splendid position on a former wharf, on the banks of the River Clyde: its fully equipped leisure area, its principal restaurant 'The Mariner', its carvery 'The Pointhouse', its cocktail bar the 'Quarter Deck'. Both of the hotel's award-winning restaurants provide standards not often encountered in large 'international' hotels. The Pointhouse is brasserie style, The Mariner (which has two AA Rosettes) fine dining. The style of cooking is modern, fresh and elegant: Scottish produce and international techniques.

Open all year
- 🏤 Rooms: 283 with private facilities
- 🛏 DB&B from £65   B&B £53–£125
- ✗ Food available all day (Pointhouse) ££
- ✗ Note: Buffet also available
- ✗ Lunch (Mariner) except Sun Sat ££-£££
- ✗ Dinner (Mariner) except Sun £££
- Ⓥ Vegetarians welcome
- 🕯 Children welcome
- ♿ Facilities for disabled visitors
- 🚭 No smoking areas in restaurants

Soufflé of crab and salmon with essence of vanilla. Loin of roe deer, shallot purée, jus of blackcurrants. Honey and praline mousse with oatmeal wafers.

STB Highly Commended 👑 👑 👑 👑 👑
- 💳 Credit cards: Mastercard/Eurocard, American Express, Visa, Mastercharge
- 👤 General Manager: Mrs Jela Stewart

PAPINGO RESTAURANT

104 Bath Street
Glasgow
G2 2EN
Tel: 0141 332 6678
Fax: 0141 332 6549

City centre, parallel to Sauchiehall Street and next block to shopping centre.

A city centre restaurant with a tremendous buzz.

- Basement of office building.
- Modern Scottish cooking.
- "I loved eating in this restaurant with a busy but unhurried atmosphere."

Situated in the basement of an old office building this restaurant celebrates its eighth anniversary this year, proving it is one which is here to stay. The decor is fresh and clean-cut with clever use of mirrors to give the illusion of more space. Papingo is the old Scots word for parrot and these abound in various styles and unusual places. The menu offers good value for money, lots of alternatives and is nicely balanced with lovely Scottish concoctions of fish, game, poultry, lamb and vegetarian dishes. All in all – first class. Papingo has 1 AA Rosette.

Open all year except 1 + 2 Jan
✗ Food available all day £-££
✗ Lunch except Sun £
✗ Dinner ££
Ⓥ Vegetarians welcome
⚘ Children welcome before 8pm
⚯ Separate no smoking area

Roasted vegetables on dressed leaves with honey, balsamic vinegar and garlic. Roast breast of chicken with tomato and sweet chilli sauce and grilled feta. Passion fruit tart with crème fraîche.

▣ Credit cards: Mastercard/Eurocard, American Express, Visa, Diners Club, Mastercharge, Switch, Delta
Ⅺ Owner: Alan C Tomkins

THE PUPPET THEATRE

Ruthven Lane
Glasgow, Hillhead
G12 9BG
Tel: 0141 339 8444
Fax: 0141 339 7666

In Ruthven Lane – off Byres Road in Glasgow's West End. Ruthven Lane opposite Hillhead underground station.

Excellent cuisine in a restaurant of individuality.

- Converted mews house.
- Modern Scottish cooking.
- "The Puppet Theatre offers intimate dining in several small rooms with Victorian ambience and excellent cuisine."

In converted mews premises behind Byres Road, this little restaurant is made up of little rooms providing intimate dining in a Victorian setting with the modern addition of a stylistic conservatory bringing the restaurant into the 1990s. The furnishings in the 'old' room are Victorian whilst the conservatory is 'modern' with a 'designer' feel to it. Opened in 1994 the Puppet Theatre has become one of the best restaurants in Glasgow with booking required weeks in advance for the weekends. The cooking is described by our Inspector as "first class" with best Scottish produce presented in modern Scottish style which looks great and with tastes that match expectation! One of 14 establishments shortlisted for The Macallan Taste of Scotland Awards 1997.

Open all year except Christmas Day, Boxing Day, New Year's Day + 2 Jan
Closed Mon
✗ Lunch except Mon Sat £-££
✗ Dinner except Mon £££
Ⓥ Vegetarians welcome
⚘ Children 12 years and over welcome
♿ Facilities for disabled visitors
⚯ Smoking area, if requested

Twice baked Stilton soufflé with poached pears in mulled red wine. Saddle of venison, fondant potatoes, root vegetables and game and chocolate sauce. Sweet crêpes (toffee, banana and pineapple).

▣ Credit cards: Mastercard/Eurocard, American Express, Visa, Mastercharge, Switch, Delta
Ⅺ Manageress: Giovanna Drovandi

RESTAURANT BOUZY ROUGE

111 West Regent Street
Glasgow
G2 2RU
Tel: 0141 221 8804
Fax: 0141 221 6941

City centre location on corner of West Regent and
Wellington Street. Approach via M8 from Charing
Cross and follow one-way system from Sauchiehall
Street.

**A vibrant city centre restaurant for casual and
gourmet dining.**

- Semi-basement corner site in heart of city
  centre.
- Scottish with international influence.
- "A restaurant full of fun, atmosphere and really
  good food."

Established in 1994, Restaurant Bouzy Rouge has
become the place for the 'in crowd' in Glasgow.
Unique designer furniture specially made to set the
scene accentuates the atmosphere of rich-
coloured walls, stone floors, bright tiles and
mosaics with complementary table settings and
glassware centred round a superb horseshoe bar
constructed from the same magnificently built
woodwork. The menu offers loads of options for
both special occasions and day-to-day business
and whilst using the best Scottish produce
introduces international dishes and themes. Look
out for the speciality nights also. Booking essential
despite being open all day and evening.

    Open all year except Christmas Day +
    New Year's Day
✗ Food available all day ££
✗ Lunch £-££
✗ Dinner ££
Ⓥ Vegetarians welcome
✦ Children welcome
♿ Facilities for disabled visitors

**Trio of Scottish puddings with an Orkney Cheddar
sauce. Seafood platter of lobster, dressed crab,
king prawns, oysters and smoked salmon with
frizzy leaves and new potatoes. Spiced peach
crème brûlée.**

▣ Credit cards: Mastercard/Eurocard, American
    Express, Visa, Diners Club, Mastercharge,
    Switch, Delta, Solo, Electron
⚑ Proprietors: Alan & Audrey Brown

STRAVAIGIN

28 Gibson Street
Hillhead
Glasgow G12 8NX
Tel: 0141 334 2665
Fax: 0141 334 4099

From M8 junction 17. From city centre take A82,
Great Western Road. Turn left down Park Road,
right onto Gibson Street. 200 yards on right hand
side.

Informal city restaurant in Glasgow's West End.

- Basement bistro restaurant.
- Eclectic menus.
- "Buzzing restaurant serving a wide range of
  dishes including Scottish influenced."

Stravaigin is situated in the basement beneath its
busy bar, popular with locals and students. The
name 'Stravaigin' means to wander, gather, and this
is the philosophy of proprietor Colin Clydesdale who
has collected new ideas and ingredients and adds
them to naturally produced local ones. The decor is
bistro style using bright pastel shades on walls and
wooden table partitions round walls. The walls are
hung with colour prints of Eastern scenes and
pictures of chillies and peppers – all of which
indicates the Eastern influence in the menus. There
is a vibrant atmosphere and cheerful and informal
service. The menus are eclectic and offer good
value for money. The cooking is highly-skilled and
dishes are presented with flair. Stravaigin has 2 AA
Rosettes.

    Open all year except Christmas Day,
    Boxing Day, 31 Dec + 1 Jan
    Closed Sun lunch
✗ Food available all day ££
✗ Lunch except Sun £
✗ Dinner ££
Ⓥ Vegetarians welcome
✦ Children welcome

**Pan-fried wild Scottish mushrooms with barley
risotto and a rich chicken and Madeira jus. Fillets
of Inverbervie mullet, roast onion celeriac mash,
fresh tomato and Arran grain mustard concasse.
Drambuie and heather honey ice cream with a wild
strawberry and elderberry syrup.**

▣ Credit cards: Mastercard/Eurocard, American
    Express, Visa, Diners Club, Switch, Delta
⚑ Manager: Carol S Wright

TWO FAT LADIES RESTAURANT

88 Dumbarton Road
Glasgow
Strathclyde
G11 6NX
Tel: 0141 339 1944
Fax: 0141 959 0957

In the heart of Glasgow's West End, 500 metres from Kelvingrove Museum/Park towards Byres Road.

An unpretentious fish restaurant in Glasgow's West End.

- Small contemporary restaurant.
- Fish a speciality, but offers meat and vegetarian as well.
- "Informal and straightforward style, producing skilfully cooked fresh dishes."

A small, busy restaurant at 88 Dumbarton Road (hence the name), in the contemporary modern style. The atmosphere is intimate, informal and cheerful. Chef/patron Calum Matheson's cooking is also very contemporary – 'Riverside Cafe-ish' – relying on utterly fresh ingredients, a searingly hot grill and the skilful use of fresh herbs. The results are extremely successful, the flavours of the fresh fish coming through well. The menu is table d'hôte (six starters, six main courses) and includes poultry, meat and vegetarian dishes. Pre-theatre supper Monday to Saturday. Advisable to pre-book.

Open all year except 1 to 12 Jan + Bank Holidays
Closed Sun
♀ Table licence
✘ Lunch Fri Sat only ££-£££
♨ Private Lunch Parties – by arrangement
✘ Dinner except Sun £££
Ⓥ Vegetarians welcome
ᕷ Children welcome
ᕫ Facilities for disabled visitors
⌇ No cigars

Japanese fish broth. Steamed sea trout with caviar, dill and vermouth sauce. Dark and white chocolate terrine with passion fruit sauce.

⊞ Credit cards: Mastercard/Eurocard, Visa, Switch
ℕ Proprietor: Calum Matheson

UBIQUITOUS CHIP

12 Ashton Lane
Glasgow G12 8SJ
Tel: 0141 334 5007
Fax: 0141 337 1302

Behind Hillhead underground station, in a secluded lane off Byres Road in the heart of Glasgow's West End.

One of Glasgow's best restaurants – a perennial favourite.

- A restaurant of character.
- Modern Scottish cooking.
- "Its appeal today is as good as when it first opened – wonderful food and surroundings to match."

The Ubiquitous Chip, known affectionately by its regulars as 'The Chip', was established in 1971 by Ronnie Clydesdale – it has been described as a 'legend in its own lunchtime'. It has also received a Michelin Red M, an award never before bestowed upon a Glasgow restaurant. The Chip is situated in a cobbled mews in Glasgow's West End. It has a spectacularly green and vinous courtyard area with a trickling pool and a more traditional dining room. The cuisine marries the traditional and original in innovative recipes and this variety is complemented by a wine list rated among the top 10 in Britain for quality and value.

Open all year except Christmas Day, 31 Dec + 1 Jan
✘ Food available all day
✘ Lunch ££
✘ Dinner £££
Ⓥ Vegetarians welcome
ᕷ Children welcome
ᕫ Facilities for disabled visitors

Pan-fried scallops on a roasted potato cake, stewed garlic and a chambery coral sauce. Marinated haunch of Argyllshire venison, sweet marag, saffron potatoes and wild mushrooms. Caledonian oatmeal ice cream with fresh fruit compote.

⊞ Credit cards: Mastercard/Eurocard, American Express, Visa, Diners Club, Mastercharge, Delta
ℕ Proprietor: Ronnie Clydesdale

YES BAR & RESTAURANT
22 West Nile Street, Glasgow G1 2PW
Tel: 0141 221 8044
Fax: 0141 248 9159

City centre between Gordon Street and
St Vincent Street. 2 minutes from Central
and Queen Street Stations.

Spacious, stylish and first-class city centre restaurant.

- Restaurant with public and private dining room, bar and brasserie.
- Modern Scottish cooking.
- "An outstanding restaurant with style and wonderful food."

Among his many accolades including Master Chef, Ferrier Richardson has led both the Scottish and British national culinary teams to international success in prestigious events. This restaurant in Glasgow's fashionable city centre bears his stamp both in the high standards of the food and wine served and the venue's stylishness and originality. As you would expect, food is outstandingly good, embodying the distinctive approach and innovative techniques that have established Ferrier Richardson as a master. The finest of Scottish dishes emerge beautifully presented to delight the taste buds. His wine list complements the menu with a balance and choice of wines to suit varied budgets. Given the quality of what is on offer here, prices are more than reasonable.

Note: Bar + Brasserie closed Christmas Day,
Boxing Day, 1 + 2 Jan
Restaurant closed all public holidays
Closed Sun
Restaurant + Brasserie closed Sun
✕ Food available all day (Brasserie) except Sun £
✕ Lunch (Restaurant) except Sun ££
✕ Dinner (Restaurant) except Sun £££
Ⓥ Vegetarians welcome
⚘ Children welcome
♿ Facilities for disabled visitors in Brasserie
🐄 Member of the Scotch Beef Club

Vodka cured salmon and caviar with baked new potatoes and sour cream. Roast peppered duck on a corn cake with rhubarb, apple and ginger reduction. Mango and apple jelly infused with lemon grass and served with coconut ice cream.

💳 Credit cards: Mastercard/Eurocard, American Express, Visa, Diners Club, Switch
👤 Managing Director: Ferrier Richardson

BEARDMORE HOTEL
Beardmore Street, Clydebank
Glasgow G81 4SA
Tel: 0141 951 6000 Fax: 0141 951 6018

Between Glasgow and Loch Lomond. Off A82, 8
miles from M8 junction 19 over Erskine Bridge or
approach from Glasgow along Dumbarton Road.

A modern, international hotel in an attractive setting (adjacent to HCI Medical Centre).

- Newly built within its own grounds, with views over the River Clyde.
- Award-winning, imaginative, international cuisine.
- "Modern state-of-the-art hotel providing luxury and comfort."

The Beardmore Hotel is ideally situated only 15 minutes from Glasgow city centre and the airport. Loch Lomond is just 25 minutes by car. Executive Chef, James Murphy, who trained with Anton Mossiman at the Dorchester, oversees both restaurants. The Waterhouse offers a well-stocked buffet in a light bright room with river views; and The Symphony Room, The Macallan Taste of Scotland Restaurant of the Year 1996, re-creates the atmosphere of a private dinner party at home. The service is efficient, friendly and relaxed.

Open all year
🛏 Rooms: 168 with private facilities
🛌 DB&B £50–£135   B&B £35–£120
SP Special rates available
✕ Food available all day ££
✕ Lunch from ££
✕ Dinner from ££
Ⓥ Vegetarians welcome
⚘ Children welcome
♿ Facilities for disabled visitors
🚭 Smoking area in restaurant

Symphony: Oak smoked sole, fondant potato and rioja essence. Guinea fowl breast, foie gras, Boudin, celeriac and kohl rabi. Nectarine 'milady'.

STB De Luxe 👑 👑 👑 👑 👑
💳 Credit cards: Mastercard/Eurocard, American Express, Visa, Diners Club, Mastercharge, Switch
👤 Director & General Manager: David Clarke

FIFTY FIVE BC

128 Drymen Road
Bearsden
Glasgow G61 3RB
Tel: 0141 942 7272
Fax: 0141 570 0017

On the main Drymen Road at Bearsden Cross.

A well-established bar and restaurant popular with locals.

- Small restaurant attached to a large wine bar.
- Modern Scottish cooking, with French influences.
- "This restaurant is a gem, offering wonderful cuisine – well worth a visit."

Fifty Five BC was, of course, the date that Julius Caesar first arrived in Britain: the restaurant has adopted this date as its name on account of the Roman remains that have been found nearby. Gary Fletcher, Head Chef, has continued to maintain the high standards for which Fifty Five BC has become known. His short à la carte menus are imaginative; his creations make ingenious use of fresh local produce and are beautifully presented and delicious. Robust bar meals (potato skins, burgers, pasta) are served daily. The style of the place is modern, light and airy. Service is casual. Fifty Five BC is particularly popular locally and deserves to be better known.

- ✗ Open all year except New Year's Day
- ✗ Lunch £-££
- ✗ Dinner £££
- Ⓥ Vegetarians welcome
- ☆ Children welcome
- ♿ Facilities for disabled visitors
- ⚞ No smoking area – bar food only

Chicken Caesar salad. Fillet of bream with sauce niçoise. Warm chocolate fondant with pistachio ice cream.

- 💳 Credit cards: Mastercard/Eurocard, American Express, Visa, Diners Club, Mastercharge, Switch, Delta, JCB
- 🗎 Proprietor: Hamish McLean

GLEDDOCH HOUSE HOTEL & COUNTRY ESTATE

Langbank, Renfrewshire PA14 6YE
Tel: 01475 540711
Fax: 01475 540201

M8 towards Greenock. Take B789 Langbank/ Houston exit. Follow signs to left and then right after ½ mile – hotel is on left.

Country house hotel in its own sporting estate overlooking the Clyde.

- First class country house hotel in lovely grounds.
- Modern Scottish cooking.
- "An elegant house offering outstanding food and impeccable service."

Gleddoch House Hotel was once the home of the shipping baron, Sir James Lithgow. It stands in a 360 acre estate with dramatic views across the River Clyde to Ben Lomond and the hills beyond. The estate allows the hotel to offer a variety of outdoor pursuits including an 18-hole golf course, horse riding, clay pigeon shooting and off-road driving. Public and private rooms are all decorated and furnished to a very high standard. The restaurant is spacious and gracious; the four course, table d'hôte menu is succinct but superbly cooked and presented by a highly professional chef. The hotel also has conference and private dining facilities and has been awarded 2 AA Rosettes.

- Open all year
- 🛏 Rooms: 39 with private facilities
- 🛏 DB&B £92.50–£127.50   B&B £60–£95
- SP Special rates available
- ✗ Food available all day £-££££
- ✗ Lunch ££
- ✗ Dinner ££££
- Ⓥ Vegetarians welcome
- ☆ Children welcome
- 🐄 Member of the Scotch Beef Club

King scallops and Oban mussels in pastry set on Pernod and chive cream. Seared Guinea fowl breast with Italian risotto. White chocolate and raspberry Delia.

STB Highly Commended 🏵 🏵 🏵 🏵 🏵
- 💳 Credit cards: Mastercard/Eurocard, American Express, Visa, Diners Club, Switch
- 🗎 General Manager: Leslie W Conn

THE HOLLY TREE HOTEL
Kentallen
Near Glencoe
Argyll
PA38 4BY
Tel: 01631 740 292
Fax: 01631 740 345

From Glasgow take the A82 to Glencoe, continue towards Ballachulish Bridge, then take the A828 Oban road to Kentallen. Hotel is 2 miles down this road on right hand side beside loch.

Beautifully converted former Edwardian railway station, set in a spectacular setting on the shores of Loch Linnhe.

- Converted Edwardian railway station.
- Modern Scottish.
- "Unique in architecture, this is a relaxing family hotel."

Lovingly restored in the classical 'Charles Rennie Mackintosh' style, the fixtures and fittings are of particular interest. All rooms overlook Loch Linnhe to the mountains of the Morvern Peninsula and beyond, as does the comfortable restaurant which also overlooks the floodlit gardens. Excellent quality fresh local produce, prepared with imagination, together with a friendly atmosphere, combine to make this a most relaxing place to enjoy the astounding scenery and location. *(See advert Page 28.)*

Open 1 Mar to 31 Nov
- ⌂ Rooms: 10 with private facilities
- 🛏 DB&B £50–£78   B&B £30–£57.50
- SP Special rates available
- ✕ Food available all day
- ✕ Lunch from £
- ✕ Dinner from £££
- V Vegetarians welcome
- ☀ Children welcome
- ♿ Facilities for disabled visitors
- ⌫ No smoking in restaurant

Grilled oysters topped with Isle of Mull cheese. Venison set on ginger parsnip purée with redcurrant and Moniack wine sauce. Drambuie iced parfait.

STB Commended 👑 👑 👑 👑
- ⊞ Credit cards: Mastercard/Eurocard, Visa, Switch, Delta
- ☒ Manager: Annette McFatridge

THE GLENISLA HOTEL
Kirkton of Glenisla
Alyth, by Blairgowrie
Perthshire PH11 8PH
Tel/Fax: 01575 582223
e-mail blake@easynet.co.uk

From south take A93 to Blairgowrie then A926 to Alyth (4 miles). Bypass Alyth to roundabout follow signs to Glenisla (12 miles). From north take B951 off A93 – follow signs to Glenisla (5 miles).

A 17th century coaching inn in a pretty glen.

- Historic old stone country inn.
- Imaginative home cooking.
- "A very friendly and welcoming inn set in beautiful surroundings."

Kirkton of Glenisla is two-thirds of the way up the glen, on the old Perth-Braemar coach route. The current inn buildings have been standing since at least 1750, and the inn itself may be older. Today it is a friendly local with an excellent pub. There is also a tastefully decorated small restaurant, with Georgian windows overlooking the glen. Simon and Lyndy Blake are justifiably proud hosts and welcome their guests warmly. The cooking reflects a degree of flair and style which has won the hotel an enviable local reputation. The menu changes daily with excellent use of local produce a feature – watch out for wicked puddings!

Open all year except Christmas Day + Boxing Day
- ⌂ Rooms : 6 with private facilities
- 🛏 DB&B £40–£55   B&B £32.50–£45
- SP Special rates available
- ✕ Lunch £
- ✕ Dinner ££
- V Vegetarians welcome
- ☀ Children welcome
- ♿ Limited facilities for disabled visitors
- ⌫ No smoking in dining room + bedrooms

A medley of smoked Glenisla venison and smoked breast of duck with a mango salad. Wild Esk salmon on a bed of Angus asparagus with a saffron sauce. Chocolate truffle cake and cream.

STB Commended 👑 👑 👑
- ⊞ Credit cards: Mastercard/Eurocard, Visa, Switch, Delta
- ☒ Proprietors: Simon & Lyndy Blake

MINMORE HOUSE
Glenlivet
Banffshire AB37 9DB
Tel: 01807 590 378 Fax: 01807 590 472

Take A95 from Grantown-on-Spey. Right after 15 miles B9008 – follow signs to The Glenlivet Distillery.

A country house hotel in the heart of whisky country.

- Converted Scottish country house with fine views over the River Livet.
- Imaginative country house cooking.
- "A delightful meal, friendly atmosphere, with peaceful setting."

The original home of the founder of The Glenlivet Distillery and standing adjacent to it, Minmore House lies in its own grounds close by the River Livet. The house retains very much the feel of a Scottish country house thanks to period furnishings and atmospheric decor. Roaring log fires and comfortable armchairs are welcoming features of the hotel's public rooms. Minmore has earned a well-deserved reputation for the quality of its cooking, drawing inspiration from the abundance of fresh locally produced ingredients, and serves a set menu that is changed daily. The cheeseboard is something of a speciality with a wide selection of Scottish cheeses attractively presented. To finish the evening, guests have the pleasure of choosing a night-cap from over 100 malt whiskies stocked at the bar. Weekly terms and short breaks available.

    Open 1 May to mid Oct
🏠 Rooms: 10 with private facilities
🛏 DB&B £50–£65   B&B £45
SP Special rates available
🍴 Bar + picnic lunches can be arranged for residents £
✗ Dinner 5 course menu £££
Ⓥ Vegetarians welcome
🧒 Children welcome
🚭 No smoking in dining room

Spinach roulade with basil, sundried tomato and pinenuts, Local salmon with watercress hollandaise. Fresh raspberry soufflé.

STB Highly Commended 👑 👑 👑 👑
£ Credit cards: Mastercard/Eurocard, Visa

BALBIRNIE HOUSE HOTEL
Balbirnie Park, Markinch Village
by Glenrothes, Fife KY7 6NE
Tel: 01592 610066 Fax: 01592 610529

½ hour equidistant from Edinburgh and St Andrews. Just off A92 on B9130. Follow directions to Markinch Village then Balbirnie Park.

Gracious and elegant country house hotel set in delightful parkland.

- Georgian country house, restored to original splendour.
- Original and accomplished.
- "Everything at Balbirnie is a delight, with many unexpected extras."

Built in 1777 and standing in a beautiful estate of 400 acres, Balbirnie is a Grade A Listed building of great architectural and historic importance. Owned and run by the Russell family, the house and grounds have been immaculately and lovingly restored. The dining room overlooks fine formal gardens and ancient yew hedges. The hotel has a reputation for fine dining and offering interesting dishes that use fresh and local produce. Balbirnie has 2 AA Rosettes. "There is an air of quiet, friendly efficiency pervading the whole establishment – outstanding." Winner of the Macallan Taste of Scotland Hotel of the Year Award 1996. Runner-up in The Taste of Scotland Scotch Lamb Challenge Competition Category 1 1997. *(See advert Page 24.)*

    Open all year
🏠 Rooms: 30 with private facilities
🛏 DB&B £79.50–£109.50   B&B £80–£112.50
SP Special rates available
✗ Lunch ££
✗ Dinner £££
Ⓥ Vegetarians welcome
🧒 Children welcome
♿ Facilities for disabled visitors
🐄 Member of the Scotch Beef Club

Steamed fillet of salmon with pearls of vegetables, basil, peas and white wine. Sautéed noisette of roe deer with spiced pear, wild mushroom tartlet, sauce of Arran mustard, honey, cream and red wine. Raspberry and Drambuie parfait.

STB Deluxe 👑 👑 👑 👑 👑
£ Credit cards: Mastercard/Eurocard, American Express, Visa, Diners Club
🅺 Proprietors: The Russell Family

DALMUNZIE HOUSE HOTEL
Spittal of Glenshee
Blairgowrie
Perthshire PH10 7QG
Tel: 01250 885 224
Fax: 01250 885 225

Approx 22 miles from Blairgowrie.

The hotel in the hills.

- Country house hotel.
- Traditional Scottish cooking.
- "The perfect location to relax and enjoy genuine Scottish hospitality."

Dalmunzie House Hotel is a substantial Victorian baronial mansion standing in its own 6,500 acre mountain estate. It has its own 9-hole golf course (every Sunday there is a 'Golf Marathon', non-golfers are partnered with good golfers); fishing, stalking and grouse shooting are available, and the ski slopes of Glenshee are not far away. The Winton family who own the hotel have lived in the glen for decades and are genuine and experienced hosts. The house has a wonderfully friendly atmosphere, with log fires and comfy chairs and is hospitable and informal – the tone set by Simon and Alexandra Winton. The menu is table d'hôte (four-five choices) with a couple of à la carte supplements. The cooking is homestyle but imaginative; everything is fresh and cooked to order.

Open 28 Dec to 1st wk Nov
🏠 Rooms: 17, 16 with private facilities
🛏 DB&B £63–£70 (3 to 6 days)   B&B £44–£57
SP Special rates available
✕ Lunch £
✕ Dinner ££-£££
V Vegetarians welcome
🕈 Children welcome
♿ Limited facilities for disabled visitors

Fresh West Coast mussels on a saffron and mixed herb risotto. Paupiette of local venison with a sorrel and garlic stuffing served with a wild mushroom and sloe gin jus. Blairgowrie raspberry cranachan cheesecake.

STB Commended 👑 👑 👑
💳 Credit cards: Mastercard/Eurocard, Visa
🅜 Owners: Simon & Alexandra Winton

ARDCONNEL HOUSE
Woodlands Terrace
Grantown-on-Spey
PH26 3JU
Tel/Fax: 01479 872 104

On A95, south west entry to town.

A carefully restored guest house.

- Elegant Victorian house furnished with antiques.
- French cooking using Scottish produce.
- "Comfortable and relaxing with a good meal to look forward to at the end of the day."

Ardconnel House, standing in its own mature gardens, is owned and run by Barbara and Michel Bouchard who recently took over the house which is elegantly furnished and decorated in keeping with the Victorian style. Michel is French and brings flair and skill to very good local produce whilst Barbara tends to the front of the house. Menus have a strong French influence yet stress the locality at the same time. Ardconnel offers excellent value for money and makes an interesting base in this popular part of the country.

Open Easter to 31 Oct
🏠 Rooms: 6 with private facilities
🛏 DB&B £42–£50   B&B £25–£33
SP Special rates available
✕ Residents only
🍽 Dinner – by arrangement ££
🕈 Children over 10 years welcome
🚭 No smoking throughout

Pheasant and pigeon terrine served with a port and wild blackberry jelly. Coq au vin in a burgundy and brandy sauce. Amaretto clafoutis maison.

STB Deluxe 👑 👑 👑
💳 Credit cards: Mastercard/Eurocard, Visa
🅜 Proprietors: Michel & Barbara Bouchard

THE ARDLARIG
Woodlands Terrace
Grantown-on-Spey
Moray PH26 3JU
Tel: 01479 873245

On A95 south west entry to town.

Comfortable and friendly country guest house with very good food.

- Carefully maintained Victorian country house.
- Fine Scottish cooking.
- "Relaxing and quiet surroundings with good service and food."

The Ardlarig is a fine country house, set in a large garden, built at the turn-of-the-century. It retains the grandeur and splendour of that time offering warm traditional Scottish hospitality, well-appointed rooms and fine food. Neil Cairns is an accomplished owner/chef – and excellent food, freshly prepared and presented, emerges from the kitchen making for a very pleasant Scottish experience. At dinner, table d'hôte and à la carte menus are available. Typical of the area – a large selection of Speyside and island malts are offered. Neil will often join guests for a glass of wine or a 'wee dram'. Please note that Neil also shares his home with two Persian cats.

Open all year except Christmas Day,
Boxing Day + New Year's Eve
- 🏠 Rooms: 7, 4 with private facilities
- 🛏 DB&B £38–£48   B&B £22.50–£25.50
- SP Special rates available
- 🍴 Picnic hampers/packed lunch only ££
- 🍽 Dinner – booking essential for non-residents ££
- V Vegetarians welcome
- ⚘ Children welcome
- ⚭ No smoking throughout

Highland broth laced with a Spey malt. Wild mountain hare pan-fried with a whisky and green peppercorn sauce and seasonal vegetables. Drambuie soufflé with raspberry coulis.

STB Highly Commended 👑 👑 👑
- 💳 No credit cards
- 👤 Owner/Chef: Neil Cairns

CULDEARN HOUSE
Woodlands Terrace, Grantown-on-Spey
Moray PH26 3JU
Tel: 01479 872106
Fax: 01479 873641

Entering Grantown on A95 from south west, turn left at 30 mph sign. Culdearn faces you.

A country house on the outskirts of Grantown.

- Victorian country house.
- Traditional home cooking.
- "Superb welcome and service with excellent Scottish cooking."

This charming deluxe establishment has achieved many accolades for the style in which it is run. Alasdair and Isobel Little are enthusiastic hosts, and quickly put their guests at ease. Their house itself is elaborately and expensively furnished throughout; service is professional and attention to detail meticulous. Isobel is a talented chef and prepares local produce in classic Scots ways. Fifty malt whiskies now on offer and an interesting wine list.

Open 1 Mar to 30 Oct
- 🏠 Rooms: 9 with private facilities
- 🛏 DB&B £45–£60
- SP Special rates available
- ✗ Residents only
- ♀ Restricted licence
- 🍴 Picnic lunches to order
- ✗ Dinner – residents only
- ⚭ No smoking in dining room
- 🐂 Member of the Scotch Beef Club

Smoked salmon terrine in cucumber and dill sauce. Pan-fried wild venison with port and juniper sauce and fresh vegetables. Raspberry and hazelnut roulade with fresh cream. Coffee and mints.

STB Deluxe 👑 👑 👑
- 💳 Credit cards: Mastercard/Eurocard, American Express, Visa, Diners Club, Mastercharge, Switch, Delta, JCB
- 👤 Proprietors: Isobel & Alasdair Little

MUCKRACH LODGE HOTEL & RESTAURANT
Dulnain Bridge
Morayshire PH26 3LY
Tel: 01479 851257
Fax: 01479 851325

3 miles from Grantown-on-Spey on A938 Dulnain Bridge – Carrbridge Road, 400 yards from Dulnain Bridge.

Traditionally built Victorian country house.

- Former shooting lodge.
- Modern Scottish cooking.
- "A worthwhile new addition to Taste of Scotland for 1998!"

Muckrach Lodge was formerly a Victorian shooting lodge. The house stands in ten acres of landscaped grounds overlooking the River Dulnain and has been tastefully refurbished in keeping with the style of the period, whilst allowing for modern requirements. The cooking is 'the' priority here, with the emphasis on interesting and flavoursome combinations, well-balanced and of excellent quality. The chef is young and enthusiastic about his subject. There are two restaurants here – the dining room and the Conservatory, both of which are well-furnished and tastefully appointed. James and Dawn Macfarlane, proprietors, have owned the lodge since late 1996 and are very much 'hands on' ensuring that their guests enjoy their stay at Muckrach. Muckrach Lodge has 1 AA Rosette.

    Open all year
- Rooms: 13 with private facilities
- DB&B £68–£78   B&B £45–£55
- Special rates available
- Lunch £
- Dinner £££
- Vegetarians welcome
- Children welcome
- Facilities for disabled visitors
- No smoking in restaurants

Terrine of veal sweetbreads and chicken livers. Wood pigeon on a pearl barley and chanterelles risotto with a beetroot jus. Chocolate Marquise with Amaretto ice cream.

STB Highly Commended 👑 👑 👑 👑
- Credit cards: Mastercard/Eurocard, American Express, Visa, Diners Club, Switch
- Proprietors: James & Dawn Macfarlane

GREYWALLS
Muirfield, Gullane, East Lothian EH31 2EG
Tel: 01620 842144
Fax: 01620 842241

At the eastern end of Gullane village (on the A198), signposted left as a historic building.

A historic hotel offering great charm and quiet elegance.

- An Edwardian architectural masterpiece.
- Refined country house cuisine.
- "A delightfully serene atmosphere envelops you as you cross the Greywalls threshold."

This charming, grand but understated house was designed at the turn-of-the-century by Sir Edwin Lutyens and his collaborator Gertrude Jekyll to be a holiday home for the Hon Alfred Lyttelton. It was one of the architect's favourite buildings and is deservedly listed as being of national importance. It became a hotel in 1948, and is still family-owned. Greywalls has a wonderful situation overlooking Muirfield Golf Course and the Firth of Forth. The hotel's lovely walled garden complements the serenity of the house itself, which still has the feel of a family home: relaxed, refined, elegant ... a perfect backdrop for the discreetly attentive service one meets with in this distinguished hotel. Chef Paul Baron's menus are table d'hôte. His cooking is deft and light, with classical influences: "a refreshing combination of well-chosen ingredients, interestingly blended." The wine list is exceptional. Greywalls has 2 AA Rosettes.

    Open mid Apr to mid Oct
- Rooms: 22 with private facilities
- B&B £87.50–£95
- Lunch ££
- Dinner ££££
- Vegetarians welcome – prior notice required
- Children welcome
- Facilities for disabled visitors
- No smoking in dining room

Warm white truffle risotto with crisp air-dried ham. Roast loin of venison with morel mushrooms and a Madeira sauce. Rich chocolate roulade with chocolate sauce.

STB Highly Commended 👑 👑 👑 👑
- Credit cards: Mastercard/Eurocard, American Express, Visa, Diners Club, Switch
- Manager: Sue Prime

MAITLANDFIELD HOUSE HOTEL
Sidegate, Haddington, East Lothian EH41 4BZ
Tel: 01620 826513
Fax: 01620 826713

Haddington on A1, take route to town centre. At east end of High Street take Sidegate (signposted Gifford and Lauder B6368) – about 300 yards – opposite St Mary's church.

This large modern hotel offers a high degree of comfort and two restaurants.

- A recently renovated and expanded large townhouse.
- Modern and classic Scottish cooking.
- "Relaxing country venue for a family meal."

Maitlandfield House Hotel is set in landscaped gardens within minutes of the centre of Haddington. The hotel provides high standards of accommodation and facilities. The 16 Kings Restaurant – named after the number of kings who have visited Haddington since 1124 – has a tent-like, canopied ceiling and offers candlelit dinner on polished wooden tables. The table d'hôte menus here use fresh local produce. Chef Mike Scotford trained at the Waldorf in London and offers a balanced menu with interesting influences. The Conservatory Bistro is more informal. The hotel also has a beer garden and children's play area.

Open all year
🏠 Rooms: 22 with private facilities
🛏 DB&B £39–£75   B&B £30–£60
SP Special rates available
✕ Food available all day ££
✕ Lunch £
✕ Dinner £££
Ⅴ Vegetarians welcome
🧒 Children welcome
♿ Facilities for disabled visitors

Confit of wood pigeon on a bed of roasted polenta. Fillet of turbot on crispy seaweed and tomato and butter sauce. Warm apricot tart served with home-made pink gin ice cream.

STB Commended 😋 😋 😋 😋
💳 Credit cards: Mastercard/Eurocard, American Express, Visa, Mastercharge, Switch, Delta
🧍 General Manager: Jacqui Scotford

MANSFIELD HOUSE HOTEL
Weensland Road, Hawick
Roxburghshire TD9 8LB
Tel: 01450 373988
Fax: 01450 372007

On the A698 Hawick to Kelso road. On the outskirts of the town.

An attractive newly extended mansion overlooking the outskirts of Hawick.

- Family-run small country house hotel.
- Traditional Scottish and contemporary cooking.
- "The MacKinnon family have run this hotel for over 12 years and continue to offer the same hospitality and commitment year upon year."

A Victorian mansion overlooking the River Teviot and the town itself and standing in 10 acres of well-kept terraced lawns and mature shrubs and trees. Approached by a private drive, the hotel is secluded and quiet, yet it is within walking distance of the town centre. The building retains many of its original features – panelled doors, open fireplaces, ornate plasterwork – and a modern extension provides a large open bar and terrace. The hotel has been owned and run by the MacKinnon family for the past 12 years and under their supervision Chef David Tate presents well-priced à la carte and 'business lunch' menus in the formal dining room, and bar meals are also available. As well as the usual grills, the à la carte menu features some unusual combinations and meats (hare, kid and duck livers). *(See advert Page 31.)*

Open all year except 26, 27 Dec, 1 + 2 Jan
🏠 Rooms: 12 with private facilities
🛏 DB&B £45–£75   B&B £30–£55
SP Special rates available
✕ Lunch £
✕ Dinner ££
Ⅴ Vegetarians welcome
🧒 Children welcome
♿ Facilities for disabled visitors
🚭 No smoking area in restaurant

Salad of smoked Teviot chicken. Grilled darne of salmon with a creamed celeriac, mussel and vegetable broth. Strawberries, lemon curd ice cream with a warm raspberry mousse.

STB Commended 😋 😋 😋
💳 Credit cards: Mastercard/Eurocard, American Express, Visa, Diners Club
🧍 Owners: Ian & Sheila MacKinnon

BONNERS

41 West Clyde Street
Helensburgh
Dunbartonshire G84 8AW
Tel: 01436 677677

On seafront between James Street and Colquhoun Street. Almost opposite Henry Bell Monument.

An informal little restaurant serving simply the best.

- Scottish tenement building.
- Modern Scottish cooking.
- "This is a delightful little jewel in the 'front street' of Helensburgh."

Bonners overlooks the Clyde, and is almost hidden in the row of tenement shops and ethnic restaurants. Walls are half-panelled, the wood painted French blue and the tops in clover pink hung with an assortment of contemporary pictures and Art Deco lights. There are many special little touches which make this a particularly pleasant place to enjoy a meal whether for business, pleasure or both! The menu places strong emphasis on the flavours and there are additional daily specials which Andy Bonner describes with pleasure, clearly loving the fresh Scottish produce on offer from Chef Alex Needham.

Open all year except Boxing Day, 1 + 2 Jan
✗ Lunch – by special arrangement + during Dec ££
✗ Dinner ££
Ⓥ Vegetarians welcome
☆ Children welcome

Loch Etive mussels cooked in a creamy cheese and leek sauce with bread chunks. Garden herb crumbed pork fillet with smoked cheese and bacon stuffing, enhanced with cider and caramelised red onion sauce. Bonners devilishly good chocolate timbale with blackcurrant coulis.

▣ Credit cards: Mastercard/Eurocard, Visa, Mastercharge, Switch, Delta
▨ Partner: Andrew Bonner

KIRKTON HOUSE

Darleith Road, Cardross
Dunbartonshire G82 5EZ
Tel: 01389 841 951
Fax: 01389 841 868
e-mail kirktonhouse@compuserve.com

Cardross is mid way between Helensburgh and Dumbarton on the north bank of the Clyde. At west end of Cardross village turn north off A814 up Darleith Road. Kirkton House drive ½ mile on right.

Pleasant family-run accommodation in tranquil location by the River Clyde.

- Old farm guest house.
- Home cooking.
- "A charming family-run guest house offering warm hospitality."

Kirkton House is a converted, late 18th century farmhouse built around a courtyard – described by its owners, Stewart and Gillian Macdonald, as a residential farmstead hotel. Stewart and Gillian are relaxed and friendly, and set out to make your stay as pleasant as possible. The public rooms have their original stone walls and rustic fireplaces – the fire in the lounge is lit on chilly evenings. Kirkton House has all the facilities of a small hotel, serves a homely dinner and a wonderful breakfast.

Open all year except 20 Dec to 13 Jan
🏠 Rooms: 6 with private facilities
🛏 DB&B £39–£53   B&B £28.50–£38.50
ⓢⓟ Special rates available
✗ Residents + friends of residents only
♀ Restricted licence
✗ Snacks served throughout day – residents only
✗ Dinner 4 course menu ££
Ⓥ Vegetarians welcome
☆ Children welcome
♿ Facilities for disabled visitors – downstairs rooms only
🚭 No smoking in dining room

Cockles and mussels in a brandy cream sauce. Pork in a light ginger sauce. Banana foster: banana flambé.

STB Highly Commended ♛ ♛ ♛
▣ Credit cards: Mastercard/Eurocard, American Express, Visa, Delta
▨ Proprietors: Stewart & Gillian Macdonald

NAVIDALE HOUSE HOTEL
Helmsdale
Sutherland KW8 6JS
Tel: 01431 821258
Fax: 01431 821531

¾ mile north of Helmsdale on main A9 road overlooking the sea.

A country house hotel in its own gardens and grounds overlooking the Moray Firth.

- Comfortable and friendly small hotel in dramatic Sutherland.
- Excellent home cooking with flair.
- "Country house hotel with excellent fish dishes."

Built as a shooting lodge for the Dukes of Sutherland in the 1830s, Navidale retains that atmosphere. Public rooms are elegant, spacious and well-appointed. Set in seven acres of woodland and garden that lead down to the sea Navidale affords dramatic views over the Moray Firth and the Ord of Caithness, alongside modern comforts. The hotel caters in particular for fishermen and outdoor enthusiasts. The property was acquired in 1997 and its new owners, with their professional team, aim to ensure that your stay at Navidale is a memorable one.

	Open 11 Jan to 1 Nov
♨	Rooms: 15 with private facilities
🛏	DB&B £45–£63　　B&B £24–£42
SP	Special rates available
⏬	Packed lunch available
✕	Lunch £
✕	Dinner £££
Ⓥ	Vegetarians welcome
✶	Children welcome
♿	Limited facilities for disabled visitors
🚭	No smoking in restaurant

Fresh Navidale langoustines served with crisp salad and garlic dressing. Prime Caithness sirloin served with a whisky, cream and mushroom sauce. Forest fruits crème brûlée.

STB Commended 👑 👑 👑 👑
- 💳 Credit cards: Mastercard/Eurocard, Visa, Switch
- Ⓜ Director: Guy Bailey

THE OLD MANSE OF MARNOCH
Bridge of Marnoch, by Huntly
Aberdeenshire AB54 7RS
Tel/Fax: 01466 780873

On B9117, less than 1 mile off A97 midway between Huntly and Banff.

A delightful country house hotel on the river Deveron in unspoilt Aberdeenshire.

- Secluded and peaceful, a small hotel of rare distinction.
- Outstanding creative cuisine.
- "Warm hospitality in this secluded elegant country house"

Renowned for its solitude and peace, this fine Georgian house was built in the 1780s as the manse for the ministers of Marnoch Old Church. Its owners Patrick and Keren Carter have preserved the Georgian elegance in a tasteful and sympathetic conversion to an intimate country house hotel. Using fresh local produce and, in season, herbs and vegetables from their own four acre garden, Keren Carter deserves her growing reputation for imaginative, fine cooking. Her four course dinner changes every day. Her breakfasts are unrivalled. For a small establishment, the wine list is a triumph, both familiar and adventurous and always reasonably priced. Fluent German spoken. The hotel has 2 AA Rosettes. The restaurant is being extended for 1998.

	Open all year except 2 wks Nov, Christmas + New Year
♨	Rooms: 5 with private facilities (2 further bedrooms to be added)
🛏	DB&B £69.30–£74　　B&B £42.30–£47
▤	Reservations essential for non-residents
✕	Dinner 4 course menu £££
Ⓥ	Vegetarians welcome – prior notice required
✶	Children over 12 years welcome
🚭	No smoking in dining room

Twice-baked goats cheese and herb soufflé. Pan-fried noisettes of lamb with a lavender-scented sauce. Honey and walnut tart with cardamom crème fraîche.

STB Deluxe 👑 👑 👑
- 💳 Credit cards: Mastercard/Eurocard, Visa, Delta
- Ⓜ Proprietors: Patrick & Keren Carter

TRAQUAIR ARMS HOTEL
Traquair Road, Innerleithen
Peebles-shire EH44 6PD
Tel: 01896 830 229 Fax: 01896 830 260

On A72 midway between Peebles and Galashiels.
Midway along Innerleithen High Street take B709
Yarrow. Hotel 150 yards on left.

**Friendly country hotel offering warm welcome in
attractive Borders village**

- An attractive Victorian village inn.
- Good home cooking.
- "Good Scottish fayre in welcoming and
  comfortable atmosphere."

A pleasant family-owned hotel close to the centre of
this small Borders town. It is a sturdy stone building in a
quiet street with a well-kept garden. The town, made
famous by Sir Walter Scott, is popular with visitors,
especially those looking for the cashmeres and tweeds
for which these parts are renowned. Hugh and Marian
Anderson run their hotel in a relaxed and friendly
manner with genuine concern for the comfort of their
guests. Extensive imaginative menus use fresh local
produce, and everything is cooked to order. You can
eat, depending on the weather, in the charming
secluded garden or beside the blazing fire in the dining
room. The bar prides itself in its real ales and there is a
range of full meals available all day. *(See advert Page
235.)*

Open all year except Christmas Day,
Boxing Day, 1 + 2 Jan
- ⌂ Rooms: 10 with private facilities
- ⊨ DB&B £39–£55   B&B £26–£42
- SP Special rates available
- ✕ Food available all day £
- ✕ Lunch £
- ✕ Dinner £££
- Ⓥ Vegetarians welcome
- ⚲ Children welcome
- ⚿ Facilities for disabled visitors – dining only
- ⚬ No smoking in dining room

Shetland smoked salmon. Fillet of Aberdeen Angus
Beef Hjatland. Scottish cheeseboard.

STB Commended 🌣 🌣 🌣
- ⊞ Credit cards: Mastercard/Eurocard, American
  Express, Visa, Diners Club, Switch, Delta
- ℕ Owners: Hugh & Marian Anderson

GORDON'S RESTAURANT
Main Street, Inverkeilor
by Arbroath, Angus DD11 5RN
Tel: 01241 830364

A92 Arbroath to Montrose, turn off at sign for
Inverkeilor

Cottage style restaurant with two rooms.

- Victorian terrace house.
- Classic/Scottish cooking.
- "A delight – fresh local produce cooked with
  skill, imagination and dedication."

This small restaurant is run by Maria and Gordon
Watson and their son Garry. Over the years they
have built up a reputation for excellent food. Being
so close to Arbroath and Lunan Bay, Gordon's
Restaurant has access to fresh catches; soft fruits
come from the berry fields which surround them;
herbs from their own herb garden. Chefs Gordon
and Garry are both in the kitchen, cooking from
scratch using classic recipes. Gordon is an
exponent of modern Scottish cooking and his
presentation is an art. The à la carte menu changes
regularly according to seasonal availability and the
range of dishes covers the spectrum of good
Scottish foods. Gordon's has 2 AA Rosettes.

Open all year except last 2 wks Jan
- ⌂ Rooms: 2 with private facilities
- ⊨ DB&B £38–£55   B&B £25–£30
- ✕ Closed Mon – residents only
- ✕ Lunch except Mon – residents only ££
- ✕ Dinner except Mon – residents only £££
- Ⓥ Vegetarians welcome
- ⚲ Children welcome
- ⚿ Facilities for disabled visitors
- ⚬ No smoking area in restaurant

En croûte terrine of chicken liver, layered with
pheasant and venison. North Sea halibut on a bed
of leaf spinach, with a citrus butter cream.
Chocolate and cognac mousse with a 'chrust'
biscuit.

STB Commended 🌣 🌣
- ⊞ Credit cards: Mastercard/Eurocard, Visa
- ℕ Proprietors: Gordon & Maria Watson

BUNCHREW HOUSE HOTEL

Inverness, Inverness-shire IV3 6TA
Tel: 01463 234917
Fax: 01463 710620

On A862 Inverness-Beauly, c. 10 minutes from centre of Inverness.

17th century country mansion set on the beautiful shores of the Beauly Firth.

- 17th century mansion.
- Excellent Scottish cooking with an imaginative modern flair.
- "The award-winning chef Walter Walker offers exquisite cuisine with first-class presentation."

Bunchrew House Hotel is a short way out of Inverness nestling on the shores of the Beauly Firth, in 20 acres of woodland. The magnificent dining room overlooks the sea where menus are innovative and interesting, and, like the rest of the house, the attention to detail is painstaking. Chef Walker's cooking embraces a variety of traditional and modern styles, with a penchant for deliciously complex sauces. Bunchrew has a well-deserved reputation for offering the finest food under Chef Walker's skilful eye and does not fail to impress. Bunchrew House Hotel has 1 AA Rosette. *(See advert Page 25.)*

Open all year
🏠 Rooms: 11 with private facilities
🛏 B&B £40–£70
SP Special rates available
✗ Food available all day £££
✗ Lunch ££
✗ Dinner £££
Ⓥ Vegetarians welcome
🕯 Children welcome
♿ Facilities for disabled visitors
🚭 No smoking in dining room
🐄 Member of the Scotch Beef Club

Salad of lobster and sole mousse with dill and lime mayonnaise. Assiette of birds served with a honey and clove sauce. Caramelised lemon tart with Armagnac sauce.

STB Highly Commended 👑 👑 👑 👑
💳 Credit cards: Mastercard/Eurocard, American Express, Visa
🗡 Proprietors: Stewart & Lesley Dykes

CAFE 1

75 Castle Street
Inverness
IV2 3EA
Tel: 01463 226200
Fax: 01463 716363

Centrally located on Castle Street near castle.

City restaurant.

- Intimate yet modern restaurant.
- Modern Scottish cooking.
- "A unique dining experience."

Cafe 1 is a modern designed restaurant with a classical slant. Head Chef Barry MacKenzie uses Scottish products giving them an international application which results in high quality, well-presented dishes which are just that little bit different. Menus change with the seasons and are served with market vegetables of the day. A most interesting place to enjoy lunch or dinner in Scotland's capital of the Highlands.

Open all year except Christmas Day, Boxing Day + New Year's Day
Closed Sun Nov to Jun
✗ Lunch £
✗ Dinner ££-£££
Ⓥ Vegetarians welcome
🕯 Children welcome
🚭 Smoking discouraged before 2.30 pm (Lunch) + 9.30 pm (Dinner)

Tian of squat lobsters, lettuce and tomato, with paprika and lemon crème fraîche. Marinated pan-seared salmon, served with spring onion Thai noodles, finished with a jus naturale. Crisp brandy snap basket filled with a selection of home-made ice cream.

💳 Credit cards: Mastercard/Eurocard, American Express, Visa, Switch, Delta
🗡 Head Chef: Barry MacKenzie

CULLODEN HOUSE HOTEL
Inverness, Inverness-shire IV1 2NZ
Tel: 01463 790461
Fax: 01463 792181

3 miles from the centre of Inverness, off the A96 Inverness to Aberdeen road.

Historic and deluxe country house hotel.

- Georgian Palladian mansion.
- Country house cooking.
- "First class food and wine enjoyed in very elegant surroundings."

Culloden House Hotel is an upmarket country house hotel in lovely grounds. The atmosphere is formal but comfortable, and there is a majestic splendour and romance about the place. The hotel is now managed by Richard Gillis who continues to develop the excellent reputation held by Culloden in the past. The standard of cooking is high, prepared by a chef obviously committed to high quality and who understands his subject well and cooks with enthusiasm. The hotel is steeped in history, having been occupied by the Jacobite army in 1746. It is therefore an excellent place from which to explore the surrounding area whilst enjoying luxurious surroundings and excellent hospitality. Culloden House Hotel has 1 AA Rosette.

Open all year
- 🏨 Rooms: 28 with private facilities
- 🛏 DB&B £170–£320   B&B £135–£250
- 𝖲𝖯 Special rates available off season
- ✗ Food available all day ££££
- ✗ Lunch ££
- ✗ Dinner ££££
- 𝖵 Vegetarians welcome
- ⚘ Children welcome
- ✗ No smoking in dining room
- 🐄 Member of the Scotch Beef Club

Terrine of game made with pigeon, rabbit, venison and wild mushrooms, wrapped in bacon and served with a rowan and port sauce. Tournedos of venison topped with a wild mushroom and pistachio mousse covered in a pastry mantle served on a light juniper berry jus. Cranachan: a rich cream sweet made with whisky, raspberries and oatmeal.

STB Deluxe 👑 👑 👑 👑 👑
- 💳 Credit cards: Mastercard/Eurocard, American Express, Visa, Diners Club, Mastercharge, Switch, Delta
- ✎ General Manager/Director: Major R H Gillis

DUNAIN PARK HOTEL
(On The A82) Inverness IV3 6JN
Tel: 01463 230512
Fax: 01463 224532

On A82, 1 mile from the Inverness town boundary.

A country house hotel in a beautiful setting, offering outstanding cuisine, cooked by a Master Chef.

- A handsome 19th century 'Georgian Italianate' hunting lodge.
- First rate Scottish cooking, with assured French influences.
- "A wonderful stay! The cooking, service and comfort are all excellent."

Dunain Park is a fine Georgian country house, standing in six acres of gardens and woodlands, overlooking the Caledonian Canal. The large kitchen garden supplies herbs, vegetables and soft fruit. Ann and Edward Nicoll have won a high reputation for their establishment and several awards. Public and private rooms are immaculately furnished – and there is an indoor swimming pool and sauna. But it is for its food that Dunain Park is particularly renowned – the hotel has 1 AA Rosette. Ann Nicoll goes to great lengths to source top quality local produce – the only beef she will use is from Highland cattle or Aberdeen Angus – and her style of cooking brings out the flavour of fresh produce, and enhances it with wonderfully assured sauces.

Open all year
- 🏨 Rooms: 14 with private facilities
- 🛏 DB&B £94–£110   B&B £69–£85
- 𝖲𝖯 Special rates available
- ✗ Dinner £££
- 𝖵 Vegetarians welcome
- ⚘ Well-behaved children welcome
- ♿ Facilities for disabled visitors – residents only
- ✗ No smoking in dining room
- 🐄 Member of the Scotch Beef Club

Mousseline of smoked haddock and whiting served with a sabayon sauce. Breast of duck served with le puy lentils, crispy bacon and a balsamic dressing. Whisky oatmeal cream with a butterscotch sauce.

STB Deluxe 👑 👑 👑 👑
- 💳 Credit cards: Mastercard/Eurocard, American Express, Visa, Diners Club, Switch, Delta
- ✎ Owners: Ann & Edward Nicoll

GLEN MHOR HOTEL
& RESTAURANT
9-12 Ness Bank
Inverness IV2 4SG
Tel: 01463 234308
Fax: 01463 713170

On river bank below castle.

Family-run hotel in Inverness.

- Handsome buildings dating back to c. 1850.
- Both modern Taste of Scotland cooking and traditional Scottish and cosmopolitan.
- "A quiet and centrally located hotel overlooking the River Ness."

The family-run Glen Mhor Hotel is situated in the centre of Inverness just below the castle. It is a large 19th century townhouse which offers full private facilities in its 30 bedrooms, which are chintzy and mellow, one with four-poster. The public rooms are comfortable and furnished with a baronial Scottish theme. The Riverview Seafood Restaurant, overlooking the River Ness, offers an extensive à la carte menu stressing seafood, but with other meat and game choices. The Bistro, Nico's, which offers a less complex range of dishes, from char-grilled steaks to traditional Scottish and cosmopolitan dishes, vegetarian options available.

Open all year
Note: Riverview Restaurant closed Sun evenings Oct to Apr
🏠 Rooms: 29 with private facilities
🍴 DB&B from £59   B&B from £36
SP Special rates available
✗ Residents only
✗ Lunch (Nico's) £-££:
(Riverview Restaurant) – by arrangement
✗ Dinner (Riverview Restaurant) £££
V Vegetarians welcome
🕯 Children welcome
♿ Facilities for disabled visitors
🚭 No smoking area in Nico's

Giant seafood platter. Neptune's pot pourri of local seafood. Almond basket with Glayva cream and fresh fruit.

STB Commended 🛏 🛏 🛏 🛏
💳 Credit cards: Mastercard/Eurocard, American Express, Visa, Diners Club, Switch
👤 Proprietors: Nicol & Beverley Manson

GLENDRUIDH HOUSE HOTEL
by Castle Heather
Old Edinburgh Road South
Inverness IV1 2AA
Tel: 01463 226499 Fax: 01463 710745

2 miles from Inverness centre. ½ mile south off Sir Walter Scott Drive. At the 2nd roundabout turn left and take the first right at the 'Hotel 300 yds' sign.

A quiet oasis two miles from Inverness, with extensive grounds, comfortably furnished bedrooms, and good quality cooking.

- A most unusual building, dating mainly from the 1850s.
- Traditional Scottish cooking.
- "Tranquil location, exquisite surroundings in the Highland capital"

This is an unusual and attractive small country house set in three acres of woodland and lawns overlooking the Moray Firth: seclusion and privacy within minutes of Inverness, and a haven for non-smokers – smoking is prohibited even in the grounds. The Druid's Glen Bar provides an excellent range of whiskies and the relaxing sitting room has the unusual feature of being completely circular, its windows and doors shaped to the contour of the room. The elegant dining room (residents only) has an Italian marble fireplace and overlooks the tidy gardens. Christine Smith's well-balanced table d'hôte menus change daily and offer classic dishes employing local game and fish.

Open all year except Christmas Day
🏠 Rooms: 7 with private facilities
🍴 DB&B £44.50–£69.50   B&B £25–£45
SP Special rates available
✗ Lunch – residents only ££
✗ Dinner – residents only ££-£££
V Vegetarians welcome
🕯 Children welcome
♿ Limited facilities for disabled visitors
🚭 No smoking throughout

Locally smoked hill venison, salad and wild rowanberry jelly. Guinea fowl suprêmes roasted and served with a rich Madeira wine sauce. Apple and cranberry pie.

STB Highly Commended 🛏 🛏 🛏
💳 Credit cards: Mastercard/Eurocard, American Express, Visa, Diners Club, Switch, JCB
👤 Proprietors: Michael & Christine Smith

MOYNESS HOUSE

6 Bruce Gardens, Inverness IV3 5EN
Tel/Fax: 01463 233836

From A9 (north + south) and A862 Beauly, follow signs for A82 Fort William holiday route. Through Tomnahurich Street to Glenurquhart Road (A82), turn into Bruce Gardens diagonally opposite Highland Regional Council offices.

Lovely Victorian house in the centre of Inverness – close to Eden Court Theatre and Balnain House.

- A detached villa built in 1880, formerly the home of Neil Gunn, the celebrated Scottish author.
- First class home cooking.
- "Stylish dishes contrasting with the traditional surroundings of Inverness."

Moyness House is situated in a quiet residential part of Inverness, within ten minutes walk of the town centre and Eden Court Theatre. It is tastefully decorated and appointed in a way which respects the Victorian nature of the house, and retains its elegance. The bedrooms are charmingly decorated and have en suite facilities; the principal rooms are smart and spacious. A large garden to the rear of the house is also available for guests to enjoy. Moyness House is run by Jenny and Richard Jones – with Jenny being responsible for the cooking and her daily changing menus show flair and imagination. She goes to great lengths to source high quality Scottish produce, and treats her ingredients imaginatively, within a classic context – just as her many regular guests like it!

Open all year except Christmas wk
- 🛏 Rooms: 7 with private facilities
- 🍴 DB&B £44–£52   B&B £26–£34
- 🆂🅿 Special rates available
- ✗ Residents only
- ♀ Residents licence
- ✗ Dinner ££
- Ⓥ Vegetarians welcome
- 🧒 Children welcome
- 🚭 No smoking in restaurant

Smoked mackerel pâté with oatcakes. Medallions of venison with port wine sauce and onion marmalade. Warm raspberry and white chocolate cake with red fruit coulis.

STB Deluxe 👑 👑 👑
- 💳 Credit cards: Mastercard/Eurocard, Visa, Switch, Delta
- 👤 Proprietors: Richard & Jenny Jones

THE RIVERHOUSE RESTAURANT

1 Greig Street
Inverness IV3 5PT
Tel: 01463 222033 Fax: 01463 811729

Situated on the corner of Greig Street and Huntly Street, on the west side of the River Ness close to Balnain House.

An attractive, small restaurant situated on the banks of the River Ness, close to the centre of Inverness.

- Ground floor of a converted Victorian building.
- A blend of traditional and contemporary Scottish cooking.
- "An enjoyable and leisurely way to pass an evening in Inverness."

Ideally situated in a converted Victorian building, on the banks of the River Ness, the Riverhouse Restaurant is small, intimate and stylishly decorated. Chef/Patron, Marcus Blackwell, prepares meals in the open plan kitchen, in full view of the guests, which leaves no doubts as to the skill and level of work in the production of each dish. Eating at the Riverhouse is a leisurely experience and although there is an interesting and appetising range of fish dishes, meat and game dishes are certainly worthy of a mention. Food products from throughout the Highlands and Islands can be found in Inverness, and Marcus, along with his wife Colleen, take full advantage of this, enabling them to source the quality of produce they require for the restaurant.

Open 1 Feb to 30 Dec except Christmas Day + Boxing Day
N.B. From 1 Apr open 7 days closed Mon Tue lunch (closed Mon Tue during Winter)
- ✗ Lunch except Mon Tue from 1 Apr to 30 Oct ££
- ✗ Dinner except Mon Tue from 1 Nov to 30 Mar – except for arranged parties £££
- Ⓥ Vegetarians welcome
- 🧒 Children welcome
- ♿ Facilities for disabled visitors
- 🚭 No smoking throughout

Fish platter: squat lobster tails, smoked salmon, oysters, winkles, marinated herring, velvet crab, taramasalata. Pan-seared venison fillet medallions with crushed peppercorns, with a red wine and fresh blackcurrant sauce. Drambuie crème brûlée.

- 💳 Credit cards: Mastercard/Eurocard, Visa, Mastercharge, Switch, Delta
- 👤 Owner: M Blackwell

PITTODRIE HOUSE HOTEL
Chapel of Garioch
by Inverurie, Aberdeenshire AB51 5HS
Tel: 01467 681444
Fax: 01467 681648

Off A96 just north of Inverurie 21 miles north of Aberdeen, 17 miles north of airport.

A country house hotel offering indoor and outdoor recreational facilities.

- Scottish baronial mansion, incorporating many architectural details of its long history.
- Well-cooked Scottish cuisine.
- "Imaginative cuisine and a relaxed atmosphere in an historic hotel."

Standing in the shadow of Bennachie, in 3,000 acres of gardens and parkland, Pittodrie House originally belonged to a branch of the family of the Earls of Mar, the estate being granted to them by Robert the Bruce for their loyalty at the Battle of Bannockburn. The house was built in 1480, and added to in the baronial style in 1850. The latter influence is reflected in the opulent interiors of the public rooms, and the period atmosphere has been carefully maintained throughout the hotel. In the dining room the robust table d'hôte menus are well-balanced and offer just the kind of dishes one would expect in a grand country house, accompanied by herbs and vegetables from the hotel's own garden and a delicious selection of desserts. *(See advert Page 27.)*

Open all year
- ⋒ Rooms: 27 with private facilities
- ⊨ DB&B £62.50–£72.50   B&B £70–£80
- SP Special rates available
- ✗ Food available all day £-££
- ✗ Lunch £-££
- ✗ Dinner £££
- V Vegetarians welcome
- ⚹ Children welcome
- ↳ No smoking in dining room

Seared king scallops on a petite salad with raspberry vinaigrette. Rack of Scottish lamb, parsnip galette, shallot and rosemary jus. Pecan pie with fresh vanilla custard.

STB Commended ♛ ♛ ♛ ♛
- ⊡ Credit cards: Mastercard/Eurocard, American Express, Visa, Diners Club, Mastercharge, Switch, Delta
- Ⓜ Managing Director: Terry Moran

APPLE LODGE
Lochranza
Isle of Arran KA27 8HJ
Tel/Fax: 01770 830229

From Brodick, head north and follow the road to Lochranza (around 14 miles). As you enter the village pass the distillery and Apple Lodge is situated 300 yards on the left opposite golf course.

Attractive country house in charming island village.

- Edwardian house with adjoining cottage.
- High quality home cooking.
- "A genuinely warm welcome awaits the visitor to this delightful location."

Originally the village manse, Apple Lodge is tranquilly located on the northern part of Arran in the delightful village of Lochranza, where the ferry from Kintyre docks. Set in its own appealing gardens, both the lodge – and the south-facing suite addition – Apple Cottage – are furnished beautifully to a very high standard. One can relax in the comfortable surroundings watching wild deer graze a few yards from the garden, whilst an eagle soars overhead. Meanwhile, Jeannie Boyd will be creating a deliciously mouth-watering dinner for all to enjoy.

Open all year except Christmas wk
- ⋒ Rooms: 4, 3 with private facilities (+ 1 suite)
- ⊨ DB&B £40.50–£49.50   B&B £25–£34
- SP Special rates available
- ✗ Residents only
- UL ♀ Unlicensed – guests welcome to take own wine
- ⊞ Packed lunches £
- ✗ Dinner ££
- V Vegetarians welcome
- ⚹ Children over 12 years welcome
- ↳ No smoking in dining room + bedrooms

Tomato, apple and celery soup with caraway bread. Turbot Steak with pink grapefruit and asparagus. Pears in pastry lattice with spiced orange and butterscotch sauce.

STB Highly Commended ♛ ♛ ♛
- ⊡ No credit cards
- Ⓜ Proprietor/Chef: Jeannie Boyd

ARGENTINE HOUSE HOTEL

Shore Road, Whiting Bay
Isle of Arran KA27 8PZ
Tel: 01770 700662
Fax: 01770 700693

8 miles south of ferry terminal. First hotel on seafront at village entrance.

Family-run guest house with comfortable bedrooms.

- Victorian seaside villa.
- Scottish produce with a continental touch.
- "The panoramic views from this interesting and comfortable hotel are matched by the skilled, colourful cuisine."

Assya and Bruno bring an interesting blend of their Swiss hospitality combined with skilful use of Scottish produce to create meals with a lightly continental touch to delight the palate of their guests. Ideally located on the promenade there is the feeling of being invited into Assya and Bruno's home. From the moment you walk up the path, past a colourful array of flags on their three flag poles, European hints as to your hosts' nationality abound. Assya's impressive cooking mirrors this with appealing menus brimming over with local produce, including organically home-grown ingredients, and is influenced by her native Switzerland and neighbouring countries.

Open Feb to mid Jan
- Rooms: 6 with private facilities
- DB&B £38–90   B&B £23–£71
- SP Special rates available
- ✗ Non-residents – by arrangement
- UL ♀ Unlicensed – guests welcome to take own wine
- ✗ Dinner ££
- V Vegetarians welcome
- ✗ No smoking in dining room

Tartar of vegetables on a spicy crème fraîche served in basil leaves. Roasted Kildonan lamb larded with garlic and anchovies on a courgette and tomato gratin, garlic cream filled vol-au-vents and barley risotto. Fresh noodles with poppyseed, vanilla and heather honey sauce on a berry purée.

STB Highly Commended 😀 😀 😀
- Credit cards: Mastercard/Eurocard, Visa
- Owners: Assya & Bruno Baumgartner

AUCHRANNIE COUNTRY HOUSE HOTEL

Brodick
Isle of Arran KA27 8BZ
Tel: 01770 302234
Fax: 01770 302812

One mile north of Brodick Ferry Terminal and 400 yards from Brodick Golf Club.

Country house hotel and country club in Brodick.

- 19th century mansion, with substantial additions.
- Country house cooking.
- A grand and welcoming hotel in a superb location."

Auchrannie House is a pink sandstone Victorian country house, formerly the home of the Dowager Duchess of Hamilton. The hotel is furnished in a reproduction period style with modern comforts. A number of self-catering 'lodges' have been built in the grounds, STB Deluxe 5 Crowns, (each accommodating up to six people), also a state-of-the-art leisure complex with 20m pool. Brambles Bistro is a popular venue for families for snacks and meals, and the Garden Restaurant (which extends the original dining room with a conservatory) offers more formal dining. The sizeable table d'hôte menu offers a good range of local Scottish meat and fish dishes complemented by fresh vegetables and a daily vegetarian speciality. Auchrannie has 2 AA Rosettes.

Open all year
- Rooms: 28 with private facilities
- DB&B £46.50–£74.50   B&B £30–£54.50
- SP Special rates available
- ✗ Food available all day £
- ✗ Lunch £
- ✗ Dinner £££
- V Vegetarians welcome
- ✗ Children welcome
- ♿ Facilities for disabled visitors
- ✗ No smoking in Garden Restaurant
- ✗ Smoking area in Brambles Bistro

Marinated red mullet, fried basil and sauce vierge. Tenderloin pork centred by an apricot mousse with Aegean prunes and Armagnac sauce. Cloutie dumpling with Drambuie parfait.

STB Highly Commended 😀 😀 😀 😀 😀
- Credit cards: Mastercard/Eurocard, American Express, Visa, Switch
- Managing Director: Iain Johnston

BRODICK CASTLE RESTAURANT

The National Trust for Scotland
Brodick, Isle of Arran
KA27 8HY
Tel: 01770 302202
Fax: 01770 302312

2 miles north out of Brodick on the Lochranza Road. Follow signs for the castle.

Delightful restaurant amidst National Trust splendour.

- Converted old servants hall on ground floor of castle.
- Home cooking and baking.
- "Enjoy the delights of home cooking while you rest."

Visitors wind their way 150 metres from the reception centre and well-stocked shop to the castle which is situated on a plateau overlooking Brodick Bay and surrounded by glorious woodland gardens and terraced lawns. In the castle itself is the restaurant which, during the season, is open all day providing very reasonable priced tasty home cooked meals and light snacks, the ingredients of which are all locally sourced on the island. The mouthwatering display and array of home baking is hard to resist. On a sunny day visitors may also sit outside to eat on the terrace and enjoy magnificent views. *(See advert Page 24.)*

Open 1 Apr to 31 Oct
Ω Licensed
✗ Food available all day £
✗ Lunch £
Ⓥ Vegetarians welcome
☆ Children welcome
& Facilities for disabled visitors
⚥ No smoking throughout

Smoked mackerel pâté with oat fingers. Casserole of venison with seasonal vegetables. Dippin dumpling.

STB Commended Visitor Attraction
⊞ Credit cards: Mastercard/Eurocard, Visa, Mastercharge
𝕂 Administrator: Mrs Veronica Woodman

CREELERS SEAFOOD RESTAURANT

The Home Farm, Brodick
Isle of Arran KA27 8DD
Tel: 01770 302810
Fax: 01770 302797

From Brodick Pier, go north following coast road towards Brodick Castle and Corrie for 1½ miles. Restaurant on right.

Seafood bistro within Arran Visitors Centre.

- Sophisticated seafood bistro.
- Fish and modern Scottish cooking.
- "A gastronomic experience well worth sampling."

Creelers Seafood Restaurant is based in the old bothy of the Brodick Castle Home Farm. Tim and Fran James have established it as an excellent seafood restaurant, where the decor is simple and colourful and the atmosphere has something continental about it. Tim once a trawlerman on the West Coast still provides much of the shellfish through his own boat. The rest of the produce is either purchased on the quayside of Kintyre or carefully sourced on the island or the mainland. There is also their own smokery adjacent, with the resulting produce appearing on the menu or for sale. Daily changing menus appear on blackboards, and are extremely good value. Service is friendly and efficient. Chef Stewart Gilchrist is professional and enthusiastic, and the style of his cooking is minimalistic, with flashes of colour and fascinating textures. Winner of Taste of Scotland Special Merit Award 1993.

Open mid Mar to 31 Oct
Closed Mon except Bank Holidays + during Aug
✗ Lunch except Mon £-££
✗ Dinner except Mon ££
Ⓥ Vegetarians welcome
☆ Children welcome
& Facilities for disabled visitors

Soufflé of monkfish tail on tomato salsa. Filo parcel of prime Scottish salmon on Champagne butter sauce and tomato concassé. Butterscotch meringue with a duo of sauces.

⊞ Credit cards: Mastercard/Eurocard, Visa
𝕂 Proprietors: Tim & Fran James

DUNVEGAN HOUSE HOTEL

Shore Road
Brodick
Isle of Arran KA27 8AJ
Tel: 01770 302811

Situated on the coast road, 500 yards from Ferry.

A well-run small hotel, right on the seafront at Brodick.

- Traditional red sandstone seafront hotel overlooking Brodick Bay on the Isle of Arran.
- Daily changing table d'hôte menu offering good traditional cooking.
- "Offering a combination of care and comfort with delicious and enjoyable food."

Dunvegan House Hotel is set back from the village's waterfront promenade by its own garden, and affords good views across the bay to Brodick Castle and Goatfell. David and Naomi Spencer arrived here from England eight years ago with no experience of the hotel business. They have learned fast, do all of the work with the help of a small dedicated team, and maintain a very high standard. Dunvegan is a past winner of the Booker Prize for Excellence – judged Best Hotel/Guest House in the UK. The dinner menus offer seasonally available local produce in a small choice of familiar dishes. The breakfasts are memorable, especially the locally smoked kippers.

Open Mar to Jan
🏠 Rooms: 9 with private facilities
🍴 DB&B £42   B&B £28
✗ Residents only
♀ Restricted licence
✗ Dinner ££
Ⓥ Vegetarians welcome
⚡ Children welcome
✗ No smoking in bedrooms

Haggis in a cream and onion sauce. Arran lamb with rosemary gravy. Traditional puddings with home-made creamy custard.

STB Highly Commended 👑 👑 👑
Ⓔ No credit cards
Ⓜ Proprietors: Mr David Spencer & Mrs N Spencer

GLEN CLOY FARMHOUSE

Glencloy Road, Brodick
Isle of Arran KA27 8DA
Tel: 01770 302351

On heading out of Brodick, towards Brodick Castle, turn left up the road with the post box on the wall. Follow signs for Glen Cloy – road becomes farm track.

A family-run farm guest house on Arran.

- Old farmhouse.
- Home cooking.
- "Offering a tranquil combination of care and comfort."

This is a charming old sandstone building in a little glen on the road to Brodick Castle. The bedrooms have a very homely air about them and two have private facilities. Mark and Vicki Padfield run the house and also do the cooking. They bake their own bread, and the vegetables and herbs come from the garden. The food is traditional fare, locally sourced and carefully prepared and is served in the attractive, homely dining room overlooking the countryside. Coffee is served in the drawing room where one is surrounded by interesting local books, Vicki Padfield's embroideries, family photos, etc. – a most relaxing and enjoyable experience.

Open 1 Mar to 7 Nov
🏠 Rooms: 5, 2 with private facilities
🍴 DB&B £33.50–£39   B&B £20–£25
Ⓢ Special rates available
Ⓤ♀ Unlicensed – guests welcome to take own wine
✗ Dinner ££
Ⓥ Vegetarians welcome
⚡ Children welcome
♿ Facilities for disabled visitors
✗ No smoking in dining room

Cream of mushroom and Arran mustard soup. Roast leg of Arran lamb with redcurrant and port wine jus. Glen Cloy gooseberry and elderflower fool.

STB Commended 👑 👑
Ⓔ No credit cards
Ⓜ Proprietors: Mark & Vicki Padfield

KILMICHAEL COUNTRY HOUSE HOTEL
Glen Cloy, by Brodick
Isle of Arran KA27 8BY
Tel: 01770 302219
Fax: 01770 302068

From Brodick Pier take road north 1½ miles, then turn inland at golf course following signs about ¾ mile.

Charming country house hotel set in a beautiful glen.

- Historic house with great period character.
- Superb modern cooking.
- "The ultimate in gracious comfort and impeccable cuisine."

Kilmichael is believed to be the oldest house on Arran – the present building is late 17th century, but there was an early christian cell on the site. Described as a 'mansion' in the records, in fact it is an elegant and compact lodge, exquisitely furnished by its present owners (oriental antiques are a feature), who engagingly describe its attractions in order of importance as "... comfort, tranquillity, books and home-made ice cream." It is the only hotel on Arran graded 'Deluxe' by the STB and has two Red entries in Michelin and 2 AA Rosettes. The menus presented in the dining room are very interesting and demonstrate French and Italian influences. A five course table d'hôte menu and à la carte menu are available at dinner. Every dish has something unique and authentic about it, with piquant flavours and delicately spiced sauces. One of 14 establishments shortlisted for The Macallan Taste of Scotland Awards 1997.

	Open all year except Christmas wk
🛏	Rooms: 6 with private facilities
🛏	DB&B £65–£87　B&B £40–£62
SP	Special rates available
✕	Dinner £££
�	Dinner for non-residents – booking essential
V	Vegetarians welcome
⅄	Facilities for disabled visitors
⤬	No smoking in dining room + bedrooms

Mille-feuille of Arran king scallops seared in Pernod with a wasabi beurre blanc. Valentines of lamb with Grenadine pomegranate sauce and Glen Cloy chanterelles. Soured crème brûlée with strawberries and rhubarb in gin.

STB Deluxe 👑 👑 👑 👑
- 💳 Credit cards: Mastercard/Eurocard, Visa
- 👤 Partners: Geoffrey Botterill & Antony Butterworth

NEW FARM RESTAURANT WITH ROOMS
New Farm, Mount Stuart
Isle of Bute PA20 9NA
Tel: 01700 831646

Just 6 miles from the ferry and 1 mile from Mount Stuart House and Gardens.

Whitewashed converted cottage farmhouse on working dairy and sheep farm.

- Whitewashed farmhouse.
- Enthusiastic, adventurous and talented cooking.
- "The superb quality of cuisine and hospitality offered here enhances the warm friendly atmosphere of the farmhouse."

New Farm is set on a 1,000 acre farm on the beautiful Island of Bute. Formerly four cottages it is now home to Carole and Michael Howard and their three children. The views from the farmhouse are magnificent and the warm welcome and homely atmosphere ensure that guests quickly settle in. On arrival you are offered home-baked afternoon tea – Carole is an accomplished baker. Her cooking is tackled with enormous enthusiasm and interest and produces imaginative and tasty meals making full use of locally sourced supplies. As Carole says "if we are unable to grow it, make it or rear it we will certainly source it locally from our island, the Isle of Bute." Guests can choose to eat on their own but most people prefer to join the other guests and have an interesting and convivial evening after being welcomed in Gaelic to the table.

	Open all year
🛏	Rooms: 3
🛏	DB&B £32.50–£35　B&B £20–£22.50
UL ⚲	Unlicensed – guests welcome to take own wine
✕	Lunch – reservation essential ££
✕	Dinner – reservation essential £££
V	Vegetarians welcome
⅄	Children welcome
⅄	Facilities for disabled visitors

Home-made broths served with home-baked bread. Honey glazed New Farm lamb casseroled on a bed of apricots and fresh tarragon. Bournville baked bananas served in a 'puddle' of cream.

- 💳 No credit cards
- 👤 Proprietor: Carole Howard

ALLAN COTTAGE GUEST HOUSE

Tarbert
Isle of Harris HS3 3DJ
Tel: 01859 502146

From ferry turn left, then hard first right on to the main village street.

An attractive family-run guest house in Harris' main village.

- A deceptively small house full of warmth and charm.
- Carefully prepared food using the best of local produce.
- "A house to return to with confidence."

This attractive old building has been interestingly converted maintaining many of the original features. It has been extended to form a house of unusual charm; quiet and homely. Rooms are all well-furnished in cottage style and the bedrooms have private facilities. Bill and Evelyn Reed are wonderfully enthusiastic and look after guests with true island hospitality. The dinner menu is discussed with guests in the morning, so that individual preferences can be taken into account. The cooking is interesting and imaginative and of a very high standard; Bill makes use of fresh local produce whenever it can be obtained. A charming little establishment.

Open 1 Apr to 30 Sep
- 🏨 Rooms: 3 with private facilities
- 🛏 DB&B £44–£48   B&B £26–£30
- SP Special rates available
- ✗ Residents only
- UL Unlicensed
- ✗ Dinner 4 course menu ££
- V Vegetarians welcome – by prior arrangement
- ☆ Children welcome
- ✗ No smoking in dining room + bedrooms

Smoked Harris salmon with asparagus cream sauce. Pan-fried collops of local venison with cassis sauce. Raspberry and apple crumble with wholemeal and hazelnut topping.

STB Highly Commended 👑 👑 👑
- 💳 No credit cards
- 🗈 Proprietors: Bill & Evelyn Reed

ARDVOURLIE CASTLE

Isle of Harris HS3 3AB
Tel: 01859 50 2307 Fax: 01859 50 2348

¼ mile off A859. 24 miles from Stornoway, 10 miles from Tarbert.

A lovingly restored house run by Derek and Pamela Martin, with four elegant and comfortable bedrooms.

- Recently restored 19th century hunting lodge on the island of Harris.
- Innovative Scottish cooking.
- "Idyllic setting, wonderful food, absolute comfort – a little bit of heaven."

Ardvourlie Castle stands on the shores of Loch Seaforth under the imposing crags of Clisham. It was built in 1863 by the Earl of Dunmore but fell into a semi-ruinous state in recent years – which makes the achievement of Derek and Pamela Martin all the more remarkable. They have restored the place magnificently, with sensitivity and outstandingly good taste. The castle is furnished in keeping with its period. The dining room offers views over the wilderness beyond and it uses designs and furniture from the Victorian and Art Nouveau periods. Here you will encounter the Martins' fine cooking. Much of the raw materials that are unavailable locally are very carefully sourced on the mainland which comprises dishes to suit all tastes using as much local produce as is available on this remote island, and where necessary fresh foods are brought in by sea from the mainland.

Open 1 Apr to 31 Oct
- 🏨 Rooms: 4
- 🛏 DB&B £70–£85   B&B £45–£60
- ✗ Residents only
- ♀ Restricted licence
- ✗ Dinner 4 course menu £££
- V Vegetarians welcome – advance notice essential
- ☆ Children welcome
- ♿ Facilities for disabled visitors
- ✗ No smoking in dining room

King prawn and orange cocktail. Kebab of island lamb, marinated in yoghurt served on a bed of basmati rice flavoured with cumin and cardamom. Deep blackberry pie and cream.

STB Deluxe 👑 👑 👑
- 💳 No credit cards
- 🗈 Owner: D G Martin

LEACHIN HOUSE

Tarbert
Isle of Harris
HS3 3AH
Tel: 01859 502157

1 mile from Tarbert on A859 to Stornoway, sign-posted at gate.

Charming Victorian house of local interest.

- Substantial lochside Victorian house.
- Modern Scottish cooking.
- "Delicious food in a stylish setting."

Linda and Diarmuid Evelyn Wood have turned Leachin House (which means house among the rocks) into a most attractive and welcoming guest house, without losing any of the charms and gracious proportions of this lovely Victorian building. Dining at Leachin is a most enjoyable experience. The views across the loch are breath-taking, the dining room itself is fascinating with its 100 year old French hand-painted wallpaper, and the skill and care with which Linda cooks and presents the food is worth a journey to Harris just to eat there! The wonderful produce of the islands, particularly lamb and seafood, feature regularly on the fixed menu and each course illustrates a well-judged mix of both simple and complex food preparation. French spoken.

Open all year except Christmas + New Year
🏠 Rooms: 3, 1 en suite, 1 with private facilities
🛏 DB&B £54–£60   B&B £34–£37
SP Special rates available
✗ Residents only
UL Unlicensed
✗ Dinner £££
🕆 Children over 10 years welcome
🚭 No smoking in dining room or bedrooms

Scallops in vermouth. Fillet of lamb with port wine and redcurrant sauce. Treacle tart with Mascarpone and nutmeg ice cream.

💳 Credit cards: Mastercard/Eurocard, Visa, Delta
👥 Owners: Linda & Diarmuid Evelyn Wood

SCARISTA HOUSE

Isle of Harris HS3 3HX
Tel: 01859 550 238 Fax: 01859 550 277
e-mail scarista@compuserve.com
website: http://www.ourworld.compuserve.com/homepages/scarista

On A859, 15 miles south-west of Tarbert (Western Isles).

Distinctive country house hotel in a peaceful island location.

- Converted Georgian manse with magnificent views.
- Modern Scottish country house cooking.
- "An unforgettable setting and a great emphasis placed on the quality of food and wine makes for a memorable stay."

Scarista House overlooks a three mile long shell sand beach on the dramatic Atlantic coast of Harris. The five bedrooms, most in a single storey annexe, all have views out to sea. This makes for an ever-changing panorama of scenery and atmosphere. The bedrooms are comfortably and traditionally furnished with bathrooms en suite. The public rooms which also include an extensive library are cheery and welcoming and the absence of radio and television is an asset not a liability. The hotel's dining room has featured in many guides worldwide and is known particularly for its superb fish and shellfish, fresh vegetables and herbs from the garden together with fresh eggs from the hotel's hens and the best of home-made bread. There is a very decent wine list chosen to complement the dishes on offer.

Open May to Sep
🏠 Rooms: 5 with private facilities
🛏 DB&B £80–£95   B&B £50–£65
♀ Residents licence
✗ Dinner £££
Ⅴ Vegetarians welcome
🕆 Children over eight years welcome
🚭 No smoking in main house, dining room + sitting rooms

Sound of Harris prawns with mayonnaise and parsley dressings. Fillets of halibut with a chive sauce, served with duchess potatoes with lovage, leeks in red wine and buttered spinach. Miniature strawberry soufflés.

STB Commended 👑 👑 👑
💳 Credit cards: Visa, Access
👥 Proprietors: Ian & Jane Callaghan

THE CROFT KITCHEN
Port Charlotte
Isle of Islay
Argyll PA49 7UN
Tel: 01496 850230

On the main road into Port Charlotte opposite the
Museum of Islay Life.

A charming family restaurant and tea-room.

- Informal village bistro style restaurant.
- Home cooking.
- "Something good for all the family."

Joy and Douglas Law took over the Croft Kitchen in
1995, having run a hotel on the island for ten years.
The Croft Kitchen itself was established 19 years
ago in a fine situation close to a sandy beach, with
views of the Paps of Jura and Loch Indaal. As well
as home baking, home-made soups, family snacks
and sandwiches, the Croft Kitchen now also offers
a good range of daily 'specials', chosen from a
blackboard, which features local scallops, oysters,
mussels, lamb and so on – at very reasonable prices.
A friendly, informal place where the whole family is
made welcome.

Open mid Mar to mid Oct
Note: Closed 2nd Thu in Aug (Islay
Show Day)
- 🔳 Unlicensed – but awaiting table licence
- ✗ Food available all day £
- ✗ Lunch £
- ✗ Dinner £
- Ⓥ Vegetarians welcome
- ⚤ Children welcome

**Loch Grunart oysters in oatmeal. Lagavulin
scallops in butter and parsley. Raspberry pancakes
with cream.**

- 💳 Credit cards: Mastercard/Eurocard, Visa
- ⚄ Joint Proprietors: Joy & Douglas Law

GLENMACHRIE FARMHOUSE
Port Ellen, Isle of Islay
Argyll PA42 7AW
Tel/Fax: 01496 30 2560

Midway on A846 between Port Ellen and Bowmore.

Comfortable guest house close by the family farm.

- Modernised farmhouse in a pretty garden.
- The best of home cooking.
- "Immaculate rooms, delicious food and every
caring attention."

Glenmachrie is a mixed farm of 450 acres, with
cattle, sheep, ponies, horses and a small fold of
Highland cattle. Rachel and Alasdair Whyte
welcome guests into their home with great warmth
and a genuine Hebridean hospitality. Generous
helpings of home cooking are cheerfully served in
the candlelit dining room. Rachel offers a choice of
dishes which include meat and game from the farm
and salmon and wild brown trout from their own
loch and river which overlooks the famous Machrie
golf links. With access to private fishing guests are
also offered the opportunity to make their own
catches.

Open all year
- 🛏 Rooms: 5 with private facilities
- 🛏 DB&B from £48   B&B from £28
- ✗ Residents only
- 🔳 ♀ Unlicensed – guests welcome to take own
wine
- ✗ Dinner ££
- ⚤ Children over five years welcome
- ♿ Facilities for disabled visitors (ground floor
bedroom)
- 🚭 No smoking throughout

**Tomatoes stuffed with haggis spiked with Islay
malt whisky. Gigot of Islay lamb roasted with
rosemary and garlic. Pears cardinal with double
cream and shortbread.**

STB Highly Commended 👑 👑 👑
- 💳 No credit cards
- ⚄ Proprietor: Rachel Whyte

KILMENY FARMHOUSE
Ballygrant, Isle of Islay
Argyll PA45 7QW
Tel/Fax: 01496 840 668

½ mile south of Ballygrant village – look for sign at road end, ¾ mile up private road.

A charming house with spectacular views.

- 19th century farmhouse.
- The best of country cooking.
- "Behind the farmhouse exterior lies a warmth of comfort and good food."

Kilmeny is a working farm of 300 acres, within easy reach of Port Askaig. Margaret and Blair Rozga have been running their guest house for over 20 years and enjoy a loyal following of guests from all over the world. The bedrooms and public rooms are very elegantly decorated, with many fine antiques and luxurious furnishings. Margaret is an accomplished cook and uses only the finest produce all of which is locally sourced. Her menus are well-planned and imaginative requiring a great deal of skill and careful organisation – all of which she accomplishes single-handedly to great effect.

Open all year except Christmas + New Year
🛏 Rooms: 3 with private facilities
🍽 DB&B £50   B&B £30
SP Special rates available
✗ Residents only
Ⓤ ♀ Unlicensed – guests welcome to take own wine
✗ Dinner except Sun ££
Ⓥ Vegetarians welcome
🜨 Children welcome
🗶 No smoking throughout

Terrine of smoked salmon, prawns and avocado. Pot-roasted Jura pheasant with hunter sauce. Little summer puddings with home-made vanilla ice cream.

STB Deluxe 👑 👑 👑
💳 No credit cards
🅽 Proprietor: Margaret Rozga

CLEASCRO GUEST HOUSE
Achmore, Lochs
Isle of Lewis HS2 9DU
Tel/Fax: 01851 860 302

A859 from Stornoway for 7 miles. Right turn onto A858. Cleascro is on right 2 miles on.

Attractive modern family-run guest house in rural Lewis.

- Modern villa.
- Skilled traditional cooking.
- "First class food can be enjoyed in this little guest house."

Cleascro is a most comfortable and welcoming small guest house, ideally situated for exploring the Isle of Lewis. Gaelic speaking Donna Murray is a gifted and imaginative cook making use of her formal training to devise menus based around the top quality local ingredients of fish, venison and lamb. All vegetables and herbs are from the garden, bread is made daily.

Open all year except Christmas Day
🛏 Rooms: 3 with private facilities
🍽 DB&B £36–£42   B&B £23–£24
SP Special rates available
✗ Residents only
Ⓤ ♀ Unlicensed – guests welcome to take own wine
✗ Dinner ££
Ⓥ Vegetarians welcome
🜨 Children welcome
🗶 No smoking in dining room

Carrot soup with ginger and honey. Fillet of salmon with parsnip rösti served with lemon grass sauce and seasonal vegetables. Pistachio meringues and fresh fruit salad with fresh cream.

STB Highly Commended 👑 👑 👑
💳 No credit cards
🅽 Owners: Donna & Geoff Murray

ESHCOL GUEST HOUSE

Breasclete, Callanish
Isle of Lewis HS2 9ED
Tel/Fax: 01851 621 357

On A858, 17 miles from Stornoway, 40 miles from Tarbert.

A guest house on the Isle of Lewis.

- A small croft in the weaving village of Breasclete.
- Home cooking.
- "Enjoy friendly service and good home cooking in this well-appointed guest house."

Isobel and Neil Macarthur run this croft on the West Coast of Lewis, within walking distance of the mysterious Stones of Callanish. There are wonderful views across Loch Roag to the island of Great Bernera and beyond, with the hills of South Uig and Harris in the distance. The three bedrooms all have their own bathrooms and have a nice simple rustic feel to them. This is a small establishment and Neil will regale you for hours (in Gaelic if you desire) with tales and folklore of the area and its past. The food here is home cooking at its best with no pretensions. Eshcol really does offer 'real island hospitality.'

Open 1 Mar to 31 Oct
🏠 Rooms: 3 with private facilities
🛏 DB&B £42–£45   B&B £25–£27
✗ Residents only
🍷 ♀ Unlicensed – guests welcome to take own wine
✗ Dinner 4 course menu ££
Ⓥ Vegetarians welcome
🏃 Children over 10 years welcome
✗ No smoking in dining room

Local smoked salmon. Chicken with tarragon sauce served with carrots, courgettes and new potatoes. Truffle torte with Amaretto cream.

STB Highly Commended 👑 👑 👑
💳 No credit cards
👤 Owners: Neil & Isobel Macarthur

HANDA

18 Keose Glebe (Ceos), Lochs
Isle of Lewis HS2 9JX
Tel: 01851 830 334

1½ miles off A859, 12 miles south of Stornoway, 25 miles north of Tarbert, Harris: last house in village of Ceos.

A hilltop house on the Hebridean island of Lewis; a small family-run guest house which provides comfortable accommodation and good food.

- This is a lovely home, furnished in pine with all modern facilities.
- Traditional Scottish home cooking.
- "Scottish hospitality at its best is to be found in this little, comfortable guest house."

This is the last house in the Hebridean haven of Keose village. It is idyllically appointed on top of a hill overlooking a private loch and ideally positioned for exploring the island and nearby Harris. Stepping from the house itself you can follow a range of pursuits from bird-watching to hill-walking and (if you are fortunate) otter sighting. The loch provides brown trout fishing and a boat and equipment can be hired from the house. The owner, Christine Morrison, runs the guest house with genuine island hospitality. Alongside traditional recipes, she does all of her own baking and uses the best of local seafood and fresh produce from her garden. Winner of The Macallan Personality of the Year Award 1995.

Open 2 May to 5 Oct
🏠 Rooms: 3, 1 with private facilities
🛏 DB&B £32–£38   B&B £17–£23
🆂🅿 Special rates available
✗ Residents only
🍷 ♀ Unlicensed – guests welcome to take own wine
✗ Dinner ££
Ⓥ Vegetarians welcome
✗ No smoking throughout

Avocado, melon and tomato in mint dressing served with garlic bread. Loch Erisort scallops flambéd, served with baby courgettes, tossed in wholegrain mustard. Meringues in 'deadly' chocolate.

STB Highly Commended 👑 👑
💳 No credit cards
👤 Owners: Murdo & Christine Morrison

THE PARK GUEST HOUSE
& RESTAURANT
30 James Street, Stornoway
Isle of Lewis, Western Isles HS1 2QN
Tel: 01851 70 2485

500 yards from ferry terminal. At junction of
Matheson Road, James Street and A866 to
airport and Eye peninsula.

**A traditional family-run guest house in the centre
of town.**

- A stone-built Victorian guest house.
- Traditional Scottish cooking with a continental
  influence.
- "It is no wonder that this restaurant sustains a
  loyal following."

A substantial stone-built B Listed building dating
from the 1880s, standing in the centre of Stornoway,
this house has a homely atmosphere and Roddy and
Catherine Afrin are friendly hosts. Catherine was
trained in interior design at the Glasgow School of
Art, and the house has benefited from her skill and
good taste. Note the original Glasgow-style
fireplace in the dining room. Roddy was formerly
head chef on an oil rig in the North Sea. His robust
à la carte menus use fresh fish from Stornoway and
the West Coast fishing boats, and local lamb and
venison. Each dish is cooked to order. The
restaurant is popular with local people.

Open all year except 24 Dec to 5 Jan
Note: Restaurant closed Sun Mon to
non-residents
🏨 Rooms: 8, 3 with private facilities
🛏 DB&B £38.50–£54   B&B £24–£29
🍴 Packed lunches available £
✘ Dinner – residents only ££-£££
✘ Dinner (Restaurant) Tue to Sat £££
Ⓥ Vegetarians welcome
⚤ Children welcome
♿ Facilities for non-residential disabled visitors

**Hebridean shellfish bouillabaisse. Pan-fried
venison loin on the bone with a wild mushroom
and rich red wine gravy. Summer fruits crêpe with
home-made Drambuie ice cream.**

STB Commended 🏅 🏅
💳 Credit cards: Mastercard/Eurocard, Visa, Delta
👤 Proprietor: Catherine Afrin
👤 Chef/Proprietor: Roddy Afrin

ARDFENAIG HOUSE
by Bunessan, Isle of Mull
Argyll PA67 6DX
Tel/Fax: 01681 700210

2 miles west of Bunessan on A849, turn right on
private road to Ardfenaig House, ½ mile.

**A lovely old country house hotel surrounded by
woodland, sea and moorland on the Isle of Mull.**

- Originally an estate factor's house then shooting
  lodge in a glorious position on the shores of Loch
  Caol on the Ross of Mull.
- Assured country house cooking.
- "A creative style of cuisine can be enjoyed in this
  comfortable and elegant country house."

Ardfenaig House stands in the southwest corner of
Mull midway between Bunessan and Fionnphort.
The house is home to Malcolm and Jane Davidson,
hospitable and welcoming hosts who look after you
charmingly. It has five en suite bedrooms and the
newly refurbished Coach House by a small burn 50
yards away provides additional self-catering
accommodation for four to six people. In front of the
house is a small jetty and Malcolm will be happy to
take you for a sail in the bay or an early morning
fishing trip. The drawing room has magnificent
views over Loch Caol and a conservatory dining
room was added in 1997. The excellent food is
freshly prepared in the kitchen from fresh local
produce and is beautifully presented. Menus are
short but imaginative, and since the Davidsons have
a share in a French vineyard, the wine list is rather
special.

Open 1 Apr to 31 Oct
🏨 Rooms: 5 with private facilities
🛏 DB&B £74–£88
♀ Restricted licence
✘ Dinner 4 course menu £££
Ⓥ Vegetarians welcome
🚭 No smoking in dining room + bedrooms

**Fresh local prawns with garlic mayonnaise.
Noisettes of Scottish lamb with a mint and
redcurrant sauce. Pecan pie with vanilla ice
cream.**

STB Highly Commended 🏅 🏅 🏅
💳 Credit cards: Mastercard/Eurocard, Visa
👤 Owners: Malcolm & Jane Davidson

ARDRIOCH FARM GUEST HOUSE

Dervaig, Isle of Mull
Argyll PA75 6QR
Tel/Fax: 01688 400264

1 mile from Dervaig on Calgary road (B8073).

A delightful farm guest house with four bedrooms and pine-panelled annexe in an informal garden setting, with wonderful views.

- A modern bungalow/farmhouse on a working 70 acre farm.
- Scottish home cooking.
- "Delicious home cooking enhances the sincere warmth and friendly atmosphere."

This cedar-built bungalow on the west coast of Mull can accommodate eight guests. It is the pleasant, comfortable home of Jenny and Jeremy Matthew – tastefully furnished with antiques, good pictures and lots of books. It is redolent of cedar wood and you will find yourself living very much amongst the busy clutter of a warm family home. Jenny's meals are delicious and homely; all dishes use fresh local produce. The day's menu is fixed, according to what is available, but she is more than happy to accommodate any preferences or requests from her guests where possible, if you ask her in advance. The house is two miles from Croig harbour, where Ardrioch's inter-island day cruises depart for wildlife and sightseeing trips.

....

    Open 1 Apr to 30 Oct
🏠 Rooms: 5, 2 with private facilities
🛏 DB&B £33.50–£36   B&B £18.50–£21
✗ Residents only
🍷 Unlicensed – guests welcome to take own wine
✗ Dinner ££
Ⓥ Vegetarians welcome
👶 Children welcome
🚭 No smoking throughout

Salad of Mull smoked trout and mussels with avocado mayonnaise. Scottish gammon with quince orange sauce and local vegetables. Raspberry meringue with cranachan.

STB Commended 👑 👑
💳 No credit cards
👤 Owners: Jenny & Jeremy Matthew

ASSAPOL HOUSE HOTEL

Bunessan
Isle of Mull
Argyll PA67 6DW
Tel: 01681 700 258
Fax: 01681 700 445

From Craignure-A849 towards Fionnphort. When approaching Bunessan, pass village school on the right, take first road on left signed Assapol House.

A delightful, spacious old house in a sheltered corner of Mull.

- Small country house hotel.
- Stylish country cooking.
- "A tranquil and genuinely hospitable country hotel with excellent cuisine."

The feature that immediately impresses the visitor to Assapol is the care and attention to detail that your hosts, the Robertson family, manifest in every department: fresh flowers in the bedrooms, beds turned down, sewing kits supplied, etc. Assapol House, itself a former manse, is 200 years old and overlooks the loch of the same name, with the Burg Peninsula, the Treshnish Isles and Staffa beyond. Wildlife, secluded beaches and historical sites abound in this delightful corner of Mull. The dinner menu offers a choice of starters and puddings and a set main course. The food is locally sourced and features local delicacies; it is sensitively cooked and imaginatively presented; and it is extremely good value. Assapol House Hotel has 1 AA Rosette.

....

    Open Apr to Oct
🏠 Rooms: 6 with private facilities
🛏 DB&B £47–£56
🆂🅿 Special rates available
✗ Residents only
🍷 Restricted hotel licence
✗ Dinner ££
Ⓥ Vegetarians welcome – by prior arrangement
👶 Children over 10 years welcome
🚭 No smoking in dining room

Salad of smoked Highland venison, beef and duck. Roast pork loin with a mustard and wild mushroom sauce. Blackcurrant, apple and calvados crumble tart.

STB Highly Commended 👑 👑 👑
💳 Credit cards: Mastercard/Eurocard, Visa, Switch, Delta
👤 Partners: Onny, Thomas & Alex Robertson

CALGARY FARMHOUSE HOTEL

Calgary, nr Dervaig
Isle of Mull, Argyll
PA75 6QW
Tel/Fax: 01688 400256

About 4½ miles from Dervaig on B8073, just up hill from Calgary beach.

A farm guest house with tea-room and gallery.

- Converted farm steadings.
- Home cooking.
- "A relaxed and attractive place in which to enjoy locally sourced ingredients skilfully cooked and presented."

Calgary Farmhouse is just up the hill from the beautiful white sands of Calgary Beach. The farm buildings and courtyard have recently been sensitively converted by Julia and Matthew Reade into nine bedrooms with private facilities, and two public rooms. Exposed stonework, wooden furniture and wood-burning stoves all contribute to a warm and cosy environment. The Dovecote Restaurant offers an à la carte menu which changes four times a week according to the seasonal produce available. The accent is on simple, home cooking in an informal atmosphere while the family's fishing connections ensure a wonderful supply of Mull's bountiful catches. There is also a tea-room, The Carthouse Gallery, charmingly converted and open throughout the day for light lunches and home baking. A changing exhibition of pictures by local artists is displayed here, many of them for sale. Runner-up in The Taste of Scotland Scotch Lamb Challenge Competition Category 1 1997.

Open Apr to Oct incl
🏠 Rooms: 9 with private facilities
🛏 DB&B £48–£58   B&B £29.70–£33
✗ Lunch £
✗ Dinner ££
Ⅴ Vegetarians welcome
✶ Children welcome
✗ Smoking discouraged whilst others are eating

Local crab with citrus fruit and light ginger and coriander dressing. Fillet of wild salmon with crisp risotto cake and asparagus sauce. Traditional baked cheesecake with sultanas and nutmeg.

STB Commended 👑 👑 👑
💳 Credit cards: Mastercard/Eurocard, Visa, Switch
👤 Proprietors: Matthew & Julia Reade

DRUIMARD COUNTRY HOUSE

Dervaig, Isle of Mull
Argyllshire PA75 6QW
Tel: 01688 400345/400291
Fax: 01688 400345

Situated adjacent to Mull Little Theatre, well signposted from Dervaig village.

A small country house hotel run by husband and wife.

- A restored Victorian manse.
- Modern Scottish cooking.
- "The combination of care and comfort together with truly talented cooking reflects great commitment."

Druimard is just on the outskirts of the pretty village of Dervaig, eight miles from Tobermory. The old house has been beautifully restored by Haydn and Wendy Hubbard, who run their hotel with the standards of comfort one would expect from a country house: service is professional, the en suite bedrooms are very comfortable, the restaurant has a strong reputation, and has been recognised by the award of 2 AA Rosettes. The table d'hôte and à la carte menus have moved with the current eating trends towards a large choice of fish which is locally caught and meat which is traditionally reared. The cooking is assured, fresh and imaginative with unusual sauces and everything is prepared to order.

Open end Mar to end Oct
🏠 Rooms: 6 with private facilities
🛏 DB&B £57.50–£68.50   B&B £37.50–£48.50
SP Special rates available
♀ Restaurant licence only
✗ Lunch – residents only £
✗ Dinner – non-residents except Sun £££
Ⅴ Vegetarians welcome
✶ Children welcome
✗ No smoking in restaurant

Avocado terrine with plum tomato and basil salad. Noisette of lamb on bed of creamed spinach with garlic, lemon and mint sauce. Sticky pear pudding with ginger wine and brandy sauce and cardamom scented custard.

STB Highly Commended 👑 👑 👑 👑
💳 Credit cards: Mastercard/Eurocard
👤 Partners: Mr & Mrs H R Hubbard

KILLIECHRONAN HOUSE
Isle of Mull
Argyll PA72 6JU
Tel: 01680 300403
Fax: 01680 300463

Leaving ferry turn right to Tobermory A849. At Salen turn left to B8035. After 2 miles turn right to Ulva ferry B8073. Killiechronan House on right after 300 metres.

A comfortable and secluded corner in one of the prettiest parts of Mull.

- Small Victorian country house hotel.
- Best of Scottish and European.
- "Elegant cuisine can be enjoyed in this gracious and charming country house."

Killiechronan is the lodge house of its own 5,000 acre estate. Six charming en suite bedrooms offer comfort and style in a peaceful setting, while the dining room and two distinctively furnished lounges are a quiet haven to relax and enjoy. The house has a happy and relaxed atmosphere, reflected also by the staff under the professional eye of Patrick and Margaret Freytag, who moved here from The Manor House, Oban. The food here is excellent, deserving its 2 AA Rosettes, and customers every needs are well-catered for with menus made available early afternoon so that any dietary requirements can be met. Ideal for a relaxed holiday in a wonderful setting.

Open 4 Mar to 31 Oct
- 🛏 Rooms: 6 with private facilities
- 🛏 DB&B £46–£80
- 💲 Special rates available
- ⚲ Residents licence
- ✕ Lunch Sun only ££
- ✕ Dinner £££
- Ⓥ Vegetarians welcome
- ⚞ No smoking in dining room

Loch na Keal oysters with fennel and honey. Isle of Mull venison with juniper berry sauce and black cherries. Parfait Flora Macdonald with Drambuie sauce.

STB Highly Commended 👑 👑 👑 👑
- 💳 Credit cards: Mastercard/Eurocard, American Express, Visa, Switch, Delta
- 👤 Managers: Patrick & Margaret Freytag

THE OLD BYRE HERITAGE CENTRE
Dervaig
Isle of Mull PA75 6QR
Tel: 01688 400229

1½ miles from Dervaig. Take Calgary road for ¾ mile, turn left along Torloisk road for ¼ mile, then left down private road following signs.

A large gift shop, tea-room and heritage centre on the Isle of Mull.

- Converted barn with self-service restaurant.
- Home cooking and baking.
- "A popular place to visit on the island and enjoy a light meal and delicious home baking."

A remotely situated, picturesque old cattle byre in Glen Bellart (near Dervaig) has been restored and converted into a heritage centre which explores the traditions and natural history of the Isle of Mull, from the first settlers to the present day. There are audio-visual displays and exhibits as well as a gift shop with souvenirs and crafts for sale. The licensed tea-room offers a range of light meals and home baking and daily specials, using fresh Mull produce. By prior arrangement meals can be arranged for groups and vegetarians are well catered for.

Open 5 Apr to 30 Oct
- ✕ Light meals served throughout day £
- ⚲ Licensed
- Ⓥ Vegetarians welcome
- ⚹ Children welcome

Vegetarian lentil soup. Smoked Tobermory trout and salad with a warm roll and butterballs. Almond millionaires shortbread.

STB Commended Visitor Attraction
- 💳 No credit cards
- 👤 Joint Owners: Ursula & Michael Bradley

THE WESTERN ISLES HOTEL
Tobermory
Isle of Mull PA75 6PR
Tel: 01688 302012
Fax: 01688 302297

High above the little town the hotel is reached in a few minutes by a steep side road out of the main seafront shopping area.

Fine old Victorian hotel in superb position above the harbour.

- Town hotel of Scottish baronial architecture.
- Substantial Scottish cooking.
- "Guests can relax in this comfortable hotel with its stunning views overlooking Tobermory Bay and be assured of impeccable service and excellent cuisine."

The hotel occupies one of the finest positions in the Western Isles set above the village of Tobermory with glorious views over the Sound of Mull. You can enjoy the ever-changing, dramatic scenery from all of the hotel's public rooms and many of the bedrooms. There is a choice of three places in which to eat here – the dining room; Spices Restaurant; and the conservatory which is a particularly delightful spot and is popular with guests and visitors to the island who drop in for lunch or even coffee. The bar lunch menu is extensive with a very wide choice, from soup of the day and filled sandwiches to a full three or four course meal of hot and cold dishes and salads. The dinner menu offers four courses on a table d'hôte menu of good, traditional Scottish cooking accompanied by a reasonably priced wine list.

Open 1 Feb to 18 Dec
- 🏨 Rooms: 23 with private facilities
- 🛏 DB&B £60–£110   B&B £38–£87
- SP Special rates available
- ✕ Lunch £
- ✕ Dinner £££
- V Vegetarians welcome
- ✭ Children welcome
- ⌣ No smoking in dining room

Smoked fine slices of local venison on different lettuce. Lightly poached supreme of Mull salmon on a fresh dill cream sauce. Quenelles of dark chocolate mousse on white chocolate sauce.

STB Highly Commended 👑 👑 👑 👑
- 💳 Credit cards: Mastercard/Eurocard, American Express, Visa, Switch
- 🗝 Proprietors: Sue & Michael Fink

CLEATON HOUSE HOTEL
Cleaton
Westray
Orkney KW17 2DB
Tel: 01857 677508
Fax: 01857 677442
e-mail cleaton@orkney.com

Signposted 5 miles from Rapness (Westray) Ferry terminal on road to Pierowall Village.

A friendly, family-run hotel on the Island of Westray.

- Victorian manse of distinctive 'ink bottle' design.
- Orcadian produce – modern cooking.
- "An island retreat with exquisite fresh food, quality and standards to match."

A regular roll-on, roll-off ferry service connects Westray to Kirkwall, and Cleaton's owner, Malcolm Stout, is happy to meet you at the pier. Such personal concern for guests is manifested in every aspect of this delightful small hotel which includes the addition of a lounge for residents use only. Chef Lorna Reid combines her many years working in 'top class' kitchens, with outstanding local ingredients, to produce quality cuisine.The hotel has splendid views and is an excellent base from which to explore Westray's beaches, cliffs and Heritage Centre – and the second largest sea-bird colony in Britain.

Open all year except New Year's Day
- 🏨 Rooms: 5 with private facilities
- 🛏 DB&B £45–£55   B&B £29–£32
- SP Special rates available
- ✕ Lunch £
- ✕ Dinner ££
- V Vegetarians welcome
- ✭ Children welcome
- ⌣ Facilities for disabled visitors
- ⌣ No smoking in dining room

Terrine of monkfish and haddock. A combination of local seafood in dill and lime sauce, encased in fresh herb pancakes. Butterscotch and toffee cheesecake.

STB Highly Commended 👑 👑 👑
- 💳 Credit cards: Mastercard/Eurocard, Visa, Delta
- 🗝 Proprietor: Malcolm Stout

CREEL RESTAURANT & ROOMS
WINNER MACALLAN PERSONALITY OF THE
YEAR 1997 – ALAN CRAIGIE
Front Road, St Margaret's Hope, Orkney KW17 2SL
Tel: 01856 831 311

Take A961 south across the Churchill Barriers
into St Margaret's Hope. 14 miles from Kirkwall.

**Alan Craigie consistently achieves a very high
standard and is rightfully acknowledged for his
culinary achievements.**

- Historic seafront house, stark, whitewashed
  and gabled, overlooking St Margaret's Hope.
- Innovative modern cooking with strong
  influences of traditional Orcadian recipes.
- "Alan and his wife Joyce run an excellent
  place here which never disappoints."

The clean white walls of the Creel shine out on
the quayside; a small, family-run restaurant with
an international reputation. Chef/owner Alan
Craigie presents a short menu which changes
daily according to the availability of local produce
and features Orcadian specialities. He cooks with
great skill, respecting textures and flavours, creating
original and unusual sauces, and spectacular
desserts. The atmosphere of the place is informal
and friendly; the restaurant has three spacious
and comfortable bedrooms, with bathrooms en
suite. The Creel has become a place of pilgrimage
for gourmets, but its cheerful understated
ambience has not changed, its unique works from
Orkney artists on the walls – nor its incredibly
reasonable prices. The Creel has 1 AA Rosette.

Open weekends Oct to Mar except Jan:
daily Apr to Sep – advisable to book,
especially in low season
Closed Christmas Day + Boxing Day, Jan +
2 wks Oct
- 🏠 Rooms: 3 with private facilities
- 🛏 B&B £30–£35
- ✕ Dinner £££
- Ⓥ Vegetarians welcome
- 🧒 Children 5 years and over welcome
- 🚭 No smoking in restaurant

**Smoked rump of beef with home-made rhubarb
chutney. Orcadian fish stew with halibut, salmon
and scallops seared in a cast pan and served on
a vegetable stew. Clootie dumpling parfait.**

- 💳 Credit cards: Mastercard/Eurocard, Visa
- Ⓜ Owners: Joyce & Alan Craigie

FOVERAN HOTEL & RESTAURANT
Foveran, St Ola
Kirkwall, Orkney
KW15 1SF
Tel: 01856 872389
Fax: 01856 876430

On A964 Orphir road, 2½ miles from Kirkwall.

Rural modern hotel in the Isles of Orkney.

- Scandinavian style, purpose-built hotel.
- Traditional Scottish cooking.
- "Orcadian fresh produce cooked to perfection."

This is a modern Scandinavian bungalow, purpose-
built as a hotel, with views over Scapa Flow. The
interior is warm and inviting, and the Corsies are
happy and charming hosts. Their menus rely heavily
on the outstanding fresh seafood and meat of the
islands, and familiar dishes are given a local twist
(rich sauce laced with Highland Park whisky,
Orkney Raven Ale sauce, etc.). There is a separate
vegetarian menu with a delicious looking range of
dishes: this in itself is indicative of the attention you
will encounter here. The Pine Restaurant and chef
Clare Cooper are achieving an excellent reputation
for the quality of cooking here. Restaurant requires
to be booked in advance.

Open all year except Christmas Day + Jan
Closed Sun – residents only
- 🏠 Rooms: 8 with private facilities
- 🛏 B&B £35–£45
- ✕ Dinner except Sun £££
- Ⓥ Vegetarians welcome
- 🧒 Children welcome
- ♿ Facilities for disabled visitors
- 🚭 No smoking in restaurant

**Arbroath smokies served hot with butter. King of
scallops served with a cheese and garlic sauce.
Orkney bouillabaisse.**

STB Commended 👑 👑 👑 👑
- 💳 Credit cards: Mastercard/Eurocard, Visa,
  Switch, Delta
- Ⓜ Owners: Bobby & Ivy Corsie

WOODWICK HOUSE

Evie
Orkney
KW17 2PQ
Tel: 01856 751 330
Fax: 01856 751 383

From the A965 turn off to Evie. After 15 minutes, drive c. 7 miles turn right at sign to Woodwick House. Turn first left, pass by farm on left and continue to the burn and tress ahead. Go over small bridge.

A peaceful retreat with good food.

- Country house hotel.
- Traditional Scottish cooking.
- "Fresh Orkney produce, friendly host, and views overlooking the Island of Gairsay."

Woodwick House is situated on the west mainland of Orkney, just 20 minutes from both main towns of Kirkwall and Stromness. Built in 1912 it is an attractive country house with delightful views, sitting in 12 acres of woodland with a burn which runs down to the bay. The style of the house is tasteful and effective with the commitment to Orkney hospitality evident throughout. The cooking is very good with interesting, well-balanced menus extremely well-presented. There is an obvious commitment to the use of local produce. This is an excellent place from which to explore the locality and those looking for that little bit more should ask for the programme on concerts lectures and courses available.

    Open all year
🏠 Rooms: 8, 4 with private facilities
🛏 DB&B £37.50–£67   B&B £23–£37
SP Special rates available
✘ Lunch £
✘ Dinner ££–£££
V Vegetarians welcome
⚘ Children welcome
♿ Facilities for disabled visitors
🚭 No smoking in dining room

Orkney farmhouse cheese with tomato and fresh basil. Smoked salmon wrapped in fresh tarragon and plaice with a white wine sauce. Woodwick raspberry Atholl brose.

STB Commended 👑 👑 👑
💳 No credit cards
👤 Co-Proprietor: Ann Herdman

BUSTA HOUSE HOTEL

Busta, Brae
Shetland ZE2 9QN
Tel: 01806 522 506
Fax: 01806 522 588

On the Muckle Roe road, 1 mile off A970 Hillswick road.

Historic Shetland house with wonderful views.

- 16th century laird's house.
- Scottish produce with modern influences.
- "A superb establishment in a uniquely stunning location."

The history of Busta House is full of superstition, ghosts and family feuds. Fear not, as the hospitality and enthusiasm of Peter and Judith Jones make you welcome to their tastefully restored home. One of the few Listed buildings in Shetland, it has many interesting features, amongst which are its walled gardens and private pier. Enjoy an aperitif in the Long Room before dinner, gently absorbing the atmosphere of the historic Busta House. Cooking is Scottish and international using local produce where possible, all freshly cooked.

    Open all year except 22 Dec to 2 Jan
🏠 Rooms: 20 with private facilities
🛏 DB&B £59–£70.50   B&B £40–£68
SP Special rates available
✘ Lunch £-££
✘ Dinner ££-£££
V Vegetarians welcome
⚘ Children welcome
🚭 No smoking in dining room

Busta gravlax. Scallops wrapped in filo pastry with wild mushrooms and dill. Drambuie parfait with ruby grapefruit syrup and a caramel cage.

STB Commended 👑 👑 👑 👑
💳 Credit cards: Mastercard/Eurocard, American Express, Visa, Diners Club, Switch, Delta
👤 Owners: Peter & Judith Jones
👤 Manageress: Jeanette Watt

ARDVASAR HOTEL

Ardvasar, Sleat
Isle of Skye IV45 8RS
Tel: 01471 844223

15 miles south of Broadford, ½ mile south of
Armadale/Mallaig ferry.

**A small roadside hotel in the 'Wild Garden
of Skye'.**

- Traditional whitewashed coaching inn.
- Innovative home cooking.
- "The village inn and the local bar with an
  established reputation for wholesome food."

Ardvasar Hotel is situated at the south end of the
Sleat Peninsula, near Armadale (the ferry point for
Mallaig) and enjoys lovely views over the Sound of
Sleat to the mountains of Knoydart. The hotel is run
by Bill and Greta Fowler who show personal
concern over their guests' comfort and well-being,
and encourage many to become regular visitors.
Bill cooks imaginatively and with great attention to
detail, with local fresh produce complemented by
unusual sauces and accompaniments. An appetising
à la carte menu is presented in the restaurant and
bar food is also available. Ardvasar Hotel has
1 AA Rosette.

Open 1 Mar to 28 Oct
🏨 Rooms: 10 with private facilities
🛏 DB&B £60–£80   B&B £45–£60
✗ Lunch ££
🍴 Dinner – reservations please £££
Ⓥ Vegetarians welcome
🏃 Children welcome
🚭 Smoking discouraged

**Fresh Sleat seafood cocktail with yoghurt
mayonnaise. Sauté fillet of halibut with scallops
and Pernod cream. Heather honey and whisky with
almond biscuit.**

STB Commended 👑 👑 👑
💳 Credit cards: Mastercard/Eurocard, Visa, Delta
👤 Partners: Bill & Greta Fowler

ATHOLL HOUSE HOTEL
& CHIMES RESTAURANT

Dunvegan
Isle of Skye IV55 8WA
Tel: 01470 521 219
Fax: 01470 521 481

In the centre of the village of Dunvegan. From the
bridge – follow A850 to Sligachan, turn left to
Dunvegan – 22 miles.

A small hotel in 'heart of the village'.

- Late 19th century manse now a comfortable
  small hotel.
- Modern Scottish cooking with care.
- "Small and friendly in a village setting."

Situated at the head of Loch Dunvegan, the Atholl
House Hotel looks out on to the twin flat-topped
mountains – the Macleod's Tables. Built in 1910 the
Atholl House Hotel is a former manse which retains
many of the original features. The atmosphere is
friendly and the cooking accomplished using much
of the excellent local Skye produce.

Open all year except Jan + Feb
🏨 Rooms: 9 with private facilities
🛏 DB&B £40–£56   B&B £24–£40
SP Special rates available
♀ Full hotel licence
✗ Food available all day £££
🥪 Packed lunch available
✗ Lunch £
✗ Dinner £££
Ⓥ Vegetarians welcome
🏃 Children welcome
♿ Facilities for disabled visitors
🚭 No smoking in restaurant

**Tart of smoked haddock and spinach with grain
mustard hollandaise. Poached salmon and
langoustines in a tomato and saffron consommé.
Warm feuillette of pear with a butterscotch sauce
and crème anglaise.**

STB Commended 👑 👑 👑
💳 Credit cards: Mastercard/Eurocard, American
   Express, Visa, Switch
👤 Owner: Joan M Macleod MHCIMA

BOSVILLE HOTEL
Bosville Terrace
Portree
Isle of Skye IV51 9DG
Tel: 01478 612846
Fax: 01478 613434

Town centre above Portree Harbour and Cuillin Mountains.

A bustling hotel in the centre of Portree village.

- Town centre hotel.
- Stylish Scottish cuisine.
- "Refreshing and appealing menus."

Centrally situated on a busy corner in Portree, the Bosville Hotel has old fashioned award-winning Highland hospitality. Recently refurbished and tastefully decorated, the hotel is achieving high standards in the culinary field due to the skills of Chef Craig Roger. The popular restaurant fronts the street; diners come and go and locals drop in for a chat, or to deliver goods and fresh produce. The hotel stands on a brae and commands fine views across the harbour, with the Cuillin Mountains beyond. Table d'hôte lunch and dinner menus are presented, using local produce wherever possible and featuring a number of Scottish specialities. *(See advert Page 22.)*

Open all year
🏨 Rooms: 15 with private facilities
🛏 DB&B £45–£65   B&B £25–£45
SP Special rates available
✗ Food available all day £
✗ Lunch £
✗ Dinner ££
Ⓥ Vegetarians welcome
🧍 Children welcome
♿ Facilities for disabled visitors
🚭 No smoking throughout

Highland terrine of veal sweetbreads and Scottish lobster studded with pistachio, placed on a lime and Pernod vinaigrette. Layers of spinach, sole, salmon, king scallops lightly steamed and glazed with a tomato and basil butter. Poached pear with honey cream, vintage port and lime syrup.

STB Commended 👑 👑 👑 👑
💳 Credit cards: Mastercard/Eurocard, American Express, Visa, Mastercharge, Switch, Delta
🛎 Hotel Manager: Donald W MacLeod MHCIMA

DUNORIN HOUSE HOTEL
Herebost
Dunvegan
Isle of Skye IV55 8GZ
Tel/Fax: 01470 521488

From Kyleakin A850 to Sligachan, then A863 to Dunvegan. 2 miles south of Dunvegan turn left at Roag/Orbost junction, 200m on right.

A small and modern, family-run hotel in a beautiful corner of Skye.

- Purpose-built with modern comforts in mind.
- Scottish cooking with island recipes/hotel cooking.
- "Immaculate accommodation, and great care taken by these caring friendly hosts."

Dunorin House is the brainchild of Gaelic-speaking native islanders Joan and Alasdair MacLean. Built in 1989, it offers comfortable accommodation in ten en suite rooms. The hotel enjoys panoramic views across Loch Roag to the Cuillin Hills. All bedrooms and public rooms are on ground level with wide corridors and so are specially suitable for the disabled. In the evenings, Joan and Alasdair's son Darren, a Gaelic Festival winner, entertains guests with traditional Scottish music. With many local recipes, the hotel's à la carte menu seeks to make the most of fresh local produce such as scallops, venison and salmon. It also offers more routine hotel fare. The wine list is reasonably priced and varied.

Open 1 Apr to 15 Nov except 2 wks Oct
🏨 Rooms: 10 with private facilities
🛏 DB&B £48–£60   B&B £30–£42
SP Special rates available
🍴 Non-residents – bookings only
♀ Restricted hotel licence
✗ Dinner £££
Ⓥ Vegetarians welcome
🧍 Children welcome
♿ Facilities for disabled visitors
🚭 No smoking in dining room

Highland haggis laced with Talisker. Noisettes of Scotch lamb with provençal sauce. Traditional cloutie dumpling with custard, fresh cream or ice cream.

STB Highly Commended 👑 👑 👑
💳 Credit cards: Mastercard/Eurocard, Visa
🛎 Partners: Alasdair & Joan MacLean

FLODIGARRY COUNTRY HOUSE HOTEL
& THE WATER HORSE RESTAURANT

Staffin, Isle of Skye
Inverness-shire IV51 9HZ
Tel: 01470 552203
Fax: 01470 552301

A855 north from Portree to Staffin, 4 miles from
Staffin to Flodigarry.

Country hotel at the north end of Skye.

- Historic house with unsurpassed views.
- Scottish cuisine.
- "A place to relax whilst exploring Skye."

This historic country house hotel nestles between
the towering pinnacles of the Quiraing and has
panoramic sea views over Flodigarry Island, and
across Staffin Bay to the mainland. Its 19th century
castellate additions lend it the air of folklore,
especially being so close to the mysterious 'Fairy
Glen', and adjacent is Flora Macdonald's cottage
(now converted to provide seven luxury en suite
rooms, five with sea view). In the Water Horse
Restaurant, residents and non-residents can enjoy
a daily changing table d'hôte menu, featuring
traditional dishes, or choose from an à la carte
menu. Bar meals are served in the conservatory
and on the terrace. Winner of The Macallan Taste
of Scotland Country House Hotel of the Year Award
1995. *(See advert Page 245.)*

Open all year
🏠 Rooms: 19 with private facilities
🛏 DB&B £70–£99   B&B £49–£79
🆂🅿 Special rates available
✕ Lunch (Restaurant) ££
✕ Dinner 4 course menu £££
Ⓥ Vegetarians welcome
🕭 Children welcome
♿ Facilities for disabled visitors
🚭 No smoking in restaurant, conservatory
    or bedrooms

**Skye dulse broth accompanied by home-made
tattie scones. Roast wild grey hare garnished with
a caramelised pear and coated with a fresh
rosemary and Madeira sauce. Highland cloutie
dumpling.**

STB Highly Commended 👑 👑 👑 👑
💳 Credit cards: Mastercard/Eurocard, Visa,
    Switch, Delta
🅽 Proprietors: Andrew & Pamela Butler

GLENVIEW INN & RESTAURANT

Culnacnoc, Staffin
Isle of Skye
Inverness-shire IV51 9JH
Tel: 01470 562 248
Fax: 01470 562 211

12 miles from Portree on the Staffin road –
signposted off the A855.

A comfortable West Highland inn near Staffin.

- Restaurant with rooms.
- Good quality cooking of fresh local seafood.
- "Delicious food and friendly attention."

Tucked into a sheltered corner up in the north end
of the island, this little hostelry is big in all the home
comforts. The fresh sea catch of the day is quickly
brought to the table, while in the afternoon, home
baking is a temptation to linger over. Whatever the
time of day – the Glenview will rise to the occasion.
Paul's cooking uses local produce and eclectic
techniques to produce well-priced and varied
meals selected from an à la carte menu and blackboard featuring daily specials – from fresh local
seafood and game to vegetarian and ethnic dishes.

Open mid Mar to early Nov
🏠 Rooms: 4 with private facilities
🛏 DB&B £37.50–£47.50   B&B £25–£35
🆂🅿 Special rates available
✕ Lunch ££
✕ Dinner £££
Ⓥ Vegetarians welcome
🕭 Children welcome
🚭 Smoking restricted to certain areas

**Warm salad of Skye scallops, cockles and squat
lobster tails with dulse. Fricassée of pheasant with
oyster mushrooms, leeks, apple, cream and
vermouth with pilau rice and warm pitta bread.
Slice of home-made hot chocolate fudge pie.**

STB Commended 👑 👑 👑
💳 Credit cards: Mastercard/Eurocard, Switch
🅽 Owners: Paul & Cathie Booth

HARLOSH HOUSE
by Dunvegan
Isle of Skye IV55 8ZG
Tel/Fax: 01470 521 367

Off A863, 4 miles south of Dunvegan.

A small hotel in a remote setting on the shores of Loch Bracadale.

* Charming 18th century tacksman's house with six bedrooms.
* Skilful restaurant cooking.
* "A dedicated chef, wonderful location and charming place to stay."

This converted farmhouse is not far south of Dunvegan in the north-west of the island, and has splendid views of the Cuillin and the islands which speckle the sea loch it sits beside. It has a relaxed atmosphere inspired by its owners, Peter and Lindsey Elford who also prepare and serve the dinners. Peter cooks, making use of the fresh seafood, which is predominant in the restaurant. His attention to detail is meticulous (he also makes his own breads, desserts and chocolates) and the dishes on his menus are complex with subtle flavours. Harlosh House has 3 AA Rosettes Food Award.

Open Easter to end Oct
🏨 Rooms: 6 with private facilities
🛏 DB&B £60–£72.50   B&B £35–£47.50
✗ Dinner £££
⚘ Children welcome
✍ No smoking in restaurant + bedrooms

Local crab and coriander kedgeree. Roast monkfish with a confit of shallots and a rosemary beurre blanc. Wild apricot strudel with cinnamon ice cream.

STB Highly Commended 👑 👑 👑
💳 Credit cards: Mastercard/Eurocard, Visa, Switch
👤 Owners: Peter & Lindsey Elford

HOTEL EILEAN IARMAIN
Sleat, Isle Ornsay
Inverness-shire IV43 8QR
Tel: 01471 833 332
Fax: 01471 833 275

From Mallaig/Armadale ferry turn right on to A852 for 8 miles, then right at sign Isle Ornsay, hotel is down at waters edge. From Skye Bridge take road to Broadford and turn off at junction signed A852 to Armadale.

Gaelic charm at 'The Inn on the Sea'.

* Small whitewashed island hotel.
* Modern Scottish cooking.
* "Warmth and character and flavoursome cooking."

Hotel Eilean Iarmain (Isle Ornsay Hotel) stands on the small rocky bay of Isle Ornsay in the south of Skye, with expansive views over the Sound of Sleat to the hills of Knoydart. The hotel was built in 1888 and retains the charm and old-world character of a gentler age, with log fires in the public rooms and a panelled dining room. It is owned by Sir Iain Noble – who has done so much for Gaelic culture and language: staff and locals are all Gaelic speakers. The award-winning restaurant serves a four course table d'hôte menu (in Gaelic, but translated) which features local shellfish (landed only yards from the hotel), game and vegetables. The restaurant has an AA Rosette. One of 14 establishments shortlisted for The Macallan Taste of Scotland Awards 1997. *(See advert Page 27.)*

Open all year
🏨 Rooms: 12 with private facilities
🛏 DB&B £76.50–£99   B&B £47.50–£70
SP Special rates available
🍴 Lunch – booking essential ££
🍴 Dinner – advance reservation advisable £££
V Vegetarians welcome
⚘ Children welcome
✍ No smoking in restaurant

Locally dived scallops sautéed with Stornoway black pudding and apple. Monkfish baked in its own juices with garlic and fennel. Crème brûlée served with berries and fresh dairy cream.

STB Commended 👑 👑 👑
💳 Credit cards: Mastercard/Eurocard, American Express, Visa, Mastercharge,
👤 Proprietors: Sir Iain & Lady Noble

KINLOCH LODGE

Isle Ornsay, Sleat
Isle of Skye IV43 8QY
Tel: 01471 833214
Fax: 01471 833277

8 miles south of Broadford on A851. 10 miles north of Armadale on A851. 1 mile off A851.

The home of the High Chief of Clan Donald and Lady Macdonald.

* Country house hotel in Sleat.
* Outstanding traditional cooking with innovative influences.
* "Prepare to pamper your taste buds in an absolutely delightful setting."

Kinloch Lodge was built in 1680, as a farmhouse, and was expanded into a sporting lodge in the 19th century. As the home of Lord Macdonald of Macdonald, it is full of portraits of ancestors, old furniture and family treasures. It is very much a family home, with two comfortable drawing rooms, log fires and a variety of bedrooms. Lady Claire Macdonald is one of the best known cooks in Scotland: an award-winning journalist and the author of 12 cookbooks. Assisted by a small team she presents a five course table d'hôte menu each night which uses only fresh seasonal produce. The breakfasts are a very special treat.

Open Mar to Nov incl
🏠 Rooms: 10 with private facilities
🛏 DB&B £70–£130   B&B £45–£95
SP Special rates available
✗ Dinner 5 course menu ££££
Ⓥ Vegetarians welcome – prior notice required
🕇 Children welcome by arrangement
🚭 No smoking in dining room
🐄 Member of the Scotch Beef Club

Smoked haddock soufflé with cream, saffron and chive sauce. Char-grilled venison fillet with port, redcurrant jelly and mushroom gravy. Dark chocolate nemesis.

STB Highly Commended 🏆 🏆 🏆 🏆
💷 Credit cards: Mastercard/Eurocard, Visa
🔪 Proprietors: Lord & Lady Macdonald

LOCHBAY SEAFOOD RESTAURANT

Stein, Waternish
Isle of Skye IV55 8GA
Tel: 01470 592235

Take B886, 4 miles down single track road to village of Stein. Last house in the village.

A small fish restaurant in Waternish, with two en suite bedrooms.

* Two restored 18th century cottages with gorgeous views over to the Outer Isles.
* Seafood handled with loving care.
* "A tiny restaurant with a big reputation for fresh fish, simply cooked."

Situated in the old fishing village of Stein and located just 30 yards from the pier with some lovely unspoilt views, these fisherman's cottages have been restored rather than converted. The old black range is still there, (and working), the copper kettle on the hob; whitewashed walls and original pine panelling. The place has great charm, and this is enhanced by the hospitality of its owners, Peter and Margaret Greenhalgh. The fish and shellfish is brought up from the pier and cooked simply and deliciously by Margaret – it simply could not be fresher. Bookings essential in the evenings.

Open Easter to end Oct incl Easter Sat
Closed Sat
🏠 Rooms: 2
🛏 B&B £20–£25
✗ Food available all day except Sat ££
✗ Lunch except Sat £
✗ Dinner except Sat ££
Ⓥ Vegetarians welcome
🕇 Children welcome
🚭 No smoking throughout

Squat lobster. Fresh mussels cooked in virgin olive oil and white wine. Cloutie dumpling.

💷 Credit cards: Mastercard/Eurocard, Visa
🔪 Proprietors: Margaret & Peter Greenhalgh

ROSEDALE HOTEL

Beaumont Crescent, Portree
Isle of Skye IV51 9DF
Tel: 01478 613131
Fax: 01478 612531

Down in the actual harbour, 100 yards from village square.

A small hotel in Skye's principal village with views directly over the harbour.

- Harbourside fishermen's cottages comfortably converted to accommodate this friendly hotel.
- Modern Scottish.
- "A village atmosphere in its waterfront setting."

The Rosedale Hotel was originally a row of William IV cottages adjacent to the harbour in the heart of old Portree. The hotel now spread its wings in all directions so that it now occupies practically all of one side of the Portree waterfront. Growth was in response to demand and demand was created by satisfied guests returning yet again for another stay. There are many unique and interesting features – not least of which is finding your way to the first floor restaurant! – from which there are splendid views out over the bay. Chef Tony Parkyn presents a daily changing table d'hôte dinner menu which offers a good choice of imaginative dishes (there is always a speciality vegetarian main course), based upon fresh local produce whenever it is available. The Rosedale Hotel has 1 AA Rosette.

Open 11 May to 1 Oct
🏨 Rooms: 23 with private facilities
🛏 DB&B £65–£71   B&B £40–£46
✖ Lunch – residents only
✖ Dinner ££££
Ⓥ Vegetarians welcome
🚭 No smoking in restaurant

Smoked haddock pasta rolls with lemon butter sauce. Pan-fried breast of duck with cranberries and a parsnip purée. Rhubarb and elderflower syllabub with shortbread.

STB Highly Commended 👑 👑 👑 👑
💳 Credit cards: Mastercard/Eurocard, Visa, Mastercharge, Switch, Delta
👤 Manager: Keith White

SKEABOST HOUSE HOTEL

Skeabost Bridge, Isle of Skye IV51 9NP
Tel: 01470 532 202
Fax: 01470 532 454

4 miles north of Portree on Dunvegan road.

An imposing family-run hotel on the shores of Loch Snizort.

- A 19th century hunting lodge set in lovely grounds.
- Skilled contemporary cooking.
- "A delightful place for relaxation and fine food."

Built in 1870 this former hunting lodge has been a family-run establishment by the Stuart and McNab families for over 27 years (granny, aged 85, still prepares the traditional afternoon teas). It is an oasis of cultivated serenity within the wild and rugged terrain of Skye. Positioned in 12 acres of lovely grounds which stretch down to the waterside, its well-kept gardens also incorporate a nine hole golf course. A period conservatory overlooks the loch and was added to the main building to extend the hotel's dining facilities. A buffet menu is available during the day and in the more formal surroundings of the elegant, wood-panelled dining room. Angus McNab presents daily changing table d'hôte menus which demonstrate considerable flair and skill, particularly with fish and game. *(See advert Page 32.)*

Open Mar to Nov
🏨 Rooms: 26 with private facilities
🛏 DB&B £84–£90   B&B £54–£60
🆂🅿 Special rates available
✖ Lunch £
✖ Dinner £££
Ⓥ Vegetarians welcome
🧒 Children welcome
♿ Facilities for disabled visitors
🚭 No smoking in dining room
🐂 Member of the Scotch Beef Club

Smooth chicken liver and Madeira parfait served with a cranberry and onion confit and toasted home-made brioche. Seared fillet of fresh Skye salmon with lemon beurre blanc sauce and cucumber spaghetti. Fresh Skye strawberries in a crisp biscuit basket with home-made vanilla ice cream and raspberry sauce.

STB Commended 👑 👑 👑 👑
💳 Credit cards: Mastercard/Eurocard, Visa, Switch
👤 Proprietors: Stuart & McNab

TALISKER HOUSE

Talisker
Isle of Skye
Inverness-shire
IV47 8SF
Tel: 01478 640245
Fax: 01478 640214

Take the A863 from Sligachan. Turn left towards Carbost on the B8009 at Drynoch 5 miles after Sligachan then 4 miles past Carbost at Talisker Bay

Historic country house.

- Delightful country house in spectacular location.
- Wholesome, hearty cooking.
- "A truly peaceful and secluded place where every care is taken."

Talisker House welcomes guests as warmly today as it did to Johnson and Boswell during their historic tour of the Hebrides in 1773. This is a hidden treasure of a house run by Jon and Ros Wathen who specialise in home cooking and personal service. The house is beautifully maintained as is the extensive garden. The cooking by Ros is accomplished, menus are interesting and make best use of the excellent local produce available on Skye.

Open Mar to Nov incl
- ♠ Rooms: 4 with private facilities
- ⇔ DB&B £50–£55   B&B £32–£35
- ♙ Residents only
- ⬜ Packed lunch – by request
- ✖ Dinner ££
- Ⓥ Vegetarians welcome
- ✶ Children welcome
- ♿ Facilities for disabled visitors
- 🚭 No smoking throughout

Duck egg pasta with smoked venison, pine nuts and rocket. Pan-fried hake fillet with ginger, coriander and coconut milk. Brandy alexander ice cream with fresh raspberries.

STB Highly Commended ♛ ♛ ♛
- ⊞ No credit cards
- ✗ Proprietors: Jon & Ros Wathen

THREE CHIMNEYS RESTAURANT

Colbost, by Dunvegan
Isle of Skye IV55 8ZT
Tel: 01470 511258

4 miles west of Dunvegan on B884 road to Glendale. Look out for Glendale Visitor Route signs.

Island restaurant in an idyllic setting.

- Delightful restaurant in converted crofter's cottage.
- Natural skilled Scottish cooking.
- "A meal at this memorable gem is an absolute must."

This restaurant is off the beaten track, right on the shore of Loch Dunvegan at Colbost, on the scenic Glendale Visitor Route which takes you to the most westerly point of Skye. Lunch, afternoon tea and light meals are served until 4 pm. Dinner, from 7 pm, is a really full blown occasion with a wide choice à la carte menu accompanied by a well-chosen wine list offering a good choice of New World and European wines. As you would expect, given its location, seafood is a speciality of the menu but fish, lamb, beef, game and an intriguing vegetarian option are also among the selection on offer. This is Scottish cooking at its best – simple, imaginative, delicious. Shirley is a brilliant and artistic cook – not to be missed! Disabled visitors are asked to contact the restaurant prior to visit. Three Chimneys has 2 AA Rosettes. Talisker Quality Award for finest food '93, '94, '95.

Open end Mar to end Oct
Closed Sun except Easter + Whitsun
- ✖ Afternoon tea and light meals except Sun £-££
- ✖ Lunch except Sun £-££££
- ✖ Dinner except Sun 3 course menu £££-££££
- Ⓥ Vegetarians welcome
- ✶ Children welcome
- 🚭 No smoking throughout
- 🐂 Member of the Scotch Beef Club

Squat lobster bisque. Grilled fillet of Highland lamb with mushroom and Madeira sauce and kidney croustade. Iced cranachan parfait with crushed raspberry sauce and fresh berries.

- ⊞ Credit cards: Mastercard/Eurocard, Visa, Switch
- ✗ Owners: Eddie & Shirley Spear

THE GLASSARY RESTAURANT AND GUEST HOUSE
Sandaig, Isle of Tiree
Argyll PA77 6XQ
Tel/Fax: 01879 220 684

On west coast of island. On leaving pier turn left through Scarinish to Heylipol, Middleton and Sandaig at west end of the island.

A restaurant and guest house on the beautiful Isle of Tiree.

- The restaurant is a pine-lined converted byre with large conservatory, giving panoramic view of Atlantic Ocean.
- Traditional Scottish with modern influences.
- "A pretty little guest house with a warm and friendly atmosphere."

The Glassary is situated on the picturesque west coast of the island, close to long stretches of unspoiled white sandy beaches. The name is taken from the nearby ruined kelp (seaweed) factory which operated during the last century. The house has recently been renovated, upgraded and extended offering all modern amenities including en suite facilities. Proprietor Mabel Macarthur and her son, chef Iain, create a warm atmosphere. Almost all the beef, lamb and seafood are local and you can order lobster in advance. Home-made soups are excellent and a speciality is carrageen pudding, made from kelp (on request). The menu prices are very reasonable and the cooking is imaginative with some original and inventive touches, making eating here a most enjoyable experience.

Open all year
🏠 Rooms: 5 with private facilities
🛏 DB&B £40–£50   B&B £25–£30
✗ Lunch £-££
✗ Dinner ££-£££
Ⓥ Vegetarians welcome
🏃 Children welcome
♿ Facilities for disabled visitors

Melon, prawn and smoked Tobermory trout. Gaelic steak: fillet of Aberdeen Angus beef pan-fried, served on a bed of haggis and coated in whisky sauce. Bread and butter pudding soaked in Drambuie.

STB Approved Listed
💳 No credit cards
👤 Proprietors: Mabel & Iain Macarthur

SIMPLY SCOTTISH
High Street
Jedburgh
Roxburghshire TD8 6AG
Tel: 01835 864696
Fax: 01835 822989

Centre of Jedburgh just off A68.

Modern bistro/restaurant specialising in local quality produce with cook shop and coffee shop.

- Modern bistro-style town restaurant.
- Fresh modern Scottish cooking.
- "Modern bistro restaurant with contemporary cooking in informal style."

The Simply Scottish restaurant, coffee shop and craft cook-shop has been recently converted from the old Co-op department store to very high standards, and with great effect and has become a popular local meeting place. The interior of the bistro/restaurant has a light, modern country feel with heavy pine furniture and stripped pine flooring. As the name suggests the emphasis on the food is using good freshly sourced local produce and served simply but with some interesting combinations of flavours and presented with style.

Open all year
✗ Food available all day £-££
✗ Lunch £
✗ Dinner except some week nights in winter (please phone) ££
Ⓥ Vegetarians welcome
🏃 Children welcome
♿ Facilities for disabled visitors
🚭 No smoking area

Smoked trout mousse. Medallions of Border beef with red wine, mushrooms, bacon and shallots. Dark chocolate layer with orange and Grand Marnier compote.

💳 Credit cards: Mastercard/Eurocard, Visa
👤 Proprietors: Linda Fergusson & Charles Masraff

EDNAM HOUSE HOTEL

Bridge Street, Kelso, Roxburghshire TD5 7HT
Tel: 01573 224168
Fax: 01573 226319

Situated on Bridge Street, halfway between town square and abbey.

Established family-run hotel in the Border town of Kelso.

- Georgian mansion – banks of Tweed.
- Traditional and modern Scottish cooking.
- "Traditional Scottish cooking, served in dining room overlooking the Tweed."

Standing on the banks of the Tweed in Kelso and enjoying wonderful views, this is considered to be the finest Georgian mansion in Roxburghshire. It was built in 1761 and its elegant facade is complemented by an interior with ornate ceilings, fireplaces and carved woodwork. In spite of this grandeur, Ednam is not a daunting house, and you are very warmly received. Public rooms and bedrooms are furnished and styled in keeping with the hotel. The proprietor/chef Ralph Brooks describes his cooking as 'straightforward, but along classical lines' and creates original dishes using unusual ingredients such as oxtail and wood pigeon, preferring to fashion his menus from the fresh ingredients he can obtain locally and seasonally.

Open all year except Christmas + New Year
🏠 Rooms: 32 with private facilities
🛏 DB&B £51–£80   B&B £36–£55
SP Special rates available
✗ Food available all day £-££
✗ Lunch £
✗ Dinner ££
Ⓥ Vegetarians welcome – prior notice required
🕭 Children welcome

Pearl barley paella with Loch Awe mussels. Sautéed lamb sweetbreads in a walnut and red wine sauce. Iced praline soufflé with raspberry coulis.

STB Commended 👑 👑 👑 👑
💳 Credit cards: Mastercard/Eurocard, Visa, Switch
🕭 Proprietors: R A & R W Brooks

SUNLAWS HOUSE HOTEL AND GOLF COURSE

Heiton, Kelso
Roxburghshire TD5 8JZ
Tel: 01573 450331
Fax: 01573 450611

Situated at the village of Heiton, on the A698 Kelso-Hawick road. Signposted at western end of village.

Leading country house hotel, owned by the Duke and Duchess of Roxburghe.

- Country house hotel and championship golf course.
- Traditional Scottish, with grand hotel touches.
- "Luxury country house, gracious accommodation and excellent food."

Sunlaws House Hotel is in the Scottish baronial style and stands on the banks of the River Teviot in many hundreds of acres of park and woodland. The hotel offers a variety of country pursuits and its own golf course. Although it is an imposing mansion, Sunlaws retains the common touch, the welcome is genuinely hospitable. Well-constructed table d'hôte menus are offered for lunch and dinner (an à la carte menu is also available in the evening) – offering both light and complex dishes and a good range of meat, fish and poultry. Chef David Bates gives careful thought to combinations of flavour and presentation. Sunlaws House Hotel has 2 AA Rosettes.

Open all year
🏠 Rooms: 22 with private facilities
🛏 DB&B £90–£143.50   B&B £72.50–£115
SP Special rates available
✗ Lunch ££
✗ Dinner £££-££££
Ⓥ Vegetarians welcome
🕭 Children welcome
🚭 No smoking in dining room
🐄 Member of the Scotch Beef Club

Char-grilled quail breasts on white truffle risotto with vegetable crisps. Fricassée of lobster and seafood on young spinach leaves and lobster sauce. Gratin of pears poached in Crème de Cassis with Granny Smith sorbet.

STB Highly Commended 👑 👑 👑 👑 👑
💳 Credit cards: Mastercard/Eurocard, American Express, Visa, Diners Club, Switch
🕭 General Manager: David A Webster

THE BUTTERCHURN

Cocklaw Mains Farm
Kelty, Fife
KY4 0JR
Tel: 01383 830169
Fax: 01383 831614

Just off the M90 motorway at junction 4, 500 yards west of Kelty.

Light and airy informal eatery with excellent food and craft shop.

- Converted and enhanced farm buildings.
- Home cooking.
- "Fresh foods, interesting crafts and fun for the children make this the ideal stop."

The Butterchurn restaurant not only serves delightful fresh food, but also houses an excellent craft shop with speciality Scottish foods and a children's play area to keep everyone happy. Children are also welcome to see the farmyard animals. Light meals and home baking are available all day right through to traditional Scottish high teas. Recently enlarged and refurbished to a very high standard the white-washed steading will be a welcome place for the weary traveller.

	Open all year except 25 Dec to 7 Jan
♀	Licensed
✕	Food available all day ££
✕	Lunch ££
✕	Dinner ££
Ⓥ	Vegetarians welcome
✝	Children welcome
✌	Facilities for disabled visitors

Haggis Lyonnaise. Pesto stuffed vegetables. Home-made cloutie dumpling.

▣	Credit cards: Mastercard/Eurocard, Visa, Switch, Delta
ꓘ	Proprietors: Mr & Mrs K Thomson

ARDSHEAL HOUSE

Kentallen, Argyll PA38 4BX
Tel: 01631 740227 Fax: 01631 740342

On A828 Oban road, 4 miles south of Ballachulish Bridge, about 1 mile up private road, signposted at main road.

Very comfortable and historic country house.

- A charming country house.
- Innovative country house cooking.
- "A step into the past with all the comfort and amenities of today."

Everywhere you turn, as you travel up the mile and a half long drive, there are ancient trees, and between them glimpses of sea and mountains. The original house was built by the Stewarts of Appin in the 1500s. It is beautifully appointed, with a magnificent oak-panelled hall, a traditional billiards room, a dining room and a conservatory in the garden area. Throughout it is furnished with fine antiques, and log fires burn in the sitting rooms on chilly days. All bedrooms are en suite. Neil and Philippa Sutherland have opened their family home to guests whose comfort and enjoyment is their main concern. Philippa is an accomplished cook and her husband a most attentive host. The atmosphere of the house is relaxed – the quiet of an earlier age. Winner of The Macallan Taste of Scotland Country House Hotel of the Year Award 1996.

	Open all year except Dec to Feb – when open by prior arrangement only
⌂	Rooms: 6 with private facilities
⇋	DB&B from £60 B&B from £37
✕	Dinner £££
Ⓥ	Vegetarians welcome
✝	Children welcome
✌	No smoking in restaurant

Four cheese pancake ravioli. Scallops in crisp potato shell and courgette chutney. Rhubarb and almond tart.

STB Highly Commended 👑 👑 👑 👑

▣	Credit cards: Mastercard/Eurocard, American Express, Visa
ꓘ	Proprietors: Neil & Philippa Sutherland

ARDANAISEIG HOTEL
Kilchrenan
by Taynuilt
Argyll PA35 1HE
Tel: 01866 833333
Fax: 01866 833222

1 mile east of Taynuilt, turn sharp left. Follow B845 to Kilchrenan. At Kilchrenan Inn turn left – 3 miles on single track road to Ardanaiseig.

Small luxury mansion house hotel.

- Skilfully restored early 19th century mansion.
- Beautifully presented modern Scottish cooking.
- "A remote and romantic country house overlooking Loch Awe."

Ardanaiseig is an elegantly appointed hotel offering excellent standards of care and comfort. Under its new owner, Bennie Gray, the house has been skilfully restored and furnished with beautiful antiques, paintings and eye-catching objet d'art. In the dining room true Scottish hospitality is delivered by new chef Drew Heron selects only the best local produce and presents with flair and sophistication. Everything about Ardanaiseig is exquisite from the gardens and nature reserve to the tiniest details. *(See advert Page 30.)*

- Open all year except 2 Jan to 14 Feb
- Rooms: 14 with private facilities
- DB&B £57–£121 B&B £32–£86
- ✗ Food available all day from £
- ✗ Lunch ££
- ✗ Dinner £££

Terrine of foie gras, pork knuckle and potato, salad of fine leaves and summer truffle dressing. Gâteau of Shetland salmon, scallops and langoustine, smoked pimento and cardomom sauce. Symphony of caramel with hazelnuts and chocolate.

STB Highly Commended 👑 👑 👑 👑
- Credit cards: Mastercard/Eurocard, American Express, Visa, Diners Club
- Manager: Jamie Alexander

TAYCHREGGAN HOTEL
Kilchrenan, Taynuilt
Argyll PA35 1HQ
Tel: 01866 833 211/833 366
Fax: 01866 833 244

Leave A85 at Taynuilt on to B845 through village of Kilchrenan to the loch side.

A small, excellently appointed hotel on the shores of Loch Awe.

- A highly regarded, award-winning hotel of great distinction.
- Elegant British cuisine.
- "An excellent retreat for the discerning diner."

There has been an hotel here, nestling on the shores of Loch Awe, for 300 years. Taychreggan was a drovers' inn. With its cobbled courtyard and great charm, it retains that sense of peace and history. But under proprietor Annie Paul no effort has been spared to restore and enhance the hotel's unique ambience. Her emphasis and that of her dedicated staff is to make visitors feel like house guests, even well-behaved canine ones. Award-winning chef Martin Wallace presents imaginative fine cuisine in the hotel's dining room. Simpler bar lunches are no less carefully prepared. Euan Paul's wine list is a revelation which has just been awarded the Les Routiers Corps D'Elite. The hotel also has 2 AA Rosettes.

- Open all year
- Rooms: 20 with private facilities
- DB&B £80–£100 B&B £52–£62
- Special rates available
- ✗ Lunch ££
- ✗ Dinner 5 course menu £££
- Vegetarians welcome
- No smoking in dining room
- Member of the Scotch Beef Club

Fresh Loch Etive langoustines. Loin of Argyll venison accompanied by a wild mushroom risotto and a rich redcurrant sauce. Drambuie and heather honey parfait.

STB Highly Commended 👑 👑 👑 👑
- Credit cards: Mastercard/Eurocard, American Express, Visa, Switch
- Proprietor: Annie Paul

KILFINAN HOTEL
Near Tignabruaich
Argyll
PA21 2EP
Tel: 01700 821201
Fax: 01700 821205

6 miles north of Tignabruaich on B8000, east coast of Loch Fyne.

Charming coaching inn with gourmet dining.

- 18th century whitewashed inn.
- Master Chef cuisine.
- "An exceptional dining experience in delightful surroundings."

Kilfinan Hotel is a very charming coaching inn steeped in character reached by a single-track road down the Cowal Peninsula. The hotel is set amidst spectacular Highland scenery on the shores of Loch Fyne and this location makes it the perfect all year retreat. Combine this with the Master Chef skills of Rolf Mueller in the kitchen and the dream is complete. Rolf's cooking is famed throughout Scotland for its innovative style and use of prime produce. Lynne Mueller takes care of the front of house with an expert eye. Rooms are furnished attractively and there is a sunny terrace to the rear of the building for that welcome cup of tea on arrival. Kilfinan has 2 AA Rosettes.

Open 1 Mar to 31 Jan
- 🏚 Rooms: 11 with private facilities
- 🛏 B&B £36–£46
- SP Special rates available
- ✗ Lunch £
- ✗ Dinner £££
- Ⓥ Vegetarians welcome – prior booking required
- 🕏 Children welcome – in bistro
- 🚭 No smoking in dining room
- 🐄 Member of the Scotch Beef Club

Fresh foie gras with Armagnac grapes on frisée endives. Canon of Scotch lamb with herb crust and thyme jus. Hazelnut terrine with a Grand Marnier sauce anglaise.

STB Highly Commended 👑 👑 👑
- 💳 Credit cards: Mastercard/Eurocard, American Express, Visa
- 🅺 Manager: Lynne Mueller

THE COFFEE CLUB
30 Bank Street, Kilmarnock
Ayrshire KA1 1HA
Tel: 01563 522048

City centre.

Town centre coffee shop/bistro.

- Popular and busy town restaurant.
- Home-cooking.
- "Established 37 years ago and still an institution today."

Situated in one of the oldest streets in Kilmarnock opposite the Laigh Kirk, this cheerful restaurant offers something for everyone. There is a large varied menu with lots of choice including grills and vegetarian dishes and a range of quick snack meals. Service is fast, friendly and efficient. All food is produced on the spot using fresh produce wherever possible and the home baking is a speciality. There is a welcoming atmosphere at The Coffee Club.

Open all year except Christmas Day, Boxing Day, 1 + 2 Jan
- 🅤 ⚲ Unlicensed – guests welcome to take own wine
- ✗ Food available all day £
- ✗ Lunch except Sun £
- ✗ Dinner except Sun ££
- Ⓥ Vegetarians welcome
- 🕏 Children welcome
- ♿ Facilities for disabled visitors
- 🚭 No smoking area in air-conditioned restaurant

Mushrooms in garlic, butter and cream sauce. Chicken Mexico – breast of chicken with spicy tomato sauce. Soft meringue gâteau with cream and chocolate sauce.

- 💳 Credit cards: Mastercard/Eurocard, American Express, Visa, Switch
- 🅺 Proprietor: Svend Kamming

BISTRO AT FERN GROVE
Kilmun, by Dunoon
Argyll PA23 8SB
Tel/Fax: 01369 840 334

6 miles from Dunoon on A880 on the side of the Holy Loch.

Small bistro with some bedrooms.

- Victorian villa.
- Good quality home cooking.
- "An unusual bistro in a family home."

This 19th century house was at one time the home of the Campbells of Kilmun overlooking Holy Loch. The hospitable hosts Ian and Estralita Murray have built up a strong reputation for their little bistro over the years. Simple cooking is their forte. A daily changing blackboard menu of chef's specials is supplemented by an à la carte menu of snacks. Accommodation is limited to three rooms, and plays a secondary role to the restaurant. The Bistro has 1 AA Rosette.

Open all year except Nov, weekends only Dec to 1 Apr
- Rooms: 3 with private facilities
- DB&B £36–£40   B&B £18–£25
- Special rates available
- Food available all day £
- Lunch ££
- Dinner ££
- Vegetarians welcome
- Children welcome
- Facilities for disabled visitors
- No smoking in restaurant + bedrooms

Lentil pâté and home-made savoury bread. Sliced breast of duck with caramelised apple and red wine. Warm pear and date cake with home-made ice cream.

- Credit cards: Mastercard/Eurocard, Visa
- Proprietors: Ian & Estralita Murray

MARCH HOUSE
Lagganlia, Feshiebridge, Inverness-shire PH21 1NG
Tel/Fax: 01540 651 388

From Kincraig follow B970 to Feshiebridge. Cross the bridge and climb until red telephone box on right. Turn right and follow no through road for ½ mile. Turn left down drive.

A family-run guest house, beautifully situated in Glenfeshie.

- Secluded Alpine style house.
- Traditional Scottish cooking with European overtones.
- "Friendly and informal with impeccable use of fresh ingredients."

Standing in a glade of mature pines at the mouth of lovely Glenfeshie, March House enjoys wonderful views of the Cairngorm Mountains and is an ideal base for the many outdoor pursuits that Speyside offers, such as skiing, gliding, birdwatching, etc. The house is modern and Alpine in style – with timber cladding, a large wood-burning stove and old stripped pine furniture. It has six bedrooms, all en suite and the spacious conservatory overlooking the mountains provides an idyllic setting for dinner (non-residents are welcome, but should telephone). It is owned and enthusiastically run by Caroline and Ernie Hayes, whose cooking and baking matches the clean, fresh atmosphere of March House itself. They use fresh local produce and present a very well-priced table d'hôte menu. Small party bookings also welcome.

Open all year except 26 Nov to 26 Dec
- Rooms: 6 with private facilities
- DB&B £32–£36   B&B £18–£22
- Special rates available
- Reservations essential for non-residents
- Unlicensed – guests welcome to take own wine
- Lunch – pre-arranged parties ££
- Dinner ££
- Vegetarians welcome
- Children welcome
- Smoking permitted after dinner

Salmon soufflé with salad and raspberry vinaigrette. Trout with leeks, orange and ginger stuffing. Fruit crème brûlée.

STB Highly Commended 🏵 🏵 🏵
- Credit cards: Visa
- Proprietors: Ernie & Caroline Hayes

THE CROSS

Tweed Mill Brae, Ardbroilach Road
Kingussie, Inverness-shire PH21 1TC
Tel: 01540 661166 Fax: 01540 661080

From traffic lights in centre of village, travel uphill
along Ardbroilach Road for c. 200 yards, then turn
left down private drive (Tweed Mill Brae).

Outstanding award-winning restaurant.

* Restaurant with rooms.
* Innovative Scottish cooking.
* "An inspirational meal – in a class of its own."

The Cross was built as a tweed mill in the late 19th
century and is situated in a wonderful waterside
setting. Here they have retained some interesting
features including the exposed original beams in the
dining room and the upstairs lounge with its
coombed ceilings. Ruth Hadley is a member of
the Master Chefs of Great Britain. She treats her
ingredients deftly and there is an experimental
energy behind some dishes. Where she can, she
uses less common produce such as wild
mushrooms, mountain hare, pike or fresh turbot, and
she grows her own herbs in the restaurant's four
acre garden. Tony Hadley's waiting style is
renowned; he also makes a nightly selection of
wines, from one of the best cellars in Scotland,
which will complement the menu. The Cross has
3 AA Rosettes.

Open 1 Mar to 1 Dec + 27 Dec to 5 Jan
Closed Tue
🏠 Rooms: 9 with private facilities
🛏 DB&B £85–£115
✘ Lunch – private party bookings by arrangement
✘ Dinner except Tue ££££
Ⓥ Vegetarians welcome – prior notice required
♿ Facilities for non-residential disabled visitors
🚭 No smoking in dining room + bedrooms

**Scallop mousse with a prawn and basil sauce.
Fillet of local wild red deer with port and
redcurrants. Chocolate whisky laird ... 3.5 million
calories per slice!**

💳 Credit cards: Mastercard/Eurocard, Visa,
  Switch, Delta
🔣 Partners/Proprietors: Tony & Ruth Hadley

THE OSPREY HOTEL

Ruthven Road
Kingussie
Inverness-shire PH21 1EN
Tel/Fax: 01540 661510

South end of Kingussie main street.

An attractive small hotel in a quiet Highland town.

* A stone-built town house.
* Traditional Scottish cooking with French
  influences.
* "Friendly, family-run hotel with a consistently
  high standard of imaginative food, always
  cooked to order."

Conveniently situated in the centre of Kingussie,
overlooking the memorial gardens, The Osprey
Hotel is an excellent base from which to explore
this part of the Highlands. Attention to detail, good
food and a fine cellar are all features of The Osprey
which bring so many guests back to the hotel time
after time. Aileen Burrow uses only fresh
ingredients always cooking to order with great
care, skill and imagination. Bread rolls are baked
daily on the premises and desserts are understated
and memorable. Both Robert and Aileen have an
excellent local knowledge and this combined with
their skill as friendly hosts ensures that guests
thoroughly enjoy their stay at the Osprey. The hotel
has 1 AA Rosette.

Open all year
🏠 Rooms: 8 with private facilities
🛏 DB&B £42–£56   B&B £24–£36
🆂🅿 Special rates available
✘ Dinner £££
Ⓥ Vegetarians welcome
👪 Children over 10 years welcome
♿ Facilities for disabled visitors

**Potted prawns wrapped in smoked salmon. Roast
duck breast served with grape and red wine sauce.
Baked chocolate cheesecake with Mascarpone
cream.**

STB Commended 🏆 🏆 🏆
💳 Credit cards: Mastercard/Eurocard, American
  Express, Visa, Diners Club
🔣 Proprietors: Robert & Aileen Burrow

SCOT HOUSE HOTEL
Newtonmore Road
Kingussie
Inverness-shire PH21 1HE
Tel: 01540 661351
Fax: 01540 661111

South end of main road through village of Kingussie (B9152 off A9 trunk road).

An attractive, well-appointed hotel set amid the unique natural splendour of the Highlands, within easy reach of three golf courses.

- A converted manse.
- Outstanding home cooking.
- "Good Scottish food in comfortable friendly surroundings."

George MacKenzie was a local man who made his fortune in Canada by founding the Singer Sewing Machine Company. In 1884 he provided the funds to build the village's Free Presbyterian Church manse. Converted in the 1960s, it is now the Scot House Hotel. Its present owners have recently restored and refurbished the entire building. With both table d'hôte and à la carte menus, the dining room makes the most of the area's excellent beef, fish and game yet also offers a vegetarian menu. Unpretentious and good, the hotel's cooking is matched by a varied and affordable wine list. Bar lunches and suppers are distinguished by wholesome ingredients, freshly prepared. Scot House Hotel has 1 AA Rosette.

Open 8 Feb to 6 Jan except Christmas Day + Boxing Day
- 🛏 Rooms: 9 with private facilities
- 🍴 DB&B £40–£57.50   B&B £27.50–£39
- ✘ Lunch £
- ✘ Dinner ££-£££
- Ⓥ Vegetarians welcome
- ☆ Children welcome
- ♿ Facilities for disabled visitors: entry ramp and toilets
- ✖ No smoking in dining room

Fantail of honeydew melon with fresh raspberries in a pool of Drambuie cream. Medallions of venison with a sauce of fresh rosemary and redcurrants. Ecclefechan tart with home-made ice cream.

STB Highly Commended 🏆 🏆 🏆
- 💳 Credit cards: Mastercard/Eurocard, Visa, Switch, Delta
- ⚜ Proprietors: W E Gilbert & W N McConachie

SKIARY
Loch Hourn, Invergarry
Inverness-shire PH35 4HD
Tel: 01809 511214

From Invergarry (on A82 Fort William–Inverness road) take A87 Invergarry–Kyle road. After 5 miles turn left to Kinlochourn. Proceed for 22 miles to end of single track road (allow 1 hour). You will then be met by boat by arrangement.

Remote, small guest house without mains electricity, accessible only by boat or on foot.

- A unique guest house on the shore of a dramatic West Highland sea-loch.
- Home cooking.
- "Wonderful, skilled and hearty home cooking with the added bonus of surroundings which are a walkers' and sailors' paradise, or simply a 'get away from it all' retreat."

This must be the most remote guest house in Scotland but the journey is worth it. Christina's cooking is miraculous, she uses excellent fresh local game, meat and fish. Vegetables, herbs and soft fruit come from the garden; and bread, scones and pastry are baked daily. The tiny bedrooms are charming. Views from the house are truly spectacular with an abundance of wild life to be seen. A fantastic experience, not for the faint-hearted. Dining in a new conservatory outside the cottage, overlooking the loch.

Open 1 May to 30 Sep
- 🛏 Rooms: 3
- 🍴 £370 per week Full Board £60 per night Full Board
- SP Special rates available
- ✘ Residents only
- 🍷 Unlicensed – guests welcome to take own wine
- ✘ Food available all day
- ✘ Lunch
- ✘ Dinner
- Ⓥ Vegetarians welcome
- ☆ Children welcome
- ♿ Downstairs bedroom suitable for mildly disabled visitors
- 🚫 No parking at establishment but parking at end of the road

Home-made soups. Duck with brandy and green peppercorns. Chocolate Marquise.

- 💳 No credit cards
- ⚜ Owners: John & Christina Everett

BUNRANNOCH HOUSE
Kinloch Rannoch
Perthshire PH16 5QB
Tel/Fax: 01882 632407

Turn right after 500 yards on Schiehallion road, just
outside Kinloch Rannoch off B846. White 3-storey
building on right hand side.

**A family-run country guest house in Highland
Perthshire.**

- An old hunting lodge in lovely surroundings.
- Traditional cooking.
- "A gem of a place – warm, homely and
  welcoming with magnificent cuisine."

Set amidst mature trees, Bunrannoch is a Listed
building and stands on the site of a medieval
settlement, in the shadow of the 'sleeping giant'
mountain, close to Loch Rannoch. There is an easy
informality within this comfortable family home,
making guests feel completely at ease and totally
relaxed. The cosy lounge, log fires and uninterrupted
Highland views complement the delicious aromas
from the kitchen. Jennifer Skeaping is the chef/
proprietor and her good cooking and friendly
manner assure you of an enjoyable stay. The menus
(a choice of two main courses) change daily, fresh
food is sourced locally and tastefully prepared.

Open all year except Christmas + New Year
- 🏠 Rooms: 7, 5 with private facilities
- 🛏 DB&B £32–£35   B&B £18–£20
- SP Special rates available
- ✕ Dinner ££
- V Vegetarians welcome – prior notice required
- 🚭 No smoking throughout

**Croustade of Rannoch smoked venison, avocado
and redcurrant jelly. Duck breasts marinated in soy
sauce with ginger and garlic. Heather honey and
whisky ice cream with lacy oat biscuits.**

STB Commended 👑 👑
- 💳 Credit cards: Mastercard/Eurocard, Visa
- 🗝 Proprietor: Jennifer Skeaping

THE LOMOND COUNTRY INN
Kinnesswood, by Loch Leven
Perthshire KY13 7HN
Tel: 01592 840253
Fax: 01592 840693

4 miles from Kinross. From south, M90 junction 5,
B9097 via Scotlandwell. From north, M90 Junction 7,
A911 via Milnathort.

**Family-run hotel/inn overlooking Loch Leven and
popular meeting place for locals.**

- Hotel in an historic village.
- Scottish/home cooking.
- "Friendly, family-run hotel."

This is an honest and unpretentious country hotel in
the village of Kinnesswood. People come here for
the food and the fine views as the inn is
conveniently situated just minutes off the
motorway. The food is freshly prepared and the
dishes have a traditional Scottish character. A good
wine list and some interesting real ales complement
the menus and food is available throughout the day.
The hotel has 1 AA Rosette.

Open all year
- 🏠 Rooms: 12 with private facilities
- 🛏 DB&B £37.50–£40   B&B £30–£35
- SP Special rates available
- ✕ Food available all day £
- ✕ Lunch £
- ✕ Dinner ££
- V Vegetarians welcome
- 🧒 Children welcome
- ♿ Facilities for disabled visitors
- 🚭 No smoking in restaurant

**Smoked mussel salad with honey and tarragon
dressing. Chicken breast stuffed with smoked
salmon and rolled in oatmeal. Raspberry
cranachan.**

STB Commended 👑 👑 👑
- 💳 Credit cards: Mastercard/Eurocard, American
  Express, Visa, Diners Club, Switch, Delta
- 🗝 Proprietor: David Adams

THE GROUSE AND CLARET

Heatheryford Country Centre
by Kinross
Tayside KY13 7NQ
Tel: 01577 864212
Fax: 01577 864920

20 metres from M90 at junction 6, opposite service station. 500 metres up private road.

Restaurant with rooms.

- Converted farm.
- Home/traditional cooking featuring some Thai flavours.
- "A wonderful blend of Scottish traditional cuisine with a hint of the Orient."

Situated in 25 acres of wild meadow surrounded by ten acres of water stocked with wild rainbow and brown trout, The Grouse and Claret (named after a fishing fly) offers good home cooking, with many traditional dishes appearing on the menus. Seasonal game and fresh shellfish are a speciality and vegetarians are well catered for. Meriel Cairns and her sister Vicki Futong take great pride in their successful establishment, assuring you of a warm welcome in lovely surroundings. The detached accommodation has comfortable ground floor rooms overlooking the fishing lochans. The Heatheryford Gallery has regular exhibitions of contemporary art.

....

	Open all year except 2 wks end Jan Boxing Day + New Year's Day Note: Closed Mon Jan to Apr
⌂	Rooms: 3 with private facilities
⇔	DB&B £45.50–£55.50 B&B £27.50–£34.50
♀	Table licence
✕	Lunch except Mon Jan to Mar ££
✕	Dinner except Sun Mon Jan to Mar ££-£££
Ⓥ	Vegetarians welcome
⚘	Children welcome
♿	Facilities for disabled visitors
⚞	No smoking in restaurant

A cheese soufflé with three Scottish cheeses and fresh herbs. Medallions of fillet of Scottish beef with a claret and wild mushroom sauce. Home-made ice cream in a brandy snap basket.

STB Commended ♛ ♛ ♛

⊞	Credit cards: Mastercard, Visa
⋈	Proprietor: Meriel Cairns
⋈	Manager: Vicki Futong

THE MUIRS INN KINROSS

49 Muirs, Kinross
Kinross-shire KY13 7AU
Tel/Fax: 01577 862270

M90 exit junction 6 and follow A922 Milnathort for a short distance. At 'T' junction, inn is diagonally opposite to right.

A popular village inn offering Scottish hospitality.

- Good, fresh, honest food at sensible prices.
- The best of straightforward home cooking – and more.
- "An historical inn with character."

Built in the early 19th century as a farmhouse, the Muirs Inn is near the shores of Loch Leven. Mary, Queen of Scots, was imprisoned on an island there in 1567. The inn merits its excellent and growing reputation for attention to detail and care for guests' comfort in its five bedrooms, all with private facilities. The same care is evident in the inn's food and ethos. The Maltings restaurant has a warm, homely feel and offers a vast menu from traditional pub food to Caribbean and Chinese. All are freshly prepared and well-presented. This is an establishment run by and for people who care.

....

	Open all year
⌂	Rooms: 5 with private facilities
⇔	DB&B £40–£42 B&B £27.50–£29.50
SP	Special rates available
✕	Lunch £
✕	Dinner ££/Supper £
Ⓥ	Vegetarians welcome
⚘	Children welcome
♿	Facilities for disabled visitors

Tomato filled with a smoked fish and Orkney cheese soufflé laced in leek. Venison medallions fried with apple and nutmeg, enhanced with redcurrant jus. Cloutie dumpling.

STB Commended ♛ ♛ ♛

⊞	Credit cards: Mastercard/Eurocard, Visa, Switch, Delta
⋈	Innkeepers: G M Westwood & G Philip

AULD ALLIANCE RESTAURANT
Castle Street
Kirkcudbright DG6 4JA
Tel: 01557 330569

Kirkcudbright town, opposite the castle.

Small restaurant in Kirkcudbright.

- A Listed stone terraced cottage.
- French/Scottish cooking.
- "Aptly named – good Scottish produce in French style."

This is a converted tradesman's cottage built from stones quarried from Kirkcudbright Castle on the other side of the street. The restaurant is unfussy, plain and simple inside which is just as well for the dishes cooked by Alistair Crawford will focus your attention. They are a wonderful mixture of fresh local foods cooked in opulent, classical French style – the style in which Alistair was trained. The spirit of the establishment echoes the ancient union between Scotland and France – and what better way to express the bond than through the confluence of technique and supply.

Open Easter to 31 Oct
- ✗ Sun lunch only £
- ✗ Dinner £££
- Ⓥ Vegetarians welcome
- ☆ Children welcome
- ♿ Facilities for disabled visitors

Kirkcudbright Bay king scallops, sautéed in garlic butter, syboes, fish veloute and baked in pastry. Kirkcudbright Bay queen scallops with smoked Ayrshire bacon, finished with Galloway cream. Home-made brandy jumble basket filled with apple and Drambuie 'witches foam'.

- 🝙 No credit cards
- ⚔ Proprietors: Alistair & Anne Crawford

THE SELKIRK ARMS HOTEL
High Street
Kirkcudbright
Dumfries & Galloway DG6 4JG
Tel: 01557 330402
Fax: 01557 331639

At the east end of the High Street in the old part of the town.

A gourmet restaurant in a small town hotel.

- Historic hotel in a pretty town.
- Innovative Scottish.
- "Inspirational cuisine – dining here is a delightful experience."

This place is another gem, having recently undergone some changes and with a new chef – Adam McKissock – setting new standards. The cuisine is excellent, innovative and inspired and the dishes presented are of superb quality. This is enhanced by professional and courteous service. This is a small town hotel with good facilities but with a restaurant which in the words of our 'seasoned' Inspector is "worth travelling miles for dinner." Selkirk Arms has 1 AA Rosette.

Open all year except Christmas night
- 🛏 Rooms: 16 with private facilities
- 🛏 DB&B £57–£63   B&B £40–£49
- ⓢⓅ Special rates available
- ✗ Lunch £
- ✗ Dinner £££
- Ⓥ Vegetarians welcome
- ☆ Children welcome
- ♿ Facilities for disabled visitors
- 🚭 No smoking in restaurant

Confit of duck arranged on a bed of champit potatoes surrounded by a summer berry jus. Seared tranche of salmon on a Parmesan risotto and smoked haddock fishcake accompanied by a citrus butter sauce. Crisp brandy basket filled with fresh strawberries and a whisky and oatmeal ice cream nestling on a pool of toffee sauce.

STB Highly Commended 👑 👑 👑 👑
- 🝙 Credit cards: Mastercard/Eurocard, American Express, Visa, Diners Club, Mastercharge, Switch, Delta, JCB
- ⚔ Partner: John Morris

LOCHSIDE LODGE & ROUNDHOUSE RESTAURANT
Bridgend of Lintrathen, By Kirriemuir
Angus DD8 5JJ
Tel: 01575 560340

From Kirriemuir take the B951 road, signposted The Glens. Pass through village of Kingoldrum and 5 miles down road to Lintrathen you will see Lochside Lodge signposted.

Delightful restaurant with rooms in attractive hamlet.

- Converted farm steading/roundhouse.
- Modern/traditional Scottish cuisine of a very high standard.
- "The roundhouse has character, charm and outstanding food."

Original stone walls and small wooden paned windows of the converted steading are a most attractive feature of this lodge and restaurant. The building is surrounded by mature trees and the loch is encircled by continuous beech hedge and therefore makes a delightful setting for a very special dining experience, which may be enjoyed by families as well as the discerning diner. It is expertly run by Stephen and Jackie Robertson and the interior has been thoughtfully restored in keeping with the character of the building. The atmosphere is relaxed. The style of cooking is modern, with excellent local produce well-cooked, with interesting combinations and menus that present something for everyone and offering excellent value for money.

Open all year except Boxing Day + New Year's Day
Closed Mon
- 🏠 Rooms: 4 with private facilities
- 🛏 B&B £25–£35
- SP Special rates available
- ✕ Lunch except Mon ££
- ✕ Dinner except Mon ££
- Ⓥ Vegetarians welcome
- ⭑ Children over 12 years welcome
- ⚹ Limited facilities for disabled visitors
- ⚹ No smoking in restaurant

Salmon and Dunsyre Blue cheese flan with sour cream dressing. Cutlets of Perthshire lamb with an onion and herb crust over an Arran mustard reduction. Hot treacle tart, cinnamon ice cream and vanilla sauce.

- 💳 Credit cards: Mastercard/Eurocard, Visa, Switch, Delta
- 🄽 Proprietors: Stephen & Jackie Robertson

CONCHRA HOUSE HOTEL
nr Dornie
by Kyle of Lochalsh
Ross-shire IV40 8DZ
Tel: 01599 555233
Fax: 01599 555433

From south continue westwards 1km on A87 past Dornie/Eilean Donan Castle. Follow hotel signposts turning right for ¾ mile (Sallachy/Killilan Road).

An historic 18th century hunting lodge.

- A family-run country house hotel.
- Good fresh food, plainly cooked.
- "Restful and attentive care in comfortable surroundings."

Conchra House was built in the 1760s to house the government's agent in Kintail, following the seizure of Jacobite estates after the '45 Rising. The house is most attractive, fits into the landscape well and enjoys a lovely situation overlooking Loch Long. It is full of interesting antiques and period details. Conchra means 'a fold' or 'haven' and the stated aim of Colin and Mary Deans, the hotel's resident owners, is to provide just this for their guests. They succeed in full measure. The place is wonderfully peaceful; guests are made to feel very much at home; the food is simple but intelligently cooked and appetising. A gem of a place.

Open all year except 24, 25, 31 Dec + 2 Jan
- 🏠 Rooms: 6, 3 with private facilities
- 🛏 DB&B £37.50–£57.50   B&B £25–£40
- SP Special rates available
- 🍴 Open to non-residents – by arrangement
- ♀ Restricted licence
- ✕ Lunch – by prior arrangement ££
- Ⓥ Vegetarians welcome
- ⭑ Children welcome
- ⚹ No smoking throughout

Avocado pear, grape and local goats cheese with mint vinaigrette. Loch salmon with orange hollandaise sauce. Baked nectarine cheesecake.

STB Highly Commended 👑 👑 👑
- 💳 Credit cards: Mastercard/Eurocard, American Express, Visa, Switch
- 🄽 Proprietors: Colin & Mary Deans

THE SEAFOOD RESTAURANT

Railway Station, Kyle of Lochalsh
Ross-shire IV40 8XX
Tel: 01599 534813

At Kyle of Lochalsh railway station on platform 1.
Parking on slipway to station.

An informal bistro and cafe in an unusual setting.

- Converted station waiting room.
- Freshly cooked, good quality food.
- "Good cooking at modest prices."

A railway platform is not the obvious choice of
location for a restaurant but it is worth taking the
trouble to track down The Seafood Restaurant for
you will not be disappointed. The station is right next
to the harbour in Kyle of Lochalsh close to the ferry
terminal which, before the bridge, was the main
crossing point to Skye. From your table in the
converted waiting room you can look out over the
Cuillins. The philosophy here is to present high
quality local produce, predominantly fish and
shellfish cooked simply. Although the abundant
seafood is prominent on the menu there is also an
interesting selection of meat and vegetarian dishes.
In the peak season there is a breakfast and lunch
menu with a selection of simple, home-cooked fare
which changes to give a more sophisticated à la
carte choice in the evening. You are advised to
check opening hours as they vary depending on the
time of year.

Open Easter to Oct
♀ Table licence
✗ Lunch except Sun Sat £
✗ Dinner ££
Ⓥ Vegetarians welcome
☆ Children welcome
♿ Limited facilities for disabled visitors
⊭ No smoking in restaurant

**Smoked venison and Brie with a tangy port and
cranberry sauce. Seafood kebabs: monkfish,
scallops and prawns in a dill and orange sauce.
Hazelnut meringue with rum cream.**

💳 Credit cards: Mastercard/Eurocard, Visa
🏠 Owners: Jann Macrae & Andrea Matheson

SEAGREEN RESTAURANT & BOOKSHOP

Plockton Road
Kyle of Lochalsh IV40 8DA
Tel: 01599 534388

Just immediately outside Kyle on the Duirinish to
Plockton visitor route.

**A relaxed, informal bistro combined with bookshop
and gallery.**

- Charming stone-built bistro restaurant.
- Modern Scottish cooking, innovative and of good
  quality.
- "Delicious food with a very original approach."

Situated on the outskirts of Kyle of Lochalsh this is a
very attractive complex of an open plan kitchen and
large, spacious dining area with a bookshop at one
end which sells literature and traditional music CDs
and cassettes. The dining room exhibits works of
local painters and photographers. Outside there is a
sheltered sunny garden and terrace, popular with
guests. An all day counter service offers delicious
salads, soups, home baking, etc., all made on the
premises from fresh local ingredients. The
restaurant offers very good wholefood but the
emphasis is increasingly on fish and shellfish. In the
evening a full à la carte dinner menu is served in a
separate dining room. The style of the food is
different from that served during the day with a
more   sophisticated   continental/European
influenced menu.

Open all year except 25, 26 Dec,
1 Jan, 6 Jan – Easter
✗ Lunch £
✗ Dinner ££-£££
🍽 Reservations preferred for dinner
Ⓥ Vegetarians welcome
☆ Children welcome
♿ Facilities for disabled visitors
⊭ No smoking in restaurant

**Local goats cheese soufflé, with salad leaves and
walnut dressing. Lochalsh king scallops, with
Chardonnay sauce and fresh herb crumble. Mead
and caramelised oatmeal ice creams with
strawberry sauce.**

💳 Credit cards: Mastercard/Eurocard, Visa,
Switch
🏠 Chef/Proprietor: Fiona Begg

THE OLD SMIDDY
Laide, nr Gairloch, Wester Ross IV22 2NB
Tel/Fax: 01445 731425

On the main road at Laide, on the A832 Gairloch –
Braemore road.

**Unique cottage guest house with small restaurant
in the tiny village of Laide.**

- Small guest house.
- Imaginative, creative, Scottish home cooking.
- "Cottage restaurant with great food where
  nothing is too much trouble."

Seven miles north of the famous Inverewe Gardens
and opposite the church sits The Old Smiddy, an
attractive and well-converted white cottage
(formerly the village blacksmith shop). Kate is a self-
taught enthusiastic cook assisted by her husband
Steve who ensures that menus are created around
guests desires. The trend now being towards
seafood of which there is an abundance in Wester
Ross but also encompassing all the finest Highland
produce which can be sourced locally. The dishes
are then compiled with interesting finishing sauces,
imaginative presentation using home-grown herbs.
Genuine warm hospitality in superior Highland
cottage providing a culinary oasis for those who
enjoy above average fayre.

Open Mar to mid Nov
- Rooms: 3, 2 with private facilities
- DB&B £38–£46   B&B £18–£26
- Special rates available
- Unlicensed – guests welcome to take own wine
- Dinner – early booking advisable for non-
  residents ££
- Vegetarians welcome
- Facilities for non-resident disabled visitors
- No smoking throughout

Shell and smoked fish platter accompanied by
Dunsyre Blue, tomato and olive bread. Roast
saddle of venison finished with port and wild
mushrooms. Drambuie and oatmeal parfait.

STB Highly Commended 👑 👑 👑
- Credit cards: Mastercard/Eurocard, Visa
- Proprietors: Kate & Steve Macdonald

BRISBANE HOUSE HOTEL
14 Greenock Road
Largs
Ayrshire KA30 8NF
Tel: 01475 687200
Fax: 01475 676295

On the seafront at Largs on A78. Midway between
Greenock and Irvine.

Seaside town hotel.

- Modern Georgian styled hotel.
- Accomplished cooking - seafood specialities.
- "A seaside hotel offering excellent food,
  comfortable rooms and panoramic views."

Brisbane House Hotel is a family Georgian styled
hotel located on the seafront in Largs and
overlooking the Isle of Arran and the Kyles of Bute.
The hotel is comfortable and with a well-appointed
conservatory to the front which allows visitors to
make the most of the hotel's setting. This also
extends to the cocktail bar/lounge. Menus are
varied with food well-cooked and at prices to suit
every occasion. Brisbane House Hotel has 1 AA
Rosette.

Open all year
- Rooms: 23 with private facilities
- DB&B £55-£99.75   B&B £40-£80
- Special rates available
- Food available all day £-££
- Lunch £
- Dinner ££
- Vegetarians welcome
- Children welcome
- Facilities for disabled visitors

Timbale of Cumbrae prawns wrapped in a whisky-
smoked salmon with an orange and tarragon
dressing. Marinated Perthshire venison with a
juniper and gin sauce. Raspberry and Drambuie
cranachan.

STB Commended 👑 👑 👑 👑
- Credit cards: Mastercard/Eurocard, American
  Express, Visa, Diners Club, Mastercharge,
  Switch, Delta
- Owner: Suzanne McDonald Purewal

LIVINGSTON'S RESTAURANT

High Street
Linlithgow, West Lothian
EH49 7AE
Tel: 01506 846565

At eastern end of the High Street opposite the Post Office.

A charming little restaurant in an historic town.

- Restaurant in old stone cottage.
- Modern Scottish cooking.
- "Innovative, talented cooking and warm hospitality."

This is a delightful little cottage tucked behind the High Street. Exposed stone walls and assorted tables and chairs provide a charm and warmth which is enhanced by dark red candles, table mats and napkins. The atmosphere is friendly and informal and the food and service is of the highest quality. There is also a conservatory which overlooks a pleasant little attractive garden. Chef David Williams is enthusiastic and is a skilful and imaginative cook and provides interesting menus with much evidence of fresh Scottish produce. Livingston's has 1 AA Rosette. *(See advert Page 232.)*

Open Feb to Dec except 1wk Oct
Closed Sun Mon
✗ Lunch except Sun Mon £
✗ Dinner except Sun Mon £££
Ⓥ Vegetarians welcome
⚘ Children over 8 years welcome – evenings
♿ Facilities for disabled visitors
⚲ Smoking permitted in conservatory

Bouillon of wild mushrooms with seared salmon and caviar chantilly. Saddle of venison with caramelised onions and roast brambles. Duo of caramel parfait and miniature crème caramel.

💳 Credit cards: Mastercard/Eurocard, Visa, Switch
ⓜ Manager: Fiona Livingston

ACHRAY HOUSE HOTEL

St Fillans
Perthshire PH6 2NF
Tel: 01764 685 231
Fax: 01764 685 320

On A85, 12 miles from Crieff.

Family-run rural hotel beside Loch Earn.

- Traditional white-painted hotel.
- Traditional cooking based on quality produce.
- "A warm welcome and personal service is the feature here."

Now owned and run by John and Lesley Murray, this popular and well-established hotel has a stunning lochside position with its own foreshore and jetty, in this area of outstanding natural beauty. They set impressively high standards and the food is offered across a range of menus in both bar and restaurant and provides an excellent choice. The dining room is tastefully appointed. *(See advert Page 234.)*

Open all year
🛏 Rooms: 9, 8 with private facilities
🛏 DB&B £32–£52   B&B £20–£34.50
ⓢⓟ Special rates available
✗ Lunch £
✗ Dinner ££
Ⓥ Vegetarians welcome
⚘ Children welcome
♿ Facilities for disabled visitors
⚲ No smoking in restaurant

Wide choice of Scottish produce – salmon, lamb, beef, venison, seafood. Good choice of freshly made vegetarian dishes always available. Home-made puddings a speciality.

STB Commended 👑 👑 👑
💳 Mastercard/Eurocard, American Express, Visa, Switch
ⓜ Proprietors: John & Lesley Murray

FOUR SEASONS HOTEL

St Fillans
Perthshire PH6 2NF
Tel/Fax: 01764 685 333

On A85, 12 miles west of Crieff, at west end of St Fillans overlooking Loch Earn.

Country hotel in the rural village of St Fillans.

* Edwardian building with tasteful extensions.
* Traditional/modern Scottish cooking.
* "A personal welcome awaits in this family-run hotel."

Loch Earn is one of the most beautiful Perthshire lochs, surrounded by woods and hills. The Four Seasons has a wonderful unspoiled view from where the seasons can truly be seen to change over the year. The hotel has well-maintained bedrooms and rather quaint public rooms and bar. The Scott family run the hotel very efficiently and Chef Andrew Scott produces menus which have a strong emphasis on seafood and game in the best traditions of the Taste of Scotland. On warmer days dine alfresco on the south facing terrace. The Four Seasons has 2 AA Rosettes.

Open Mar to Nov
* Rooms: 18 with private facilities
* DB&B £53.50–£65   B&B £34–£44
* Special rates available
* Lunch ££
* Dinner £££
* Vegetarians welcome
* Children welcome
* Facilities for disabled visitors
* No smoking in dining room

Terrine of venison, wood pigeon, juniper, lentils, apple chutney. Fillet of halibut with West Coast scallops and mussels. Iced rhubarb and orange parfait.

STB Commended 👑 👑 👑 👑
* Credit cards: Mastercard/Eurocard, American Express, Visa, Diners Club, Switch
* Owners: The Scott Family

CAMERON HOUSE HOTEL AND COUNTRY ESTATE

Loch Lomond, Alexandria
Dunbartonshire G83 8QZ
Tel: 01389 755565
Fax: 01389 759522

On A82 near Balloch, on the banks of Loch Lomond. At Balloch roundabout follow signs for Luss. Approx 1 mile, first right.

Luxury hotel and leisure complex on the shores of Loch Lomond.

* Converted baronial mansion with time-shared lodges and a state-of-the-art leisure complex.
* Modern contemporary cooking
* "Comfort, luxury, good food and service all wrapped up in this baronial home."

A luxury hotel resort on the southern shore of Loch Lomond, standing in 108 acres of parkland. Executive Chef Peter Fleming presents a highly sophisticated and imaginative menu in the hotel's main restaurant, the elegant Georgian Room. The bright and airy Smolletts Restaurant has a more relaxed atmosphere and offers a wide variety of dishes from an à la carte menu; bar snacks are available in the Breakers Restaurant at the Marina. Cameron House has 3 AA Rosettes.

Open all year
* Rooms: 96 with private facilities
* DB&B £95–£200   B&B £85–£185
* Food available all day £-££££
* Lunch except Sun Sat ££
* Dinner ££££
* Vegetarians welcome
* Children welcome
* Facilities for disabled visitors
* No smoking in Georgian Room
* Member of the Scotch Beef Club

Lanark Blue cheese soufflé. Roast wild salmon, Celtic cabbage and Oban scallops. Hot banana soufflé, vanilla ice cream

STB Deluxe 👑 👑 👑 👑 👑
* Credit cards: Mastercard/Eurocard, American Express, Visa, Diners Club, Mastercharge
* Executive Chef: Peter Fleming

GLENMORISTON ARMS HOTEL
Invermoriston
Inverness-shire IV3 6YA
Tel: 01320 351206
Fax: 01320 351308

At junction of A82 and A887 in Invermoriston.

A Highland sporting hotel with a village inn atmosphere; ideal location for country sports and holidays combined with spectacular scenery.

- A traditional drovers inn in Glenmoriston for over 200 years.
- Imaginative Scottish cooking featuring speciality game dishes.
- "Glenmoriston has a welcoming atmosphere with Scottish themed menus."

Glenmoriston Arms is a traditional Highland sporting hotel which has stood in Glenmoriston for over 200 years. It is situated in a beautiful part of the Highlands only a few hundred yards from Loch Ness with woodlands behind. There is an 'olde worlde' atmosphere inside with the Moriston Bar and Restaurant decorated with antique guns and fishing rods evoking a sporting theme. The restaurant menu is short and fresh with seasonally changing dishes. Resident owners Neil and Carol Scott ensure that guests enjoy their experience at Glenmoriston.

Open all year except Christmas Day
- 🏠 Rooms: 8 with private facilities
- 🛏 DB&B £49-£63   B&B £30-£40
- 🆂🅿 Special rates available
- ✖ Lunch ££
- ✖ Dinner £££
- Ⓥ Vegetarians welcome
- 🅺 Children welcome
- ♿ Facilities for disabled visitors – please telephone prior to booking
- 🚭 No smoking in restaurant

Timbale of haggis, neeps and tatties on a whisky and chive sauce. Seafood treasure chest with fresh local scallops, prawns, salmon and sole, flamed in Pernod, set in a crisp pastry puff. Ecclefechan tart served with a cinnamon crème fraîche.

STB Highly Commended 👑 👑 👑 👑
- 💳 Credit cards: Mastercard/Eurocard, Visa, Switch, Delta
- 🅽 Resident Owners: Neil & Carol Scott

CARRON RESTAURANT
Cam-Allt, Strathcarron
Ross-shire IV54 8YX
Tel: 01520 722488

Lochcarron to Kyle of Lochalsh road, 4 miles from Lochcarron village.

Restaurant overlooking Loch Carron.

- Charming purpose-built restaurant.
- Skilful home cooking.
- "A place to seek out and return to."

This restaurant lies at the side of Loch Carron and is most attractively positioned. Its appeal is enhanced by the clean-cut exterior adorned with hanging flower baskets and tubs of flowers. It is adjacent to the Carron Pottery which makes the charming hand-thrown crockery used in the restaurant. The restaurant itself is furnished in pine, and paintings for sale by local Highland artists line the walls. Apart from the daily specials which depend on local catches and seasonal produce, there is a range of dishes from substantial grills to smaller dishes like home-made salmon quiche. For travellers, the restaurant is also now open for an early hearty breakfast.

Open 1 Apr to end Oct
Closed Sun
- ✖ Food available all day £
- ✖ Lunch £
- ✖ Dinner ££
- Ⓥ Vegetarians welcome
- 🅺 Children welcome
- ♿ Facilities for disabled visitors
- 🚭 No smoking throughout

Lochcarron king scallops in garlic butter and herbs. Wild venison steak, char-grilled and served with rowan jelly. Strawberry pavlova or local cheeses.

- 💳 Credit cards: Mastercard/Eurocard, American Express, Visa
- 🅽 Proprietors : Seamus & Sarah Doyle

ROCKVILLA HOTEL & RESTAURANT

Main Street, Lochcarron
Ross-shire IV54 8YB
Tel/Fax: 01520 722379

Situated in centre of village, c. 20 miles north of Kyle of Lochalsh.

Little hotel in centre of village.

- Small family-run hotel.
- Traditional Scottish cooking.
- "A simple 'pub lunch' but with food of an excellent quality.

This is an attractive little restaurant with bar and four comfortable rooms above. The restaurant has an open outlook to the loch and hills, and Lorna and Kenneth Wheelan are attentive hosts. An à la carte dinner menu offers excellent value and gives a good choice of starters, main courses and puddings. Local specialities and traditional favourites mean that there is something for everyone. After a hearty breakfast guests are well set up for a day's walking, fishing or exploring the West Highlands with its dramatic scenery.

....

Open all year except Christmas Day + 1 Jan
- 🏠 Rooms: 4 with private facilities
- 🛏 B&B £22–£30
- SP Special rates available
- ✗ Lunch £
- ✗ Dinner ££
- Ⅴ Vegetarians welcome
- ☆ Children welcome
- ⌇ No smoking in restaurant

Filo basket of Lochcarron queen scallops with smoked bacon and Brie. Pan-fried Aberdeen Angus sirloin with whisky, cream and mushroom sauce. Cloutie Dumpling.

STB Commended 🏵 🏵 🏵
- 💳 Credit cards: Mastercard/Eurocard, Visa, Switch, Delta
- 🎴 Proprietors: Lorna & Kenneth Wheelan

THE ALBANNACH

Lochinver, Sutherland IV27 4LP
Tel/Fax: 01571 844407

From Lochinver follow signs for Baddidarroch. After ½ mile, pass turning for Highland Stoneware, turn left for The Albannach.

An excellent small restaurant overlooking Lochinver.

- Restaurant with rooms.
- Contemporary Scottish cooking.
- "Relaxed and friendly atmosphere, backed up with superb, fresh, locally sourced foods."

The Albannach is a 19th century house of considerable architectural character standing in a small glen overlooking Lochinver and the wild country beyond. It has been tastefully decorated by Colin Craig and has a Victorian feel and a cosy atmosphere. Drinks are available in the conservatory, which has a paved patio and stone balustrade beyond it. Dinner is served in the wood-panelled, candlelit dining room. Lesley Crosfield presents a set, four course dinner menu which relies entirely on the availability of fresh, free-range produce, her cooking is creative and assured. Colin Craig serves at table, resplendent in kilt and Jacobean shirt and some nights a piper plays outside before dinner.

....

Open last 2 wks Mar to 27 Dec
- 🏠 Rooms: 5 with private facilities
- 🛏 DB&B £59–£65
- SP Special rates available
- ✗ Non-residents welcome – booking essential
- ♀ Table licence
- ✗ Dinner 4 course menu £££
- Ⅴ Vegetarians welcome – by prior arrangement
- ☆ Children over 10 years welcome
- ⌇ No smoking throughout

Warm tartlet of Badnaban crab with a lime and cucumber dressing. Fillets of hare and woodpigeon on juniper kale with port and rosemary jus. Pears roasted in Chardonnay and cinnamon, with orange and Cointreau parfait.

STB Highly Commended 🏵 🏵 🏵
- 💳 Credit cards: Mastercard/Eurocard, Visa
- 🎴 Chef/Proprietors: Lesley Crosfield & Colin Craig

INVER LODGE HOTEL
Iolaire Road, Lochinver
Sutherland IV27 4LU
Tel: 01571 844496 Fax: 01571 844395

A837 to Lochinver, first turn on left after village hall.
½ mile up private road to hotel.

A new West Highland hotel in the 'grand hotel' tradition.

- A modern luxury hotel with outstanding views.
- Modern Scottish cooking, with classic/grand hotel influences.
- "What a wonderful place – fabulous setting, luxurious surroundings and professional, well-trained staff."

Inver Lodge was opened in 1988. It stands on the hill above Lochinver village and bay, and enjoys panoramic views across the Minch and the wild country of Assynt. The building itself is long, low and plain – even spartan. Inside, however, it is comfortably and tastefully appointed, with a 'highland shooting lodge' theme (it has good private fishing for salmon and trout); public rooms and bedrooms are spacious and airy, and all share the terrific view . It has a snooker room, solarium and sauna. Members of staff are uniformed in tartan, well-trained and courteous. À la carte and table d'hôte menus feature Lochinver-landed fish and shellfish and Assynt venison. The cooking is highly professional, and the presentation and service is in the 'grand hotel' style. Great care and effort goes into every aspect of Inver Lodge's hospitality. *(See advert Page 29.)*

- Open 10 Apr to 1 Nov
- 🛏 Rooms: 20 with private facilities
- 🛏 DB&B £75–£100   B&B £60–£100
- ⓈⓅ Special rates available
- ✕ Lunch £
- ✕ Dinner £££
- Ⓥ Vegetarians welcome
- ★ Children welcome
- ⅍ No smoking in dining room
- 🐄 Member of the Scotch Beef Club

West Coast mussels served with a white wine, parsley and cream sauce. Medallions of venison served with a whisky and peppercorn sauce. Highland cranachan.

STB Deluxe 👑 👑 👑 👑
- ⊞ Credit cards: Mastercard/Eurocard, American Express, Visa, Diners Club, Switch, Delta, JCB
- Ⓜ General Manager: Nicholas Gorton

SOMERTON HOUSE HOTEL
Carlisle Road
Lockerbie DG11 2DR
Tel: 01576 202583
Fax: 01576 204218

Follow High Street eastwards towards M74, 1 mile from town centre.

Small, family hotel on the edge of the town

- Sandstone mansion.
- Classic contemporary.
- "Traditional food served with modern influences."

Situated on the outskirts of town, with views to open countryside yet within easy striking distance of the M74, the hotel stands in its own spacious grounds facing the road with well-kept pretty gardens to one side and ample private parking. Inside this attractive merchant's villa/mansion has retained many of its superb original features in excellent order and combined these expertly with all the best of modern comforts making the hotel a relaxing and charming place to stay. A bar menu is served in the extensive cosy lounge and adjoining patio lounge bar while a full à la carte is served in the delightful dining room. There are plans to add a conservatory in 1997 adding a private meeting room/restaurant. The food is hearty and the dishes familiar but served with some style in these pleasant surroundings. Popular with locals and visitors alike, a warm welcome awaits guests at the Somerton.

- Open all year
- 🛏 Rooms: 7 with private facilities
- 🛏 B&B £26–£30
- ✕ Lunch £
- ✕ Dinner ££-£££
- Ⓥ Vegetarians welcome
- ★ Children welcome
- ⅍ No smoking in dining room

Lowland Ham and Haddie: a local speciality of smoked haddock and ham in a cream sauce topped with croûtons, tomato and cheese. Barbary duckling on a nest of crispy noodles surrounded by a raspberry pond. Strawberry tiramisu.

STB Commended 👑 👑 👑 👑
- ⊞ Credit cards: Mastercard/Eurocard, American Express, Visa, Diners Club
- Ⓜ Proprietors: Alex & Jean Arthur

OLD MANOR HOTEL

Leven Road, Lundin Links
Fife KY8 6AJ
Tel: 01333 320368
Fax: 01333 320911

On A915 Kirkcaldy–St Andrews, 1 mile east of
Leven, on right overlooking Largo Bay.

**An excellent comfortable and friendly hotel in a
golfer's paradise.**

- Country house.
- Contemporary Scottish cuisine.
- "Friendly and informal hotel in the heart of golf-
  country."

Owned and run by the Clark family, their commitment
to what they do here is obvious. The Clarks are a
mine of information and advice on the game of golf.
Their Aithernie Restaurant serves both à la carte and
table d'hôte dishes, based on fresh local meat and
fish, imaginatively prepared and presented. The wine
list is sound and reasonably priced. The restaurant's
success has been reflected by a number of awards
for chef Alan Brunt. The hotel's Coachman's Grill
caters for a different market, serving upmarket,
inexpensive food simply and unpretentiously. The Old
Manor has 2 AA Rosettes.

Open all year except Boxing Day +
     New Year's Day
🏩 Rooms: 25 with private facilities
🛏 DB&B £40.50–£105, B&B £25–£80
SP Special rates available
✗ Food available all day ££
✗ Lunch ££
✗ Dinner £££
V Vegetarians welcome
☆ Children welcome
⅄ Facilities for disabled visitors
⅄ No smoking in restaurant
🐂 Member of the Scotch Beef Club

**Mille feuille of peppered Shetland salmon on a
lemon butter sauce with keta. Supreme of corn fed
chicken filled with a pigeon mousse, served with a
gâteau of black pudding and apple. King William
pear poached in Pinotage, served with amaretto
ice cream.**

STB Highly Commended 👑 👑 👑 👑
💳 Credit cards: Mastercard/Eurocard, American
     Express, Visa, Mastercharge, Switch, Delta,
     JCB
🧍 Owners: Clark Family

THE PORTLAND ARMS HOTEL

Lybster
Caithness KW3 6BS
Tel: 01593 721208
Fax: 01593 721446

On A9, 12 miles south of Wick.

**A small, family-run hotel in a beautiful Caithness
village.**

- A historic roadside hotel.
- Unpretentious and wholesome cooking.
- "Homely atmosphere, hearty food served by
  friends."

This hotel was built as a staging post for the
turnpike roads in the 19th century. Today, it makes
for an excellent base from which to explore the
charms of the surrounding countryside. The
emphasis now is on attentive, cheerful service. All
bedrooms are comfortable and well-equipped.
Some even have jacuzzi baths en suite. Local
weddings and small conferences enjoy the hotel's
new function room. The menus are straightforward,
using local produce when available, and represent
good value for money.

Open all year except 1 + 2 Jan
🏩 Rooms: 19 with private facilities
🛏 DB&B £55–£65   B&B £38.50–£45
SP Special rates available
✗ Food available all day £
✗ Lunch ££
✗ Dinner £££
V Vegetarians welcome
☆ Children welcome
⅄ Facilities for disabled visitors
⅄ No smoking in dining room

**Oak-smoked salmon with dill sauce. Fillet of beef
Wellington with Madeira sauce. Baked fillet of
lemon sole with cream and prawns.**

STB Commended 👑 👑 👑 👑
💳 Credit cards: Mastercard/Eurocard, American
     Express, Visa, Diners Club, Mastercharge,
     Switch
🧍 Owners: Helen & Gerald Henderson

MARINE HOTEL
Mallaig
Inverness-shire PH41 4PY
Tel: 01687 462217
Fax: 01687 462821

Adjacent to railway station. First hotel on right off A830, and a 5 minute walk from ferry terminal.

A family-run hotel in the fishing port of Mallaig.

- Long established local small town hotel.
- Traditional wholesome cooking.
- "A reliable, long established hostelry."

Mallaig is at the end of the famous West Highland Railway Line and also marks the termination of The Road to the Isles. Once the busiest herring port in Britain, the town has still a busy fishing harbour and is the main ferry terminal to the Hebrides. The hotel has well-appointed bedrooms, 18 of which are en suite. The menus, which are offered in both lounge bar and the recently refurbished restaurant, take full advantage of freshly landed fish and shellfish. Good selection of malt whiskies available.

Open all year except Christmas Day + New Year's Day
Note: Restricted service Nov to Mar
🏠 Rooms: 19 with private facilities (1 with separate private facilities)
🛏 DB&B £40–£45   B&B £26–£30
SP Special rates available
✕ Lunch ££
✕ Dinner ££
Ⓥ Vegetarians welcome
⚘ Children welcome
🦽 Limited facilities for disabled visitors
🚭 No smoking in restaurant

Marinated seafood salad. Scallops in crème fraîche and wine sauce. Roast rack of lamb on a red wine marmalade. Cloutie dumpling with home-made ice cream.

STB Commended 👑 👑 👑
💳 Credit cards: Mastercard/Eurocard, Visa
👤 Proprietor: Dalla Ironside

LADYBURN
by Maybole, Ayrshire KA19 7SG
Tel: 01655 740 585
Fax: 01655 740 580

A77 (Glasgow-Stranraer) to Maybole then B7023 to Crosshill. Turn right at War Memorial (Dailly-Girvan). After exactly 2 miles, turn left and follow signs. 5 miles south of Maybole.

Country house hotel.

- 17th century country house.
- Home cooking.
- "Good home cooking and hospitality."

Ladyburn is an historic house set deep in 'the most beautiful valley in Ayrshire' and is the family home of Jane and David Hepburn. You are surrounded by family heirlooms and portraits, and comfortable antique furniture. There is a homely authenticity about the food served in the dining room, reflecting Jane Hepburn's commitment to produce genuine dishes cooked with original touches of flavours and textures; neither overbearing nor trendily understated. Substantial well-tried recipes cooked with care are the order of the day. Dining room open at all times for residents. Italian, French, German and Russian spoken.

Open all year except 2 wks Nov + 4 wks during Jan to Mar
🏠 Rooms: 8 with private facilities
🛏 DB&B £90–£120   B&B £70–£100
SP Special rates available
♀ Restricted licence
🅜 Reservations essential for non-residents
✕ Lunch except Mon ££
✕ Dinner except Sun Mon £££
Ⓥ Vegetarians welcome
⚘ Children over 16 years welcome
🦽 Facilities for disabled visitors
🚭 No smoking in dining room, drawing room + bedrooms

Smoked fillet of venison with brandy and orange dressing. Rack of lamb with fresh herb crust served with an apple, mint and red wine jus. Poached peaches with Amaretto.

💳 Credit cards: Mastercard/Eurocard, American Express, Visa
👤 Proprietors: Jane & David Hepburn

BURTS HOTEL

Market Square, Melrose
Roxburghshire TD6 9PN
Tel: 01896 822285 Fax: 01896 822870

A6091, 2 miles from A68, 38 miles south of Edinburgh.

A family-run 18th century hostelry.

- Delightful 18th century restored inn.
- Modern Scottish cooking.
- "No trip to the Borders would be complete without a meal here."

Burts Hotel, is a delightful 18th century Scottish inn. It stands in the centre of the square of this Borders market town, and is always bustling with activity. It is run by Graham, Anne and Nicholas Henderson, professional and friendly hosts, who make their guests feel very welcome. Their restaurant has a good local reputation. The à la carte menu is extensive and displays a thorough familiarity with contemporary eating fashions. Both it and the regularly changing table d'hôte menu are ambitious and display imaginative combinations, creative confidence and a sound appreciation of appropriate flavours. The cooking and presentation is akin to that which you would expect to find in a refined country house. Burts has 2 AA Rosettes. *(See advert Page 234.)*

Open all year except Boxing Day
🏠 Rooms: 20 with private facilities
🛏 DB&B £60–£65   B&B £44–£50
ᴾ Special rates available
✗ Lunch except Christmas Day + Boxing Day ££
✗ Dinner except Christmas Day + Boxing Day £££
Ⓥ Vegetarians welcome
🕏 Children welcome
🚭 No smoking in restaurant
🐄 Member of the Scotch Beef Club

Grilled fillet of smoked haddock laid on a pillow of spinach, crowned with a duck egg. Pave of venison with a port wine and juniper jus. Selkirk bannock pudding with shortbread ice cream.

STB Highly Commended 🏨 🏨 🏨 🏨
💳 Credit cards: Mastercard/Eurocard, American Express, Visa, Diners Club, Switch, Delta, JCB
🔑 Manager: Nicholas Henderson

MELROSE STATION RESTAURANT

Palma Place, Melrose
Roxburghshire TD6 9PR
Tel: 01896 822546

100 yards from Market Square. Take Dingleton Road signposted B6359 to Lilliesleaf – first right just before bridge.

Modern bistro restaurant in historic Border town.

- Converted 19th century station-master's house.
- Modern Scottish, with international influences.
- ""Converted station-master's house into bistro/restaurant offering interesting dishes using local produce."

Melrose Station Restaurant is situated in an A Listed building which overlooks the leafy town and famous abbey. The restaurant's style is modern and tasteful, simple and elegant, friendly and informal – the approach is bistro-style. Claire Paris was trained in Aberdeen and also gained hotel experience in Australia. Her excellent small restaurant is much patronised by locals. Head Chef Angus McIntosh is responsible for the superb cuisine, presenting a blackboard menu at lunchtime and a more formal table d'hôte menu at dinner, with steaks as a new addition. There is an option of just two courses if the full menu seems a little daunting!

Open all year except 25 Dec to 31 Dec + first 3 wks Feb
Closed Mon
✗ Lunch except Mon ££
✗ Dinner except Sun Mon Tue £££
Ⓥ Vegetarians welcome
🕏 Children welcome
♿ Facilities for disabled visitors

Roast duck breast and avocado salad with caramelised orange sauce Filo parcel of salmon, halibut, prawns, tomato and pesto topped with lemon hollandaise.

💳 Credit cards: Mastercard/Eurocard, Visa, Delta
🔑 Proprietor: Claire Paris

WELL VIEW HOTEL
Ballplay Road, Moffat
Dumfriesshire DG10 9JU
Tel: 01683 220184
Fax: 01683 220088

Leaving Moffat take A708. At crossroads, left into
Ballplay Road – hotel on right.

Family-run hotel offering first class cuisine.

- Victorian town house with gardens.
- Modern Scottish cooking.
- "Taste of Scotland in natural and modern style."

Janet and John Schuckardt run this traditional
hotel, which has a peaceful garden and stands on
the outskirts of Moffat. It is within easy walking
distance of the centre of this charming town which
sits in a fertile plain below the dramatic Devil's Beef
Tub. John has a good knowledge of wine and has
over 100 bins available. The six course menu
demonstrates an inventive approach to more
familiar dishes, accompanied by light fruity sauces
and dressings. The meat is served pink and the
vegetables al dente, which is a good sign of use of
fresh produce. The owners go out of their way to
look after their guests every need. German and a
little French spoken. Well View has 2 AA Rosettes.

....

    Open all year
🏦 Rooms: 6 with private facilities
🛏 DB&B £57–£77   B&B £30–£50
SP Special rates available
✗ Lunch except Sat ££
✗ Dinner 6 course menu £££
💺 Prior reservation essential for both lunch +
    dinner
Ⓥ Vegetarians welcome
★ Children over 5 years welcome at dinner
⤸ No smoking throughout

**Watercress and Cairnsmore cheese tartlet with
onion marmalade and salad. Roast breast of
Guinea fowl on a risotto of chicken liver, bacon
and chives with woodland mushrooms and a port
wine sauce. Sable galette of summer fruits with a
fruit coulis.**

STB Deluxe 👑 👑 👑
💳 Credit cards: Mastercard/Eurocard, American
    Express, Visa
👤 Owners: Janet & John Schuckardt

THE LINKS HOTEL
Mid Links, Montrose
Angus DD10 8RL
Tel: 01674 671000
Fax: 01674 672698

From town centre follow signs to the Links and
the beach. Links Hotel is situated in a pleasant
residential area.

**A town hotel in an attractive setting, a short walk
from the beach.**

- Town house hotel.
- Scottish cooking with French influence.
- "Interesting menus, fresh food with French flair."

The Links is a comfortable hotel overlooking a
tree-lined park, where the emphasis is on the
informal. Its location makes it ideal for golfers,
anglers, bird-watchers and general touring. All of
the 22 bedrooms have been extensively refurbished
and a multi-purpose function suite and conference
facilities are new for 1998. The cooking is good
Scottish with French influences, and Head Chef
Franc Rivault ensures that only the freshest
produce is used. Menus are interesting and offer
good value for money. This is one place which
successfully surpasses expectations.

....

    Open all year except 4 to 11 Jan
🏦 Rooms: 22 with private facilities
🛏 DB&B from £47 (value breaks) Fri-Sun only
SP Special rates available
✗ Food available all day
✗ Lunch ££
✗ Dinner ££-£££
Ⓥ Vegetarians welcome
★ Children welcome
♿ Facilities for disabled visitors

**Arbroath smokie and leek terrine. Loin of Scottish
lamb with rosemary essence. Fresh local wild
berries au gratin.**

STB Approved 👑 👑 👑 👑
💳 Credit cards: Mastercard/Eurocard, American
    Express, Visa, Mastercharge, Delta
👤 Executive Head Chef: Mr Franc Rivault

ORD HOUSE HOTEL
Muir of Ord
Ross-shire IV6 7UH
Tel/Fax: 01463 870 492

On A832 Ullapool-Marybank, ½ mile west of Muir of Ord.

A relaxed and friendly small country house hotel in beautiful surroundings.

- Country house hotel.
- Good country cooking.
- "This converted laird's house offers the best of fresh local produce."

John and Eliza Allen offer their guests the unhurried peace of a bygone age in this 17th century laird's house. Open fires and an elegant drawing room match the calm beauty of the hotel's 50 acres of grounds. Bedrooms are tastefully decorated and well-appointed. The dining room offers unpretentious and reasonably-priced honest country cooking that uses fresh meat, game and fish and vegetables, in season, from the hotel's own garden. Service is attentive without being fussy. The wine list is sound and inexpensive. Fluent French is spoken.

Open 1 May to 20 Oct
- ⌂ Rooms: 11 with private facilities
- ⇔ DB&B £55.50–£61.50   B&B £35–£41
- ✗ Lunch £
- ✗ Dinner 4 course menu ££
- Ⓥ Vegetarians welcome
- ✶ Children welcome
- ✍ No smoking in dining room

Cassoulet of wild mushrooms. Fresh-dived West Coast scallops served in the shell in a leek and mushroom sauce. Home-made banoffi ice cream in a brandy snap basket.

STB Commended ♕ ♕ ♕
- ▣ Credit cards: Mastercard/Eurocard, American Express, Visa
- ▨ Proprietors: John & Eliza Allen

CAWDOR TAVERN
The Lane, Cawdor
Nairn-shire IV12 5XP
Tel/Fax: 01667 404 777

Turn off A96 to Cawdor. Tavern is clearly signposted.

Traditional village inn with friendly atmosphere.

- An historic inn.
- Modern, freshly prepared cooking.
- "A quaint village inn with very good food and hospitality."

Cawdor Tavern is a country pub located in the quiet conservation village by Cawdor Castle. The building itself was originally the castle workshop and the old oak panelling that decorates the walls was gifted by the old laird. The Sinclair family – formerly of The Moorings Hotel in Fort William – are well-known for their skill in the hospitality business. The food here is wholesome making good use of fresh products, with a blackboard menu featuring daily speciality dishes offering good value for money. A popular place for the traveller and locals.

Open all year except 25, 26 Dec, 1 + 2 Jan
- ✗ Lunch £
- ✗ Dinner ££
- Ⓥ Vegetarians welcome
- ✶ Children welcome
- ♿ Facilities for disabled visitors
- ✍ No smoking area in restaurant

Crab and salmon fishcakes. Drynachan pheasant wrapped in bacon served with a red wine and lovage jus set on a bed of crushed potatoes. Sticky ginger pudding accompanied by home-made vanilla ice cream.

- ▣ Credit cards: Mastercard/Eurocard, American Express, Visa, Diners Club, Switch
- ▨ Proprietor: Norman Sinclair

THE GOLF VIEW HOTEL
& LEISURE CLUB
Seabank Road
Nairn IV12 4HD
Tel: 01667 452301
Fax: 01667 455267

At west end of Nairn. Seaward side of A96. Turn off at large Parish Church.

A large sporting hotel with a leisure club.

- 19th century seafront mansion converted into a modern hotel, leisure club and terrace restaurant.
- Modern Scottish cooking.
- "A spectacular view, good food and hospitality – a delightful experience."

Adjacent to the Nairn Golf Club, the appropriately named 'Golf View' is also within an hour's drive of 25 further courses. The hotel has a fully equipped leisure club has a magnificent swimming pool and multi-gym. The restaurant offers a nightly changing, invitingly descriptive, table d'hôte menu. Fish and shellfish are featured strongly, as well as locally sourced meat and game. Creative and well-made sauces complement the dishes and demonstrate the chef's expertise. Vegetarian dishes show skill and imagination, and delicious fresh bread is baked every day. The Conservatory is open all day, every day, serving food.

Open all year
- 🛏 Rooms: 47 with private facilities
- 🛏 DB&B £50–£86   B&B £47.50–£65
- SP Special rates available
- ✗ Food available all day ££
- ✗ Lunch £
- ✗ Dinner 4 course menu £££
- V Vegetarians welcome
- ☀ Children welcome
- ♿ Facilities for disabled visitors
- ⊁ No smoking in restaurant + conservatory

Home-made venison sausage with horseradish potato and Madeira sauce. Fillet of turbot with scallops, mussel and red onion stew. Chocolate and Tequila Mousse.

STB Highly Commended 👑 👑 👑 👑 👑
- 💳 Credit cards: Mastercard/Eurocard, American Express, Visa, Diners Club, Switch
- Ⓜ General Manager: Greta Anderson

CREEBRIDGE HOUSE HOTEL
Minnigaff, Newton Stewart
Wigtownshire DG8 6NP
Tel: 01671 402121
Fax: 01671 403258

From roundabout signposted Newton Stewart on A75, through the town, cross bridge over river to Minnigaff. 250 yards – hotel on left.

Country house hotel situated in pleasant gardens.

- An old Galloway family house with character and charm.
- Imaginative country house cooking.
- "Traditional Scottish country house, fresh local produce excellently prepared by chef owner Chris Walker."

Creebridge House Hotel was formerly owned by the Earls of Galloway and its present resident owners, Chris and Sue Walker, have made sure that it retains an atmosphere of unhurried elegance, peace and tranquillity. The drawing room has an ornate ceiling and period fireplace, not to mention a baby grand piano. There is a choice of eating during the day, either in the bar or in the main restaurant. Chef/proprietor Chris Walker and his Head Chef Paul Sommerville present imaginative table d'hôte menus for the Garden Restaurant and outstanding à la carte bar menus. Winner of The Taste of Scotland Scotch Lamb ChallengeCompetition Classic Section 1996. *(See advert Page 26.)*

Open all year except 24 to 26 Dec
- 🛏 Rooms: 20 with private facilities
- 🛏 DB&B £45–£60   B&B £30–£42
- SP Special rates available
- ✗ Lunch £
- ✗ Dinner ££
- V Vegetarians welcome
- ☀ Children welcome
- ♿ Facilities for disabled visitors
- ⊁ No smoking in restaurant

Open lasagne of wild forest mushrooms with fresh asparagus spears and chervil butter. Fillet of Galloway beef with horseradish crust finished with roast shallots and a rich red wine jus. Gratin of fresh Scottish raspberries with home-made Drambuie ice cream.

STB Commended 👑 👑 👑 👑
- 💳 Credit cards: Mastercard/Eurocard, American Express, Visa, Switch, Delta
- Ⓜ Proprietors: Chris & Sue Walker

KIRROUGHTREE HOUSE
Newton Stewart
Wigtownshire DG8 6AN
Tel: 01671 402141
Fax: 01671 402425

From A75 take A712 New Galloway road, hotel 300 yards on left.

Delightful, grand Scottish country hotel set in attractive grounds.

- 18th century mansion converted into a stylish, family-run country house hotel.
- Gourmet Scottish cooking.
- "Wonderful surroundings, excellent gourmet Scottish cooking."

Kirroughtree has all the grandeur and opulence of an historical mansion, it is sumptuously furnished and elegantly decorated, yet it has an atmosphere which is welcoming and considerate rather than over-formal. There are two dining rooms, reached from the panelled lounge. Head Chef, Ian Bennett, was trained by the celebrated Michel Roux, and his cooking is highly accomplished. The menus are short (three main courses at dinner, two at lunch), creative and well-balanced. Special golfing packages at sister hotel, Cally Palace and local Newton Stewart course. Kirroughtree has 2 AA Rosettes. Winner of The Taste of Scotland Special Merit Award 1993.

Open 14 Feb to 3 Jan
- ⌂ Rooms: 17 with private facilities
- ⇔ DB&B £65–£95   B&B £55–£80
- ⒮ᴾ Special rates available
- ✗ Lunch – booking essential ££
- ✗ Dinner 4 course menu £££
- Ⓥ Vegetarians welcome – prior notice required
- ⚲ Children over 10 years welcome
- ⚲ No smoking in dining rooms
- 🐂 Member of the Scotch Beef Club

Bavarois of Scottish smoked salmon with red pepper coulis and sevruga caviar. Rump of Kirroughtree venison with poached pear and grand veneur sauce. Iced apple parfait with apple fritters and Armagnac caramel.

STB Deluxe 👑 👑 👑 👑
- 💳 Credit cards: Mastercard/Eurocard, Visa, Switch
- Ⓜ Manager: James Stirling

MARINERS
81 High Street
North Berwick
East Lothian EH39 4HG
Tel: 01620 893171

Central position in High Street

Coffee shop with traditional home baking.

- Sunny coffee shop in High Street.
- Home cooking.
- "Coffee shop offering traditional home baking and traditional fare in modern style."

This new coffee shop in the main street of this seaside town is run by Rod and Lorna Bunney, formerly Taste of Scotland members in the north of Scotland. The coffee shop has a calm atmosphere and offers a good selection of dishes ranging from good home baking to some more substantial dishes throughout the day. For those wishing to enjoy the sea air – packed lunches are available. Smoked salmon, fresh herbs and Scottish cheeses also for sale.

Open all year except Christmas Day, New Year's Day, 1 + 2 Jan
- ✗ Food available all day £
- ✗ Lunch £
- ⚲ Licensed
- Ⓥ Vegetarians welcome
- ⚲ Children welcome
- ♿ Facilities for disabled visitors
- ⚲ No smoking throughout

Spicy leek and potato soup. Salmon and prawn bake with salad and crusty bread. Whisky marmalade ice cream.

- 💳 No credit cards
- Ⓜ Owners: Rod & Lorna Bunney

ARDS HOUSE

Connel, by Oban
Argyll PA37 1PT
Tel: 01631 710255

On main A85 Oban–Tyndrum, 4½ miles north
of Oban.

Family-run guest house overlooking Loch Etive.

- Victorian villa.
- Home cooking.
- "Immediate relaxation in this warm and
  genuinely friendly atmosphere."

This is a comfortable guest house standing on the
shores of a loch, with views over the Firth of Lorn
and the Morvern Hills. All the bedrooms have
private facilities and there is a happy air of the
family home here, encouraged by the owners John
and Jean Bowman, who take great trouble over
their guests. The daily changing set menu is
displayed in the afternoon and any special
requirements are easily catered for. The dishes rely
on local produce where possible, combining a taste
for detail and fresh home cooking.

	Open Feb to mid Nov
▥	Rooms: 6 with private facilities
⊨	DB&B £35–£44.50 B&B £25–£38
ⓢⓟ	Special rates available
✕	Non-residents – by arrangement
⚲	Restricted licence
✕	Dinner 4 course menu ££
Ⓥ	Vegetarians – by arrangement
⚹	Children over 12 years welcome
⅟	No smoking throughout

**Potato pancake with seared local shellfish. Roast
rack of lamb with red wine sauce. Crème de
Menthe parfait with fresh fruit and coconut
biscuits.**

STB Commended 👑 👑 👑
- ⊞ Credit cards: Mastercard/Eurocard, Visa,
  Switch, Delta
- Ⓜ Proprietors: John & Jean Bowman

DUNGALLAN HOUSE HOTEL

Gallanach Road, Oban
Argyllshire PA34 4PD
Tel: 01631 563799 Fax: 01631 566711

In Oban, at Argyll Square, follow signs for
Gallanach. ½ mile from Square.

**A fine old Victorian house offering a tranquil,
country atmosphere.**

- A small and friendly country house hotel.
- Traditional fresh Scottish/home cooking.
- "A genuine welcome enhances the warm and
  friendly atmosphere of this pleasant and tranquil
  hotel."

Set in its own five acres of mature woodland yet
close to Oban's bustling centre, Dungallan House
was built in 1870 by the Campbell family. It was
used as a hospital in the First World War and as HQ
for the Flying Boat Squadrons in the Second. Now
owned and refurbished by George and Janice
Stewart, Dungallan House enjoys magnificent
panoramic views over Oban Bay to the Island of
Mull, Lismore and the Hills of Morvern. As is
appropriate for this prime West Coast port, menus
take full advantage of the range of fresh fish and
shellfish available locally. Janice Stewart does the
cooking in person. The well-balanced table d'hôte
menu offers four/five choices for each course. The
wine list offers something to match each dish on
Dungallan's rounded menu. Dungallan has 1 AA
Rosette. *(See advert Page 28.)*

	Open all year except Nov Feb
▥	Rooms: 13, 9 with private facilities
⊨	DB&B £53–£70 B&B £33–£48
ⓢⓟ	Special rates available
✕	Lunch £
✕	Dinner £££
Ⓥ	Vegetarians welcome
⚹	Children welcome
♿	Limited facilities for disabled visitors
⅟	No smoking in dining room
🐂	Member of the Scotch Beef Club

**Squat lobsters in a hot garlic vinaigrette dressing.
Duck breast on caramelised red cabbage with
redcurrant and mango sauce. Strawberry meringue
roulade.**

STB Commended 👑 👑 👑
- ⊞ Credit cards: Mastercard/Eurocard, Visa
- Ⓜ Directors: Janice & George Stewart

THE GATHERING SCOTTISH RESTAURANT AND O'DONNELL'S IRISH BAR
Breadalbane Street, Oban
Argyll PA34 5NZ
Tel: 01631 565421/564849/566159
Fax: 01631 565421

Entering Oban from A85 (Glasgow) one-way system. Turn left at Deanery Brae into Breadalbane Street (signs for swimming pool etc.) then right at bottom of Deanery Brae.

An informal, distinctively Scottish, town restaurant.

- A popular restaurant and bar with a Celtic theme.
- Good, plain cooking.
- "Steeped in history this is an unusual and interesting place to enjoy fine Scottish food."

First opened in 1882 as a supper room for the famous annual Gathering Ball, The Gathering has a distinguished pedigree and is rightly popular with Oban's many tourists. With antlers and targes on the walls, the restaurant's ambience is decidedly and memorably Scottish. The menu offers first-class, straightforward dishes made from local meat and seafood, as well as a range of imaginative starters and popular 'lighter bites'. The wine list is well-chosen and fairly priced. Portions are generous, prices modest and service cheerful. During July to September live music is available every night in O'Donnell's Irish Bar e.g. ceilidhs, folk music and local musicians. Live music at weekends off season.

Open Easter to New Year except Christmas Day, New Year's Day + some Suns
Closed Sun off season – please telephone
Note: closed to public last Thu in Aug
✕ Lunch £-££: off season – by reservation
✕ Dinner ££-£££
Ⓥ Vegetarians welcome
✶ Children welcome
♿ Facilities for disabled visitors
⚡ No smoking in restaurant

Ocean Bounty Platter: best of fresh local seafood. Fillet of local venison charcoal grilled, with a port and tarragon sauce. Cranachan.

💷 Credit cards: Mastercard/Eurocard, Visa, Switch, Delta, JCB
Ⓝ Owner/Chef: Elaine Cameron

ISLE OF ERISKA
Ledaig, by Oban
Argyll PA37 1SD
Tel: 01631 720 371
Fax: 01631 720 531

A85 north of Oban, at Connel Bridge take A828 for 4 miles. North of Benderloch village follow signs to Isle of Eriska.

Exceptional hotel by any standards.

- An impressive, grey granite Scottish baronial house built in 1884, romantically situated on an island reached by a short road bridge.
- Gourmet country house cuisine.
- "To dine here is to experience impeccable service, superb cuisine and the gentleness of discreet courtesy."

The Buchanan-Smith family have run their home on the island of Eriska as a hotel for over 20 years and manage to combine the intimate atmosphere of a family-run country house with the highest standard of professional service. In the dining room, internationally acclaimed standards of cuisine are meticulously maintained. The hotel has a leisure complex with swimming pool, etc. Isle of Eriska has 3 AA Rosettes. Winner of The Macallan Taste of Scotland Hotel of the Year Award 1994.

Open all year except Jan + Feb
🏠 Rooms: 17 with private facilities
🛏 B&B £195–£230
✕ Open to non-residents for dinner only
✕ Lunch – residents only
✕ Dinner 7 course menu ££££
Ⓥ Vegetarians welcome
✶ Children over 10 years old welcome at dinner
♿ Facilities for disabled visitors
⚡ No smoking in dining room
🐄 Member of the Scotch Beef Club

Timbale of scallop and courgette with squat lobsters, artichoke and champagne butter sauce. Seared pave of lamb, sweetbread and rosemary mousse, chanterelle and truffle jus. Chocolate nemesis with white chocolate sorbet.

STB Deluxe 👑 👑 👑 👑 👑
💷 Credit cards: Mastercard/Eurocard, American Express, Visa, Mastercharge, Switch
Ⓝ Partner: B Buchanan-Smith

THE MANOR HOUSE
Gallanach Road, Oban
Argyll PA34 4LS
Tel: 01631 562087
Fax: 01631 563053

From Argyll Square, Oban, follow signs for
Gallanach and the car ferry. Continue for
approx ½ mile.

An historic house overlooking Oban Bay.

- Small country house hotel.
- Scottish cooking with French influences.
- "A house of great character which combines
  elegance with modern amenities."

Situated on the southern tip of Oban Bay, the Manor
House was built in 1780 by the Duke of Argyll, and
was first a factor's residence and then a Dower
House. In 1826 Oban's first bank, 'The National',
opened here and in 1845 Admiral Otter used it as his
base which conducted hydrographic surveys on the
West Coast. Latterly it was the home of the
MacLeans of Drimnin. The house retains much of
the charm and atmosphere of the past. The five
course table d'hôte dinner menu (three/four
starters, three/four main courses) changes every
day, according to what is available and seasonal.
The cooking is fresh and creative. The Manor
House has 1 AA Rosette.

Open all year
N.B. From 1 Nov to 1 Mar closed after
Sun lunch until Tue dinner time
🏨 Rooms: 11 with private facilities
🛏 DB&B £46–£80   B&B £26–£60
🆂🅿 Special rates available
✖ Lunch £
✖ Dinner 5 course menu £££
🆅 Vegetarians welcome
🚭 No smoking in dining room

**Warm scallop and bacon salad with spinach and
vegetables juliennes. Loin of venison saddle with a
compote of wildberries. Whisky and oatmeal
parfait with a honey syrup.**

STB Highly Commended 👑 👑 👑 👑
💳 Credit cards: Mastercard/Eurocard, American
   Express, Visa, Switch
👤 Manageress: Gabriel Wijker

THE SCOTTISH SALMON CENTRE
Kilninver, Oban
Argyll PA34 4QS
Tel: 01852 316202
Fax: 01852 316262

7 miles south of Oban on A816 on the shores of Loch
Feochan.

**Attractive building overlooking Loch Feochan with
shop, restaurant, and Visitors Centre.**

- Well-planned centre well worth a visit for
  all ages.
- Good Scottish cooking.
- "Good Scottish cooking with interesting
  exhibition and gift shop."

The Scottish Salmon Centre has successfully
combined a shop, educational exhibition and
restaurant, making it one of the very interesting
places to visit near Oban. The centre itself has been
carefully decorated and finished with pleasing
individual touches and the shop – which you pass
through to the restaurant – is crammed with
interesting gifts of food and non-perishables – all
that is best from Argyll and the islands. The food, as
you would expect, specialises in seafood but not
exclusively so and everything is well-cooked. There
is something to suit all pockets here and children
are especially welcome and thoughtfully catered
for. Traditional Scottish afternoon teas are a
speciality. Now open for dinner the setting is ideal
to watch the glorious West Coast sunsets
shimmering on the loch. The centre has 1 AA
Rosette.

Open Mar to end Oct
✖ Food available all day £
✖ Lunch £
✖ Dinner ££
🆅 Vegetarians welcome
🧒 Children welcome
♿ Facilities for disabled visitors

**Melon and smoked Argyll ham. Fillet steak with
local langoustine. Iced honey and whisky creams.**

STB Commended Visitor Attraction
💳 Credit cards: Mastercard/Eurocard, Visa
👤 Managing Director: Robert Provan

YACHT CORRYVRECKAN
Dal an Eas
Kilmore, nr Oban
Argyll PA34 4XU
Tel/Fax: 01631 770246

Stylish yacht exclusively designed for West Coast cruising and gourmet eating.

- Charter yacht.
- Best fresh home cooking.
- "Probably the best food afloat on a charter yacht – a superb bonus to a special holiday."

Douglas and Mary Lindsay have been offering chartered cruises on the West Coast for many years and brought all their experience to bear when they designed Corryvreckan (strictly speaking Corryvreckan II, since their earlier vessel had the same name). She is 65 feet overall, 16 feet in the beam and has a wonderfully spacious feel – standing room is available throughout. There are five double guest cabins, and the dining table seats 12 comfortably. Mary's cooking is wonderful: everything (even baking and canapés) is cooked fresh; the galley is full of potted herbs; every night is a dinner party. Guests are members of the crew and help with washing up as well as actually sailing the ship. This is a memorable experience!

Open Apr to Oct
⌂ Cabins: 5
🛏 DB&B £435–£480 per person for 1 week cruise – all incl
SP Special rates available for whole boat charter
UL ℧ Unlicensed – wine provided with dinner
⅍ No smoking below deck
🚗 Parking available

Arbroath smokies baked in cream with basil and tomato. Ragoût of venison with toasted walnuts. Bramble whisky syllabub.

⊞ No credit cards
⋈ Proprietors: Douglas & Mary Lindsay

MELDRUM HOUSE
Oldmeldrum
Aberdeenshire AB51 0AE
Tel: 01651 872294
Fax: 01651 872464

A947 Aberdeen to Oldmeldrum (15 miles). 13 miles north of Aberdeen airport.

An historic house in rural Aberdeenshire.

- Scottish baronial mansion, now a country house hotel.
- Creative Scottish cooking.
- "Scottish hospitality and very good food in a peaceful location."

Local tradition maintains that King Charles I spent part of his childhood here, when a ward of the Seton family of nearby Fyvie Castle. The historic atmosphere of the house is enhanced by antiques, portraits and faded furniture. The house stands in 15 acres of lawns and woodland, with its own small loch. The resident proprietors are Douglas and Eileen Pearson, attentive and courteous hosts who make you very welcome to their home. Residents and non-residents can enjoy an imaginative and well-constructed four course table d'hôte menu carefully overseen by enthusiastic chef Mark Will.

Open all year
🏠 Rooms: 9 with private facilities
🛏 DB&B £114–£124   B&B £105–£115
SP Special rates available
℧ Restricted licence
✗ Lunch ££
✗ Dinner £££
Ⓥ Vegetarians welcome
✶ Children welcome
♿ Facilities for disabled visitors
⅍ No smoking in restaurant

Pan-fried rainbow trout with anchovy and caper cous cous with mussel sauce. Guinea fowl breast with thyme and lemon dumpling with red wine gravy. Champagne, raspberry and Mascarpone cheesecake.

STB Commended 👑 👑 👑 👑
⊞ Credit cards: Mastercard/Eurocard, Visa, Switch
⋈ Proprietors : Douglas & Eileen Pearson

ALLT-NAN-ROS HOTEL

Onich, by Fort William
Inverness-shire PH33 6RY
Tel: 0185 582 1210
Fax: 0185 582 1462

On A82, 10 miles south of Fort William.

Highland hotel on the shore of Loch Linnhe.

- Lochside Victorian house.
- Country house cooking.
- "A very welcoming hotel where comfort and relaxation is on the menu."

Situated halfway between Ben Nevis and Glencoe, Allt-nan-Ros is an attractive 19th century shooting lodge standing in an elevated position above the loch and commanding spectacular views: a most picturesque situation. The Gaelic name means Burn of the Roses, and derives from the cascading stream which passes through the gardens of the hotel. The decoration is modern, rooms are comfortably furnished and service is personal. Dinner is served in a new conservatory. The menus offer a range of familiar Scottish dishes, prepared from locally sourced ingredients, and the style of the cooking has French influences. An accordionist serenades guests in the dining room from time to time! Allt-nan-Ros has 2 AA Rosettes.

....

Open 1 Jan to 10 Nov
🛏 Rooms: 21 with private facilities
🛏 DB&B £55–£75   B&B £34–£52.50
SP Special rates available
✕ Lunch ££-£££
✕ Dinner 5 course menu £££-££££
Ⓥ Vegetarians welcome
✗ No smoking in dining room

Roasted Mallaig scallops with basil pesto oil. Pan-fried venison with thyme and juniper sauce and rösti potatoes. Caramelised lemon tart with vodka berry sorbet.

STB Highly Commended 🏵 🏵 🏵 🏵
💳 Credit cards: Mastercard/Eurocard, American Express, Visa, Diners Club, Mastercharge, Switch
👤 Proprietor: James Macleod

CUILCHEANNA HOUSE

Onich
by Fort William
Inverness-shire PH33 6SD
Tel: 01855 821226

250 yards off A82 in village of Onich – 9 miles south of Fort William.

An attractive and welcoming West Highland hotel.

- A small country house hotel with a warm welcome and peaceful setting.
- Quality home cooking.
- "Comfortable home-from-home with good home cooking."

This is an old farmhouse (17th century foundation) now a traditional family hotel run by Russell and Linda Scott, who are most welcoming hosts. It stands in its own grounds overlooking Loch Linnhe, peacefully situated with views towards Glencoe and the Isle of Mull, and is pleasantly furnished – with piles of books of local interest and a cosy log fire in the lounge. The set four course dinner menu changes daily, and is complemented by a well thought out wine list, as well as a fine selection of quality malt whiskies. The emphasis is on genuine home-cooking and Linda makes good use of prime local produce and fresh Scottish-grown herbs. The comprehensive breakfast choice includes local favourites such as venison sausage, haggis, herring in oatmeal and Mallaig kippers.

....

Open Easter to end Oct
🛏 Rooms: 7 with private facilities
🛏 DB&B £36–£39   B&B £22–£24
SP Special rates available
✕ Residents only
✕ Dinner 4 course menu ££
Ⓥ Vegetarians welcome
✗ No smoking throughout

Smoked duck breast with a warm Inverness sauce. Baked Megrim sole with a soured cream and tomato sauce. Chocolate soufflé pudding with a coffee crème anglaise.

STB Commended 🏵 🏵 🏵
💳 Credit cards: Mastercard/Eurocard, Visa, Delta
👤 Proprietors: Linda & Russell Scott

FOUR SEASONS BISTRO & BAR

Inchree, Onich
by Fort William
Inverness-shire PH33 6SD
Tel: 01855 821393
Fax: 01855 821287

8 miles south of Fort William. Take Inchree turn-off,
¼ mile south of Corran Ferry, then 250 yards.

Casual dining in a 'log cabin' atmosphere.

- Log cabin style building.
- Modern Scottish cooking.
- "A place of casual easy eating for both locals
  and tourists."

Four Seasons Bistro and Bar is a warm and
welcoming haven in lovely leafy surroundings with
views of Loch Linnhe and Ardgour. It is a family
business and the staff are all pleasant, exuding a
happy atmosphere. The interior is unusual but suits
the timber of the building and the furniture and
decor is pleasing, complementing the style of the
establishment. The menus are interesting, food
well-cooked with much evidence of fresh, locally
caught seafood prepared and presented with care
and attention to detail.

....

    Open Christmas + New Year period
    Winter limited opening until Easter
    Closed Tue except Jul + Aug
✗ Dinner except Tue ££
Ⓥ Vegetarians welcome
⚹ Children welcome
♿ Facilities for disabled visitors
⚬ No smoking in eating areas

**Warm salad of wild mushrooms. Sauté of monkfish
with a light soy sauce on a bed of spring
vegetables. Selection of home-made desserts.**

▣ Credit cards: Mastercard/Eurocard, American
    Express, Visa
Ⅺ Manageress: Susan Heron

THE LODGE ON THE LOCH HOTEL

Onich, by Fort William
Inverness-shire PH33 6RY
Tel: 0185 582 1237
Fax: 0185 582 1238

On A82, 1 mile north of the Ballachulish Bridge.

A well-appointed hotel in beautiful gardens.

- Victorian country hotel, with modern additions.
- Traditional Scottish cooking.
- "This hotel offers top service and food at
  affordable prices."

The Lodge on The Loch Hotel is a granite Victorian
villa with new additions. It stands within yards of
Loch Linnhe and enjoys good views towards the
hills of Morvern. Guests of the Lodge on The Loch
Hotel have automatic membership of a sister hotel's
swimming pool, sauna, steam room, turbo pool,
solarium and multi-gym. The bedrooms are
comfortable and the dining room has delightful loch
views. The table d'hôte menus feature several
Scottish dishes.

....

    Open Christmas/New Year + 2 Feb to 4 Jan
🏠 Rooms: 20, 18 with private facilities
🛏 DB&B £34.50–£79.50   B&B £25–£54
ⓢ Special rates available
✗ Food available all day ££
✗ Lunch ££
✗ Dinner 4 course menu £££
Ⓥ Vegetarians welcome
⚹ Children welcome
♿ Facilities for disabled visitors
⚬ No smoking in dining room

**French pork terrine with dressed salad leaves.
Rosette of beef fillet with sauté calves liver, potato
rosti and red wine sauce. Cepes meringue dessert.**

STB Highly Commended 👑 👑 👑 👑
▣ Credit cards: Mastercard/Eurocard, Visa,
    Mastercharge, Switch, Delta
Ⅺ General Manager: Mr Iain Coulter

OBINAN CROFT

Opinan
Laide
Wester Ross IV22 2NU
Tel: 01445 731548
Fax: 01445 731635

Turn off the A832 Braemore junction-Gairloch road at Laide Post Office. Continue to Mellon Udrigle then Opinan. Obinan Croft is last house by the shore.

Small remote family-run croft with wonderful panoramic views.

- White-washed sea shore house.
- Traditional Scottish cooking.
- "Traditional Scottish hospitality, comfort and wonderful home-cooked produce."

Obinan Croft occupies a solitary position on a headland – you can see it long before you reach it. Innovative furnishings, a mix of old and new blend well together and make for very comfortable, homely and interesting surroundings. Roger and Mairi, owners and hosts, are keen climbers and the sitting room is full of interesting books and photographs. The food here is excellent – Mairi is a self-taught and talented cook and Roger a genial host. All that Taste of Scotland could ask for is offered here – excellent fresh local produce, lovingly prepared and presented in warm convivial surroundings.

Open 1 Mar to 31 Oct
🏨 Rooms: 4 with private facilities
🛏 DB&B £50–£55
✕ Residents only
🍴 Packed lunch £
✕ Dinner ££
♿ Facilities for disabled visitors
🚭 No smoking in dining room + bedrooms

Smoked blackface lamb with grape pickle and home-made wholemeal bread. Baked salmon fillet on a sorrel sauce with carrot and potato cake. Rhubarb and orange compote with stem ginger ice cream and brandy snaps.

💳 Credit cards: Mastercard/Eurocard, Visa, Switch
👤 Proprietors: Roger & Mairi Beeson

THE PEAT INN

Peat Inn, by Cupar, Fife KY15 5LH
Tel: 01334 840206 Fax: 01334 840530

At junction of B940/B941, 6 miles south west of St Andrews.

Delightful first-class restaurant with luxury accommodation.

- Restaurant with rooms in a converted village inn.
- Unpretentious top quality modern cuisine.
- "An intensely enjoyable experience – The Peat Inn oozes quality."

Food and style writers have waxed lyrical about The Peat Inn almost since the day it opened its doors. Chef and owner David Wilson has literally re-written the rule book on Scottish cooking and has created a world class restaurant whose name is synonymous with good food. His bold imaginative cooking style has gained him all the top food and wine awards including his most recent – the Scottish Chef Achievement Award. All ingredients are of the utmost freshness and quality and, with tremendous flair, they are transformed into truly memorable dishes. His wine list is formidable but provides great choice even in the lowest price range. Menus are table d'hôte, à la carte and a tasting menu of six or seven courses which must be ordered for a complete table. The Peat Inn has 3 AA Rosettes.

Open all year except Christmas Day +
New Year's Day
Closed Sun Mon
🏨 Rooms: 8 all with sitting room + private facilities
🛏 DB&B £90–£98, £65–£95
✕ Lunch except Sun Mon 4 course menu ££
✕ Dinner except Sun Mon 4 course menu £££
Ⓥ Vegetarians welcome
🧒 Children welcome
♿ Facilities for disabled visitors
🚭 No smoking in dining rooms
🐂 Member of the Scotch Beef Club

Herb salad with scallops, prawns, avocado and spicy mayonnaise. Roast saddle of venison with wild mushroom and truffle crust. White chocolate mousse with caramelised banana.

💳 Credit cards: Mastercard/Eurocard, American Express, Visa, Diners Club, Switch, JCB
👤 Partners: David & Patricia Wilson

PARK HOTEL
Innerleithen Road, Peebles
Tweeddale EH45 8BA
Tel: 01721 720451
Fax: 01721 723510

At eastern end of High Street (A72).

A peaceful country house hotel with good accommodation and food.

- Attractive baronial style country house set in parkland with views over the River Tweed.
- Traditional hotel cuisine.
- "Good food in peaceful surroundings on banks of the Tweed."

An attractive mansion standing in its own grounds on the outskirts of Peebles, on the banks of the River Tweed. It has a peaceful and relaxing atmosphere and caters primarily for the older visitor. The hotel is surrounded by well-tended gardens and lawns. The comfortable public rooms are on the ground floor. The leisure and sporting facilities of the Peebles Hydro are available to the Park's guests, who are then able to retreat from the family bustle of the larger hotel! The oak-panelled restaurant has splendid views of the Tweed and the rolling Border hills beyond, you will find a wide choice of familiar and more unusual dishes, plainly cooked and nicely presented.

Open all year
- 🏚 Rooms: 24 with private facilities
- 🛏 DB&B £50–£71   B&B £40–£61
- SP Special rates available
- ✕ Lunch £
- ✕ Dinner 4 course ££
- Ⓥ Vegetarians welcome
- 🏃 Children welcome
- ♿ Facilities for non-residential disabled visitors

Venison pâté with cranberry and Drambuie sauce. Aberdeen salmon with a creamy Arran mustard sauce. Trio of chocolate mousses on a bed of fresh raspberry sauce.

STB Commended 🛏 🛏 🛏 🛏
- 💳 Credit cards: Mastercard/Eurocard, American Express, Visa, Diners Club, Mastercharge, Switch
- Ⓜ Manager: Lawson Keay

BALLATHIE HOUSE HOTEL
WINNER MACALLAN SPECIAL MERIT AWARD 1997 – BEST LUNCH
Kinclaven, by Stanley, Perthshire PH1 4QN
Tel: 01250 883268 Fax: 01250 883396

Off A9, 2 miles north of Perth – turn off at Stanley and turn right at sign to Kinclaven.

A fine country house hotel.

- A Victorian baronial house on the River Tay.
- Award-winning modern and classic Scottish cooking.
- "One of Scotland's gems for consistently excellent food."

An elegant turreted mansion, well-seated in superb shooting country on one of the best salmon beats on the mighty River Tay. Chris Longden, Ballathie's Manager, is very experienced, and his Chef, Kevin McGillivray, presents lunches and dinners which one inspector described as 'exceptional.' His menus change daily, use local produce and offer subtle variations on classic Scottish dishes. Ballathie has 2 AA Rosettes. Winner of The Macallan Taste of Scotland Country House Hotel of the Year Award 1994. Winner of The Taste of Scotland Scotch Lamb Challenge Competition Gourmet Section and Overall Winner 1995.

Open all year
- 🏚 Rooms: 28 with private facilities
- 🛏 DB&B £80–£110   B&B £60–£90
- SP Special rates available
- ✕ Food available all day ££
- ✕ Lunch £££
- ✕ Dinner £££
- Ⓥ Vegetarians welcome
- 🏃 Children welcome
- ♿ Facilities for disabled visitors
- 🚭 No smoking in dining rooms
- 🐂 Member of the Scotch Beef Club

Ballathie's home cured Tay salmon in a citrus marinade with pickled cucumber and Arran mustard cream. Roast loin of venison, barley and leek risotto and juniper jus. Ogen melon and kirsch soup with local berries.

STB Deluxe 🛏 🛏 🛏 🛏
- 💳 Credit cards: Mastercard/Eurocard, American Express, Visa, Diners Club, Mastercharge, Switch, Delta, JCB
- Ⓜ Manager: Christopher J Longden

HUNTINGTOWER HOTEL
Crieff Road
Perth PH1 3JT
Tel: 01738 583771
Fax: 01738 583777

Signposted off A85, 1 mile west of Perth,
towards Crieff.

An elegant mansion in its own garden a mile outside Perth.

- County hotel.
- Traditional cooking with modern influences.
- "A warm welcome awaits you at this relaxing venue near Perth."

Huntingtower is a half-timbered Edwardian mansion standing in a four acre garden, with a pretty little stream meandering through it. Both the spacious conservatory and the dining room overlook the garden. The former offers unusual bar meals – including Mexican Fajitas, pasta, omelettes and filled croissants, as well as substantial meat and fish dishes. The latter is an elegant room, panelled from ceiling to floor, with crystal chandeliers, ornate cornices and a very handsome ingle-nook fireplace. Both à la carte and table d'hôte menus are offered, with table d'hôte reasonably priced and offering some unusual dishes and classic sauces. The hotel is a popular venue for weddings and business meetings. Huntingtower has 1 AA Rosette.

Open all year
🏠 Rooms: 27 with private facilities
🛏 DB&B £45–£49.50   B&B £45–£50
SP Special rates available
✗ Lunch £
✗ Dinner ££
V Vegetarians welcome
⚘ Children welcome
♿ Facilities for disabled visitors

Char-grilled smoked salmon steak set on a tossed salad of herbs with a tomato and pesto dressing. Braised brace of quail stuffed with truffle and mushroom duxelle on a port jus. Steamed chocolate sponge pudding with white chocolate ice cream and Cointreau anglaise.

STB Highly Commended 👑 👑 👑 👑
💳 Credit cards: Mastercard/Eurocard, American Express, Visa, Diners Club, Switch
Ⓜ General Manager & Director: Michael Lee

THE LANG BAR & RESTAURANT, PERTH THEATRE
185 High Street, Perth PH1 5UW
Tel: 01738 472709 Fax: 01738 624576

Perth city centre in pedestrian zone at middle section of High Street.

Restaurant and bar which is part of Perth Theatre.

- Theatre restaurant.
- Innovative/traditional Scottish cooking.
- "Culture and cuisine all at the one venue!"

Perth Theatre was built in 1900, and has recently been beautifully restored. The bar, restaurant and coffee bar benefits both from its situation and the refurbishment. The menus are changed to suit the current production (a novel touch!). However being theatrical, when the stage is 'dark' so is the restaurant. The food is of a high standard and covers the range of Scottish meat, fish and game in really rather interesting dishes with continental touches. There is a creative touch in the more traditional dishes which demonstrates chef Colin Potter's culinary energy. During the summer the restaurant is open Thursday to Saturday evening with live music adding to the atmosphere. This place is understandably popular with locals and visitors. Winner of Martini/TMA British Regional Theatre Award for Most Welcoming Theatre in Britain 1995 and winner of The Glenturret – Perthshire Tourist Board Award for the 'Most Enjoyable Restaurant Meal in 1996'.

Open all year except Christmas Day +
Public Holidays
Closed Sun
Note: Please telephone to ensure Restaurant is open
✗ Food available all day ££
✗ Lunch except Sun £
Ⓜ Dinner except Sun – booking advised ££
V Vegetarians welcome
⚘ Children welcome
♿ Facilities for disabled visitors
⚊ Smoking areas in restaurant + coffee bar

Button mushroom stuffed with hazelnut and cheese, coated in oatmeal, deep fried and served on a bed of spinach leaves. Pigeon breast in redcurrant and juniper syrup, wrapped in filo pastry and glazed with rosemary jus. Hot red cherry and almond tart.

💳 Credit cards: Mastercard/Eurocard, American Express, Visa, Diners Club, Mastercharge, Switch, Delta
Ⓜ Catering Manager: Peter Hood

LET'S EAT
WINNER MACALLAN AWARD 1997 – RESTAURANT OF THE YEAR
77/79 Kinnoull Street
Perth PH1 5EZ
Tel: 01738 643377
Fax: 01738 621464

Stands on corner of Kinnoull Street and Atholl Street, close to North Inch. 3 minutes walk from High Street.

An exceptional city bistro restaurant.

- Attractive town centre restaurant.
- Modern Scottish cooking with a continental influence.
- "A wonderful and most memorable meal."

Under the skilled hands of Tony Heath and Shona Drysdale Let's Eat is enjoying growing success in the year since it opened. Tony gained an excellent reputation and won awards for his cooking at The Courtyard in Aberdeen, and is continuing this excellence. Shona's expertise is front of house and between them they have a very successful blend of hospitality, comfortable welcoming surroundings and superb food. The style of food is bistro in style with classic influences, the atmosphere relaxed. Winner of The Scottish Chefs Association 'Best New Restaurant of the Year 1996'. Let's Eat has 2 AA Rosettes.

Open all year except 2 wks mid Jul
Closed Sun Mon
- ✘ Lunch except Sun Mon ££
- ✘ Dinner except Sun Mon ££
- Ⓥ Vegetarians welcome
- ⚥ Children welcome
- ♿ Facilities for disabled visitors
- 🚭 No smoking in restaurant area
- 🐄 Member of the Scotch Beef Club

Grilled brioche and herb crusted fillet of cod on a bed of rocket with aioli. Seared halibut with asparagus, squat lobsters, queen scallops and a Loch Etive trout caviare butter sauce. Lime tart with home-made lemon ice cream.

- 💳 Credit cards: Mastercard/Eurocard, American Express, Visa, Mastercharge, Switch, Delta
- ✗ Partners: Tony Heath & Shona Drysdale

MURRAYSHALL COUNTRY HOUSE HOTEL
Scone
nr Perth PH2 7PH
Tel: 01738 551171
Fax: 01738 552595

4 miles out of Perth, 1 mile off A94.

A country house hotel with its own golf course.

- Baronial country house set in parkland converted to a golf course.
- Elegant Scottish cuisine.
- "Dine in style overlooking beautiful Perthshire."

Golfers will feel particularly at home in this small, pink sandstone mansion house, surrounded by its own 300 acres and private, 18-hole golf course, covered bay driving range, indoor golf school, tennis etc. Bowls and clay pigeon shooting are also available in the hotel's grounds. The Old Masters Restaurant is an elegant, spacious and well-furnished room, its menus based on the best of seasonally-available produce. Many of the herbs and vegetables are grown in the hotel's own kitchen garden. Service is polished and friendly. The wine list is extensive, and in accord with the menus. Special dietary needs catered for. French spoken. The newly rebuilt country club serves informal meals at light 'oak' tables and is ideal for families and meetings.

Open all year
- 🛏 Rooms: 26 with private facilities
- 🛏 DB&B £52–£75   B&B £35–£55
- SP Special rates available
- ✘ Lunch (Clubhouse) £
- ✘ Dinner (Old Masters) ££
- Ⓥ Vegetarians welcome
- ⚥ Children welcome

Warm salad of asparagus and Proscuitto ham, pistachio chive sauce. Grilled fillet of seabass with a mussel and herb broth. Citrus tart with crème anglaise.

STB Highly Commended 👑 👑 👑 👑
- 💳 Credit cards: Mastercard/Eurocard, American Express, Visa, Diners Club, Switch
- ✗ Sales Development Manager: Lin Mitchell

NEWMILN
Newmiln Estate
by Scone Palace, Perth PH2 6AE
Tel: 01738 552364
Fax: 01738 553505

4 miles north of Perth on A93 Blairgowrie road. Follow signs for Scone Palace. 3 miles after Scone Palace, Newmiln driveway on left.

A country house and sporting estate just outside Perth.

- Country house hotel.
- Scottish/modern cooking.
- "A wonderful experience – not to be missed."

Standing within its own 700 acre estate – pheasant, duck and trap shooting are available to guests – the house is Victorian in character and dates from the 19th century. Its owner, Elaine McFarlane, succeeds in making Newmiln a 'home from home' for guests; although imposing and beautifully appointed, the house is cosy and the welcome warm. Their young and talented chef, J Paul Burns presents a sophisticated menu in the handsome dining room. Altogether a delightful experience. Newmiln has 3 AA Rosettes. One of 14 establishments shortlisted for The Macallan Taste of Scotland Awards 1997.

Open all year except Christmas Day + Boxing Day
Rooms: 7 with private facilities
DB&B £100–£160 B&B £70–£130
Special rates available
Traditional Sun lunch – other days by prior arrangement ££
Dinner – reservations essential £££
Vegetarians welcome
Children over 12 years welcome
Facilities for disabled visitors
No smoking in dining room

West Coast scallops and langoustines caramelised with nut oil and served with dill dressing. Estate shot pigeon with wild mushroom and truffle flavoured ragoût. 'Macallan' glazed local berries with a rocher of home-made ice cream.

STB Highly Commended 👑👑👑
Credit cards: Mastercard/Eurocard, American Express, Visa
Owners: James & Elaine McFarlane

NUMBER THIRTY THREE SEAFOOD RESTAURANT
33 George Street
Perth PH1 5LA
Tel: 01738 633771

Perth city centre.

A stylish city centre restaurant.

- Well-established and popular seafood restaurant in Perth.
- Formal Scottish cooking with a choice of eating styles.
- "Wonderful fresh seafood cooked with considerable skill."

Number Thirty Three has now been established in George Street for ten years, easily identified by its distinctive seahorse sign. The theme is Art Deco in muted tones of pink and grey with a clever use of sea imagery creates a stylish atmosphere, the perfect setting for an extremely good meal. The menu is based principally on fish and seafood balanced by interesting and original starters and puddings. Mary Billinghurst oversees her small team in the kitchen. There is a choice of menu with light meals available in the Oyster Bar and more formal dining in the restaurant. Whichever option you choose, the food and wine list are impressive, confirming the restaurant's well-earned reputation for quality. Number Thirty Three has 1 AA Rosette.

Open all year except 25, 26 Dec, 1, 2 Jan, also last 2 wks Jan + first wk Feb
Closed Sun Mon
Lunch except Sun Mon ££-££££
Dinner except Sun Mon ££-££££
Vegetarians welcome
Children over 5 years welcome
Guests are asked not to smoke cigars

Home-made gravadlax with dill mayonnaise. Smoked trout and apple mousse served with a crispy bacon and fried crouton salad. Chocolate roulade with coconut cream and passion fruit.

Credit cards: Mastercard/Eurocard, American Express, Visa
Proprietors: Gavin & Mary Billinghurst

ACARSAID HOTEL
8 Atholl Road
Pitlochry
Perthshire PH16 5BX
Tel: 01796 472389
Fax: 01796 473952

On main road at the Perth end of Pitlochry occupying a prominent position.

An attractively furnished town hotel ideal for theatre-goers.

- Victorian villa with later additions.
- Traditional home cooking with imagination.
- "A lovely warm, friendly atmosphere."

Acarsaid is a haven where comfort of guests and attention to detail are priorities. Attractively furnished throughout, the hotel is comfortable with care given to small details, and residents receive complimentary afternoon tea upon arrival. Of the public rooms one is 'smoking' and one 'non-smoking'. The cooking is very good offering sound, well-prepared and thought out dishes. Ina and Sandy MacArthur are attentive hosts who care for their guests comfort and this is evident throughout.

....

Open all year except 7 Jan to 5 Mar
🏢 Rooms: 19 with private facilities
🛏 DB&B £39–£52   B&B £25–£35
🆂🅿 Special rates available
✕ Food available all day ££
✕ Lunch – residents only £
✕ Dinner ££
Ⓥ Vegetarians welcome
⚹ Children over 10 years welcome
⚱ No smoking in dining room – Smoking and non-smoking lounges

Minced lamb tartlet resting on a redcurrant coulis. Poached fillet of Scottish salmon in a cream and Crabbies sauce. Home-made desserts.

STB Highly Commended 👑 👑 👑
💳 Credit cards: Mastercard/Eurocard, Visa, Switch, Delta
🅽 Partners: Sandy & Ina MacArthur

AUCHNAHYLE
Pitlochry
Perthshire PH16 5JA
Tel: 01796 472318 Fax: 01796 473657
e mail: HowmanA@aol.com

Off East Moulin Road, at end of Tomcroy Terrace. Keep going to end of farm road.

An unusual private house, in the heart of rural Perthshire.

- An 18th century farmhouse and steading with a self-catering cottage.
- Scottish home cooking.
- "A delightful eating experience and wonderful hospitality."

This delightful little 18th century farmhouse has a lovely garden which is home to the family's peacocks. The land was once owned by the monks of Dunfermline Abbey, one of the richest monasteries in Scotland. Auchnahyle is home to Penny and Alastair Howman who are attentive hosts. Penny is a skilled and accomplished cook and prepares the best of fresh farm and local produce and herbs from the herb garden to provide imaginative dishes for their guests. Dinner is served by candlelight around the family dining table and guests are offered genuine hospitality, every comfort and memorable meals. If you are a theatre-goer – pre-theatre supper is available. One of Taste of Scotland's gems.

....

Open all year except Christmas + New Year
Note: Winter months – please book well beforehand
🏢 Rooms: 3 with private facilities
🛏 DB&B £53–£57   B&B £32–£36
✕ Residents only
🆄🅻 ♀ Unlicensed – guests welcome to take own wine
🍴 Picnic lunches £
✕ Dinner 4 course menu ££
Ⓥ Vegetarians welcome – prior notice required
⚹ Children over 12 years welcome
♿ Facilities for disabled visitors
⚱ No smoking in dining room

Smoked duck breast with red onion marmalade. Baked halibut with Gruyère, cream and mustard. Coffee iced strawberry meringue.

💳 Credit cards: Mastercard/Eurocard, Visa, Mastercharge
🅽 Proprietors: Penny & Alastair Howman

BIRCHWOOD HOTEL

East Moulin Road
Pitlochry, Perthshire
PH16 5DW
Tel: 01796 472477
Fax: 01796 473951

From Perth, pass under overhead rail bridge, take 2nd right 75 metres along road at scout hall. From north, first left after police station.

A comfortable hotel with attractive accommodation.

- An Victorian stone mansion set on a wooded knoll with two acres of grounds and gardens.
- Traditional Scottish cooking.
- "Traditional cooking in a friendly atmosphere."

Birchwood is a grand country villa built in the 1870s on the south side of Pitlochry surrounded by four acres of woodland gardens. Unpretentious and welcoming, it is now run by new owners John and Viv Holmyard who, like their predecessors, are committed to making their guests welcome and providing every comfort. The previous staff remain, including the chef. Hospitality is allied to good food and spacious bedrooms, all with private facilities. The pleasant restaurant overlooks the garden and the chef uses fresh produce to create table d'hôte and à la carte menus with a strong Scottish flavour, giving good value for money. The chef is also happy to cater for personal dietary preferences.

Open 1 Mar to 31 Dec
🏠 Rooms: 12 with private facilities
🛏 DB&B £48–£60   B&B £30–£39
SP Special rates available
♀ Restricted hotel licence
✗ Dinner ££
Ⅴ Vegetarians welcome
⚘ Children welcome
♿ Limited facilities for disabled visitors
🚭 No smoking in restaurant

Crail crab parcels. Rannoch venison steaks with juniper berries and an orange and redcurrant sauce. Blairgowrie raspberry hazelnut meringue.

STB Highly Commended 🏵 🏵 🏵
💳 Credit cards: Mastercard/Eurocard, Visa, Switch, Delta
👥 Partners: John & Viv Holmyard

EAST HAUGH COUNTRY HOUSE HOTEL & RESTAURANT

Pitlochry, Perthshire PH16 5JS
Tel: 01796 473121 Fax: 01796 472473

1½ miles south of Pitlochry on old A9 road.

Charming country house hotel.

- 17th century turreted stone house.
- Elegant Scottish cooking.
- "This place lives up to its 1996 Macallan Taste of Scotland Award for Best Informal Lunch."

Built originally as part of the Atholl Estate around 300 years ago, East Haugh is a turreted stone house, standing in its own gardens. It is run by Neil and Lesley McGown who bought the property in 1989 and have converted it sympathetically – some bedrooms have four-poster beds - one with open fireplace! They are helped by their two daughters and all aim to offer a very personal service. Both Neil and Lesley are keen fishermen and Neil also shoots and stalks – these are encouraging pastimes for Neil who is the chef, since the bag or catch often appear on the menu. There is a great deal of food on offer at East Haugh, with children's menus, lunchtime and evening bistro style menus plus those offered in The Gamekeeper's Restaurant for dinner. The lunch dishes are very wide ranging and are prepared to order; dinner in the restaurant is a more formal affair, with a well-composed menu which changes every two days and features local produce. Traditional roast, Sunday lunch menu, a speciality.

Open all year except Christmas Day,
Boxing Day + first 2 wks Feb
N.B. Closed Mon to Thu for lunch during Nov,
Dec, Jan + Mar – unless by prior arrangement
🏠 Rooms: 12 with private facilities
🛏 DB&B £49–£79   B&B £25–£49
SP Special rates available
✗ Lunch ££
✗ Dinner ££-£££
Ⅴ Vegetarians welcome
⚘ Children welcome
🚭 No smoking in restaurant

West Coast scallops wrapped in bacon, chive lime butter sauce. Roast fillet of roe deer, wild mushrooms, roast shallots, port sauce. Sharp deep lemon tart, ginger cream.

STB Commended 🏵 🏵 🏵
💳 Credit cards: Mastercard/Eurocard, Visa
👥 Proprietors: Neil & Lesley McGown

THE GREEN PARK HOTEL
Clunie Bridge Road
Pitlochry, Perthshire
PH16 5JY
Tel: 01796 473248
Fax: 01796 473520

Following Atholl Road through Pitlochry, the hotel is signposted to the left at the town limits.

Lovely country house hotel overlooking Loch Faskally.

- White building dating from 1800s.
- Traditional/classical cooking.
- "Every effort is made to make guests feel welcome and at home in this extremely friendly and professionally-run establishment."

The McMenemie family took over the Green Park Hotel early in 1997 and have already established themselves in this lovely setting. The hotel is delightful and overlooks the loch. Previously running another establishment in Pitlochry the family know their customers well and make every effort to ensure that every stay is a special one. The cooking is classical with great attention to detail and the best use is made of local produce to ensure that the flavours dominate. The dining room is very tastefully decorated and overlooks the gardens.

Open all year
🏠 Rooms: 39 with private facilities
🛏 DB&B £35–£50   B&B £20–£35
[SP] Special rates available
✗ Food available all day £
✗ Lunch £
✗ Dinner ££
[V] Vegetarians welcome
🕇 Children welcome
🕭 Facilities for disabled visitors
✔ No smoking throughout

Tagliatelle of pasta and smoked venison. Poached sea bass with spring onion, peppers and mustard sauce. Yoghurt and Drambuie cheesecake with vanilla cream.

STB Commended 👑 👑 👑 👑
💳 Credit cards: Mastercard/Eurocard, Visa, Switch
🕊 Proprietors: Alistair & Diane McMenemie

THE KILLIECRANKIE HOTEL
by Pitlochry
Perthshire PH16 5LG
Tel: 01796 473220
Fax: 01796 472451
e-mail: killiecrankie.hotel@btinternet.com.uk

B8079 on old A9, 3 miles north of Pitlochry.

An attractive country house overlooking the River Garry.

- Small country house hotel.
- Modern Scottish cooking with classic influences.
- "Excellent, colourful dinner menu in lovely setting."

This is a former manse built in 1840 and stands in four acres of well-kept gardens and woodland above the River Garry and the historic Pass of Killiecrankie, where a notable battle was fought in 1689. The surrounding country abounds with wildlife and the hotel has the atmosphere of a sporting lodge. Its resident owners, Colin and Carole Anderson, have decorated and furnished the house very tastefully; and have provided a high standard of comfort. Head Chef John Ramsay's cooking is highly professional and imaginative, and his table d'hôte menus (four starters, four main courses) are well-balanced and appetising. A most attractive and well-run establishment. Killiecrankie has 2 AA Rosettes.

Open 7 Mar to 3 Jan except 1 wk mid Dec
🏠 Rooms: 10 with private facilities
🛏 DB&B from £79
[SP] Special rates available
✗ Lunch ££
✗ Dinner 5 course menu £££
[V] Vegetarians welcome
🕇 Children welcome
✔ No smoking in dining room

Baked brûlée of goats cheese served with tomato and basil salsa. Roast boneless quail stuffed with goose mousseline and served on an asparagus salad with walnut and bacon vinaigrette. Poached pear with vanilla cream and spiced syrup.

STB Highly Commended 👑 👑 👑 👑
💳 Credit cards: Mastercard/Eurocard, Visa, Switch, Delta
🕊 Owner/Proprietors: Colin & Carole Anderson

KNOCKENDARROCH HOUSE HOTEL
Higher Oakfield, Pitlochry
Perthshire PH16 5HT
Tel: 01796 473473
Fax: 01796 474068

In a commanding position, 3 minutes walk from the town centre. Take Bonnethill Road and then take first right turn.

An imposing Victorian villa with a period atmosphere.

* Victorian mansion in Pitlochry.
* Excellent classic cooking
* "Good food, warm hospitality in a wonderfully relaxing atmosphere."

Knockendarroch is a sturdy villa, built in 1870 on a steep hillock in Pitlochry, and accordingly enjoying wonderful views up the Tummel Valley to the south, and of Ben Vrackie to the north. The house is well proportioned, the public rooms well-appointed and comfortable and the bedrooms all individually furnished. The current owners are Tony and Jane Ross. The cooking is excellent in a traditional style and your hosts make every effort to make you feel at home, and succeed. Knockendarroch has 1 AA Rosette. *(See advert Page 29.)*

Open 1 Feb to 16 Nov
🏠 Rooms: 12 with private facilities
🛏 DB&B £36–£54   B&B £28–£36
SP Special rates available
🍴 Non-residents – prior booking essential
✕ Dinner £££
Ⅴ Vegetarians welcome
🧍 Children welcome
🚭 No smoking throughout

Smoked haddock mousse wrapped in smoked salmon resting on a green dressed salad. Roast breast of duck accompanied by a sauce of woodland berries and port. Drambuie and chocolate mousse with a vanilla and ginger cream.

STB Highly Commended 👑 👑 👑
💳 Credit cards: Mastercard/Eurocard, American Express, Visa, Switch, Delta
👤 Owners: Tony & Jane Ross

PITLOCHRY FESTIVAL THEATRE RESTAURANT
Port-na-Craig, Pitlochry
Perthshire PH16 5DR
Tel/Fax: 01796 473054

On south bank of the River Tummel, approx ¼ mile from centre of town. Clearly signposted.

An informal restaurant for theatre-goers with a relaxed atmosphere.

* Restaurant and coffee bar.
* Modern Scottish cooking enlivened with imaginative touches.
* "Colourful themed menus set the scene for performances."

The Pitlochry Festival Theatre is beautifully situated on the banks of the River Tummel at the gateway to the Highlands. The theatre's restaurant and coffee bar are a boon to theatre patrons as well as Pitlochry locals who drop in regularly to enjoy the home baking which is such a feature of the coffee bar in the foyer. At lunchtime the restaurant is buffet style with a choice of hot and cold dishes including local fish from the 'Summer Festival Buffet'. Portions are generous with lots of healthy eating options. In the evening table d'hôte dinner is served at 6.30 pm to accommodate theatre-goers. Booking is essential.

Open 1 May to 10 Oct
Note: open early Apr for Coffee + Lunch only
✕ Lunch £
🍴 Dinner – booking essential £-££
🍴 Note: If theatre performance Sun, buffet served – booking essential
Ⅴ Vegetarians welcome
🧍 Children welcome
♿ Facilities for disabled visitors
🚭 No smoking in restaurant during dinner
🚬 Smoking area in Coffee Bar

Scampi, scallops, salmon and prawns in a cream and dill sauce. Poached fillet of Scottish salmon with spinach and leek sauces. Mincemeat roulade filled with a Glayva flavoured cream.

💳 Credit cards: Mastercard/Eurocard, American Express, Visa, Mastercharge
👤 Catering Manager: Alistair Barr

PORT NA CRAIG INN AND RESTAURANT

Portnacraig
Pitlochry
Perthshire PH16 5ND
Tel: 01796 472777

Directly below the Pitlochry Festival Theatre on the banks of the River Tummel.

Stone built inn on the River Tummel ideal for theatre-goers.

- Delightful stone built Inn.
- Modern Scottish cooking.
- "Delicious food in beautiful location."

Port na Craig is a bistro-style restaurant with windows looking out onto the River Tummel from where you can watch the fishermen in waders, the ducks flying over and skimming the water and the fish jumping whilst you enjoy a candlelit dinner. It is one of the oldest buildings in Pitlochry, dating back some 300 years, and the inn and the restaurant have been lovingly restored. The restaurant has a buzz about it – it is busy with friendly staff and the sort of place where you can dress up or down depending upon the occasion. Cooking is excellent with good quality food interesting menus presented with imagination and flair. Weather permitting, you may dine alfresco on the patio which is situated on the banks of the River Tummel.

Open 14 Mar to 30 Nov + private parties available during off season
🏠 Rooms: 2 with private facilities
🛏 DB&B £35–£45   B&B £20–£30
🆂🅿 Special rates available
✗ Food available all day ££
✗ Lunch £
✗ Dinner ££
Ⓥ Vegetarians welcome
🅰 Children welcome
♿ Facilities for disabled visitors

Smoked mackerel pâté with a raspberry vinaigrette. Medallions of venison with a brandy and pink peppercorn sauce. Rhubarb and strawberry fool.

💳 Credit cards: Mastercard/Eurocard, Visa, Mastercharge, Switch, Delta
🅽 Partners: Bill & Andrew Bryan

QUEENS VIEW HOTEL

Strathtummel, by Pitlochry
Perthshire PH16 5NA
Tel: 01796 473 291 Fax: 01796 473 515

Take old A9 (B8079) north from Pitlochry, turn left onto B8019 signposted Kinloch Rannoch and 'Queens View' 4 miles. Hotel is ½ mile before 'Queens View' between road and Loch Tummel.

A country house hotel in a beautiful setting.

- Stone built baronial house overlooking Loch Tummel.
- Innovative, yet traditional cooking.
- "The view from the dining room is breathtaking."

The Queens View Hotel is on a fabulous position 100 feet or more above Loch Tummel. The building itself was built in several phases and dates back to the early 1800s the interior of which has a very traditional Scottish feel to it. Norma and Richard Tomlinson run the hotel using the wide experience gained in the catering business over the years and their care and professionalism shows throughout. Seven of the bedrooms are en suite and six have king-size beds. Two bedrooms form a family suite, en suite with its own bathroom. Norma's cooking is the best of Scottish with some imaginative touches and the experience to be found here was described by our Inspector as like staying as a guest in someone's home.

Open 1 Mar to mid Jan
Closed Christmas Eve, Christmas Day + Boxing Day
🅿 Note: Telephone bookings required for Jan
🏠 Rooms: 10 with private facilities
🛏 DB&B £50–£92   B&B £30–£72
🆂🅿 Special rates available
✗ Food available all day £ – full meals only at set times
✗ Lunch £-££
✗ Dinner £££
Ⓥ Vegetarians welcome
🅰 Children welcome
🚭 No smoking in dining room

Smoked haddock cream on a bed of lemon dressed salad leaves. Stuffed loin of lamb with a redcurrant mint and fresh orange sauce. Walnut tart and whisky and honey ice cream.

STB Commended 👑 👑 👑 👑
💳 Credit cards: Mastercard/Eurocard, Visa, Switch, Delta
🅽 Proprietors: Richard & Norma Tomlinson

WESTLANDS OF PITLOCHRY
160 Atholl Road, Pitlochry
Perthshire PH16 5AR
Tel: 01796 472266
Fax: 01796 473994

A924 into Pitlochry, Westlands at north end of town
on right hand side.

Attractive stone-built hotel.

- Country town hotel.
- Traditional cooking.
- "Traditional cooking with flair."

An attractive stone building with an extension, built
in keeping with the rest. The lawn, which is
bordered by mature trees, slopes down to the main
road, and Westlands has attractive views. The hotel
is personally run by its resident proprietors, Andrew
and Sue Mathieson, supported by their manager
and chef. There is a straightforward table d'hôte
menu and an à la carte menu which offers a wide
range of Scottish dishes. Both are reasonably
priced. Meals are served in the Garden Room
Restaurant, which has pleasant views of the Vale of
Atholl.

Open all year except 25, 26 Dec
🏠 Rooms: 15 with private facilities
🛏 DB&B £43–£58.50   B&B £25.50–£41
SP Special rates available
✗ Lunch £
✗ Dinner ££
Ⓥ Vegetarians welcome
♰ Children welcome
✦ No smoking in restaurant

**Griddled black pudding with apricot and onion
marmalade and seasonal leaves. Smoked haddock
on a bed of chive mash, surrounded by a light leek
and parsley sauce. Summer pudding and cream.**

STB Commended 👑 👑 👑 👑
💳 Credit cards: Mastercard/Eurocard, Visa
Ⓜ Partners: Andrew & Sue Mathieson

THE HAVEN HOTEL
Innes Street, Plockton, Ross-shire IV52 8TW
Tel: 01599 544223
Fax: 01599 544467

In the village of Plockton.

A small West Highland hotel.

- Converted 19th century merchant's house.
- Stylish Scottish cooking.
- "Once discovered, customers return for more! A
  most charming place."

Plockton is known as the 'jewel of the Highlands.'
With its palm trees along the waterfront and shining
views out over the sea, it is really one of the
country's loveliest villages. The Haven was built for
a Victorian merchant and has a pleasing simplicity
in its architecture, whinstone-fronted and harled
sides and rear. Although detached, it stands in the
terrace of traditional houses at Plockton, only yards
from the beach. The hotel continues to offer the
same high standard of cuisine for which it has long
had such a good reputation. Two suites, one with a
four-poster bed, have now been completed. Dinner
menus are table d'hôte (six choices of main course)
and combine fresh local produce with interesting
sauces, changing daily. The Haven has 1 AA
Rosette, and is a member of the Certified Aberdeen
Angus Scheme. *(See advert Page 28.)*

Open 1 Feb to 20 Dec incl
🏠 Rooms: 15, 12 with private facilities
🛏 DB&B £51–£68   B&B £35–£37
SP Special rates available
Ⓠ Restricted licence
✗ Lunch – 24 hours notice required ££
✗ Dinner 5 course menu £££
Ⓥ Vegetarians welcome
♰ Children over 7 years welcome
♿ Facilities for disabled visitors
✦ No smoking in restaurant

**Plockton prawn and scallop galantine with a lime
butter sauce. Aberdeen Angus beef and
horseradish cheese baked in filo pastry with
Talisker whisky sauce. Caledonian cream.**

STB Highly Commended 👑 👑 👑 👑
💳 Credit cards: Mastercard/Eurocard, Visa,
Switch, Delta
Ⓜ Owners: Annan & Jill Dryburgh

THE LAKE HOTEL
Port of Menteith, Perthshire FK8 3RA
Tel: 01877 385258
Fax: 01877 385671

On A81 – at Port of Menteith – 200 yards on road south to Arnprior.

A country house with Art Deco influences overlooking the lake and Inchcolm Priory.

- A well-established, comfortable and recently refurbished country hotel.
- Excellent cooking. Imaginative use of the best of Scottish produce.
- "A most comfortable hotel, steeped in the history of Mary Queen of Scots."

Standing on the southern shore of Scotland's only 'lake', the hotel enjoys splendid views towards the Trossachs. The heart of the building was a 19th century manse, but it became an hotel over 50 years ago, with many well-integrated additions, and from the outside it is a classic example of a traditional Scottish country hotel. The interior provides a surprise: the theme is Art Deco, well executed, with many original pieces of furniture. The Conservatory Restaurant is on the lakeside, entered from the spacious lounge. Like all the other rooms, it is pleasantly appointed. The table d'hôte menus (lunch and dinner) are very well-priced and offer some unusual traditional dishes which have all but disappeared from more 'precious' restaurants. The excellence of the cooking has been recognised with 2 AA Rosettes.

Open all year
🏨 Rooms: 16 with private facilities
🛏 DB&B £46–£80   B&B £30–£64
🍴 Lunch – booking essential ££
✗ Dinner 4 course menu £££
Ⓥ Vegetarians welcome
✗ No smoking in restaurant

Chicken and herb terrine with sun dried tomato dressing. Grilled halibut with spinach, saffron potatoes and an orange and aniseed sauce. Drambuie parfait with raspberry coulis.

STB Highly Commended 👑 👑 👑 👑
💳 Credit cards: Mastercard/Eurocard, American Express, Visa, Switch
✗ Manager: Douglas Little

CORSEMALZIE HOUSE HOTEL
Port William
Newton Stewart
Wigtownshire DG8 9RL
Tel: 01988 860254
Fax: 01988 860213

Halfway along B7005 Glenluce-Wigtown, off A714 Newton Stewart-Port William or A747 Glenluce-Port William.

Victorian mansion house.

- Victorian country mansion.
- Modern, Scottish cooking.
- "A comfortable country house hotel with caring hosts and good food."

This 19th century house with its own 40 acre estate is a popular venue for those who enjoy the countryside. The hotel has its own small burn, The Malzie Burn, within its garden and also lovely woodland walks. The hotel has recently extended its kitchen garden which offers fresh vegetables to complement all meals. Corsemalzie has its own fishing, both on the river and loch, and fresh game from its estate. *(See advert Page 25.)*

Open 1 Mar to 20 Jan except Christmas Day + Boxing Day
🏨 Rooms: 15 with private facilities
🛏 DB&B from £59.50   B&B £37–£47
⑤ᴾ Special rates available
✗ Lunch £-££
✗ Dinner £££
Ⓥ Vegetarians welcome
🧒 Children welcome
♿ Facilities for disabled visitors – ground floor only
✗ No smoking in dining room

Smoked salmon, avocado and orange salad. Trio of medallions with Madeira and wild mushroom sauce. Rhubarb crème brûlée.

STB Highly Commended 👑 👑 👑 👑
💳 Credit cards: Mastercard/Eurocard, American Express, Visa, Mastercharge, Switch, Delta
✗ Proprietor: Peter McDougall

GLEN ROY RESTAURANT

Monreith, nr Newton Stewart
Wigtownshire, DG8 9LJ
Tel/Fax: 01988 700466

Approximately 17 miles from A75 at Newton
Stewart. Take A714 to Port William then A747 coast
road to Monreith. Restaurant at southern end of
main street.

**Small specialist restaurant offering good food with
sea view .**

- Old fisherman's cottage.
- Modern Scottish.
- "Excellent choice of seafood presented in
  modern style."

Monreith is a tiny village set up on the cliffs
overlooking Luce Bay and the Mull of Galloway. The
restaurant is at one end of a row of tiny
white-washed old fisherman's cottages on the main
road looking out to the sea. The interior is simply
furnished with open fireplace, candles and has a
welcoming feel to it. The food is an excellent
example of contemporary cooking with seafood a
particular speciality. All produce is freshly sourced,
in particular good Galloway beef.

Open all year except 2 wks end Nov
Note: closed Tue Nov to Easter
Closed Mon
✗ Lunch except Mon £
✗ Dinner except Mon ££
Ⓥ Vegetarians welcome
⚰ Children welcome
♿ Facilities for disabled visitors
🚭 No smoking in one of two dining rooms

**Baked crab with ginger and spring onion. Fillet of
salmon in a creamy mustard, lime and chardonnay
sauce. Marrow, apple and cinnamon sponge and
custard.**

⊞ Credit cards: Mastercard/Eurocard, Visa, Delta
Ⅺ Joint Owners: Patrick & Jenny Crawley

FERNHILL HOTEL

Heugh Road, Portpatrick
nr Stranraer DG9 8TD
Tel: 01776 810220
Fax: 01776 810596

On entering Portpatrick take right fork – Heugh
Road – and hotel is c. 300 yards on left.

**A comfortable hotel overlooking the pretty seaside
village and sea.**

- Victorian house with modern conservatory
  extension.
- Modern Scottish cooking.
- "Interesting menus, served in delightful and
  friendly surroundings."

Set above the harbour of the beautiful, unspoiled
fishing village of Portpatrick, The Fernhill Hotel has
been family run by Anne and Hugh Harvie for over
30 years. It began as a single Victorian villa-
boardinghouse, and has gradually expanded in all
directions, so that it now has 20 bedrooms and a
sizeable conservatory restaurant with splendid
views over the village to the sea. The chef, John
Henry, uses locally landed fish and shellfish and
Galloway beef and lamb. His cooking is fresh and
healthy and his menus sensible and well-priced.

Open all year except Christmas Day +
Boxing Day
🛏 Rooms: 20 with private facilities
🛏 DB&B £60–£110   B&B £40–£90
ⓢⓟ Special rates available
✗ Food available all day £-££
✗ Lunch £-££
✗ Dinner ££
Ⓥ Vegetarians welcome
⚰ Children welcome
♿ Facilities for disabled visitors
🚭 No smoking in conservatory

**Smoked salmon and spinach mousse with roast
red pepper sauce. Pan-fried collops of venison
saddle with sautéd wild mushrooms and red wine
sauce. Tangy lemon cheesecake topped with
toffee meringue.**

STB Highly Commended 👑 👑 👑 👑
⊞ Credit cards: Mastercard/Eurocard, American
    Express, Visa, Diners Club, Switch, Delta, JCB
Ⅺ Proprietor: Mrs Anne Harvie

KNOCKINAAM LODGE
**WINNER MACALLAN AWARD 1997 –
COUNTRY HOUSE HOTEL OF THE YEAR**
Portpatrick, Dumfries & Galloway DG9 9AD
Tel: 01776 810471 Fax: 01776 810435

From the A77 or the A75, follow signs for
Portpatrick. 2 miles west of Lochans, Knockinaam
sign on right. Take first left turning, past smokehouse. Follow signs for 3 miles to lodge.

Luxury country house hotel with outstanding cuisine.

- A 19th century hunting lodge converted into a
  first class country house hotel.
- Best modern British cooking.
- "Deluxe country house hotel in a secluded,
  untouched corner of Galloway where dining
  is a gastronomic experience."

Knockinaam was built in 1869 and was
described 'as delightful a maritime residence as
is anywhere to be seen', remotely situated on
the Galloway coast. The public rooms are small
and cosy, with open log fires in winter; the bedrooms, varying in size, are superbly appointed.
The lodge's resident owners, Michael Bricker
and Pauline Ashworth, are attentive and
hospitable hosts, and their Head Chef Tony Pierce
prepares dishes which are both contemporary,
unusual and outstandingly successful. A
memorable place. Knockinaam has 3 AA Rosettes.

Open all year
🏠 Rooms: 10 with private facilities
🛏 DB&B £80–£130
SP Special rates available
✕ Food available all day ££
✕ Lunch £££
✕ Dinner ££££
Ⓥ Vegetarians welcome
ᐜ Children welcome
♿ Facilities for disabled visitors – restaurant only
🚭 No smoking in dining room

**Poached Luce Bay lobster with a four citrus
nage. Highland venison Wellington garnished
with cubed vegetables and a cassis and clove
jus. Chocolate soufflé served with coconut ice
cream and a pineapple anglaise.**

STB Deluxe 👑 👑 👑 👑
💳 Credit cards: Mastercard/Eurocard, American
   Express, Visa, Diners Club, Switch, Delta
🗶 Proprietors: Michael Bricker &
                Pauline Ashworth

SCIBERSCROSS LODGE
Strath Brora, Rogart
Sutherland IV28 3YQ
Tel: 01408 641246
Fax: 01408 641465

A9 over Dornoch Firth Bridge for c. 10 miles, then
A839 for 4 miles. In Rogart turn right onto single-
track road (Balnacoil) for 7 miles, lodge on left.

**An attractive sporting lodge in secluded
surroundings.**

- Country house hotel.
- Country house cooking.
- "A very friendly country house hotel with
  excellent food."

Sciberscross is the home of Peter and Kate
Hammond, and this classic Victorian sporting lodge
built for the Duke of Sutherland in 1876 is full of
homely touches – masses of fresh cut flowers,
framed photographs and family portraits and
antique furniture. The lodge stands in spectacular
scenery just across the Dornoch Firth and offers
fishing for salmon, sea trout, brown trout and char.
Kate uses whatever can be sourced locally. Her five
course dinners have set menus (choices for starter
and dessert), and her cooking is delicious. Their
motto is "Arrive as strangers, leave as friends."

Open 1 Feb to 30 Nov
🏠 Rooms: 5 with private facilities
🛏 DB&B £85 (incl wines and spirits)   B&B £40
SP Special rates available
✕ Lunch – by special arrangement ££££
✕ Dinner 5 course fully inclusive menu –
   non-residents by prior booking only ££££
Ⓥ Vegetarians welcome
ᐜ Children welcome at owners' discretion

**Dornoch Firth mussels in a rich cream and garlic
sauce. Fillet of Rogart lamb with a rosemary and
redcurrant jus. Drambuie parfait with a Highland
wild berry sauce served with Dunrobin Castle
cream.**

💳 Credit cards: Mastercard/Eurocard, Visa
🗶 Joint Resident Owner: Peter Hammond
🗶 Chef/Patron: Kate Hammond

THE GRANGE INN

Grange Road, St Andrews
Fife KY16 8LJ
Tel: 01334 472670
Fax: 01334 472604

From centre of town follow A917 Crail road past hospital to double mini roundabout. Take middle road signposted Grange – ¾ mile to Inn.

A charming country Inn overlooking St Andrews Bay.

- 17/18th century buildings.
- Modern and traditional Scottish cooking.
- "Warm and welcoming in every sense – what one would expect from a country Inn."

Charming restaurant dating back to the 17th/18th century situated on a hillside overlooking St Andrews Bay. A short distance from the historic old town of St Andrews, The Grange offers fresh Scottish produce imaginatively prepared and cooked to order. Under the capable management of Proprietor Peter Aretz, The Grange has prospered and grown busy yet still managed to retain much of its old fashioned charm and atmosphere. There are three separate dining areas where you'll find high standards of hospitality with uncomplicated, tasty, home-cooked food. A range of draught and bottled beers, spirits and liqueurs are available in the cosy, stone-flagged Caddies Bar, with a personally selected wine list.

Open all year but closed Mon Tue Nov to Apr incl
- 🛏 B&B £30–£35
- ✗ Lunch £-££
- ✗ Dinner £££
- Ⓥ Vegetarians welcome
- ⳇ Children welcome
- ⳇ No smoking in Patio Room + Bay Room

Deep-fried king prawns in a lime and ginger butter served with smoked queen scallops and a sweet pepper/coriander relish. Spiced lamb accompanied by saffron cous cous served with a mint and garlic sauce. Baked vermicelli with almonds and peach served cold with amaretto syrup.

- 💳 Credit cards: Mastercard/Eurocard, American Express, Visa, Diners Club, Switch, Delta
- 🗽 Proprietor: Peter Aretz

THE OLD COURSE HOTEL GOLF RESORT & SPA

St Andrews, Kingdom of Fife KY16 9SP
Tel: 01334 474371 Fax: 01334 477668

A91 to St Andrews on outskirts of town.

A modern resort hotel standing on the edge of the most famous golf course in the world.

- Grand resort hotel .
- Modern Scottish.
- "Unique location, breath-taking views and fine dining."

The hotel is set in a spectacular location in the home of golf overlooking the infamous 17th Road Hole and the historic Royal and Ancient clubhouse. All 125 bedrooms, including 17 suites, have unrivalled views, some looking over the Old Course to the sea, others towards the hotel's own Duke's Course and the surrounding countryside. The hotel offers its guests a unique choice of dining experiences – the Road Hole Grill with its open kitchen, the Conservatory – serving light meals throughout the day in summer, and the Jigger Inn, originally a 19th century cottage, now a popular golfing pub serving real ale and good wholesome food. Winner of The Taste of Scotland Scotch Lamb Challenge Competition Gourmet Section and Overall Winner 1996.

- Open all year
- 🛏 Rooms: 125 with private facilities
- 🛏 DB&B £130–£155   B&B £120–£180
- SP Special golf and spa rates available
- ✗ Food served £-££
- ✗ Lunch ££
- ✗ Dinner ££££
- Ⓥ Vegetarians welcome
- ⳇ Children welcome
- ♿ Facilities for disabled visitors
- ⳇ Pipe and cigar smoking not permitted in restaurants
- 🐂 Member of the Scotch Beef Club

Endive and watercress salad with goats cheese and lemon vinaigrette. Fillet of Beef with mushroom mashed potato, asparagus, Gorgonzola and garlic sauce. Carrot pudding and brandy snap canoli.

STB Deluxe 👑 👑 👑 👑 👑
- 💳 Credit cards: Mastercard/Eurocard, American Express, Visa, Diners Club, Mastercharge, Delta, JCB
- 🗽 Food & Beverage Manager: Andrew Phelan

RUFFLETS COUNTRY HOUSE & GARDEN RESTAURANT
Strathkinness Low Road, St Andrews
Fife KY16 9TX
Tel: 01334 472594
Fax: 01334 478703

On B939, 1½ miles west of St Andrews.

A most attractive country house near St Andrews.

- Country house hotel.
- Fine country house cooking.
- "A charming, friendly old country house set in beautiful countryside."

Rufflets is one of the oldest established country house hotels in Scotland, and has the distinction of being privately owned and managed by the same family since 1952. The house itself was built in 1924 and stands in formal gardens; furnishings are extremely tasteful (a mix of antique and contemporary country house); bedrooms are all individually designed and furnished. The attractive Garden Restaurant has an AA Rosette, among other awards. The daily changing menus are table d'hôte (six main courses) and the cooking combines the fresh seafood available from the East Neuk and good local meats and vegetables with imaginative sauces and stuffings. A four course, Scottish 'tasting' menu is also available. Service is smart and professional under the guidance of Manager, John Angus.

....

Open all year
- ⌂ Rooms: 25 with private facilities
- ⇔ DB&B £75–£105   B&B £60–£90
- SP Special rates available
- ✕ Lunch (Restaurant Sun Sat) ££
- ✕ Dinner £££
- Ⓥ Vegetarians welcome
- ⋏ Children welcome
- ♿ Facilities for non-residential disabled visitors
- 🐂 Member of the Scotch Beef Club

A warm salad of king scallops with ginger, spring onions and lime juice. Fillet of Scottish Lamb baked with a pine kernel crust on a Madeira wine jus. Ice cranachan parfait with a compote of local berries.

STB Deluxe ♕ ♕ ♕ ♕
- 💳 Credit cards: Mastercard/Eurocard, American Express, Visa, Diners Club, Mastercharge, Switch
- 👤 Proprietor: Ann Russell

BUCCLEUCH ARMS HOTEL
The Green
St Boswells
Roxburghshire
TD6 0EW
Tel: 01835 822243
Fax: 01835 823965

Situated on the main A68, 60 miles north of Newcastle. 40 miles south of Edinburgh.

An historic country house hotel, converted from hunting lodge.

- Sportsman's hotel/inn.
- Contemporary hotel cooking.
- "Friendly country hotel in Tweed Valley, ideally situated for fishing and golf."

The Buccleuch Arms dates from the 16th century, when it was a hunting lodge for the Dukes of Buccleuch. Situated on one of the main roads into Scotland (now the A68), beside the pretty village cricket pitch and green in the old village of St Boswells (established in the 11th century by a French monk, Boisil). Now a coaching inn, it is a popular base from which to tour the Tweed Valley, fish, shoot or golf (there are 14 golf courses within a 20 mile radius). Lunch and suppers/dinners are served in the bar and in the restaurant. The cooking is adventurous, uses as much local produce as possible and favours aromatic sauces and combinations.

....

Open all year except Christmas Day
- ⌂ Rooms: 18, 17 with private facilities
- ⇔ DB&B £42–£47   B&B £37.50–£42
- SP Special rates available
- ✕ Food available all day £
- ✕ Lunch ££
- ✕ Dinner ££
- Ⓥ Vegetarians welcome
- ⋏ Children welcome
- 🚭 No smoking in dining room

Scottish game terrine set on a warm Cumberland sauce. Breast of pheasant roasted with red lentils, smoked bacon and mushrooms. Traditionally baked pudding smothered with butterscotch sauce.

STB Commended ♕ ♕ ♕ ♕
- 💳 Credit cards: Mastercard/Eurocard, Visa
- 👤 Director: Sue Dodds

EDDRACHILLES HOTEL
Badcall Bay
Scourie
Sutherland
IV27 4TH
Tel: 01971 502080
Fax: 01971 502477

A894, 38 miles north of Ullapool, and 2 miles south of Scourie. Visible and signposted from main road.

Magnificently situated in Badcall Bay with wonderful views.

* Country house hotel.
* Traditional.
* "Superb situation, friendly staff and excellent cuisine."

Eddrachilles Hotel, formerly a manse, sits in 300 acres of delightful grounds in this beautiful part of the North West Coast of Scotland. The building is 200 years old and has been tastefully refurbished and extended to provide comfort in keeping with the surroundings. Many original features have been retained – including for example the flag stoned floors of the dining rooms. The food offered here is of excellent quality with much evidence of local produce which has been carefully cooked to retain its flavour and presented in a traditional and professional style.

Open 17 Mar to 22 Oct
** fb** Rooms: 11 with private facilities
⊨ DB&B £48–£54   B&B £38–£42
SP Special rates available
✗ Residents only
✗ Bar snacks available
✗ Dinner ££
Ⅴ Vegetarians welcome
★ Children over 3 years welcome

Loch Laxford mussels in white wine and garlic. Quarter Badcall Bay salmon, sautéed in butter. Pancakes with bramble jelly and cream.

STB Highly Commended 🏵 🏵 🏵
⊞ Credit cards: Mastercard/Eurocard, Visa, Switch, Delta
⋈ Proprietor: Mr A C M Wood

COACH HOUSE RESTAURANT
Glenfintaig
by Spean Bridge, Lochaber
PH34 4DX
Tel: 01397 712 680
Fax: 01397 712 100

From Spean Bridge take A82 to Inverness. Approx 3 miles on right hand side.

Small country restaurant in converted coaching inn.

* Stone cottage.
* Modern Scottish.
* "An intimate and informal country restaurant."

The Coach House is a charming little restaurant set off the road lovely countryside. It is very Scottish in its style with whitewashed walls, plain wooden tables decorated with fresh flowers and a warming log stove combining to make a comfortable and welcoming atmosphere. There are no pretensions here – just good food, wines and guest draught ales run by committed and enthusiastic people. The restaurant is becoming popular with locals, and, owing to its size booking, particularly in the evenings, is advisable to avoid disappointment.

Open 30 Apr to 25 Oct
✗ Lunch £
✗ Dinner ££
Ⅴ Vegetarians welcome
★ Children welcome
✁ No smoking in restaurant

Smoked salmon on a hot potato fritter with horseradish cream. Shoulder of lamb stuffed with mushrooms and ham. Flaming strawberries.

⊞ Credit cards: Mastercard/Eurocard, Visa, Mastercharge, Switch, Delta, JCB
⋈ Owners: Iain & Tarlika

CORRIEGOUR LODGE HOTEL
Loch Lochy, by Spean Bridge
Inverness-shire PH34 4EB
Tel: 01397 712685
Fax: 01397 712696

Follow A82, 17 miles north of Fort William; 47 miles south of Inverness – between Spean Bridge and Invergarry.

A charming former Victorian hunting lodge on the shores of Loch Lochy.

- A small, personally owned and managed country house hotel.
- Excellent modern Scottish cuisine.
- "A hotel full of atmosphere and home comforts."

This is a well-established hotel situated on the shores of Loch Lochy with the grounds extending through their own gardens and across the road to a private beach and jetty. The hotel is now run by new owners, Christian Kerr and her family. It is well-maintained and cared for and the addition of a conservatory dining room offers wonderful scenery. The house is full of old comfortable furniture, nice books to read, interesting bits and pieces and the additional conservatory dining room offers wonderful scenery. The food here is good, using excellent local produce with menus which change often reflecting the availability of the produce. The hotel's wine list is extensive and reasonably priced.

Open 1 Feb to 30 Nov (weekends only 1 Feb to 31 Mar) + special 3/6 day breaks at New Year
- 🛏 Rooms: 9 with private facilities
- 🍴 DB&B £49–£63   B&B £29–£36
- SP Special rates available
- 🍴 Non-residents – dinner only
- ✕ Lunch – by arrangement
- ✕ Dinner £££
- V Vegetarians welcome
- 🕭 Children over 8 years welcome
- 🚭 No smoking in restaurant

Home-made soup and pâté. Rack of Highland hill lamb with a rowanberry gravy. Cloutie dumpling with Drambuie ice cream.

STB Highly Commended 🏴 🏴 🏴
- 💳 Credit cards: Mastercard/Eurocard, American Express, Visa, Switch, Delta
- ⚉ Owner: Christian Kerr

OLD PINES RESTAURANT WITH ROOMS
Spean Bridge, by Fort William
Inverness-shire PH34 4EG
Tel: 01397 712324 Fax: 01397 712433
e-mail goodfood.at.oldpines@lineone.net

From Spean Bridge take A82 to Inverness. One mile north take B8004 next to Commando Memorial 300 yards on right.

Award-winning cuisine in this restaurant with rooms.

- Scandinavian-style log and stone chalet overlooking Glen Spean and the Nevis Range.
- Outstanding and sophisticated Scottish cuisine.
- "A relaxed family atmosphere combined with Sukie's excellent cooking – what a joy!"

Old Pines is a little jewel set amongst mature pine trees in the Great Glen. It is the family home of Bill and Sukie Barber and dinner by crystal and candlelight in the conservatory will certainly be the highlight of your stay. To dine here is to experience the very best of Scottish food, cooked superbly by Sukie who brings unlimited enthusiasm and skill to her craft. All ingredients are sourced locally, and they have their own smokehouse. Winner of the Taste of Scotland Scotch Lamb Challenge Competition Classic Section 1995 and Runner-up Category 1 1997.

Open all year except 2 wks Nov: Closed Sun to non-residents May to Sep
- 🛏 Rooms: 8 with private facilities
- 🍴 DB&B £50–£70
- SP Special rates available
- ⚉ Unlicensed – guests welcome to take own wine
- ✕ Food available all day £
- 🍴 Lunch except Sun – restaurant lunch if booked £££
- ✕ Dinner 5 course menu except Sun (supper to residents) £££
- V Vegetarians welcome – prior notice appreciated
- 🕭 Children welcome
- ♿ Facilities for disabled visitors
- 🚭 No smoking throughout
- 🐄 Member of the Scotch Beef Club

Monkfish, mussels and squat lobsters in a sauce of the sea. Roast haunch of venison with pineapple juice, thyme and juniper. Meringue with pears and Poire William liquor ice cream, red wine, bramble and cinnamon sauce.

STB Highly Commended 🏴 🏴 🏴
- 💳 Credit cards: Mastercard/Eurocard, American Express, Visa, Mastercharge, Switch, Delta
- ⚉ Proprietors: Bill & Sukie Barber

CHAPELTOUN HOUSE HOTEL

nr Stewarton, Ayrshire KA3 3ED
Tel: 01560 482696
Fax: 01560 485100

Driving south through Stewarton on A735, take
2nd right after viaduct onto B769 to Irvine. Hotel
signposted after 2 miles.

**A country house hotel deep in Ayrshire's
countryside.**

- 1900s Edwardian house.
- Modern Scottish cooking.
- "Oak panelling, open fires and hospitality in the
  best country house style."

Chapeltoun House Hotel is now owned by the
Dobson family and run by Simon Dobson who is
very much a hands on proprietor. The hotel is an
attractive house built in 1900 with all the elegance
and features of this period and stands in 20 acres of
gardens. It is comfortable and elegantly furnished
often with period furniture adding to the
atmosphere. David Auchie, who won Scottish Chef
of the Year 1997 is now Executive Chef and
prepares good, well-balanced menus offering
plenty of choices and using only the freshest local
produce. Great care is taken of the presentation
and whilst there is much evidence of Scottish
produce influences are drawn from other countries
which results in a gourmet dining experience
offering the best of everything. Chapeltoun House
Hotel has 2 AA Rosettes.

Open all year
🏨 Rooms: 8 with private facilities
🛏 DB&B £74.75–£94.30   B&B £49.95–£69.50
SP Special rates available
✕ Lunch ££
✕ Dinner £££
Ⓥ Vegetarians welcome
🕇 Children welcome
🚭 No smoking in restaurant

**Roasted scallops with baby fennel and ginger
cream. Mignons of venison with a piquant sauce
and sweet and sour cabbage. Apricot bread and
butter pudding.**

STB Highly Commended 👑 👑 👑 👑
💳 Credit cards: Mastercard/Eurocard, American
   Express, Visa, Switch, Delta
👤 Partner & Host: Simon Dobson

SCHOLARS RESTAURANT

Stirling Highland Hotel
Stirling
FK8 1DU
Tel: 01786 475444
Fax: 01786 462929

From Stirling town centre follow directions to
Stirling Castle. Stirling Highland Hotel is on the hill
approx 500 yards below the castle in Spittal Street.

**An historic A Listed building, converted from the
old high school.**

- Historic converted town hotel.
- Modern Scottish cooking.
- "Situated in the old town of Stirling, ideally
  placed as a base for touring Central Scotland."

In keeping with the rest of the hotel, Scholars
Restaurant is named with its former use in mind –
namely that of the old high school. The restaurant
adjoins the lounge bar entitled 'Headmaster's
Study' and is a formal restaurant, with fine linen,
cutlery and crockery. Menus are à la carte and
table d'hôte and offer a good selection of fresh
local produce. Chef Kieran Grant has been at the
hotel for six years and is skilled and talented. Staff
are well-trained and professional yet friendly.
Scholars Restaurant has 1 AA Rosette.

Open all year
Closed Sun evening + Sat lunch
🏨 Rooms: 78 with private facilities
🛏 DB&B £49–£59   B&B £61.50–£95
SP Special rates available
✕ Food available all day
✕ Lunch except Sat £
✕ Dinner except Sun ££
Ⓥ Vegetarians welcome
🕇 Children welcome
♿ Facilities for disabled visitors
🚭 No smoking in restaurant

**Achiltibuie smoked selection with a chive
dressing. Noisettes of venison Blairlogie.
Raspberry mille feuille with caramelised puff
pastry.**

STB Highly Commended 👑 👑 👑 👑 👑
💳 Credit cards: Mastercard/Eurocard, American
   Express, Visa, Diners Club, Mastercharge,
   Switch, JCB
👤 General Manager: Andrew G Swinton

CROMLIX HOUSE
Kinbuck, by Dunblane
Perthshire FK15 9JT
Tel: 01786 822125
Fax: 01786 825450

Off A9, B8033 to Kinbuck, through village, cross
narrow bridge, drive is second on left. From Crieff
A822 to Braco, then B8033 Kinbuck.

A baronial mansion recalling the splendours of a bygone age.

- A highly praised hotel with the atmosphere of a much loved home.
- Outstanding modern/traditional Scottish cuisine.
- "Cromlix, as always, is one of our better country house hotels with an atmosphere and class of its own."

Proprietors David and Ailsa Assenti succeed in exemplifying the true traditions of country house hospitality, treating each of their guests as a cherished individual. This is reflected in the high standard of their accommodation, which includes eight large suites with private sitting rooms. Head Chef Craig Wilson, takes only the best of fresh produce, either from the estate or procured locally, and produces imaginative meals for the discriminating palate. Menus change daily. The wine list is discerning and extensive. Cromlix is indeed a 'totally relaxing, seemingly effortless, well-run ship'. Cromlix has 2 AA Rosettes.

Open all year except 2 to 30 Jan
🏫 Rooms: 14 with private facilities
🛏 DB&B £114–£163   B&B £77.50–£125
🆂🅿 Special rates available
✕ Lunch ££
✕ Dinner 5 course menu ££££
Ⓥ Vegetarians welcome – extensive menu
🧍 Children welcome
🚭 No smoking in dining rooms
🐄 Member of the Scotch Beef Club

Freshly prepared tagliatelle with carved breast of Guinea fowl and woodland mushroom cream. Filo wafers layered with scallops and stir-fry vegetables over a lime and ginger essence. Banana and cinnamon soufflé beignets served with a butterscotch sauce.

STB Deluxe 👑 👑 👑 👑
💳 Credit cards: Mastercard/Eurocard, American Express, Visa, Diners Club, Switch
👤 Proprietors: David & Ailsa Assenti

THE TOPPS
Fintry Road, Denny (B818)
Stirlingshire FK6 5JF
Tel: 01324 822471
Fax: 01324 823099

On B818 Denny – Fintry road, off M80. 4 miles from Denny.

A family-run farm guest house in Stirlingshire.

- A farmhouse on a working sheep and cashmere goat farm.
- Excellent home cooking.
- "Homely informality with good food and wonderful views."

This is a most informal farm guest house where you cannot help but share in the day to day activities of the country. The house itself is a modern bungalow with splendid views over the Fintry and Ochil Hills, pleasantly furnished with plenty of family bric-a-brac. The atmosphere is cosy and familiar. A popular restaurant complements the guest house facilities. It has a small bar and a comfortable dining room. Scottish owners Jennifer and Alistair Steel both cook. The menus are straightforward, usually offering a choice of four main courses and as much produce as possible comes from the farm itself.

Open all year
🏫 Rooms: 8 with private facilities
🛏 B&B £20–£32
✕ Dinner ££
Ⓥ Vegetarians welcome – prior notice required
🧍 Children welcome
♿ Facilities for disabled visitors
🚭 No smoking throughout

Asparagus spears lightly cooked and served with just a brush of butter. Venison fillet served with port and raspberry sauce. Brandy baskets filled with ice cream and Blairgowrie sauce.

STB Commended 👑 👑 👑
💳 Credit cards: Mastercard/Eurocard, Visa
👤 Owners/Chefs: Jennifer & Alistair Steel

NORTH WEST CASTLE HOTEL
Portrodie, Stranraer
Wigtownshire DG9 8EH
Tel: 01776 704413
Fax: 01776 702646

Seafront – opposite ferry port.

Town hotel situated in busy seafront resort.

- 1820s town mansion.
- Traditional hotel cooking.
- "Impressive town house in which to enjoy traditional cooking presented in modern style."

This castellated townhouse was built by Sir John Ross, the Arctic explorer, in 1820. It has been owned and run as a hotel by the McMillan family for many years and has been well-maintained with comfortable accommodation and function rooms. It has the distinction of being the first hotel in the world with its own indoor curling rink and also has bowling, swimming pool (with spa bath), sauna, sunbeds and multi-gym. The games room offers snooker, pool and table tennis. Overlooking Loch Ryan the large 'Regency' dining room has a grand hotel atmosphere with pianist playing each evening and both the à la carte and table d'hôte menus offer traditional Scottish dishes, treated in a creative way. The kitchen goes to great lengths to find fresh local produce.

Open all year
🏵 Rooms: 71 with private facilities
🛏 DB&B £46–£88 (min 2 nights stay), B&B £35–£77
SP Special rates available
✗ Lunch ££
✗ Dinner ££££
Ⓥ Vegetarians welcome
🧍 Children welcome

Timbale of local oak-smoked salmon filled with a smoked trout mousse, accompanied by a cucumber and yoghurt sauce. Roast saddle of venison served with a red wine and juniper game sauce. Warm Ecclefechan tart accompanied by a light caramel sauce.

STB Highly Commended 🏵 🏵 🏵 🏵 🏵
💳 Credit cards: Mastercard/Eurocard, Visa, Switch, Delta
🗑 Proprietor: H C McMillan

COUL HOUSE HOTEL
Contin, by Strathpeffer
Ross-shire IV14 9EY
Tel: 01997 421487
Fax: 01997 421945

North of Inverness, continue on A9 over Moray Firth Bridge. After 5 miles take second left at roundabout on to A835. Follow this road for about 12 miles until you reach the village of Contin. Hotel is ½ mile up private drive to the right.

A country house near Strathpeffer.

- 19th century mansion.
- Country house cooking.
- "This mansion house hotel has great food, hospitality and staff."

This elegant country house hotel commands fine views over unspoiled Highland scenery, little changed since its original inhabitants, the Mackenzies of Coul lived here. The spacious public rooms have open log fires and the recently refurbished en suite bedrooms are comfortable and tastefully decorated. Home to Martyn and Ann Hill, whose warm Highland welcome is only matched by their loveable Labradors. The bar lunches are notable – and the 'Kitchen Bar' itself is very popular with locals. Mackenzie's Taste of Scotland Restaurant offers table d'hôte and à la carte lunch and dinner menus which focus on Scottish specialities. Coul House has 1 AA Rosette. *(See advert Page 26.)*

Open all year
🏵 Rooms: 20 with private facilities
🛏 DB&B £49.50–£73.25   B&B £35–£49.75
SP Special rates available
🍴 Lunch £-££ (Restaurant – prior booking only)
✗ Dinner 5 course menu ££££
Ⓥ Vegetarians welcome
🧍 Children welcome
♿ Facilities for disabled visitors
🚭 No smoking in restaurant
🐄 Member of the Scotch Beef Club

Home smoked venison with avocado fan and pigeon, cranberry parfait. Char-grilled salmon, monkfish and scallops, lemon and watercress cream. Layered apple, raspberry, cinnamon crisp and chantilly cream.

STB Highly Commended 🏵 🏵 🏵 🏵
💳 Credit cards: Mastercard/Eurocard, American Express, Visa, Diners Club, Switch, JCB
🗑 Proprietors: Martyn & Ann Hill

CREAGAN HOUSE
RESTAURANT WITH ACCOMMODATION
Strathyre
Perthshire FK18 8ND
Tel: 01877 384638
Fax: 01877 384319

On A84, ¼ mile north of Strathyre.

Family-run restaurant with accommodation.

- 17th century farmhouse.
- Innovative Scottish cooking.
- "Wonderful local food served in a magnificent baronial dining room."

Creagan House dates from the 17th century, and has been sympathetically restored to provide a 'baronial' dining room and five letting bedrooms. The house is eclectically furnished with all sorts of interesting pieces, and one of the bedrooms has a unique four-poster bed. Gordon and Cherry Gunn have been awarded an AA Rosette for their cooking. Guests choose from the 'menu of the day' or the 'chef's favourites menu'. The emphasis of the cooking is to allow the fresh local ingredients to emerge, with herbs from the garden, meats sourced from within Perthshire and interesting Scottish cheeses. The care and attention to detail in preparation, cooking and presentation is obvious and the overall effect is excellent.

Open all year except 3 to 28 Feb + 1 wk Oct (Scottish half term)
- ⏏ Rooms: 5 with private facilities
- ⇋ DB&B £52.50–£57.50   B&B £35
- SP Special rates available
- ⅌ Booking essential for all meals
- ✕ Lunch Sun ££ (Mon to Sat – lunch parties can be arranged)
- ✕ Dinner ££-£££
- Ⓥ Vegetarians welcome – with prior notice
- ⅋ Children welcome
- ⅍ No smoking in dining hall + bedrooms

Monkfish with braised fennel and pineapple with port wine glaze. Loin of lamb and rabbit with paprika on a redcurrant and orange sauce. Toblerone soufflé with local raspberries.

STB Deluxe 👑 👑 👑
- 🎴 Credit cards: Mastercard/Eurocard, American Express, Visa
- ⅄ Chef/Proprietor: Gordon Gunn
- ⅄ Co-Proprietor: Cherry Gunn

KILCAMB LODGE HOTEL
Strontian
Argyll PH36 4HY
Tel: 01967 402257
Fax: 01967 402041

On A861, 13 miles from Corran Ferry (A82, 15 miles south of Fort William).

Charming, small country house hotel in stunningly beautiful loch-side setting.

- Small country house hotel.
- Good quality modern Scottish cuisine.
- "First class Scottish country house with energetic and ardent cooking and service."

Kilcamb Lodge is a charming, substantial West Highland dowager house, with extensions at each end. Its situation is superb – standing in 28 acres of lawns and woodland, with half a mile of shoreline along Loch Sunart. The hotel is family-owned and run by Anne and Peter Blakeway. The excellence of the food has been recognised by the award of 2 AA Rosettes. Peter Blakeway cooks, presenting a short and highly professional table d'hôte menu which changes daily and uses the best of the produce available that day. This is a family business with real style – the perfect setting for any hotel and the way it is run enhances it further.

Open mid Mar to early Nov
- ⏏ Rooms: 11 with private facilities
- ⇋ DB&B £62–£85   B&B £44.50–£60
- ✕ Light Lunch £
- ✕ Dinner 4 course menu £££
- Ⓥ Vegetarians welcome – prior notice required
- ⅋ Children welcome
- ⅍ Facilities for non-residential disabled visitors
- ⅍ No smoking in restaurant

Seared Morar scallops with avocado salsa. Fillet of Angus Beef with pickled walnut café au lait. Butterscotch pudding with toffee ice cream.

STB Deluxe 👑 👑 👑
- 🎴 Credit cards: Mastercard/Eurocard, Visa, Switch, Delta
- ⅄ Directors: Peter & Anne Blakeway

THE WHEATSHEAF HOTEL
WINNER MACALLAN AWARD 1997 –
HOTEL OF THE YEAR
Main Street, Swinton
Berwickshire TD11 3JJ
Tel: 01890 860 257
Fax: 01890 860 688

On B6461 Kelso-Berwick-upon-Tweed, 12 miles west of Berwick or a few miles east of A697.

Country inn with rooms in Border village.

- A small country inn on the village green.
- Modern Scottish cooking.
- "Excellent food using local produce cooked in a modern style."

That a great deal of care has been taken to preserve the character of a genuine country inn is evident. The result is a welcoming, comfortable and intimate atmosphere, the sort that takes years to acquire. Bedrooms are prettily furnished, light and airy with en suite bathrooms. The menu is surprisingly extensive, very reasonably priced and changes quarterly with the seasons. Excellent local produce is given added flavour by the chef's individuality and flair. The Wheatsheaf has 1 AA Rosette.

Open all year except last wk Oct + last 2 wks Feb
Closed Mon
🏠 Rooms: 5, 4 with private facilities
🛏 B&B £32–£52
SP Special rates available
✕ Lunch except Mon £££
✕ Dinner except Mon £££
Ⅴ Vegetarians welcome
🕂 Children welcome
⅁ Facilities for disabled visitors
⅂ No smoking in restaurant

Fillet of smoked haddock served on a leek and potato cake with a butter and chive sauce. Fillet of Highland venison on a port and redcurrant sauce with spiced red cabbage.

STB Highly Commended 👑 👑 👑
💳 Credit cards: Mastercard/Eurocard, Visa, Switch
👤 Proprietors: Alan & Julie Reid

MANSFIELD HOUSE HOTEL
Scotsburn Road, Tain
Ross-shire IV19 1PR
Tel: 01862 892052
Fax: 01862 892260

Approaching Tain from south, ignore first entrance and continue north on A9 to second turning, signposted to police station and Royal Academy.

A family-run luxury country house hotel

- 19th century baronial house.
- Good Scottish cooking.
- "With the best use of local food and ideal peaceful surroundings this is a wonderful place to stay."

Visitors to the Royal Burgh of Tain, chartered in 1066, are able to enjoy many architectural features of interest. Mansfield House was built in 19th century baronial style by Donald Fowler, the former Provost of Tain between 1898 and 1912. The house has been lovingly maintained and offers every comfort for travellers. The kitchen prides itself in preparing well-chosen Scottish produce for a selection of familiar and popular dishes. There is a friendly and relaxed atmosphere and the Lauritsen family, highly skilled and experienced, are excellent hosts – assisted by their two golden retrievers! *(See advert Page 32.)*

Open all year
🏠 Rooms: 18 with private facilities
🛏 B&B £35–£60
SP Special rates available
✕ Food available all day £-£££
✕ Lunch £
✕ Dinner £-£££
Ⅴ Vegetarians welcome
🕂 Children welcome
⅁ Facilities for disabled visitors
⅂ No smoking in restaurants

Entremets of avocado and fresh crab with tomato and coriander dressing. Scottish lamb topped with Brie and leeks. Hot chocolate tart with vanilla sauce.

STB Highly Commended 👑 👑 👑 👑 👑
💳 Credit cards: Mastercard/Eurocard, American Express, Visa, Switch
👤 Proprietors: Norman, Norma & David Lauritsen

AN TAIRBEART HERITAGE CENTRE
Tarbert
Argyll PA29 6SX
Tel: 01880 820190
Fax: 01880 820102

2 minutes south of Tarbert on the main A83 to Campbeltown.

- Heritage centre including farm shop, delicatessen and restaurant.
- Excellent Scottish cooking.
- "A creative style of Scottish cuisine delights the eye as well as the palate – you will visit again and again."

An Tairbeart nestles at the base of native woods through which paths lead the visitor to see ponies, farmed deer, sheep and Highland cattle. The attractive timber and glass building houses the licensed restaurant, farm shop and delicatessen. Talented Alison Sykora, along with her enthusiastic team produces highly accomplished fare to suit all tastes and pockets. The cooking offers a wide range of dishes and includes an attractive menu for children – one could have a light snack or take a full three course lunch – all skilfully cooked, presented and professionally served.

Open all year except Christmas Day + New Year's Day
✗ Food available all day £-££
✗ Lunch £-££
✗ Dinner (min booking of 12+ during winter) £-££
Ⓥ Vegetarians welcome
⚘ Children welcome
♿ Facilities for disabled visitors
✄ No smoking throughout

Fresh marjoram and tomato soup. Smoked salmon kedgeree. Bread and malt whisky butter pudding.

STB Commended Visitor Attraction
▱ Credit cards: Mastercard/Eurocard, Visa, Switch, Delta
Ⓜ Manager: Alison Sykora

THE ANCHORAGE RESTAURANT
Harbour Street
Tarbert, Argyll
PA29 6UD
Tel: 01880 820 881

Towards the end of main street in Tarbert, fronting the harbour.

- Small seafood restaurant at the harbour side.
- Skilled modern cooking.
- "A talented chef with the abundance of fresh Tarbert seafood to call upon."

The re-opening of the premises known as 'The Anchorage' in Tarbert, Argyll will come as welcome news to lovers of fine cooking on the West Coast. Nathalie and Russell Burns , the new owners are well experienced in the trade and in their new premises in March this year they received the Booker prize for Excellence 96/97 Best Restaurant UK – a prestigious start to their latest venture. Although seafood dominates, good local meat is also treated with care and a most distinctive style. The restaurant is small so booking is always advisable.

Open all year except Boxing Day + New Year's Day
✗ Dinner ££
Ⓥ Vegetarians welcome
⚘ Children welcome

Warm salad of prawns topped with melted Mozzarella cheese and toasted pine kernels, served with a citrus dressing. Brochette of Isle of Jura monkfish and wild salmon, served with saffron rice. Hot gaufrette filled with fresh strawberries and cream.

▱ Credit cards: Mastercard/Eurocard, Visa, Switch, Delta
Ⓜ Owners: Nathalie & Russell Burns

THE COLUMBA HOTEL

East Pier Road, Tarbert
Argyll PA29 6UF
Tel/Fax: 01880 820808

On East Pier Road, ½ mile to the left around the harbour. Hotel on roadside.

A well-appointed family-run hotel close to harbour at Tarbert.

- A Victorian waterfront hotel refurbished by the present owners as a comfortable and pleasant establishment.
- Scottish modern cooking.
- "A warm and friendly hotel with panoramic views over the hills and Loch Fyne."

This small hotel overlooks Loch Fyne at the entrance to Tarbert Harbour. It has been a labour of love to Gina and Bob Chicken, who have worked hard at sympathetically refurbishing this Victorian hotel and continue to do so. The decor is in keeping with the building; there is a cosy bar with an open fire, which is popular for its wholesomely different bar food (and its 30 malt whiskies). The restaurant has been elegantly restored; it offers a relaxed atmosphere and a menu which makes imaginative use of the excellent local produce – fish and shellfish from the harbour; game from Inveraray Castle. *(See advert Page 234.)*

....

Open all year except 25, 26 Dec
🛏 Rooms: 10 with private facilities
🍴 DB&B £38.95–£51.95   B&B £31.95–£37.95
SP Special rates available
✗ Lunch £
✗ Dinner ££
Ⓥ Vegetarians welcome
🕭 Children welcome
✂ No smoking in restaurant

Argyllshire smoked ham and lemon chicken mousse. Lightly poached scallops and monkfish with fresh fennel sauce. Hazelnut and butterscotch meringue with Drambuie and orange iced cream.

STB Commended 👑 👑 👑
💳 Credit cards: Mastercard/Eurocard, Visa
Ⓜ Partners: Bob & Gina Chicken

TAYVALLICH INN

Tayvallich
Argyll PA31 8PL
Tel: 01546 870282
Fax: 01546 870333

On B8025 (via B841 [Crinan] off B816 at Cairnbaan).

An informal bistro style restaurant with an enviable reputation.

- Both a popular local hostelry and a destination for the discerning.
- Simple treatment of freshest ingredients.
- "A peaceful haven with a well deserved reputation for excellent cuisine."

Under the same dedicated ownership of John and Pat Grafton for 19 years, Tayvallich Inn has earned the reputation of being a firm favourite. Beautifully situated with a spectacular outlook onto Tayvallich Bay, its many regular customers are drawn to its friendly atmosphere and excellent cooking. The reasonably-priced menus concentrate on the abundance of local seafood – scallops, prawns, mussels, crab and oysters – but does equally well for carnivores and vegetarians. The cooking is simple, straightforward and unpretentious. Service is cheerful and relaxed.

....

Open all year
Note: Closed Mon Nov to Mar
✗ Lunch £
✗ Dinner ££
Ⓥ Vegetarians welcome
🕭 Children welcome
✂ No smoking area in bar (meal times)

Loch Swealch mussels marinière. Pan-fried Sound of Jura scallops. Apple crumble.

💳 Credit cards: Mastercard/Eurocard, Visa, Mastercharge, Switch
Ⓜ Proprietors: John & Pat Grafton

TRIGONY HOUSE HOTEL
by Thornhill
Dumfries
DG3 5EZ
Tel: 01848 331211
Fax: 01848 331303

Situated off A76, 13 miles north of Dumfries. 1 mile south of Thornhill on the Dumfries-Ayr trunk road.

An Edwardian country house standing in its own gardens.

- An attractive converted shooting lodge standing in its own gardens.
- Simple, elegant Scottish cooking.
- "An elegant place to find fine cuisine and excellent hospitality."

Trigony is a small country house hotel built of pink sandstone, standing amidst its own four acres of mature trees and lawns. It was once the home of the oldest woman in Scotland, Miss Frances Shakerley, who lived to be 107, and became an hotel 18 years ago. Its owners, Robin and Thelma Pollock take justifiable pride in their hotel and provide homely comfort and good food made from local produce. Public and private rooms are bright and airy, prettily decorated and with charming views over the surrounding country. *(See advert Page 32.)*

Open all year
- Rooms : 8 with private facilities
- DB&B £52.50–£62.50   B&B £35–£45
- Special rates available
- ✕ Lunch £
- ✕ Dinner ££
- Ⓥ Vegetarians welcome
- Children over 8 years welcome
- No smoking in dining room

Sauté of mushrooms with Dunsyre blue cheese, garlic and cream. Fillet of salmon in white wine and a lime and ginger sauce. Crème caramel.

STB Highly Commended 👑 👑 👑 👑
- Credit cards: Mastercard/Eurocard, Visa
- Proprietors: Robin & Thelma Pollock

LION & UNICORN
Main Street, Thornhill
by Stirling FK8 3PJ
Tel: 01786 850204
Fax: 01786 850306

On A873, 9 miles west of Stirling, between Blair Drummond Safari Park and Aberfoyle.

A popular old coaching inn dating back to the 1600s.

- Informal restaurant and bar.
- Modern and traditional Scottish cooking.
- "An informal and friendly village pub."

The Lion & Unicorn was built in 1635 as a coaching inn – with low ceilings, stone walls and open log fires. It is family-run and friendly: a popular local pub. A good range of reasonably priced dishes featuring fresh produce is offered on a blackboard. Vegetarian and children's options are also available. The lay out of the pub allows for there to be both smoking and non-smoking areas in the restaurant. Chef/owner Walter MacAulay is experienced and forthright, and his wife Ariane is Dutch and also speaks German. Walter speaks reasonable French!

Open all year
- ✕ Lunch ££
- ✕ Dinner ££
- Ⓥ Vegetarians welcome
- Children welcome
- Facilities for disabled visitors
- No smoking in restaurant

West Coast queen scallops with Pastis and pinenut sauce. Loin of Perthshire lamb with a pistachio and herb crust with roasted garlic jus. Spiced banana tartlet with white chocolate sauce.

- Credit cards: Mastercard/Eurocard, American Express, Visa, Diners Club, Mastercharge, Switch, JCB
- Proprietors: Walter & Ariane MacAulay

FORSS COUNTRY HOUSE HOTEL
by Thurso
Caithness
KW14 7XY
Tel: 01847 861201/202
Fax: 01847 861301

4 miles from Thurso heading west on A836.
Secluded setting at Bridge of Forss.

Country house hotel set in 20 acres of woodland.

- Country house hotel.
- Traditional Scottish cooking.
- "A tranquil country hotel offering quality food."

Forss Country House Hotel has been run by the MacGregor family for the past few years Jamie MacGregor is 'mein host' looking after guests from arrival and even playing the bagpipes on special occasions for his guests. Jackie MacGregor does all the cooking and is accomplished in this task. Best use of local produce is made, in particular locally caught fish brought to the kitchen by Jamie. This is a most welcome addition to Taste of Scotland and an excellent place from which to enjoy the splendour of the Highlands.

Open 5 Jan to 23 Dec
🏠 Rooms: 10 with private facilities
🛏 DB&B £62–£69   B&B £42.50–£49.50
SP Special rates available
✗ Food available all day ££
✗ Lunch - residents only £-££
✗ Dinner ££
Ⅴ Vegetarians welcome
† Children welcome
♿ Facilities for disabled visitors
✗ No smoking in dining room

Venison pâté served with a crisp salad, Orkney oatcakes and hawthorn jelly. Local sirloin steak stuffed with haggis and presented on a bed of Glenmorangie sauce. Burnt raspberry creams: Scottish raspberries topped with a secret recipe and lightly grilled.

STB Highly Commended 👑 👑 👑 👑
💳 Credit cards: Mastercard/Eurocard, American Express, Visa
⛏ Proprietors: Jamie & Jackie MacGregor

BEN LOYAL HOTEL
Main Street, Tongue
Sutherland IV27 4XE
Tel: 01847 611216
Fax: 01847 611212

At junction of A838 and A836, midway between John o' Groats and Cape Wrath – in village centre.

A family-run hotel offering the best of hospitality with wonderful views of Ben Hope and Ben Loyal.

- Highland village hotel.
- Modern Scottish cooking.
- "The hotel to visit for sport, relaxation or touring."

Standing in a splendid location overlooking the Kyle of Tongue, this hotel seems to have been designed with the sole intention of enabling guests to enjoy stunning panoramas from the comfortably furnished lounge to the beautifully appointed bedrooms, nine of which are en suite, with their pine furniture, pretty fabrics and four-poster bed. But perhaps the best views of all can be had from the dining room, where you will find your loyalties torn between relishing the view and savouring the food. Only fresh local produce – much of it home-grown – is used in the preparation of traditional dishes presented in a modern way. Ben Loyal has 1 AA Rosette. *(See advert Page 22.)*

Open 1 Mar to 31 Oct
🏠 Rooms: 12, 9 with private facilities
🛏 DB&B £34–£60   B&B £18–£40
SP Special rates available
✗ Lunch (Restaurant lunch by prior arrangement only) £
✗ Dinner ££
Ⅴ Vegetarians welcome
† Children welcome
♿ Limited facilities for disabled visitors
✗ No smoking in dining room

Smoked salmon and artichoke ravioli with a light balsamic cream. Roast haunch of Highland venison with a juniper berry sauce. Shetland whipkull with local berries.

STB Highly Commended 👑 👑 👑
💳 Credit cards: Mastercard/Eurocard, Visa, Switch, Delta
⛏ Proprietors: Mel & Pauline Cook

PIERSLAND HOUSE HOTEL
15 Craigend Road, Troon
Ayrshire KA10 6HD
Tel: 01292 314747
Fax: 01292 315613

South corner of Troon, opposite Royal Troon
Golf Club.

A fine country house hotel in the town of Troon.

- A beautifully restored Tudor style mansion in the heart of Ayrshire golfing country.
- International cuisine.
- "Country house hotel with impressive cuisine and service."

Piersland was built for Sir Alexander Walker, grandson of the Johnnie Walker who founded the whisky firm of the same name. Tudor outside, and very impressive, the house has some fine Jacobean-style features. It stands in four acres of immaculate grounds that include a Japanese water garden. The hotel also has 13 cottage suites for guests wanting that little bit extra. All have their own lounge and twin-bedroom and are fully equipped. With ten championship courses within a 30 minute drive, this is a golfers' paradise. In the dining room the fixed price a la carte menu justifies the hotel's reputation for fine and varied cuisine. The Garden Room caters for private functions. The hotel has 1 AA Rosette.

Open all year
- ⊞ Rooms: 28 with private facilities
- ⊯ DB&B £75–£90   B&B £55–£70
- SP Special rates available
- ✕ Lunch ££
- ✕ Dinner ££
- Ⓥ Vegetarians welcome
- ⚓ Children welcome
- ♿ Facilities for disabled visitors

Ragoût of wild mushrooms with spring leaves laced with a Drambuie sauce. Medallions of Highland venison layered with black pudding, masked by a mild black peppercorn sauce. Hot raspberry soufflé presented with shortbread fingers.

STB Highly Commended 👑 👑 👑 👑
- 💳 Credit cards: Mastercard/Eurocard, American Express, Visa, Diners Club, Mastercharge, Switch
- 🅜 Manager: Karel Kuhler

MALIN COURT HOTEL
Turnberry
Ayrshire KA26 9PB
Tel: 01655 331457
Fax: 01655 331072

On A719 Ayr-Girvan, south of Maidens.

A modern country hotel with spectacular views.

- Popular, purpose built country hotel.
- Modern Scottish cooking.
- "Attentive, friendly hospitality and very enjoyable cuisine."

Overlooking the famous Turnberry Open Championship Golf Course and close to Culzean Castle, Malin Court enjoys an attractive situation on the Ayrshire coast with a marvellous outlook over to the Isle of Arran. Accommodation is comfortable and well-furnished with every facility you could wish for. In the Carrick Restaurant, Andrea Beach has developed a successful blend of modern cooking combined with traditional Scottish dishes. Menus are imaginative and complemented by a short, well-priced wine list. The pleasure of dining is enhanced by spectacular sunset views of Arran. The hotel has 1 AA Rosette. *(See advert Page 31.)*

Open all year
- ⊞ Rooms: 17 with private facilities
- ⊯ DB&B £65–£95   B&B £52–£82
- SP Special rates available
- ✕ Food available all day ££
- ✕ Lunch ££
- ✕ Dinner £££
- Ⓥ Vegetarians welcome
- ⚓ Children welcome
- ♿ Facilities for disabled visitors

Spiced lentil pâté, toasted brioche and a tomato chutney. Medallions of beef, woodland mushrooms on a rosemary and onion jus. Steamed vanilla pudding and raspberry sauce with flakes of bitter chocolate.

STB Highly Commended 👑 👑 👑 👑
- 💳 Credit cards: Mastercard/Eurocard, American Express, Visa, Diners Club, Switch, Delta
- 🅜 General Manager: W R Kerr

TURNBERRY HOTEL
Turnberry, Ayrshire KA26 9LT
Tel: 01655 331000
Fax: 01655 331706

A77 – 17 miles south of Ayr. 2 miles after Kirkoswald.

One of Scotland's most exclusive hotels.

- Resort hotel of international standing.
- Grand hotel cooking; also spa and grill-room styles.
- "A justifiably famous and exceedingly special place."

Turnberry was purpose built as a golfing resort hotel at the turn-of-the-century, and retains many opulent Edwardian features. Service is gracious and supremely professional, yet friendly. The hotel's main restaurant offers the best classical cooking using fresh, local ingredients. Chef Stewart Cameron who is a member of the Academie Culinaire de France was awarded The Macallan Personality of the Year 1996. During the week lunch is served in the Bay Restaurant where a blissful menu for the health-conscious is presented. The Turnberry Clubhouse serves roasts, grills, fries and sandwiches. Turnberry has 2 AA Rosettes.

Open all year
- Rooms: 132 with private facilities
- DB&B £123.50–£187.50   B&B £80–£142.50
- Special rates available
- Food available all day ££
- Lunch £££
- Dinner ££££
- Vegetarians welcome
- Children welcome
- Facilities for disabled visitors
- Member of the Scotch Beef Club

West Coast scallops and scampi tails sautéed with garlic and cardamom. Cutlet of Highland venison with celeriac mousse, poached pear, cranberries and lavender game sauce. Caramelised apple with hot cider butter, chilled calvados parfait and almond macaroon.

STB Deluxe ♛ ♛ ♛ ♛ ♛
- Credit cards: Mastercard/Eurocard, American Express, Visa, Diners Club, Mastercharge, Switch
- Resident Manager: A R W Furlong

FIFE ARMS HOTEL
The Square, Turriff
Aberdeenshire AB53 7AE
Tel: 01888 563124

Situated in Turriff town square on A947. 10 miles from Banff, 17 miles from Oldmeldrum.

A pleasant and relaxing restaurant offering traditional and modern dishes.

- Old market square building.
- Freshly cooked local produce.
- "A popular, traditional inn offering delicious food."

There is a tradition of a hostelry on this site since the early 1900s. Situated at the top of the square the Fife Arms with its Poachers Restaurant offers a cosy and informal venue for travellers and locals alike. The restaurant menu is written on a blackboard and changes daily, according to availability of local produce, particularly the seafood which comes from Macduff. The lounge bar is a relaxing place with oak beams, stained glass windows and open fire, and friendly service. Bedrooms are being renovated.

Open all year
- Rooms: currently being renovated
- Food available all day – bookings only £-££
- Lunch £
- Dinner £-££
- Vegetarians welcome
- Children welcome
- No smoking in restaurant

Mussels cooked in white wine, tomato, herbs and fresh ground pepper. Red deer fillet, char-grilled and served with a red wine and juniper berry sauce. A changing selection of home-made sweets.

- Credit cards: Mastercard/Eurocard, Visa, Delta
- Chef/Manager: John Ferrier

THE TOWIE TAVERN
Auchterless
nr Turriff
Aberdeenshire AB53 8EP
Tel: 01888 511201

On main A947, 4 miles from Fyvie Castle, 4 miles from Turriff.

An old coaching inn with restaurants.

- Village inn.
- Traditional country style cooking.
- "Excellent food and fine Scottish hospitality can be found in this old coaching inn."

The Towie Tavern is a charming old coaching inn, built about 1800, standing close to the beautifully restored early 16th century Towie Barclay Castle. It has two restaurants – the Barclay (for dinners) and the Castle (for suppers). Lunches are served in both; there is a smaller chamber – the Post Room – off the Barclay for private parties, family gatherings, etc., and there is also a diner's bar and a lounge bar. The cooking makes use of the best of Grampian produce; à la carte menus are offered, and there are daily 'Towie Treats' of both supper and dinner dishes.

Open all year except 1 + 2 Jan
- ✗ Lunch £
- ✗ Dinner ££
- Ⓥ Vegetarians welcome
- ✦ Children welcome
- ♿ Facilities for disabled visitors
- ⚟ No smoking in restaurants

Fresh Inverawe mussels steamed with tomato, cider, garlic and onion. Fillet steak with onion, bacon, red wine, Arran mustard and cream. Home-made desserts.

- ⊞ Credit cards: Mastercard/Eurocard, Visa, Mastercharge
- ⋈ Proprietors: Douglas & Eileen Pearson

THE CLIFTON COFFEE HOUSE
Tyndrum
Central Scotland FK20 8RY
Tel: 01838 400271
Fax: 01838 400330

On A85 to Oban and Fort William. 5 miles north of Crianlarich.

Excellent self-service restaurant.

- Craft and souvenir shopping eaterie.
- Home cooking.
- "A great self-service restaurant – popular with tourists and walkers."

What began as a simple self-service restaurant has become a tourist attraction in its own right. The shopping complex which has grown up around it sells books, crafts, woollens, gifts and food, but the restaurant is still the focal point. The owners constantly review their standards, service is friendly and reliable, offering good home baking and cooking and a wide variety of traditional Scottish meals and snacks. Very popular with visitors to Glencoe.

Open 8 Feb to 4 Jan except Christmas Day, Boxing Day + New Year's Day
- ✗ Food available all day £
- ✗ Lunch £
- Ⓥ Vegetarians welcome
- ✦ Children welcome
- ♿ Facilities for disabled visitors
- ⚟ No smoking area in restaurant

Curried apple and parsnip soup. Hebridean leek pie. A large variety of home baking.

- ⊞ Credit cards: Mastercard/Eurocard, American Express, Visa, Diners Club, Mastercharge, Switch, Delta
- ⋈ Partners: DD, LV & IL Wilkie/L P Gosden/ F D Robertson

DUNDONNELL HOTEL
Little Loch Broom
Ross-shire IV23 2QR
Tel: 01854 633204
Fax: 01854 633366
e-mail - selbie@dundonnellhotel.co.uk.

On A832 by Little Loch Broom, midway between
Ullapool – 26 miles and Gairloch 30 miles.

**An established country hotel in the North West
Highlands.**

- Fine stone-built hotel with loch-side location.
- Modern Scottish cooking.
- "High standards of comfort and good Highland
  hospitality."

This converted roadside coaching inn dates back
for over a century and has been owned by the
Florence family for more than 30 years during which
time they have modernised and built additional
bedrooms. The hotel is comfortable, pleasantly
decorated and offers an ideal spot for touring
Wester Ross. Cooking is of a high standard and
offers a good range of dishes presenting local
produce in comfortable surroundings. The hotel
also has a recently built conference suite.
Dundonnell Hotel has 1 AA Rosette. *(See advert
Page 26.)*

Open 1 Feb to 3 Jan
🍴 Rooms: 28 with private facilities
🛏 DB&B £42.50–£75 B&B £30–£55
SP Special rates available
✗ Lunch ££
✗ Dinner £££
Ⓥ Vegetarians welcome
👍 Children welcome
🚭 No smoking in dining room

**Smoked salmon, prawn and avocado gâteau.
Medallions of Highland venison, minted apple
potato cake with port wine and redcurrant jus.
Whisky marmalade ice cream with shortbread
hearts.**

STB Highly Commended 👑 👑 👑 👑
💳 Credit cards: Mastercard/Eurocard, American
  Express, Visa, Switch
👤 Owner: Selbie Florence

MOREFIELD MOTEL AND MARINERS RESTAURANT
North Road, Ullapool, Ross-shire IV26 2TQ
Tel: 01854 612161
Fax: 01854 612171

After c. 1 mile leaving village heading north (A835)
turn left immediately over the river bridge. Follow
hotel signs.

**An unpretentious hotel and restaurant with a well-
earned reputation for fish and shell-fish.**

- An inexpensive motel, good pub and restaurant.
- Specialists in seafood, but offer a variety of
  cooking.
- "Expertly cooked fresh locally-landed fish and
  shellfish is the main attraction of this genial
  establishment."

The Morefield is an excellent base from which to
enjoy this beautiful part of Scotland. The Mariners
Restaurant deserves its popularity, serving the best
of freshly-caught seafood, cooked with flair and
imagination, and outstanding Scottish meat. The
Lounge Bar and air-conditioned conservatory, offer
pub grub that proves just how good this kind of
cooking can be. Bookings advisable for dinner during
high season. Accommodation closed Nov to mid
March.

Open all year except Christmas Day,
Boxing Day, 1 + 2 Jan
🍴 Rooms: 10 with private facilities
🛏 B&B £22.50–£25
SP Special rates available
✗ Food available all day £-££
✗ Lunch £
✗ Dinner (Mariners Restaurant) ££
Ⓥ Vegetarians welcome
👍 Children welcome
♿ Facilities for disabled visitors
🚭 No smoking in restaurant

**Fresh mussels sautéed with white wine, chopped
onion and fresh garlic. Whole fresh chicken
cooked with wine and mushrooms and finished
with a light cream and fresh herb sauce. Apple
granny cake: fresh apple and toffee served hot with
ice cream.**

STB Commended 👑 👑 👑
💳 Credit cards: Mastercard/Eurocard, American
  Express, Visa, Mastercharge, Switch
👤 Proprietor: David Smyrl

Achray House Hotel

Stunning Lochside position in St Fillans – an area of outstanding natural beauty.
Well established, family run hotel, known for its wide selection of good food, service & a caring attitude that brings people back year after year.
The perfect base for sightseeing, golf, walking, field & watersports.
From £32.00/night, en-suite,
B & B per night.

Contact:
Lesley or John Murray
Achray House Hotel
Loch Earn, St Fillans,
Perthshire PH6 2NF
Tel 01764 685231
Fax 01764 685320

AA ★★

STB Commended

See entry Page 185
See entry Page 125

BURTS HOTEL

Melrose, Roxburghshire,
Scotland TD6 9PN
Tel: 01896 822285 Fax: 01896 822870

Distinguished family run Town House Hotel built in 1722. 21 well appointed Bedrooms all with modern facilities. Elegant Restaurant offering both à La Carte and Table d'Hôte Menus beautifully prepared and presented by our Chef Gary Moore and his Dedicated Brigade using the Best of Produce from Scotland's Natural Larder. Popular Lounge Bar serving Imaginative Bar Lunches and Suppers daily with a Gantry furnished with over 50 single Malt Whiskies and a good selection of Real Ales!

Burts Hotel is the ideal centre for Touring the Beautiful Scottish Borders Countryside with an abundance of Castles, Gardens and Stately Homes and 16 golf courses all within easy reach of the Hotel.

RAC★★★

AA ★★★ ⊛ ⊛

EGON RONAY'S GUIDES

recommended

See entry Page 192
See entry Page 227

SUPERB CUISINE

---◆---

IN INTIMATE VICTORIAN SURROUNDINGS

BUTTERY

652 Argyle Street, Glasgow, G3 8UF
Telephone 0141 221 8188
Fax 0141 204 4639

THE Columba Hotel

Tranquil Lochside position with stunning views over Loch Fyne.

Log fired bars with local Malt Whiskies.

Local produce imaginative prepared.

Extensive, but not expensive, Wine List.

STB
Commended

Logis of Great Britain

Tarbert, Kintyre,
Argyll PA29 6UF
Tel 01880-820 808

234

Balmoral

SET IN A BEAUTIFUL FORESTED AREA OF DEESIDE
OFF THE A93, BETWEEN BALLATER AND BRAEMAR

REGIONAL CAR PARK NEAR
MAIN GATES

1998 ADMISSION CHARGES:
Adults £3.50, Senior Citizens £2.50,
Children (5-16) £1.00

Enquire at Main Gate for facilities
for the disabled.

1998 OPENING DATES:
The Grounds, Gardens and Exhibitions are
open to the public from
10am to 5pm

Friday 10th April until
Saturday 30th May,
Monday to Saturday Only

Monday 1st June until
Sunday 2nd August
Open Daily

GARDENS, COUNTRY WALKS,
GIFT SHOPS, CAFETERIA,
PONY TREKKING, PONY CART RIDES (WHEN
PONIES AVAILABLE)

Exhibition of paintings and works of art in
the Castle Ballroom

The remainder of the Castle is closed to the
Public

**FOR FURTHER INFORMATION
TELEPHONE (013397) 42334/5
FAX (013397) 42271**

See entry Page 142

STB *Commended*

TRAQUAIR ARMS HOTEL

Innerleithen, Peebleshire, EH44 6PD
Facsimile: 01896 830260 Telephone: 01896 830229

Slow down a little, relax a lot at
the Traquair Arms Hotel, a
cosy friendly family-run hotel
situated in Innerleithen, in the
peaceful Tweed Valley with
splendid hills rising on either side.
We offer comfortable bedrooms, attentive service and an approach to
food that is a delight.

Imaginative menus created from
the finest of Scottish produce and
served in an informal, unhurried
atmosphere, beside our blazing log
fires in either lounge bar.

The 1999 Taste of Scotland Guide

s scheduled to be published in November 1998.

To reserve a copy at a special post inclusive price, just complete the coupon below indicating your method of payment and send it to:

Taste of Scotland (Guide Sales)
33 Melville Street
Edinburgh EH3 7JF

You will be placed on the priority list to receive the Guide as soon as it is published. For your convenience, we accept MASTERCARD and VISA.

Tel: 0131-220 1900. Fax: 0131-220 6102

--- ✂

To: Taste of Scotland (Guide Sales), 33 Melville Street, Edinburgh EH3 7JF

Please send_____copy/copies of the Taste of Scotland 1999 Guide and debit my MASTERCARD/VISA (please delete as appropriate)

Card No. ☐☐☐☐☐☐☐☐☐☐☐☐☐☐☐☐☐☐☐☐

Expiry Date   Month_____Year_____

Account Name: _____

Signature _____

Please ✓ appropriate amount:

to addresses		
in UK	£8.50	
in Europe	£9.50	
in North America (Airmail)	£11.00	

Note: cheques in £ sterling also accepted

Name: _____

Address: _____

_____

_____

Post Code: _____Country: _____

BLOCK CAPITALS, PLEASE

Post inclusive prices to other countries availabile on request

Comments on meals in places listed in
The Taste of Scotland Guide are welcomed.
Send to Taste of Scotland, 33 Melville Street, Edinburgh EH3 7JF

Establishment visited _____

Date of visit _____ Meal(s) taken _____

Comments _____

_____

_____

_____

_____

_____

_____

_____

Name _____

Address _____

_____

_____

✂ -

Comments on meals in places listed in
The Taste of Scotland Guide are welcomed.
Send to Taste of Scotland, 33 Melville Street, Edinburgh EH3 7JF

Establishment visited _____

Date of visit _____ Meal(s) taken _____

Comments _____

_____

_____

_____

_____

_____

_____

_____

Name _____

Address _____

_____

_____

The Macallan Taste of Scotland Awards 1998

Send to: Taste of Scotland, 33 Melville Street, Edinburgh EH3 7JF

I nominate _____ (Establishment)

for a Macallan Taste of Scotland Award for the following category:
(Please tick one category only)

☐ Hotel of the Year   ☐ Country House Hotel of the Year   ☐ Restaurant of the Year

☐ Special Merit for _____   ☐ Personality of the Year _____

Name _____

Address _____

_____

_____

Date of visit _____

Meal (if appropriate) _____

Closing date for entries: 30 June 1998

-- ✀

The Macallan Taste of Scotland Awards 1998

Send to: Taste of Scotland, 33 Melville Street, Edinburgh EH3 7JF

I nominate _____ (Establishment)

for a Macallan Taste of Scotland Award for the following category:
(Please tick one category only)

☐ Hotel of the Year   ☐ Country House Hotel of the Year   ☐ Restaurant of the Year

☐ Special Merit for _____   ☐ Personality of the Year _____

Name _____

Address _____

_____

_____

Date of visit _____

Meal (if appropriate) _____

Closing date for entries: 30 June 1998

Comments on meals in places listed in
The Taste of Scotland Guide are welcomed.
Send to Taste of Scotland, 33 Melville Street, Edinburgh EH3 7JF

Establishment visited _____

Date of visit _____Meal(s) taken _____

Comments _____

_____

_____

_____

_____

_____

_____

_____

Name _____

Address _____

_____

_____

✂ -

Comments on meals in places listed in
The Taste of Scotland Guide are welcomed.
Send to Taste of Scotland, 33 Melville Street, Edinburgh EH3 7JF

Establishment visited _____

Date of visit _____Meal(s) taken _____

Comments _____

_____

_____

_____

_____

_____

_____

_____

Name _____

Address _____

_____

_____

Reputation for Excellence

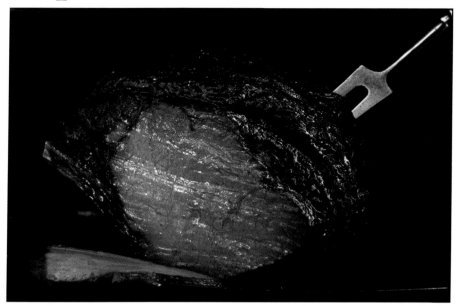

As with all other products which have earned a reputation for excellence it takes time, skill and dedication to produce Specially Selected Scotch Beef and Lamb.

Taste of Scotland members have a commitment to quality, reflected in their presentation of Scotland's own natural foodstuffs. Two of those, Specially Selected Scotch Beef and Lamb, are the end-products of a chain of traceability which reaches out from Scottish farmers to the finest tables in the land.

Specially Selected Scotch Beef and Lamb are available from accredited stockists around Britain so if you would like to learn more about the traditional production standards, now coupled to the pioneering assurance schemes of Scotland's farmers, hauliers, auctioneers and meat plants, and have details of your local retail stockists, then please contact

Scotch Quality Beef and Lamb Association,
Rural Centre - West Mains,
Newbridge, Midlothian EH28 8NX.
Tel: 0131 472 4040; Fax: 0131 472 4038

The Scotch Lamb

Scotch Lamb – Naturally one of the
Traditional Tastes of Scotland…

THE GLORIES OF SCOTLAND'S NATURAL LARDER are acclaimed by chefs and diners alike. Our country generously yields an abundance of excellence – game from both land and air; fish from sea, rivers and lochs; fruits and berries, the barley for our national drink; and our Scotch beef and Scotch lamb. The Taste of Scotland Scheme is itself an on-going celebration of Scotland cornucopia. Scotch Lamb is, arguably, the traditional taste of Scotland and, like other cuisines our traditional dishes reflect the needs of an often harsh rural past, and the constraints of one-pot cooking. Food was the fuel for heavy labour, ingredients were solely those available in season.

Today's Scotch lamb is the end-product of those same husbandry skills which are on record as being notable even in the Middle Ages, now coupled with the high standards of quality assurance provided by a modern Scottish meat industry. But, though tradition still rightly influences many a Bill of Fare, today's tastes, appetites, chefs' skills, and culinary expectations are firmly of the 20th century. It was this which six years ago prompted the Scotch Quality Beef and Lamb Association – an organisation whose strong links with the Taste of Scotland Scheme date back to the early days of both bodies – to offer sponsorship of an annual chefs' competition for Scotch lamb. One objective of the competition was to develop a cannon of contemporary recipes for this versatile meat.

For many of the world's top chefs Scotland is an instinctive choice when sourcing beef or lamb for their restaurants – they know that the traditional stock rearing skills are linked to high standards of quality assurance. For all chefs working in Taste of Scotland restaurants, large or small, the Scotch Lamb Challenge offers an opportunity to further demonstrate their skills and creativity in this prestigious competition. Many of the dishes developed for the competition have become regular features on members' menus.

The competition grows in importance… 1997 saw six finalists – from an initial field of over 80 chefs – competing for the honour of winning Scotch Quality Beef and Lamb Association's Taste of Scotland Scotch Lamb trophies and titles.

Challenge 1997

———— **Winner Category 1** ————
Leslie Brown of Dunlaverock House, Coldingham Bay

———— **Winner Category 2** ————
and Overall Winner of The 1997 Taste of Scotland Scotch Lamb Challenge 1997
John Mark Rutter of the Atrium, Edinburgh (now Head Chef at the Blue Bar Cafe, Edinburgh)

Runners-up in both categories were:
Sukie Barber, Old Pines Restaurant with Rooms, Spean Bridge.
Gail Struthers, Calgary Farmhouse Hotel, Calgary, Isle of Mull.
Scott Dougall, Balbirnie House Hotel, Glenrothes.
Lorraine Ferguson, Martins Restaurant, Edinburgh.

Roast Loin of Scotch Lamb, Tomato Fondue Crest, Artichoke Polenta, Aubergine Roquet, Wild Mushroom Tian, Garlic Jus

John Rutter, Sous Chef
Winner Category 2 and Overall Winner – Scotch Lamb Challenge Competition 1997
The Atrium, Edinburgh

INGREDIENTS

2 Boned Racks of Scotch Lamb

Tomato Fondue Crust
6 plum tomatoes
2 cloves garlic
salt and pepper
100g fine breadcrumbs
25g cheddar
25g pinenuts
50g olive oil

Aubergine Tian
1 aubergine
100g wild mushrooms
150g roquet

Artichoke Polenta
1 artichoke
250ml water
110g polenta
25g butter
1 shallot

Garlic Jus
4 shallots
1 bulb garlic
500ml stock, made from
 lamb bones
¼ bottle red wine

METHOD

1 Bone out rack of lamb and keep all trimmings. Cut into four pieces.
2 Blanch and skin tomatoes then cut into pieces. Sweat tomatoes, garlic, salt and pepper and olive oil until reduced to a pulp.
3 Robocoup breadcrumbs, cheddar, pinenuts and olive oil until it becomes a fine crumble.
4 Peel artichoke and cook until al dente. Slice into fine strips.
5 Bring water to the boil. Add butter and shallot, add artichoke then stir in polenta. Pour out onto a tray and allow to set. Finely slice aubergine, season with salt and sugar and pan fry until crisp.
6 Wash roquet, clean and slice wild mushrooms. For the jus, sweat shallots, garlic and lamb trimmings. Add red wine and stock, reduce by half.

PRESENTATION

Roast lamb until pink GM7/220°C/425°F for approx. 10 minutes, spread tomato fondue and sprinkle crumble on top. Cut four squares of polenta and pan-fry until crisp. Sauté mushrooms and layer aubergine, mushroom and roquet tian. Strain jus and correct seasoning. Grill lamb until brown crust forms, cut in half to show pinkness. Place on top of crisp polenta. Place tian opposite lamb. Pour jus around lamb and tian.

Serves 4

Noisettes of Scotch Lamb with Kibbeh Stuffing and a Minted Garlic Cream

Leslie Brown, Owner/Chef
Winner Category 1 – Scotch Lamb Challenge Competition 1997
Dunlaverock House, Coldingham Bay

INGREDIENTS

1 Boned Loin of Scotch Lamb

Stuffing
50g bulgar wheat
25g butter
1 medium onion, finely chopped
2 cloves garlic, crushed
75g no-soak dried apricots –
   finely chopped
50g sultanas
25g pinenuts
2 tablespoons fresh mint –
   finely chopped
1 tablespoon coriander –
   finely chopped
½ teaspoon ground cumin
½ teaspoon ground mixed spice
good pinch cayenne pepper

Sauce
25g butter
3–4 cloves garlic, crushed
50g red wine
250g lamb stock
2 teaspoons runny honey
250g double cream
3 tablespoons fresh mint –
   chopped fine
½ teaspoon ground cumin
salt & freshly ground pepper

METHOD

To make the stuffing, soak the bulgar wheat in 300g of cold water for 30 minutes.

Melt the butter in a large frying pan and cook the onion over a medium heat until soft. Add the crushed garlic and continue cooking for another minute. Remove from heat and stir in the apricots, sultanas, pinenuts, mint, coriander, cumin, mixed spice and cayenne.

Drain the bulgar wheat well and stir into the apricot mixture. Preheat oven to GM4/180°C/ 350°F. Place the stuffing down the centre of the lamb and close the loin around the stuffing, tying with string at regular intervals. Place the stuffed lamb loin in a roasting pan and cook in a pre-heated oven for 1¼ hours or until it registers as cooked on a meat thermometer.

Sauce – melt the butter in a frying pan and add crushed garlic. Cook over medium heat for 1 minute. Add red wine. Turn heat up and cook until reduced to about 2 tablespoons. Add stock and honey and cook over a medium heat until reduced and syrupy. Add cream and cook until sauce thickens. Add mint, cumin and salt and pepper to taste.

To serve, remove lamb to a cutting board, cover and let rest for 5 minutes. Remove string and cut into 1.5cm slices. Put a spoonful of sauce on each warmed serving plate, and put 2 noisettes on the sauce. Decorate with mint leaves. Serve with home-made apple mint chutney.

Serves 4

Smoked Salmon and Avocado Cheesecake on a Crunchy Oatcake Base Accompanied with a Tomato and Orange Vinaigrette

John Henry, Head Chef
Fernhill Hotel, Portpatrick

INGREDIENTS

100g Scottish smoked salmon
200g Philadelphia cheese
1 avocado
lemon juice
tabasco
1 packet of 4 oatcakes
seasoning to taste
1 orange
white wine vinegar
100ml olive oil
35g tomato purée
small bunch celery leaves

METHOD

1 Blend 75g of the smoked salmon with the avocado, cheese, lemon juice and tabasco.
2 Chop remaining smoked salmon and put on the bottom of four moulds.
3 Pipe the cheese mixture onto the salmon using a plain nozzle.
4 Crunch up the oatcakes and lightly bind with the butter.
5 Gently press some of the crumb on top of the cheese mixture and chill for a couple of hours.
6 For the vinaigrette – blend 140g of peeled plum tomatoes and 35g of tomato purée with the juice and rind of one orange, salt, pepper and white wine vinegar, then add 100ml of olive oil.
7 Turn out the cheesecake and decorate with segments of orange and celery leaves and drizzle the vinaigrette round the plate.

Serves 4

A Gâteau of Salmon Carpaccio, Asparagus and Parmesan Wafers with a Saffron, Red Pepper and Spring Onion Dressing

Malcolm Warham, Head Chef
36, Edinburgh

INGREDIENTS

Marinade

150g Scottish salmon fillet, skinned and boned
juices of 1 lemon and 1 lime
150ml extra virgin olive oil
5ml finely crushed green peppercorns
4ml finely crushed coriander seeds
15g chopped fresh coriander
90ml balsamic vinegar

Dressing

2 poached eggs, firm
good pinch of saffron stamens
50ml white wine
2 shallots
25ml white wine vinegar
125ml olive oil
1 red pepper
½ bunch spring onions

Parmesan Wafers

70g finely grated parmesan
20g plain flour
black pepper
10 pieces of fine asparagus
½ a head of celeriac –
cut into round discs

METHOD

1 Slice salmon thinly and place into a tray allowing 2 slices per portion. Prepare marinade and pour over salmon making sure all of the salmon is covered. Cover and leave in marinade for approximately 45 minutes, turning salmon after 20 minutes. Remove salmon from marinade and keep covered.

2 Prepare wafers – mix grated parmesan, flour and black pepper together, sprinkle over template and bake in a hot oven for approximately 6–8 minutes. Leave to cool.

3 Prepare asparagus – blanch in boiling salted water, refresh and cut into small spears. Re-heat in hot griddle pan and keep warm.

4 Prepare dressing – poach eggs in acidulated water and cook until just firm. Refresh in iced water. Infuse saffron with white wine, white wine vinegar and shallots, leave to cool. Meanwhile, cut pepper into brunoise and chop spring onions finely. Place eggs into a bowl and break up with a fork. Add saffron infusion and emulsify with olive oil, add peppers and spring onions. Season to taste.

5 Pan fry discs of celeriac in olive oil and roast in oven until just cooked. Keep warm. To present dish – layer wafers with salmon carpaccio asparagus and celeriac disc to form gâteau, spoon dressing around plate and serve.

Serves 4

Filo Lasagne of Seared Shetland Salmon with Wilted Spinach, Roast Peppers and a Basil Sauce

Robert Richardson, Head Chef
Busta House Hotel, Brae, Shetland Isles

INGREDIENTS

12 (10cm x 10cm) squares of filo pastry
8 x 100g salmon escalopes, skinned and boned
200g fresh spinach leaves
1 green pepper, diced
1 yellow pepper, diced
8 tomatoes, skinned, deseeded and chopped
2 shallots, finely chopped
1 clove of garlic, crushed
1 glass of white wine
squeeze of lemon
bunch of fresh basil
salt and pepper to season
olive oil

METHOD

1 Brush the peppers with a little of the olive oil, sprinkle with salt and pepper. Place on a baking tray into a hot oven GM8/230°C/450°F until they start to blister.
2 Place the filo squares on a greased tray and sprinkle with salt. Bake until golden brown, approximately 3-4 minutes.
3 Soften the shallots and garlic in a little oil. Add the tomatoes, white wine, squeeze of lemon and salt and pepper. Simmer for 3-4 minutes then add the chopped basil and keep warm.
4 Fry the salmon escalopes quickly – 2 minutes each side and keep warm on a separate tray.
5 In the same pan as the salmon was cooked (it should still be warm) gently wilt the spinach leaves.
6 To serve, place a sheet of filo in the centre of the plate. Top with spinach and escalope of salmon and a little sauce. Repeat this step once more finishing with a sheet of filo. Arrange the roast peppers around the edge with a little of the sauce.

Serves 4

Medley of Seafood with Dill and Chive Sauce

Wendy Barrie, Food Stylist

INGREDIENTS

225g Scottish salmon fillet
225g monkfish fillet
8 fresh Scottish scallops
8 clams
4 crayfish
15ml sunflower oil
25g butter
freshly milled salt
1 teaspoon pink & green peppercorns
1 small glass dry white wine
150ml double cream
15ml each of dill & chives
Italian parsley/dill to garnish

METHOD

1 Prepare the seafood prior to cooking, trim any skin from salmon and monkfish and cut into cubes. Clams should be checked to see that the shells are closed and rinsed in cold water, pulling off any beard, weed or sand. The scallops can be sliced horizontally, leaving the coral with one half. Pierce the coral with the tip of a knife to prevent it bursting on cooking.

2 Heat butter and oil in frying pan and lightly sauté salmon and monkfish, first for 2–3 minutes, tossing to achieve a golden colour. Add the scallops for the final 2 minutes cooking time to ensure they are not overcooked. Remove seafood from pan and keep hot.

3 Meanwhile, bring to the boil a pan of water with a steamer on top. Plunge the crayfish into the boiling water for 3–4 minutes whilst the clams are steaming above. Discard any clams that have not opened on cooking.

4 Quickly deglaze the pan with cream, wine and flavourings. Stir and reduce for a minute. Divide salmon, monkfish, scallops and clams between four heated plates. Pour over sauce and garnish with crayfish and herbs.

Delicious with crusty bread. This can be served as a main course for 4 people.

Serves 8

Steamed Seabass with Seared Scallops and Julienne of Vegetables Laced with a Warm Rhubarb and Coriander Vinaigrette

Craig Wilson, Head Chef
Cromlix House, Kinbuck by Dunblane

INGREDIENTS

4 fillets of seabass (approx. 200g each)
12 fresh scallops
50g butter
1 lemon
200ml fish stock – optional
rock sea salt and ground black pepper

For Vinaigrette	**For Julienne Vegetables**
200g rhubarb	1 large carrot
small bunch fresh coriander – chop half	1 red pepper
freshly squeezed lemon juice	1 yellow pepper
4 shallots – finely chopped	1 courgette
200ml dry white wine	75g bean sprouts
2 tablespoons white wine vinegar	6 baby corns
1 tablespoon dark brown sugar	150g mangetout
2 tablespoons olive oil	

METHOD

1 To prepare the seabass – remove scales and fillet the fish making an incision behind the head and cut along the back bone (or your fishmonger will fillet them for you). Season fish with rock sea salt & ground black pepper.

2 Place on greased tray with a little white wine, squeezed lemon juice and a knob of butter. Place a piece of foil over the top ready for the oven (making your own steamer). Steam seabass in oven for about 10 minutes at GM4/180°C/350°F.

3 Prepare all your vegetables by cutting into thin strips.

4 To prepare the vinaigrette – preheat pan and place chopped rhubarb, shallots, white wine, sugar and half the coriander. Stew together for about 10 minutes and pass through a fine sieve. Whisk in vinegar, olive oil and seasoning.

5 To prepare the scallops – leave whole or cut in half (depending on size). Season with plenty of black pepper and salt. Preheat pan until smoking with a little olive oil and pan fry scallops. Add a little lemon juice before removing from pan, they will only take 3–4 minutes to cook. Be careful not to overcook them. Remove from the pan.

6 Add a little more olive oil and add the vegetables, cooking very quickly, keeping them crisp. Serve onto a preheated plate, the julienne of vegetables, then the scallops with the seabass resting on top, surrounded by the warm vinaigrette. Garnish with the remaining coriander leaves.

Serves 4

Fillet of Highland Venison on Spiced Red Cabbage with Port

John Keir, Head Chef
The Wheatsheaf Hotel, Swinton

INGREDIENTS

4 x 125g venison fillets

Marinade
400ml red wine
10 juniper berries
25g finely diced shallots
2 bay leaves
50ml olive oil

Sauce
600ml reduced beef stock
1 tablespoon redcurrant jelly
50ml ruby port
2 tablespoons arrowroot

Vegetables
4 x fondant potatoes
8 turned carrots
8 roasted shallots
1 small celeriac
4 broccoli florets
fresh coriander
10g butter
25g finely diced shallot
2 cloves
50g diced apple
1 teaspoon honey
2 tablespoons balsamic vinegar
200g finely sliced red cabbage

METHOD

1   Marinate venison fillets for at least 24 hours.
2   Pat dry the venison fillets, then seal in a sauté pan and place in oven at GM6/200°C/400°F for 5 minutes.
3   Once meat has cooked, leave to rest.
4   To make fondant potatoes – take 4 even sized potatoes and shape into 4 barrel style shapes. Brush with butter and place in a roasting tray. Half cover with white stock and place in the oven until cooked (approximately 15-20 minutes) until all stock has been absorbed. Brush with butter before serving.
5   For the sauce – add stock, redcurrant jelly and port. Heat through, boil and thicken slightly with arrowroot until correct consistency is achieved.
6   Grate half of the celeriac and sauté with 10g of butter and coriander, reserving the other half of the celeriac for garnish (fried julienne).
7   Sauté shallots, apple and cabbage. Add the vinegar, cloves and honey. Leave to simmer.
8   Re-heat venison, then carve and arrange on cabbage. Garnish with the broccoli and carrots cooked al dente and serve with the sauce around the venison.

Serves 4

Steamed Parcels of Tay Salmon with a Seaweed and Crab Stuffing, accompanied with a Quenelle of Fromage Frais and Coriander Leaves

Colin Potter, Head Chef
The Lang Bar and Restaurant, Perth Theatre, Perth

INGREDIENTS

500g salmon, cut into 8 thin escalopes
6-8 seaweed strips, soaked and steamed if dried
10ml peanut oil
40g shallots
125g crab meat
1 small clove garlic, crushed
2 tablespoons chopped parsley
1 tablespoon chopped chives
½ teaspoon paprika
50-100g breadcrumbs
10ml lemon juice
4 whole black peppercorns, crushed
100g fromage frais
1 tablespoon shredded coriander leaves
1 carrot & 1 onion, finely sliced
1 bayleaf
20ml vermouth
20ml water
6 coriander leaves
6 watercress leaves

METHOD

1 Heat a small pan, add peanut oil, peppercorns, garlic and shallots, and cook for 30 seconds.
2 Remove from heat and add half of parsley and chives, paprika, chopped seaweed, crab meat and lemon juice.
3 Mix in breadcrumbs, but do not allow mixture to become too firm, as after cooking will become too dry.
4 To make the parcels – lay salmon escalopes flat and season. Divide the stuffing between the salmon escalopes, placing in the centre.
5 Roll the front edge of salmon over the stuffing, tuck in the sides and finish rolling the escalope.
6 Place on a bed of carrots and onions in an ovenproof dish. Sprinkle with vermouth and an equal quantity of water, put in the bayleaf and cover with a tight lid or foil.
7 Place in a hot oven for 10–12 minutes.
8 To make the sauce – fold the rest of the parsley and all the coriander into the fromage frais, adding black pepper. Serve as a quenelle with the salmon parcels. Garnish with lemon, coriander leaves and watercress.

Serves 4

Millefeuilles of Shortbread and Strawberries

Craig Rodger, Head Chef
Bosville Hotel and Chandlery Restaurant, Isle of Skye

INGREDIENTS

600g fresh strawberries
20g icing sugar

For the Shortbread

50g icing sugar, sifted
1 egg yolk
100g unsalted butter, creamed
a pinch of salt
135g plain flour, sieved

For the Raspberry Sauce

250g fresh raspberries
40g caster sugar
juice of ¼ lemon

Craig's Tip   The shortbread pastry must be made at least 2 hours in advance and can be prepared the day before. The type of pastry is suitable for freezing.

METHOD

1   To make the shortbread – mix together the icing sugar, egg yolk, creamed butter and salt. Add the flour and rub together using your fingertips until sandy in texture. Press together to a fairly soft dough.

2   Lightly flour work surface and place the dough on it. Knead with the palm of your hand until well blended. Wrap in cling film and chill for 2 hours (this allows the pastry to firm up).

3   Pre-heat the oven to GM3/160°C/325°F. On a lightly floured surface, roll the shortbread out to a rectangle. With a fluted pastry cutter cut out 12 discs. Place on a baking tray and bake for 10–15 minutes or until lightly blonde. Allow to cool on a wire rack.

4   To make the sauce – place the raspberries, sugar and lemon juice in a bowl and slightly mash with a fork. Marinate for about an hour then liquidise in a blender and sieve. Reserve the liquid in a refrigerator.

5   To serve – place the 4 shortbread discs on plates. Place half the strawberries evenly on the discs and place another disc on top. Using the remaining raspberries place another layer on top of the second disc. Dust the remaining four discs with icing sugar and place on top of the second layer of strawberries. Pour the raspberry sauce around the desserts and serve.

Serves 4

Warm Chocolate Gingerbread and Fromage Frais Ice Cream

Nicholas Laurent, Executive Chef
and Philippe Wagenfuhrer, Executive Sous Chef
The Sheraton Grand Hotel, Edinburgh

INGREDIENTS

Gingerbread	**Ice Cream**
100g icing sugar	200g milk
40g plain flour	20g milk powder (0% fat)
50g almond powder	85g sugar
80g egg white	30g egg yolk
100g nut brown butter	30g dextrose
25g confit orange skin	30g sugar
25g nibbed almonds	10g stabiliser
3g gingerbread spices	500g fromage frais
2g baking powder	
85g caraque chocolate	
(Valrhona) melted	
juice of half a lemon	

METHOD

1 Put icing sugar, plain flour, ground almond and egg white together and mix until a smooth consistency.

2 Add hot nut brown butter and then cool the mixture down a little bit, but do not put into the refrigerator.

3 Into another bowl mix the confit orange, nibbed almond and ginger spice with the baking powder.

4 Pour in the nut brown butter mix and the melted chocolate, then finally the lemon juice.

5 Pour into small individual moulds of any shape and bake in oven at GM4/180°C/350°F for about 6–8 minutes.

6 Serve warm and soft in the middle.

7 For the ice cream – in a saucepan bring the milk, milk powder, sugar and dextrose to 85°C. Add the egg yolk and bring back to 85°C again for 20 minutes. Leave in the refrigerator for twelve hours.

8 The following day cook the sugar and stabiliser at 40°C, then add to the first mix.

9. Finally, incorporate the fromage frais.

This ice cream can be held for two days only in the freezer.

Serves 4

Orange Charlotte with Tuile and Mixed Berries

Denis Dwyer, Chef/Proprietor
The Cabin Restaurant, Glasgow

INGREDIENTS

Chocolate Sponge
4 eggs
80g caster sugar
50g cornflour
50g plain flour
20g good cocoa powder

Charlotte
250ml double cream
50g sugar
2 leaves gelatine
3 egg yolks
4 oranges and zest

Tuile Mix
25g melted butter
pinch of ground cinnamon
25g flour
25g egg whites
50g sugar

Glaze
2 oranges
1 leaf gelatine

METHOD

1   For chocolate sponge – whisk egg yolks and sugar. Mix dry ingredients together. Add dry ingredients slowly to egg mix. Pour into a tray and bake at GM5/190°C/375°F, for 15-20 minutes.

2   For tuile mix – mix eggs and sugar, then add flour, cinnamon and melted butter.

3   To glaze – heat fresh orange juice and gelatine.

4   For charlotte – whip cream to ribbon. Whisk yolks and add sugar until white. Melt gelatine. Add orange juice to yolks, then cream, then the gelatine and zest.

5   Make the sponge and spread thinly on a tray and bake at GM5/190°C/375°F for 5 minutes. Cut into shape (1cm x 4cm), and put into a circular cutter. Pour in charlotte and let it set, then glaze. For the tuile, add one teaspoon of treacle. Spread mix on template thinly. Bake for 45 seconds approximately. Shape while hot.

Serves 4

DAVID **FRAME** CREATIVE
design for communication

THE ESSENTIAL INGREDIENT

GRAPHIC DESIGN · ILLUSTRATION · COPYWRITING · PRINT MANAGEMENT

1–3 South East Circus Place Edinburgh EH3 6TJ   Telephone 0131 225 6540 Fax 0131 225 6779

ISDN 0131 226 2484   e-mail dfc@compuserve.com

Designers of the Taste of Scotland Guide

FLODIGARRY
COUNTRY HOUSE HOTEL
& *Flora MacDonalds Cottage*

1895 to 1995
but timeless

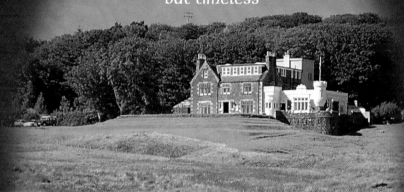

Unspoilt by progress the hotel is a warm sheltered haven amidst the dramatic scenery of northern Skye. Set in five acres of gardens and mixed woodland the fine 19th century mansion house is steeped in history and has strong Jacobite associations. Built as a private house in 1895 by Alexander Livingstone MacDonald on a site adjacent to the cottage where his legendary ancestor Flora MacDonald had once lived and an hotel since 1928, its originality has been carefully preserved. Today, hotel guests can still enjoy old fashioned hospitality in its unique atmosphere and beauty.

The award-winning highland hospitality and homeliness of Flodigarry also extends to its renowned cuisine. Residents and non-residents alike can enjoy traditional Scottish dishes and other tempting specialities, all of which are prepared daily using fresh and where possible local produce. Supplementing the full four course Table d'Hôte menu in the dining room are excellent bar and conservatory meals available throughout the daytime and evening.

STAFFIN   ISLE OF SKYE   SCOTLAND   IV51 9HZ
TELEPHONE 01470 552 203   FACSIMILE 01470 552 301

TALISKER AWARDS · BEST SERVICE · BEST ACCOMMODATION
MACALLAN AWARD · COUNTRY HOUSE HOTEL OF THE YEAR

Index

New Member for 1998★★

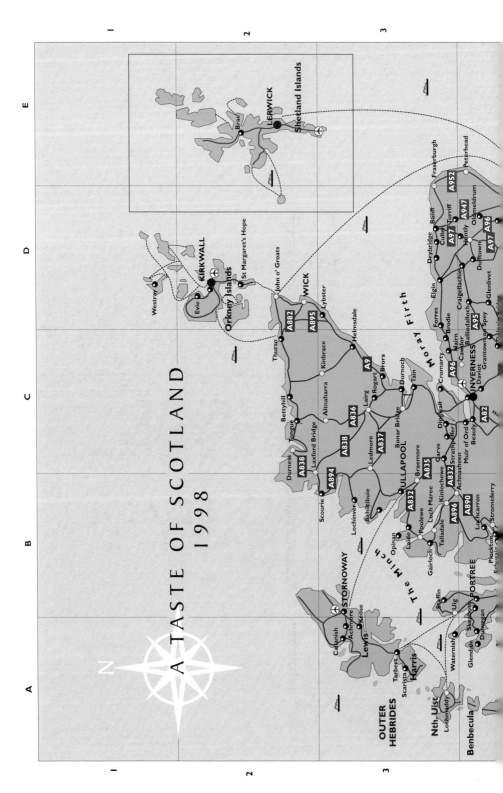

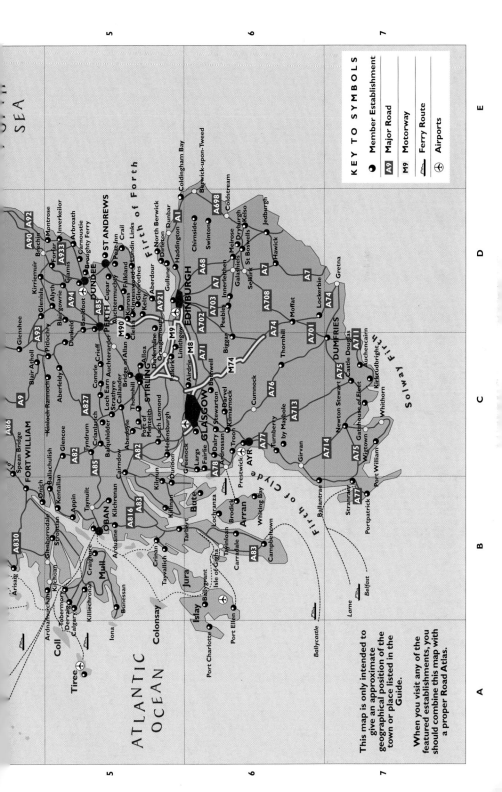

The Taste of Scotland Guide 1998

Editorial
Amanda Clark, Angela Nealon, Tracey Brown

Published by
Taste of Scotland Ltd
A non-profit making company limited by guarantee trading as Taste of Scotland

Design, Illustration & Typesetting
David Frame Creative, Edinburgh

Printed by
Macdonald Lindsay Pindar plc

With particular thanks for editorial assistance
Jim Middleton, David Frame Creative, Edinburgh

Cover Photography
Main photograph courtesy of Dumfries and Galloway Area Tourist Board
(Threave Castle, Castle Douglas)
Inset Food Photo by Graham Lees, Glasgow
Food Styling by Wendy Barrie

Editorial Photography courtesy of
Scottish Area Tourist Boards (see page 11 for contact details)
Scotch Quality Beef and Lamb Association
John Boak, East Lothian

The details quoted in this Guidebook are as supplied to Taste of Scotland Scheme Limited and to the best of the company's knowledge are correct. They may have been amended subsequently and all users are advised in their own interest to check when making a reservation.

Taste of Scotland Scheme Limited accepts no responsibility for any errors or inaccuracies.

Taste of Scotland Scheme Limited
33 Melville Street Edinburgh
Tel: 0131 220 1900 Fax: 0131 220 6102

ISBN 1-87144-509-4